Integrated Security and Safety of Intelligent Computing Networks

Cheng Wang • Hao Tang

Integrated Security and Safety of Intelligent Computing Networks

Springer

Cheng Wang
Tongji University
Shanghai, China

Hao Tang
Tongji University
Shanghai, China

ISBN 978-981-95-5024-1 ISBN 978-981-95-5025-8 (eBook)
https://doi.org/10.1007/978-981-95-5025-8

This Springer imprint is published by the registered company Springer Nature Singapore Pte Ltd.
The registered company address is: 152 Beach Road, #21-01/04 Gateway East, Singapore 189721, Singapore

Preface

With the rapid development of the digital economy, particularly since 2020, there has been an increasing demand for massive connectivity, high computing power, and strong security, which has driven the evolution of the "computing + network" integration in the information and communication technology (ICT) industry. In this context, intelligent computing networks (ICNs) have emerged as a key direction for the development of network computing services. ICNs integrate multiple dimensions, including cloud computing, networking technologies, algorithms, data, edge computing, and terminal devices, aiming to build a multilayered computing infrastructure system that supports coordinated collaboration between networks, clouds, and edge devices, as well as promoting green intelligence. This multidimensional, multi-field collaboration creates new business models in network computing, involving the integration and application of data, computing power, and algorithms across domains and categories.

However, as the architecture of ICNs continues to evolve, security issues have become more prominent. New network computing services not only span various elements, such as data, computing power, and algorithms, but also involve the cross-domain flow of these elements between terminals, edge devices, and cloud servers. This complex business model leads to longer risk management chains, making the entire system more vulnerable to security threats, as the attack surface expands. In particular, the presence of security weaknesses, such as identity verification vulnerabilities or flaws in authorization mechanisms, allows attackers to exploit these weaknesses, thus widening the attack surface and compromising the security of the entire business process. Intelligent computing networks not only require the collaboration of computing power, data, and algorithms but also feature a stronger coupling between these elements, making security issues more complex and interrelated. As intelligent computing networks continue to evolve, new security threats emerge continuously and effectively safeguarding and managing risks within a multi-layered and multi-field collaborative environment has become a critical challenge. To address these challenges, it is essential to consider the complexity of the network computing environment and foster innovations in security technologies and management methods, ensuring that intelligent computing networks can meet modern application needs while effectively mitigating increasing security risks.

The purpose of this book is to present representative research on trustworthy ICNs by systematically examining the structural coupling among data, computing power, and algorithms, and by proposing coupling-aware methodologies that enhance system security and safety. This book is structured in four coherent parts that reflect the logical progression from foundational concepts to practical solutions. The first part (Chaps. 1) provides a historical and architectural overview of ICNs, tracing their evolution from early client-server systems through cloud, fog, and edge computing models to the current era of computing-network integration. The second part (Chaps. 2) establishes a theoretical paradigm centered on the triadic interaction of data, computing power, and algorithms, introducing a fine-grained behavioral knowledge graph as the core modeling framework for security and safety. The third part (Chaps. 3, 4, and 5) maps the challenges of ICN security onto three distinct dimensions, namely system, data, and algorithmic, allowing for a structured decomposition of risks and threat surfaces specific to each dimension. This perspective not only clarifies the technical characteristics and security demands unique to each dimension but also highlights the cross-dimension dependencies that must be jointly addressed to achieve trustworthy and resilient ICN operations. The final part (Chaps. 6) presents an integrated security and safety platform built upon modular and extensible components, demonstrating how cross-layer coordination and semantic analysis can support intelligent responses to threats in real-world domains such as finance, industry, and healthcare. Together, these four parts offer a comprehensive and unified perspective on designing and operating intelligent computing networks that are both efficient and trustworthy.

This book provides a systematic exploration of the security and safety challenges in intelligent computing networks from the perspective of triadic resource coupling. By introducing a behavior-driven and semantically grounded modeling paradigm, it offers a unified framework for analyzing and mitigating risks that emerge across data, computing, and algorithmic layers. The work bridges theoretical insights with practical architectures, advancing the discourse on integrated system trust in increasingly autonomous and data-constrained environments. It serves as both a conceptual foundation and a forward-looking reference for researchers, system architects, and practitioners working at the intersection of intelligent infrastructure, cybersecurity, and complex systems engineering.

Shanghai, China Cheng Wang

Competing Interests The authors have no competing interests to declare that are relevant to the content of this manuscript.

Contents

Chapter 1
Intelligent Computing Networks

Abstract This chapter reviews the evolution and current state of Intelligent Computing Networks (ICNs), a fundamental component for the efficient operation of the digital society. It traces the progression of computing paradigms, from centralized client-server models to distributed systems such as fog and edge computing, highlighting their impact on resource management, service deployment, and scheduling logic. The chapter also examines the role of national strategies, such as the "East Data, West Computing" initiative, in shaping the development of ICNs, enhancing coordination efficiency and resource integration. It presents the three core elements of ICNs: computing power, algorithms, and data, and discusses their increasing interdependence. The chapter also reviews key enabling technologies, including software-defined networking, network function virtualization, containerization, and privacy mechanisms, along with the challenges faced during deployment. The chapter concludes by offering insights into future trends, emphasizing the growing complexity of resource scheduling, the shift toward demand-aware scheduling, and the integration of computing, algorithms, and data. It also addresses challenges related to standardization, security, and coordination.

1.1 Historical Evolution of Computing Networks

The development of ICNs has not occurred overnight, rather, it has undergone multiple stages of technological paradigm shifts and integration over the past several decades as illustrated in Fig. 1.1. Computing paradigms began in the late twentieth century with client-server and peer-to-peer (P2P) models. They then progressed through grid computing, which emphasized resource sharing, and later evolved into cloud computing for massive-scale data processing. Throughout this evolution, these paradigms have continually refined their operational logic and extended their service boundaries. Each iteration of computing models has represented not only a leap in technological advancement but also a response to evolving societal demands for more efficient computing resource distribution, service responsiveness, and system flexibility. With the convergence of technology and societal transformation, ICNs have gradually evolved into a new paradigm characterized by computing-network

C. Wang, H. Tang, *Integrated Security and Safety of Intelligent Computing Networks*, https://doi.org/10.1007/978-981-95-5025-8_1

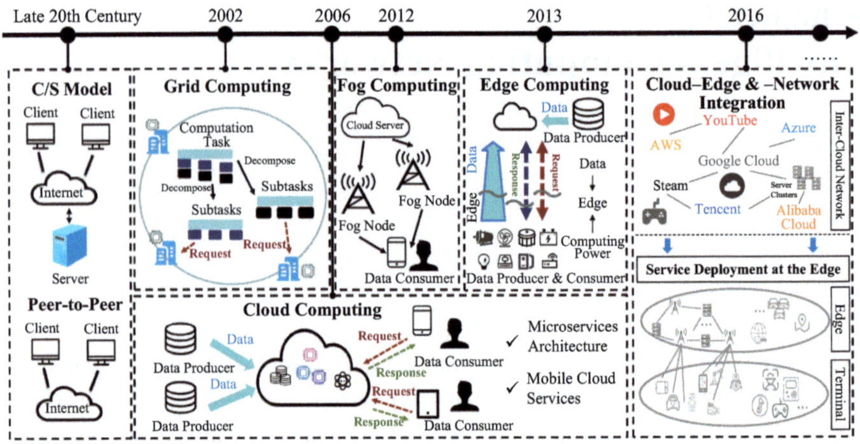

Fig. 1.1 Historical evolution of intelligent computing networks

integration. This section follows a chronological timeline to trace the step-by-step evolution of ICNs, analyzing the core technical concepts at key historical stages and laying a foundation for understanding their formation logic.

1.1.1 Client-Server Model and Peer-to-Peer Computing

1.1.1.1 Origin of Computing Networks

At the end of the twentieth century, computing networks began exploring models for resource sharing and remote services. However, limited by the hardware, bandwidth, and management technologies of the time, early computing networks had to strike a balance between centralized control and node autonomy. As a result, two classic computing network architectures emerged: the client-server model and the peer-to-peer model. The client-server model, known for its simplicity and intuitive structure, was widely adopted. It is a centralized computing architecture in which clients request resources or services from a server, and the server, acting as a central hub, exposes interfaces and processes requests. In contrast, the peer-to-peer model adopts a completely decentralized architecture. In this model, each node acts both as a consumer and a provider of services. Although these two architectures are fundamental, each has its advantages in different scenarios. They laid a solid foundation for the development of more complex architectures such as grid computing and cloud computing.

1.1.1.2 Client-server Architecture

As a centralized computing architecture, the client-server (C/S) mode typically features a star-shaped network topology centered around the server. Clients and servers are often located on physically distant machines. The client software sends user requests to the server and presents the processed results in the required format; the server application accepts requests from clients, handles them as needed, and returns the final output.

A basic client-server database system includes two main components, namely the client-side application and the database server module, which are commonly referred to as the frontend and backend. The device that executes the server program functions as the application server. After being launched, the server program continuously listens for requests from client applications and responds accordingly. The client software runs on the user's local computer and automatically connects to the server whenever a database operation is required, sending requests that the server responds to based on predefined rules. In this structure, the application server bears a relatively light data load.

Client-server mode is widely used in email systems, enterprise management systems, and online game clients. Taking online games as an example, the client handles graphical rendering and user input, while the game server manages player data synchronization, world state maintenance, mission logic, and more.

The client-server model requires dedicated client installations and careful maintenance of communication between client and server software. One major drawback is its limited scalability. Client software developed for Windows cannot run on Linux-based machines, and even Operating System (OS) updates may cause compatibility issues. As a result, client software must support multiple platform versions and stay up-to-date with operating system changes. Moreover, the client-server model heavily relies on the server's availability. When the server goes offline, it creates a single point of failure and may cause major service disruptions, which in turn impose heavy requirements on server maintenance.

1.1.1.3 Peer-to-peer Architecture

As a decentralized computing architecture, the peer-to-peer (P2P) mode features a completely different logical topology and role definition from the client-server model. In P2P mode, each node acts both as a consumer and a provider of services, and there is no fixed central node in the overall network topology [1]. In fact, P2P networks can be categorized into centralized peer networks and unstructured distributed networks. The former relies on a central directory server and essentially still contains a central node and transmission bottlenecks, with poor scalability, and thus will not be elaborated here. In the commonly understood P2P mode, there is no central server; all nodes connect to the network through communication with neighboring nodes. When a node searches for needed resources, its request propagates outward through neighboring nodes. To prevent unchecked flooding of requests, a time-to-live (TTL) value is typically set, which decreases during query propagation until it reaches zero and stops spreading.

The advantages of peer-to-peer are evident. It avoids the single point of failure seen in client-server mode; the failure of one node does not significantly impact the overall network service, especially in large-scale networks. P2P networks are highly scalable and can grow flexibly. Moreover, the peer-to-peer model introduced the concept of resource sharing, covering both data and computing power.

In terms of data sharing, the BitTorrent protocol is one of the most successful applications of the peer-to-peer model. Traditional file downloads rely on a single server as the data source, concentrating bandwidth pressure and creating bottlenecks. In contrast, the BitTorrent system splits files into multiple small pieces, which are distributed across all participating nodes. Each node is both a downloader (client) and an uploader (server), simultaneously downloading and uploading data blocks to other nodes. This design greatly reduces bandwidth concentration, improves overall download efficiency, and provides strong fault tolerance and scalability, ensuring file accessibility even if some nodes go offline.

In terms of computing power sharing, the emergence of blockchain technology has further extended the boundaries of the peer-to-peer model. Taking the Bitcoin network as an example, every node can participate in transaction validation and block generation through mining, contributing its computing resources. Unlike traditional systems where centralized servers validate transactions, blockchain uses distributed consensus mechanisms, such as Proof of Work (PoW), allowing any node with sufficient computing power to equally participate in network maintenance. This enhances decentralization and ensures the immutability and high security of transaction data, forming a highly resilient, self-organizing, and self-verifying intelligent network infrastructure.

However, the drawbacks of the peer-to-peer model are also significant. It depends heavily on the number of online nodes and stable bandwidth connections. Additionally, challenges arise in terms of data consistency, authentication, and security. Without a central control entity, maintaining consistent data replicas across nodes becomes extremely difficult. Risks include data lag, tampering, or loss between nodes. Moreover, identity verification and access control are more complex in a decentralized environment, as malicious nodes may interfere with network operation through identity spoofing, poisoning attacks, denial-of-service attacks, and more. Therefore, how to retain the flexibility of decentralization while enhancing the stability, security, and manageability of peer-to-peer systems remains a key issue in their practical application.

1.1.2 Grid Computing

1.1.2.1 Origins and Conceptual Foundations

With the growing demand in the industry for scientific computing and research collaboration, grid computing emerged. The design goal of grid computing is to enable distributed, cross-rack resource sharing and collaborative computation. The term "grid" in grid computing is derived from the "Electric Grid", signifying the vision that computing resources, like electricity, should be accessible to users on demand, without concern for their physical location or underlying complexity. This metaphor was later extended to cloud computing and edge computing, but the core concepts of "on-demand sharing" and "unified standards" were first proposed and implemented in grid computing. Ian Foster, known as the founder of grid computing, defined three key criteria for a system to be considered a grid [2]:

- Resources are coordinated in a manner that avoids centralized management.
- It relies on universal, transparent protocols and interfaces designed for broad applicability.
- The system ensures significant and high-quality service capabilities.

1.1.2.2 Protocol Stack and Architectural Layers

The fabric layer is the lowest layer in the grid computing architecture, responsible for interfacing with and abstracting underlying hardware resources such as computing, storage, and networking. This layer does not define new protocols but instead utilizes existing local resource managers (such as Portable Batch System (PBS), Condor and Slurm) and storage systems (such as Network File System (NFS) and General Parallel File System (GPFS)) to enable operations on local resources. It provides interfaces to upper-layer protocols, ensuring smooth execution of scheduling, monitoring, and data access tasks under heterogeneous physical conditions.

The connectivity layer establishes secure communication channels and authentication mechanisms between nodes in the grid. Its core protocol is the Grid Security Infrastructure (GSI). Based on the X.509 certificate system, GSI supports features such as Single Sign-On and Proxy Certificates, allowing users seamless access to resources across organizational domains. This layer ensures secure and trustworthy data exchange in an open environment and serves as the foundation for trusted collaboration within the grid.

The resource layer defines the protocols for publishing, discovering, scheduling, monitoring, and utilizing individual resources in the grid. It is the central component of grid computing. Key protocols include: Grid Resource Allocation and Management (GRAM) for remote job submission and status control; GridFTP for high-performance large data file transfers; and RSL (Resource Specification Language) for describing resource request parameters. This layer standardizes underlying resource capabilities for collective-level scheduling and upper-level application invocation.

The collective layer focuses on the coordinated scheduling and management of resource collections across the entire grid system. It provides capabilities such as directory services, global job scheduling, and collaborative resource allocation. Typical components include: Monitoring and Discovery Service (MDS) for resource registration and discovery; Condor-G and Nimrod-G for cross-domain job matching and execution; and Community Authorization Service (CAS) for access authorization control within virtual organizations. The collective layer is the key bridge that extends grid computing from "single-point resource access" to "multi-point collaborative sharing."

The application layer is the top layer of the grid protocol stack, directly serving end users and supporting a variety of scientific and engineering applications based on grid infrastructure. Representative examples include science gateways (such as the TeraGrid Science Gateway), which provide users with unified web interfaces for submitting computing tasks, and workflow systems (such as Swift and Kepler) that support the orderly orchestration and automated execution of complex computational tasks. This layer typically offers services through graphical interfaces or service portals, shielding users from underlying complexity and improving usability.

1.1.2.3 Core Technologies

The development of grid computing relies on a set of key middleware and coordination mechanisms that support its operation. Among them, the most representative middleware is the Globus Toolkit, which served as the de facto standard framework. It provided core modules covering GSI, GRAM, and GridFTP, laying the foundation for the early implementation of the grid protocol stack. Globus was designed with an emphasis on modularity and standardization, greatly facilitating cross-platform resource interoperability.

At the mechanism level, grid computing achieves cross-administrative domain resource sharing through the construction of Virtual Organizations (VOs). Each VO is essentially a logical collaboration entity composed of users and resources from different institutions, operating cooperatively based on trust mechanisms. In terms of task scheduling, grids commonly adopt a batch processing model, utilizing Local Resource Managers (LRMs) such as PBS or Condor in combination with the GRAM protocol to enable remote job submission and execution management.

Moreover, with the exponential growth of scientific data, the concept of the Data Grid emerged. Through the mechanism of "virtual data", it enables location transparency, format transparency, and reproducible management of data, providing essential support for data-intensive tasks.

1.1.2.4 Representative Platforms

In practical applications, grid computing has been widely employed in large-scale computation and data analysis tasks centered around scientific research. These platforms and projects are mostly maintained by governmental or official organizations.

One of the most representative grid platforms is TeraGrid, led by the National Science Foundation in the United States. It integrates supercomputing resources from multiple universities and national laboratories, providing powerful computational support for scientific projects such as climate modeling and genome analysis. Another notable platform is the Open Science Grid (OSG), which primarily supports high-throughput task scheduling and data processing in high-energy physics experiments. These platforms fully demonstrate the core value of grid computing in cross-institutional collaboration, heterogeneous resource integration, and the development of scientific infrastructure.

1.1.2.5 Limitations and Challenges

Although grid computing offers unique advantages in cross-institutional resource sharing and the construction of research infrastructure, it also faces numerous limitations in practical applications. First, as task scheduling is primarily based on batch processing models, grid systems struggle to support interactive and low-latency computing tasks, making them unsuitable for applications that require rapid responsiveness. Additionally, the resources integrated within a grid often come from different institutions, resulting in high heterogeneity and complex scheduling, which increases the cost of system deployment and maintenance.

Moreover, due to the slow progress in standardization and the diversity of platform interfaces, grid computing has yet to establish a clear and viable commercial service ecosystem. Most large-scale grid platforms are maintained by government or official organizations, forming a stark contrast with the widespread adoption of cloud computing. Despite this, grid computing retains strong control capabilities in areas such as security, identity management, and resource authorization. However, its support for modern computing features like virtualization and elastic scaling is relatively limited, making it difficult to meet the demands of complex coupled tasks or large-scale service-oriented applications.

1.1.3 Cloud Computing

1.1.3.1 Origins and Conceptual Foundations

The concept of cloud computing can be traced back to 1961, when computing pioneer John McCarthy predicted that "computing may someday be organized as a public utility." This idea also inspired the naming of grid computing. It gradually became a reality in the early twenty-first century, especially against the backdrop of the rapid rise of Web 2.0 and surging demand for enterprise IT infrastructure. Cloud computing emerged as a new computing paradigm characterized by resource-as-a-service and elastic provisioning. Compared to early distributed and grid computing, cloud computing shifted the focus from resource connectivity and sharing to service encapsulation, dynamic scalability, and economically driven models.

From a definitional perspective, cloud computing is generally regarded as a large-scale, virtualized, and on-demand distributed computing paradigm. Built on economies of scale, it uses virtualization technologies to abstract and encapsulate underlying computing, storage, and platform resources, ultimately delivering services to external clients through standardized interfaces. These services can range from basic infrastructure (such as compute and storage resources) to development platforms and complete application systems, forming the three classic delivery models: Infrastructure-as-a-service (IaaS), Platform-as-a-service (PaaS), and Software-as-a-service (SaaS) [3]. As noted by Foster and others, the rapid development of cloud computing has been driven by three key factors: (1) the sharp decline in hardware costs and the rise of multicore architectures; (2) the exponential growth of data volumes; and (3) the widespread adoption of service computing and web applications.

Although the architecture and operational mechanisms of cloud computing differ significantly from those of grid computing, the core vision remains unchanged: to achieve centralized management and elastic provisioning of computing resources through standardized platforms, ultimately reducing user costs while improving system reliability and resource utilization. Unlike grid computing, the success of cloud computing has largely depended on massive investment and data center construction by commercial companies such as Amazon, Google, and Microsoft. This has enabled capabilities such as "access to hundreds of thousands of servers worldwide with just a credit card", truly realizing the public-facing model of "computing as a service".

1.1.3.2 Evolution from Grid Computing

Grid computing had already addressed, to some extent, the challenges of distributed computing and resource sharing. Cloud computing inherited many of the core principles of grid computing, including resource sharing, remote scheduling, and heterogeneous access, but introduced fundamental reconstructions and optimizations in implementation path, system architecture, user interface, and business model. As Foster and others have noted, although cloud and grid computing share a common vision, which is to transform computing resources into on-demand services [2]. However, cloud computing places greater emphasis on economies of scale, service encapsulation, and platform unification, rather than merely federated coordination across organizations. This has led to the rapid adoption and stronger commercialization of cloud computing.

Architecturally, grid computing focused on collaboration among multiple organizations, relying on standardized protocols, authentication mechanisms, and highly heterogeneous systems. In contrast, cloud computing is built upon unified platforms within private or public data centers, utilizing virtualization to achieve resource pooling and elastic scalability, with services targeted at mass-market and commercial applications. Thus, cloud computing can be seen as a continuation of grid computing that has undergone "inward consolidation" and "platformization" on a technical basis, shifting the focus from "how to connect" to "how to encapsulate", and from "federated resource coordination" to "centralized resource provisioning".

From the user's perspective, grid computing is typically geared toward research communities, with resource allocation governed by project-based quotas and application procedures, requiring a high level of technical expertise. In contrast, cloud computing is defined by "on-demand usage and pay-as-you-go" principles, with standardized and graphical service interfaces that greatly lower the entry barrier, promoting the widespread adoption of the computing-as-a-service paradigm.

1.1.3.3 Cloud Computing Architecture and Service Model

The architecture of cloud computing can be broadly defined in four layers: (1) fabric, (2) unified resource, (3) platform, and (4) application layers. The fabric layer consists of the underlying physical computing, storage, and network resources, forming the foundational infrastructure of the cloud platform. The unified resource layer abstracts and pools these resources through virtualization technologies, presenting them as logical computing nodes, distributed file systems, and object storage systems with enhanced manageability and elasticity. The platform layer builds on this foundation to provide middleware and development environments that support application deployment and execution. The application layer serves end users directly, delivering various SaaS-level services that represent the final goal of cloud computing delivery.

The IaaS delivery model primarily provides users with virtualized computing power, storage resources, and network interfaces. Users can deploy operating systems, customize middleware, and implement business logic on IaaS platforms, enjoying control capabilities similar to local deployments. IaaS offers high flexibility and manageability, with typical platforms including Amazon EC2, Microsoft Azure VM, and Alibaba Cloud ECS. It is suitable for enterprise application hosting, dynamic resource scheduling, and multi-tenant isolation scenarios.

PaaS provides developers with highly integrated environments for application development and execution, abstracting away the complexity of underlying resource management. Users can focus solely on business logic without worrying about VM configurations, network topology, elastic scaling, or load balancing. PaaS typically includes function computing, message queues, database services, and application deployment tools, significantly improving development efficiency and system maintainability. Representative platforms include Google App Engine, Microsoft Azure

App Service, and Huawei Cloud AppCube, making PaaS ideal for rapid deployment, small-team collaboration, and microservice architecture implementation.

SaaS is a service model of cloud computing that most directly targets end users. Complete application software is encapsulated as remote services and accessed via web or Application Programming Interface (API) interfaces, eliminating the need for local installation or maintenance. SaaS platforms are widely used in areas such as office collaboration, customer relationship management, content sharing, and online education. Examples include Microsoft 365, DingTalk, and Tencent Docs. SaaS reduces the barrier to software usage and drives the transformation of IT into a service-oriented business model, making it the most mature and commercialized layer of cloud computing.

1.1.3.4 The Key Driving Force

The rapid development of cloud computing has been primarily fueled by the maturity and accumulation of foundational technologies. The declining unit cost of computing hardware has made the construction of large-scale data centers feasible. More critically, virtualization technologies (such as VMware, Xen, and Kernel-based Virtual Machine (KVM)) have reached practical applicability, enabling computing resources to be abstracted into elastic, controllable, and securely isolated logical units. The convergence of these technologies laid a solid foundation for key cloud computing capabilities such as resource pooling, automated scheduling, and multi-tenant isolation [4].

The explosive growth of data has placed increasing demands on computing, storage, and distributed processing capabilities. Traditional local deployments struggle to accommodate such growth, while cloud computing, with its elasticity and integrated resources, has become the ideal solution for supporting big data applications and distributed computation.

A significant driving force behind cloud computing's rapid expansion is the shift in service demand models. The Web 2.0 era gave rise to a proliferation of interactive, social, and real-time internet services, which require platforms to support high concurrency, high availability, and rapid iteration. These are capabilities that traditional IT architectures struggle to deliver flexibly. Cloud computing, with its standardized APIs and elastic resource provisioning, is well-suited to these emerging needs and has become the mainstream approach for modern application deployment.

The involvement of commercial capital has further propelled the development of cloud computing. Technology giants such as Amazon, Google, and Microsoft not only commercialized their own infrastructure but also fostered rich ecosystems of PaaS and SaaS offerings, accelerating the productization and industry penetration of cloud services. The vast market demand and economies of scale have, in turn, reinforced platform development, driving the global proliferation of cloud computing.

1.1.3.5 Limitations and Challenges

Although cloud computing has greatly advanced the centralization and service-oriented transformation of computing resources, it has also revealed a series of structural limitations in practical applications. Chief among these is the inherent latency caused by centralized architectures. In scenarios that demand extremely high real-time performance and low latency, such as industrial control, autonomous driving, and remote healthcare, the response speed of cloud platforms often falls short of expectations. Centralized data processing also poses challenges in data transmission, as the bandwidth burden and cost of uploading massive amounts of data to centralized cloud centers have become increasingly prominent bottlenecks in Internet of Things (IoT) environments. In addition, concerns around privacy compliance and edge autonomy are becoming more pronounced, with users and enterprises placing growing emphasis on local processing and storage capabilities to enhance control over their data [3].

These challenges have prompted both academia and industry to explore new computing paradigms, such as fog computing and edge computing, which aim to push computing power downward from the central cloud to edge locations closer to the data source. This enables a more distributed, real-time, and autonomous computing model.

1.1.4 Fog Computing

1.1.4.1 Key Characteristics of Fog Computing

Fog computing is a new computing paradigm proposed following cloud computing, designed to meet the emerging needs of scenarios such as the IoT that demand low latency, high bandwidth, and location awareness. Unlike traditional cloud computing, which relies on centralized data centers, fog computing pushes computing, storage, and networking capabilities down to the edge of the network [5]. This includes access points, edge routers, local servers, or smart devices, effectively bringing services closer to the data source. This significantly reduces transmission latency and improves system responsiveness [6]. The architecture is particularly well-suited for applications that require high levels of real-time performance and stability, such as intelligent transportation, industrial control, and smart homes.

Fog computing nodes typically possess location awareness and can dynamically optimize resource allocation and task scheduling based on users' geographic positions, offering more context-adaptive services. In terms of mobility support, fog computing is better equipped to handle data requests from frequently moving endpoints, such as vehicles, wearable devices, and drones, due to its flexible deployment and proximity to terminals. At the same time, fog computing retains the advantage of elastic scalability from cloud computing. It enables preliminary data filtering, aggregation, and processing at the edge, thereby significantly reducing the load on central clouds and improving overall system bandwidth efficiency and resource allocation flexibility.

Fog computing not only extends the service boundaries of cloud computing but also provides critical support for the evolution of ICNs.

1.1.4.2 Comparison of Fog and Cloud Computing

Although fog computing originates from cloud computing in terms of technical architecture, the two differ fundamentally in areas such as response latency, mobility support, data processing location, and network load. These differences critically shape their respective application scenarios.

Cloud computing services primarily rely on data centers centrally deployed within the core network. While these data centers offer powerful computing and storage capabilities, end devices must communicate with remote cloud nodes across multiple layers of network paths, resulting in significant transmission latency. This issue becomes especially pronounced in scenarios requiring frequent data uploads and rapid responses. In contrast, fog computing deploys computing resources at the network edge, such as access points and regional nodes, allowing tasks to be executed locally or nearby, thereby drastically reducing end-to-end response times. This "proximate computing" mechanism is critical for use cases such as real-time video analytics, industrial control, and intelligent transportation systems, which are domains where cloud computing often proves inadequate.

Traditional cloud computing architectures exhibit clear limitations in environments with frequent endpoint mobility and constantly changing network conditions. With centralized control logic and distant computing resources, cloud platforms are often unable to perceive or respond to dynamic changes in endpoint location or behavior in real time. Fog computing, by contrast, naturally supports location awareness and localized decision-making, enabling it to perform resource scheduling and access control at the edge. This ensures continuous connectivity and service availability for fast-moving terminals such as vehicles, wearable devices, and drones. As such, fog computing plays a pivotal role in enabling the next generation of mobile IoT applications and addresses the cloud's shortcomings in managing "edge dynamism".

Fog computing establishes an intermediate layer between cloud and end devices, offloading part of the computational burden to the network edge. This facilitates collaborative operation between cloud and edge, reducing the load on the cloud while enhancing the system's overall responsiveness and flexibility. Nonetheless, fog computing still depends on cloud resources, especially for global scheduling, large-scale storage, and model training. In this sense, fog computing paves the way toward a more thoroughly "distributed and edge-autonomous" paradigm represented by edge computing. The two models are both connected and distinct in the architectural evolution path, and this relationship will be explored further in the following sections.

1.1.4.3 Representative Application Scenarios

In intelligent transportation systems, roadside units (RSUs), traffic lights, cameras, and in-vehicle devices generate large volumes of real-time data. If this data were transmitted directly to the cloud for processing, network congestion and physical distance could introduce excessive latency, making it difficult to meet the demands of dynamic traffic response. By deploying fog nodes, such as edge servers or smart traffic light controllers, at the roadside, the system can locally perform tasks like video stream analysis, vehicle speed detection, and pedestrian recognition. For example, when a camera detects the flashing lights of an ambulance, the fog node can immediately determine the situation and switch the nearby traffic light to green, creating a fast-response corridor. Such immediate reaction is nearly impossible in a cloud-only architecture. Moreover, fog nodes can coordinate with one another to form a "green wave", synchronizing signals along the direction of vehicle travel to improve traffic flow efficiency. This combination of local autonomy and horizontal collaboration makes fog computing a key enabler of reliable, low-latency intelligent transportation systems.

In modern industrial systems, a wide array of sensors and actuators continuously generate high-frequency data streams for monitoring equipment status, environmental changes, or product quality. Traditional cloud architectures struggle with such high-frequency, latency-sensitive applications, such as anomaly detection and real-time control. Fog computing addresses this gap by pushing critical control logic and preliminary data analysis down to fog nodes located near workshops or production lines. For instance, in a smart manufacturing facility, temperature sensors and motor vibration monitors transmit data in real time to a nearby edge server for analysis. If overheating or abnormal vibrations are detected, the fog node can respond within milliseconds by sending control signals to shut down the equipment, preventing damage and production downtime. This "edge processing" model reduces bandwidth dependency, enhances system robustness and data security, and is especially suitable for industrial environments where network conditions are unstable or safety requirements are high.

1.1.4.4 Challenges in Platform Design and Deployment

Although fog computing offers an ideal architectural complement to ICNs, its platform design and deployment in practice face multiple technical challenges. One of the foremost issues is the choice of virtualization technology. Given the heterogeneous hardware capabilities of fog nodes, selecting between lightweight and efficient containers (such as Docker) and more feature-complete virtual machines (such as KVM) becomes a critical early design decision. Poor choices in this area can directly affect the system's ability to support elastic scheduling and resource reuse.

Fog computing is intended to serve low-latency applications, yet its geographically distributed nature introduces cumulative latency in task partitioning, data aggregation, and resource scheduling. Particularly under sudden workloads or high-frequency device requests, resource-constrained fog nodes may suffer from delayed scheduling responses, resulting in service jitter and undermining the very advantages fog computing is meant to provide.

Security and privacy also pose significant barriers to fog platform deployment. Fog nodes are often located in physically untrusted environments, making them vulnerable to risks such as man-in-the-middle (MITM) attacks, node tampering, and data leakage [7]. Furthermore, their local processing characteristics make traditional centralized authentication and access control mechanisms difficult to apply. Designing lightweight authentication mechanisms suitable for distributed environments and ensuring trustworthy data processing are urgent frontiers for future fog computing platforms.

These challenges have, in turn, accelerated the development of edge computing. Unlike fog computing, which emphasizes coordination and control through a platform-based architecture, edge computing focuses more on extreme real-time demands near the terminal, aiming to push computing power as close as possible to the data source.

1.1.5 Edge Computing

1.1.5.1 The Emergence and Concept of Edge Computing

With the rapid proliferation of mobile devices, IoT terminals, and the advancement of high-speed access technologies such as 5G, traditional cloud computing architectures face growing challenges, including increased bandwidth pressure, high response latency, and elevated risks of privacy leakage. In this context, "Edge Computing" has emerged as a new computing paradigm. It advocates deploying computing and storage resources closer to the data source, specifically at the edge of the network, in order to achieve lower latency, higher bandwidth efficiency, and stronger real-time processing capabilities.

The concept of edge computing can be traced back to the late 1990s with Akamai's introduction of Content Delivery Networks (CDNs), but it only evolved into an independent architectural model more recently, driven by the rise of 5G and IoT technologies [8, 9]. Compared to traditional cloud computing, edge computing does not aim to replace the centralized cloud but rather complements it: while cloud centers excel at centralized high-performance processing and storage, edge nodes are better suited for handling local tasks that are sensitive to latency and bi-directional data volume.

1.1.5.2 Key Architectures of Edge Computing and Comparison with Cloud/Fog

Edge computing is not a singular structure but a ubiquitous computing paradigm that encompasses multiple implementation forms, all aimed at deploying computing and storage capabilities closer to data sources to achieve low latency, high bandwidth utilization, and enhanced user experience. In both academic research and industrial practice, four representative edge computing architectures have emerged. Multi-access Edge Computing (MEC), proposed by European Telecommunications Standards Institute (ETSI), is deployed near base stations or access nodes and emphasizes location awareness and network context awareness, making it a core solution in 5G scenarios. Fog Computing focuses more on collaborative processing among lower-layer network devices, utilizing widely distributed nodes to handle lightweight, high-frequency data tasks common in IoT systems. Cloudlet computing, originating from academia, refers to "micro data centers" deployed within one network hop of terminals, offering stronger computing and storage capabilities suitable for tasks such as Augmented Reality (AR)/Virtual Reality (VR) and edge inference. Mobile Cloud Computing (MCC) emphasizes offloading tasks from mobile devices to remote clouds or edge nodes via wireless networks to overcome limitations in mobile computing power and battery life. Despite differences in deployment and resource configuration, these architectures together form the backbone of today's edge computing ecosystem.

Edge computing and cloud computing are not functionally exclusive but rather complementary. Cloud computing, with its centralized architecture and massive resource pool, excels at large-scale data storage, deep model training, and global analytics. However, it struggles with latency-sensitive applications, high bandwidth consumption, and local data privacy concerns. Edge computing addresses these issues by offloading certain computing and storage tasks to the edge of the network, greatly shortening data transmission paths and response times, making real-time applications such as vehicular networks, industrial control, and augmented reality feasible. Due to its proximity to heterogeneous end devices, edge computing favors lightweight virtualization (such as containers) and device-level isolation, emphasizing flexibility and deployment efficiency [10]. In contrast, cloud computing relies on heavyweight virtual machines and centralized scheduling, better suited for stable, long-duration tasks. From a service paradigm perspective, cloud computing is data-driven and platform-centered, whereas edge computing focuses more on user experience and scenario adaptation, representing a shift toward localized and distributed computing resources.

Edge computing and fog computing are often used interchangeably, but they differ significantly in technical pathways and implementation logic. Edge computing typically emphasizes computing resource offloading to the terminal side or access point, centering on "local processing" and "distributed response", which is ideal for scenarios requiring fast decision-making and localized services. Fog computing, by contrast, tends to build a layered, collaborative processing architecture within the middle layers of the network, such as routers, gateways, and edge servers, focusing

Table 1.1 Comparison of cloud, fog, and edge computing

Dimension	Cloud computing	Fog computing	Edge computing
Architecture	Centralized large-scale data centers	Distributed intermediate nodes (e.g., routers, gateways and edge servers)	Distributed devices near end-users (e.g., base stations and access points)
Primary objective	Massive storage, deep learning model training, global analytics	Data aggregation, filtering, relaying, collaborative resource scheduling	Local processing, rapid response, task offloading
Deployment location	Central cloud	Middle layer of network	User-side or near access points
Processing granularity	Large-scale batch processing	Lightweight, high-frequency data tasks (e.g., IoT)	Real-time inference and response (e.g., AR/VR and V2X)
Typical applications	Long-term stable tasks, big data training	Smart city, environmental monitoring, energy management	Latency-sensitive, inference-intensive applications (e.g., AR/VR and V2X)

on information aggregation, filtering, and forwarding, with a more pronounced "intermediary" role. The two differ in node placement, processing granularity, and autonomy. Fog computing emphasizes inter-node connectivity and collaborative resource scheduling, while edge computing prioritizes local task execution and rapid response.

From an application perspective, fog computing is often applied in smart city scenarios such as environmental monitoring and energy management, which require wide-area coverage. Edge computing is more suited for latency-critical, inference-intensive applications like image recognition, AR inference, and Vehicle-to-Everything (V2X) communication. The two are not mutually exclusive in deployment but can form a synergistic architecture, together building a layered and complementary ICN.

A summarized comparison of the characteristics of cloud computing, fog computing, and edge computing is presented in Table 1.1.

1.1.5.3 Representative Applications and Deployment Scenarios

Due to its low latency, high bandwidth utilization, and local responsiveness, edge computing demonstrates unique value across various application domains. Two representative scenarios are highlighted here.

The first is V2X communication in intelligent transportation systems. In traditional architectures, inter-vehicle communication often relies on remote cloud centers for relay and processing, resulting in noticeable network delays that fall short of the millisecond-level response required in high-speed driving environments.

Edge computing addresses this by deploying MEC servers at roadside units or base stations, pushing computing and sensing capabilities to the "communication edge." This enables local processing and rapid forwarding of information between vehicles and roadside infrastructure, supporting real-time traffic alerts, cooperative obstacle avoidance, and optimized signal scheduling, significantly enhancing road safety and traffic efficiency. In comparison, fog computing can also be deployed at transportation nodes but focuses more on coordination among multiple sensing points, making it suitable for large-scale scenarios such as urban traffic flow analysis and historical behavior modeling. Overall, edge computing excels at low-latency, near-end control tasks, while fog computing emphasizes wide-area coordination and data aggregation; the two can complement each other within the V2X ecosystem.

The second representative application is AR interaction systems. AR applications require intensive computation for image processing, pose sensing, and scene rendering. Relying solely on local devices may compromise the experience due to limited resources, while complete dependence on remote cloud computing may introduce frame stutter and latency jitter due to network fluctuations. To address this, edge computing utilizes Cloudlet nodes deployed in public spaces, such as shopping malls, subways, and exhibition halls, to provide high computational support within one network hop of users. This allows image recognition and model rendering tasks to be executed near the user, ensuring real-time and seamless AR experiences. In contrast, fog computing nodes typically offer weaker computational power and are more suited to data pre-processing and event triggering tasks, making them less capable of supporting AR's high concurrency inference demands. Thus, in such high-computation-density scenarios, edge computing offers a better fit with its powerful processing and short communication paths, while fog computing can play a supportive role in environmental sensing and boundary security, forming a multi-layer collaborative system.

1.1.5.4 Limitations and Evolution Toward Integrated Architectures

Although edge computing demonstrates significant value across various scenarios through its advantages in low latency, near-source deployment, and localized processing, it still faces several key challenges in large-scale practical applications. First, edge nodes are typically heterogeneous devices with limited computing and storage capabilities, making it difficult to continuously support complex models and high-concurrency tasks. Second, the lack of unified scheduling, orchestration, and management mechanisms in edge computing leads to suboptimal resource utilization. Finally, the wide geographic distribution and environmental variability of edge nodes significantly increase the difficulty of network security, privacy protection, and device maintenance.

More fundamentally, edge computing alone cannot sustain a complete ICN ecosystem. It must collaborate with the cloud's centralized high-performance computing and global perspective. As a result, the industry is increasingly shifting toward hybrid architectures such as cloud-edge collaboration and cloud-network convergence. These architectures aim to establish unified frameworks for resource scheduling, task orchestration, and data pipelines, enabling functional complementarity and intelligent coordination among cloud, edge, and terminal layers. This integrated development trend marks a critical direction in the evolution of ICNs and will be further explored in the next section.

1.1.6 Cloud-Edge Collaboration and Cloud-Network Integration

1.1.6.1 Advantages and Features

Cloud-edge collaboration and cloud-network convergence represent key evolutionary directions in response to the rapid growth of compute-intensive and latency-sensitive applications. Compared to traditional centralized cloud computing models, cloud-edge collaboration enables the offloading and processing of tasks closer to the data source, thereby ensuring faster service response while significantly reducing network backhaul traffic. Furthermore, edge nodes possess the ability to sense their environment and process local data, allowing them to maintain basic system services even when the cloud is unreachable or communication is interrupted, thus enhancing overall network resilience and reliability.

In cloud-network convergence architectures, underlying network resources and upper-layer computing resources are jointly scheduled. Technologies such as SDN and NFV enable unified resource management and dynamic orchestration, breaking the traditional "functional silo" between computing and networking. This collaborative system lays a critical foundation for building agile, efficient, and elastic ICNs.

1.1.6.2 Key Architectures

Current cloud-edge collaboration and cloud-network convergence architectures generally adopt a three-layer distributed model consisting of cloud, edge, and terminal layers. The cloud layer is responsible for global management and policy generation, the edge layer handles real-time computation and preliminary data processing, and the terminal layer serves as the front line for data collection and control execution.

Scheduling systems typically follow a hybrid strategy combining centralized control and edge autonomy. At the global level, the control center formulates initial allocation plans based on task priority, resource load, and network conditions. At the local level, edge nodes perform dynamic adjustments and resource reuse based on real-time contextual awareness. In recent years, the adoption of AI-based scheduling techniques, such as deep reinforcement learning and attention mechanisms [11], has significantly advanced the intelligence of cloud-edge collaborative scheduling. These approaches enable perception of high-dimensional dynamic states and optimization of complex task assignments. As a result, such scheduling strategies not only improve task completion rates and resource utilization but also demonstrate strong generalization capability and robustness.

1.1.6.3 Limitations and Challenges

Despite significant progress in cloud-edge collaboration and cloud-network convergence, several challenges remain in large-scale deployment and cross-domain scheduling. On one hand, the limited physical capabilities and heterogeneous runtime environments of edge nodes make it difficult to design unified scheduling strategies that suit all scenarios, increasing the complexity of resource virtualization and interface standardization. On the other hand, multi-layer architectures often involve long task migration paths and high latency in state synchronization, which adversely affect task real-time performance and overall system scheduling efficiency. Moreover, there is still a lack of flexible and efficient coordination mechanisms between edge nodes and cloud resources, particularly in task offloading decisions and data consistency assurance. Most current scheduling algorithms focus on optimizing a single objective, making it difficult to simultaneously balance multiple constraints such as user experience, system load, and energy efficiency. There is an urgent need for more unified, intelligent, and evolvable scheduling frameworks to support deeper integration in cloud-edge collaborative environments.

1.1.7 Computing Network Convergence

1.1.7.1 Concept and Connotation

"Computing-network integration" refers to the agile, intelligent, and secure interconnection of cloud, edge, and terminal computing resources through a unified network infrastructure, enabling centralized scheduling, elastic orchestration, and efficient delivery of computing power. Its core goal is to break down isolated computing silos, enhance the overall utilization of distributed computing resources, and provide computing services via the network in a manner as ubiquitous and accessible as utilities like water and electricity. Compared to traditional centralized computing models, computing-network integration emphasizes the ubiquitous deployment and on-demand invocation of computational resources. It leverages the network as a medium to "transport" computing power, schedule resources, and ensure service quality-driving computation from static central hubs toward dynamic network edges.

1.1.7.2 Distinction from Cloud-network Integration

Computing-network integration is an evolution and expansion based on the concept of cloud-network integration. Cloud-network integration primarily emphasizes "cloud-driven network adjustment" and "network following the cloud", focusing on the coordinated configuration of cloud computing and network resources, with an emphasis on optimizing the coupling between cloud service deployment and network paths. While computing-network integration elevates "computing" to a core capability, it encompasses a wider range of heterogeneous computing forms (such as GPU, NPU, and FPGA), enables elastic provisioning across diverse scenarios and services, and introduces unified computing power metrics and orchestration mechanisms. This facilitates a deeper level of integration among computing, services, and networks.

In terms of service objectives, cloud-network integration prioritizes connection quality assurance, while computing-network integration places greater emphasis on the reachability, adjustability, and serviceability of computing resources.

1.1.7.3 Architectural Layers and Key Capabilities

Computing-network integration generally comprises four architectural layers:

- Infrastructure convergence layer, which provides physical connectivity and coordination between network and computing resources.
- Platform convergence layer, which enables unified management of computing power and service provisioning.
- Application convergence layer, which delivers ubiquitous computing services tailored to vertical industries.
- Security convergence layer, which ensures trustworthiness and isolation during the computing resource scheduling process.

In terms of key capabilities, computing-network integration features computing resource awareness, intelligent network routing, SLA-driven scheduling, and heterogeneous computing orchestration. It supports real-time, end-to-end "computing-network path" selection and service delivery based on business demands.

1.1.7.4 Challenges

Although computing-network integration outlines a forward-looking blueprint for the development of computing infrastructure, its implementation still faces multiple challenges. The foremost issue is the lack of mature unified modeling and measurement frameworks for different types of computing resources, which hinders generalized orchestration. Additionally, cross-domain scheduling involves complex mechanisms for resource awareness and real-time coordination, yet currently lacks standardized interfaces and efficient protocol support. Furthermore, concerns around computing security, service isolation, and data compliance impose higher demands on integrated platforms. Moving forward, continuous efforts are needed in areas such as standard system development, key technology research, and system-level architectural design to advance computing-network integration from concept to large-scale practical deployment.

1.2 Current Status of Intelligent Computing Networks

This section focuses on the current state of development in ICNs, providing a systematic overview of their strategic context, technological pathways, and architectural frameworks. Driven by the global wave of digital transformation and major national initiatives such as the "East Data, West Computing" project in China, significant changes are underway in the deployment strategies, resource organization models, and service provisioning forms of computing networks. A cloud-edge-terminal collaborative architecture is gradually taking shape, forming the foundational framework for multi-tier resource scheduling and service delivery. Building upon this framework, the system integrates the three core elements of computing power, algorithms, and data into a heterogeneous resource infrastructure spanning all layers, with strong integration capabilities and service elasticity in real-world applications. Meanwhile, key enabling technologies such as software-defined networking, containerization, cloud-network collaboration, and edge intelligence are evolving continuously, propelling the computing network ecosystem toward greater intelligence and convergence. This section provides the practical context and technological background necessary for the subsequent discussions on the convergence-oriented scheduling of the three elements and future development trends.

1.2.1 Strategic and Technical Background of ICNs

1.2.1.1 The Era of Data-driven Digital Transformation

Since the beginning of the twenty-first century, the world has experienced a wave of digital transformation driven by data. With the continuous evolution of emerging technologies such as cloud computing, the Internet of Things, 5G, and artificial intelligence, the generation and application of massive amounts of data have become key factors in promoting social progress and industrial upgrading. Research institutions predict that the total volume of global data will continue to grow rapidly in the coming years, with a high average annual growth rate. How to efficiently store, process, and analyze this vast amount of information has become a core issue that must be addressed in the era of the digital economy.

Against this backdrop, the new generation of technologies presents unprecedented challenges for computing power. The development of artificial intelligence has driven an exponential increase in the demand for computing resources in applications such as deep learning and large-scale model training, with the number of parameters in individual AI models continuing to rise. 5G technology provides high-bandwidth and low-latency data transmission capabilities, supporting the demand for real-time data analysis and processing in intelligent manufacturing, intelligent transportation, and other fields. The rapid proliferation of Internet of Things devices has further led to massive and distributed real-time data generation, with the number of global IoT devices and the total amount of data expected to continue to grow significantly in the future. The combined effect of these technologies has led computing architectures to evolve from centralized large-scale computing at single points to distributed, heterogeneous, and multi-level collaborative computing networks.

Faced with the challenges that traditional centralized computing architectures cannot meet, ICNs have emerged as an innovative infrastructure and have become a key path to meet diverse computing power demands. ICNs achieve ubiquitous deployment and flexible scheduling of computing resources through the collaboration of diversified computing nodes such as central clouds, edge clouds, and edge gateways. On one hand, computing networks solve problems such as imbalanced distribution of computing power between different regions and between Internet and traditional industries, thereby improving the overall utilization of computing resources. On the other hand, ICNs have transformed computing power into a basic societal resource that can be accessed on demand, much like electricity and water, promoting industrial intelligence and informatization transformation.

Many practical cases in the industry have demonstrated the significant value of ICNs. In the manufacturing sector, BMW has used digital twin technology and the Nvidia Omniverse platform to build and optimize factory production lines in virtual space, significantly improving production efficiency and cost control capabilities. In the transportation sector, intelligent V2X solutions combine in-vehicle sensors with the collaborative capabilities of computing networks. This achieves multi-dimensional real-time data processing and driving strategy optimization. These optimizations apply to interactions between vehicles, between vehicles and infrastructure, and within vehicles themselves. In the healthcare industry, the National Health Service (NHS) of the United Kingdom has introduced the Heartflow Analysis platform, which uses non-invasive coronary imaging and 3D model reconstruction technology to achieve more accurate cardiovascular disease screening and significantly reduce medical costs.

It is worth noting that the strategic position of computing power is increasingly becoming a critical national infrastructure for international competition. The United States launched the National Strategic Computing Initiative (NSCI) as early as 2015, clearly proposing to enhance the research and deployment of high-performance computing capabilities through policy and technological measures. In recent years, China has actively promoted the construction of an integrated nationwide computing network infrastructure through national strategies such as the "East Data, West

Computing" project, striving to achieve green, low-carbon, flexible, and intelligent supply of computing resources. Standard-setting work for computing and network convergence (CNC) is also underway, laying the foundation for global ICNs. This effort is being launched by key international organizations, such as the International Telecommunication Union (ITU), 3rd Generation Partnership Project (3GPP), and the Internet Engineering Task Force (IETF).

The explosive growth of global data and the diverse application scenarios of emerging technologies have created a strong and sustained demand for computing power. As a new generation of infrastructure, ICNs have fundamentally changed the way computing power is supplied and allocated, and have become a crucial cornerstone of national strategic competition in the era of the digital economy, providing strong support for subsequent technological innovation and social development.

1.2.1.2 The "East Data, West Computing" Project

To address the imbalance of computing power resources between eastern and western regions of China and the excessive energy consumption challenges, the country officially launched the "East Data, West Computing" project in 2022. The goal is to build data centers and new computing infrastructure in the central and western regions to systematically redirect the massive data generated in the east to the west for processing and storage, thereby promoting the efficient circulation and coordination of national computing resources. This project has been hailed as a milestone strategic initiative following other large-scale national resource allocation projects such as the South-to-North Water Diversion Project, the West-to-East Electricity Transmission Project, and the West-to-East Gas Pipeline Project. It demonstrates China's strong commitment to building new infrastructure for the digital economy.

The implementation of the "East Data, West Computing" project aligns with China's strategic goals for digital economic development during the 14th Five-Year Plan period. Currently, with the rapid development of emerging technologies such as 5G, the Internet of Things, and artificial intelligence, the explosive growth of massive data has generated unprecedented demands for computing power. However, the eastern regions face serious constraints in land and electricity resources, making it difficult to continue expanding data center construction. In contrast, the western regions have abundant renewable energy and land resources, making them suitable as national computing hubs to undertake data processing tasks from the east. According to research by national institutions, the energy consumption of data centers has become a critical bottleneck restricting the development of digital infrastructure in the east, and there is an urgent need to optimize resource allocation nationwide through the orderly transfer of computing resources [12, 13].

In terms of policy design, the East Data, West Computing project has designated two sets of infrastructure. First, it named eight national computing power hubs: the Beijing-Tianjin-Hebei region, the Yangtze River Delta, the Guangdong-Hong Kong-Macao Greater Bay Area, Chengdu-Chongqing, Inner Mongolia, Guizhou, Gansu, and Ningxia. Second, it designated ten national data center clusters, including Zhangjiakou, Guian, and Qingyang. Among them, regions such as Inner Mongolia, Guizhou, Gansu, and Ningxia mainly undertake non-real-time computing tasks (e.g., background processing, offline analysis, and backup storage). In contrast, regions like Beijing-Tianjin-Hebei and the Yangtze River Delta focus on large-scale real-time computing tasks, supporting the digital development of critical industries and metropolitan clusters.

The project has played a key role not only in enhancing national computing power but also in supporting China's dual carbon goals of peaking carbon emissions and achieving carbon neutrality. Research shows that the energy consumption of Chinese data centers has reached very high levels, becoming a major factor restricting the further expansion of digital infrastructure and imposing higher requirements for carbon emissions control. By building green, low-carbon data centers in the west, adopting efficient power supply technologies, liquid cooling technologies, and directly using renewable energy, the project can effectively reduce the power usage effectiveness (PUE) values and promote the green transformation of data centers.

The project has already achieved significant initial results. On one hand, it has stimulated large-scale infrastructure investments and driven the development of related upstream and downstream industries. On the other hand, the scale of data centers in the western regions has grown rapidly, and computing resources have started to transfer orderly from east to west, alleviating the long-standing issue of regional development imbalance. For example, Guizhou has proposed the construction of data industry clusters in five areas, namely pilot areas, pioneer areas, demonstration areas, and reserve areas. Gansu has built a Northwest artificial intelligence data center cluster and a data governance base to actively undertake the computing needs of the eastern regions.

In addition, the project has strengthened the national integrated big data center collaborative innovation system, providing both technological and policy foundations for the integration and circulation of data resources across levels, regions, and systems. Relevant national departments are also studying the establishment of standardized assessment and evaluation systems to ensure the smooth progress and effectiveness of the project's implementation.

In the future, as more detailed policies and technical standards are introduced, the "East Data, West Computing" project is expected to further optimize the distribution of national computing resources and enhance China's overall strength in global digital economic competition.

1.2.1.3 The Rise of Cloud-edge-end Collaborative Architectures

To address data transmission bottlenecks, enhance business flexibility, and achieve optimized resource allocation, the cloud-edge-end collaborative architecture has emerged. This architecture distributes computing, storage, network, and other resources across the cloud, edge, and terminal devices as needed. It achieves multilevel collaborative processing and provides strong technical support for fields such as the Internet of Things, the Internet of Vehicles, the Industrial Internet, and intelligent manufacturing [14].

The technological foundation of the cloud-edge-end collaborative architecture originates from the development of multiple cutting-edge technologies. Cloud computing provides powerful centralized resource pools and large-scale data processing capabilities, serving as the core for global resource management and business scheduling. Edge computing reduces data transmission latency and bandwidth consumption by offloading computing tasks from central nodes to network edges closer to data sources, thereby enhancing data privacy and system robustness. Terminal devices, as the source of data generation and the execution units for real-time response, possess sensing, control, and local intelligent processing capabilities, forming the foundation for autonomy and collaboration at the device level.

This collaborative architecture is typically divided into three layers: the cloud layer, the edge layer, and the end layer. In a typical practice within the field of industrial control systems (ICS), the cloud platform is responsible for dynamic global resource scheduling, business analysis, and data model training. Edge IoT agents, located near end users, handle real-time data processing, transmission, and storage tasks. Terminal devices, including smart sensors and industrial gateways, are responsible for data acquisition, status sensing, and execution control. This hierarchical design effectively realizes business load balancing and optimized resource allocation, enhancing the overall reliability and responsiveness of the system. In actual deployments, terminal devices transmit data to edge nodes for preprocessing, which then forward partial data or processing results to the cloud for further analysis and model optimization. The optimized models are subsequently distributed from the cloud to the edge and terminal layers, realizing bidirectional collaboration between data and models, as illustrated in Fig. 1.2.

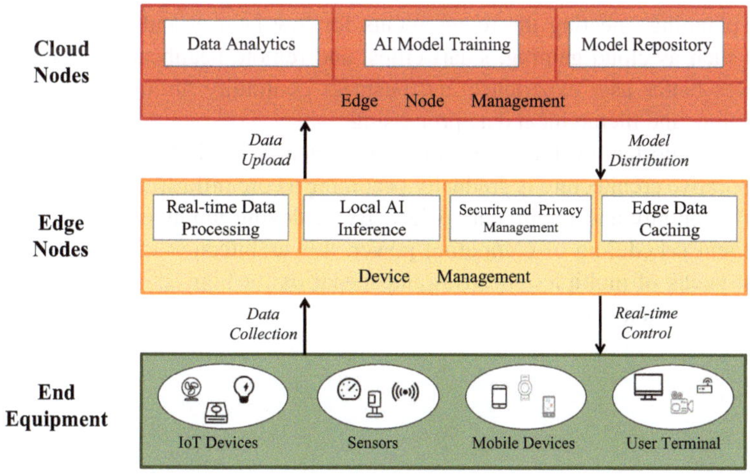

Fig. 1.2 Cloud-edge-end collaborative computing framework

In practical applications, the cloud-edge-end architecture exhibits multiple typical interaction modes, including edge-end collaboration, cloud-edge collaboration, and cloud-end collaboration. Edge-end collaboration focuses on enabling real-time local data processing by terminal devices and feedback to edge devices, significantly reducing the load on the cloud. Cloud-edge collaboration aggregates regional data onto the cloud platform for big data analysis and decision-making, and then transmits scheduling results back to edge nodes for execution. Cloud-end collaboration is mainly used for special or high-priority tasks, where the cloud platform directly dispatches terminal devices to achieve precise control and data sharing.

The China Academy of Information and Communications Technology has systematically reviewed the development status of the Cloud-Edge-End Architecture in China in its report on integrated Cloud-Edge-End development. It proposed six major directions for integrated development: resource integration, operation and maintenance integration, data integration, application integration, scheduling integration, and security integration. Resource integration shields the underlying distributed heterogeneous resources to achieve unified resource pool management. Operation and maintenance integration improves the visualization and automation of distributed device monitoring and maintenance. Data integration breaks data silos and realizes full lifecycle management of data. Application integration promotes the unified development, deployment, and governance of distributed cloud-native applications. Scheduling integration improves resource utilization and business experience through intelligent algorithms. Security integration establishes a comprehensive multi-level security protection system from device authentication and data encryption to cloud security posture awareness.

The cloud-edge-end collaborative architecture has been applied in various industry scenarios. In intelligent manufacturing, edge devices preprocess industrial on-site data, reducing transmission pressure and enabling local intelligent control. In the Internet of Vehicles, edge nodes assist vehicles with real-time perception and route planning, meeting the requirements for low latency and high reliability. In fields such as cloud gaming, smart cities, and remote healthcare, the architecture achieves better user experience and business continuity through elastic resource scheduling and hierarchical data processing.

As an important evolutionary form of next-generation ICNs, the cloud-edge-end collaborative architecture is gradually becoming a core infrastructure supporting the digital economy and intelligent society. By achieving ubiquitous deployment and intelligent scheduling of computing power, this architecture effectively meets the urgent needs of multiple industries and scenarios for high-reliability, low-latency, and high-elasticity computing.

1.2.2 *Current Architectural Status of the Three Core Elements in Intelligent Computing Networks*

1.2.2.1 Current Synergistic Operations and Role Overlaps

In current ICN systems, computing, algorithm, and data serve as the three core elements forming the foundational resource framework that supports intelligent services. Although overlaps among these elements have emerged in certain applications, they still maintain relatively distinct functional roles at the architectural level. Each element fulfills a specific responsibility, working together to accomplish sensing, computation, and decision-making. This section provides a systematic overview of the present collaboration patterns and structural characteristics of these elements, focusing on three aspects: functional roles, coordination mechanisms, and boundary interactions.

From the perspective of functional division, computing, algorithm, and data currently exist as relatively independent resource layers in most intelligent systems, corresponding to different types of infrastructure and service models. Computing resources are typically hosted on centralized or distributed heterogeneous platforms and are responsible for tasks like model training, inference, and data processing. Algorithms are encapsulated as pre-trained models, rule-based systems, or online inference services, and are deployed through middleware or microservice platforms to provide core intelligent functions. Data is organized and managed through offline warehouses, real-time streaming frameworks, or distributed data lakes, serving as input, feedback, and labeled information sources for algorithmic processes. These elements each play a distinct role and have not yet been integrated at the physical or control-layer level.

In terms of coordination mechanisms, interactions among computing, algorithm, and data are primarily enabled by orchestration platforms, middleware, and standardized service interfaces, resulting in a modular and policy-driven collaborative model. In most practical deployments, these three elements are jointly scheduled through platform-level orchestration systems. For example, an algorithmic task may be assigned by a scheduler to a computing node with suitable resources, while corresponding data fragments are retrieved for execution. In this process, container orchestration platforms such as Kubernetes manage computing resources and service deployments, while data access is handled by data middleware or unified APIs. These coordination mechanisms are highly configurable and abstract, enabling rapid deployment and elastic scaling of algorithmic services, as well as greater controllability and observability in data processing pipelines.

It is important to note that while the current coordination mechanisms enable the elements to interact effectively, they are primarily realized through pipeline-style integrations such as interface calls, data transfers, and container registration. Unified modeling and scheduling across all three elements at the underlying level are still absent. In other words, these interactions are more accurately described as process-level coupling supported by platforms, rather than ontological fusion among the elements themselves. State information, optimization logic, and scheduling policies for each element remain bound to separate systems, requiring bridge-layer logic to synchronize states and coordinate resources. Although this architecture offers flexibility and maintainability, it also introduces coordination overhead and latency in cross-system operations.

From the perspective of role boundaries, some systems have begun to exhibit overlaps in the functional responsibilities of computing, algorithm, and data. However, these overlaps mostly occur at the interface or service abstraction level and have not yet evolved into full architectural integration. For instance, data resources today not only provide input but also serve as feedback for model tuning, contributing to closed-loop algorithm refinement. Likewise, some algorithm modules have been service-oriented and embedded into computing platforms, supporting on-demand loading and task-driven deployment under the concept of Algorithm-as-a-Service (AaaS). Computing nodes are increasingly equipped with autonomous capabilities to select appropriate algorithm containers and data paths based on task types. Nonetheless, these overlaps largely rely on protocols and service-layer middleware rather than unified logical or structural integration across the three elements.

In summary, computing, algorithm, and data in ICNs currently exhibit clear functional separation, structured coordination patterns, and partial overlaps in their roles. The collaboration among them is facilitated through platform mechanisms and scheduling logic that support stable system operation. However, their integration is still based on modular linkage and interface interaction, without a unified abstraction or operational model. While this structure has improved the overall efficiency and flexibility of intelligent systems, it also reveals inherent bottlenecks in cross-domain coordination and unified scheduling. As new AI systems, heterogeneous computing resources, and complex application scenarios continue to emerge, the demand for deeper integration among the three elements is rising.

1.2.2.2 Infrastructure Status Supporting the Three Elements

Currently, the infrastructure of computing power, algorithms, and data in ICNs is exhibiting a dual trend of rapid evolution and deep integration. From hardware resources and software platforms to data support systems, a multi-layered infrastructure covering cloud, edge, and terminal levels is being established globally to provide a solid physical and technical foundation for frontier applications such as artificial intelligence, big data, and the Internet of Things.

In terms of computing power infrastructure, hyperscale data centers have become the primary carriers of global computing capacity. Multi-location hub data centers form powerful heterogeneous computing pools. They do this through the centralized deployment of diverse computing resources. A key example is China's East Data, West Computing project. This project has built an integrated computing network across eastern and western regions to achieve complementary and dynamically scheduled computing resources between areas. The project utilizes feature encoders to convert unstructured data into tensor formats and applies algorithm containerization technologies to enhance model transfer and reuse efficiency. Intelligent scheduling systems dynamically allocate computing resources based on real-time business demands, significantly improving overall resource utilization levels.

The construction of edge computing facilities is rapidly addressing the “last mile” gap in computing networks. Edge servers, micro data centers, and intelligent gateways deployed near data sources enable local data processing and real-time response capabilities, substantially reducing data backhaul bandwidth and system latency. For example, intelligent manufacturing enterprises have deployed GPU edge nodes inside factories, which, combined with sensor data streams and reinforcement learning algorithms, have established complete factory-level digital twin systems. These systems realize automated optimization and anomaly detection of production processes, improving system energy efficiency while ensuring real-time performance.

In terms of algorithm infrastructure, leading global cloud service providers are actively building AaaS platforms centered on artificial intelligence. Platforms such as Google Cloud AI Platform, Amazon SageMaker, Microsoft Azure Machine Learning, Huawei ModelArts, and Baidu PaddlePaddle provide users with comprehensive services for algorithm development, model training, inference deployment, and lifecycle management. The cloudification of algorithm infrastructure has greatly lowered the technical threshold for algorithm research and deployment, promoting tighter integration between algorithms and computing resources. For example, the financial industry has introduced federated learning architectures to achieve cross-institutional, distributed collaboration of computing resources and algorithm models, significantly enhancing model generalization capabilities and risk identification performance [15].

As the cornerstone of the three-element integration, data infrastructure is evolving from traditional centralized storage toward distributed data lakes, big data clusters, and real-time data stream processing systems. National-level data centers, enterprise-level data lakes such as AWS Lake Formation and Azure Data Lake Storage, and IoT real-time data platforms together form the foundation for multi-source heterogeneous data management and analysis. For instance, the “East Data, West Computing” project uses distributed data storage systems to achieve large-scale data synchronization and sharing, thereby improving the efficiency and security of data flow. Additionally, supported by computing-power and electricity collaborative scheduling technologies, green data centers dynamically optimize server workloads based on wind power prediction data, task priority, and electricity price fluctuations. This enhances the use of clean energy and reduces energy consumption, setting an exemplary model for the construction of green and low-carbon data centers.

The current infrastructure development of ICNs shows a clear transformation from single-dimension capabilities to multi-dimensional coordination and from centralized architectures to distributed edge architectures. As shown in Fig. 1.3, computing power infrastructure forms a hierarchical computing capability across cloud, edge, and terminal levels. Algorithm infrastructure achieves standardized

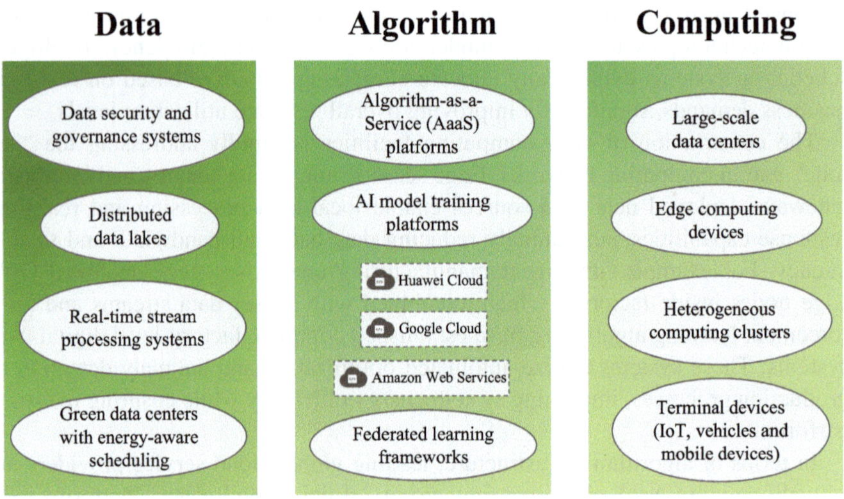

Fig. 1.3 Infrastructure of computing, algorithm, and data

research and deployment through cloud service platforms. Data infrastructure enhances data accessibility and availability through distributed storage and real-time stream processing. The high level of coordination among the three in real-world systems is gradually breaking down traditional technical boundaries and is forming a solid foundation for future intelligent applications. It is foreseeable that, with the continuous development of 5G, artificial intelligence, big data, and computing network technologies, the collaborative optimization capabilities of the three-element infrastructure will continue to strengthen, propelling ICNs toward a more efficient, greener, and smarter new stage of development.

1.2.3 Current Status of Key Technologies

1.2.3.1 Software-defined Networking and Network Function Virtualization

As ICNs continue to demand greater flexibility, scalability, and optimized resource allocation, traditional network architectures have become insufficient to meet the service requirements of large-scale, multi-type terminals and diverse applications. Against this backdrop, SDN and NFV have emerged as critical foundational technologies within ICNs.

SDN introduces a centralized network control plane by decoupling control logic from traditional network devices such as routers and switches and transferring it to a unified controller. This approach enables centralized management and programmable control of the entire network. Network administrators can dynamically configure and optimize network resources through software, greatly improving network flexibility and programmability. In ICNs, SDN provides strong support for the coordination of multi-level heterogeneous networks across cloud, edge, and terminal environments, and has shown wide application value particularly in data centers, 5G networks, and edge computing scenarios.

NFV further advances the virtualization of network services. By running proprietary network functions traditionally hosted on hardware devices, such as firewalls, load balancers, and intrusion detection systems, as software on general-purpose computing platforms, NFV has greatly reduced equipment procurement and maintenance costs [16]. It has also improved the flexible deployment and rapid scalability of network services. In ICN environments characterized by dynamic resource changes and diverse business requirements, NFV works synergistically with SDN to achieve elastic and efficient service chain orchestration and management [17].

However, the development of SDN and NFV still faces some challenges. The centralized control architecture of SDN presents potential single points of failure and security risks, while NFV's virtualized environments may experience performance degradation and issues related to multi-tenant isolation. These concerns place higher demands on future technological advancements [18]. Current research focuses on multi-controller collaboration, distributed SDN architecture design, optimization of NFV at the edge, and AI-assisted adaptive network management [19–23].

Therefore, as key components of ICNs, SDN and NFV are driving network infrastructure toward a more open, flexible, and efficient direction, laying a solid foundation for the construction of next-generation high-performance ICNs.

1.2.3.2 Containerization and Container Orchestration Technologies

With the rapid development of technologies such as cloud computing, big data, and the Internet of Things, applications within ICNs have become highly distributed, modular, and microservice-oriented. Traditional virtual machine technologies, due to their high resource overhead and low migration efficiency, can no longer meet the current demands for elastic scaling and rapid deployment. Against this backdrop, containerization and container orchestration technologies have emerged as important means to improve computing resource utilization and operational efficiency.

Containerization packages applications and runtime environments into lightweight, portable images, greatly enhancing consistency in software development and deployment. Compared with virtual machines, containers offer lower system resource consumption, faster startup times, and greater portability, leading to their widespread adoption in enterprise-level cloud computing platforms and edge computing environments.

However, as large-scale container clusters have become prevalent, efficiently managing tens of thousands of container instances has become a new challenge. Container orchestration technologies have been developed to address this issue.

Kubernetes (K8s), currently the most representative open-source container orchestration platform, has become the de facto industry standard in ICNs [24].

Originally developed by Google, Kubernetes is now a core project of the Cloud Native Computing Foundation (CNCF) community. It provides comprehensive cluster management capabilities, including automated deployment, scaling, load balancing, rolling updates, and self-healing recovery of containers, significantly reducing the operational complexity of distributed applications. The design philosophy of Kubernetes emphasizes declarative configuration and automated control; users only need to define the desired state, and the system automatically converges to that state, greatly enhancing system maintainability and scalability.

In practical applications of ICNs, the capabilities of Kubernetes have extended from traditional data centers to edge computing and cloud-edge-end collaborative scenarios. Through lightweight derivatives such as K3s, Kubernetes can automate the deployment and management of microservices even on resource-constrained edge devices. In addition, the rich ecosystem of Kubernetes plugins, such as Istio for service mesh implementation [25], Prometheus for monitoring, and Helm for application management, provides strong support for building complex distributed intelligent computing platforms.

Although Kubernetes has demonstrated strong application potential, challenges remain in areas such as multi-tenant isolation, security policy configuration, and cross-domain multi-cluster management. Current research efforts are focused on improving Kubernetes performance in heterogeneous environments, enhancing security [26], and deeply integrating AI-driven adaptive resource scheduling algorithms [27]. Containerization and Kubernetes have provided ICNs with efficient, flexible, and scalable application hosting and resource scheduling capabilities, serving as essential foundational technologies for realizing cloud-edge-end integrated service architectures.

1.2.3.3 Cloud-network Collaboration and QoS Assurance Mechanisms

As the scale and complexity of ICNs continue to grow, optimizing either computing or network resources alone is no longer sufficient to meet the diverse and high-reliability business requirements. To achieve global collaborative optimization of computing, storage, and network resources, cloud-network collaboration has become a critical direction for current research and practical implementation. This technology breaks the traditional isolation between cloud computing and network systems, enabling dynamic joint orchestration of resources, guaranteeing business priority, and improving overall service performance.

In traditional cloud computing models, computing resources are typically concentrated in data centers, while networks serve only as passive data transmission channels. Cloud-network collaboration introduces intelligent control at the network layer, enhancing application awareness and resource scheduling flexibility. Technologies such as SDN and NFV provide strong foundational support for cloud-network collaboration by enabling on-demand dynamic allocation of computing resources and network bandwidth, thus achieving a truly service-driven network.

Within the cloud-network collaboration system, Quality of Service (QoS) assurance mechanisms play a key role in ensuring the prioritized transmission of critical services [28–30]. QoS improves the reliability and predictability of network transmission through strategies such as bandwidth guarantees, delay control, packet loss rate limitation, and jitter suppression [31]. Various service-oriented strategies and algorithms have been proposed, such as SDN-based traffic engineering technologies that automatically adjust link allocation according to service priority to reduce transmission latency for critical tasks.

Additionally, the development of edge computing has further advanced the evolution of cloud-network collaboration architectures. By offloading part of the computing and storage tasks to edge nodes, the transmission path of data within core networks is reduced, effectively lowering overall latency and improving real-time system responsiveness. Particularly in low-latency, high-bandwidth scenarios such as the Internet of Vehicles, the Industrial Internet of Things, and AR/VR applications, cloud-edge-end collaborative architectures demonstrate significant performance advantages.

However, cloud-network collaboration still faces several technical challenges. There is a lack of interoperability between devices and systems from different vendors, and the absence of unified interface standards and protocols affects seamless cross-domain resource scheduling. In addition, ensuring QoS and secure isolation in multi-tenant environments requires further research and optimization. In the future, AI-assisted adaptive QoS scheduling, cross-domain resource orchestration, and collaborative optimization algorithms for multi-service scenarios will become key research areas.

In summary, cloud-network collaboration and QoS assurance mechanisms play a crucial role in improving resource utilization, service continuity, and user experience in ICNs. They serve as important technological foundations for realizing integrated intelligent services across cloud, edge, and terminal environments.

1.3 Development Trends of Intelligent Computing Networks

This section discusses the developmental trends of ICNs, with a focus on three core dimensions: the increasing complexity of resource scheduling, the paradigm shift in task-resource matching, and the convergence of computing power, algorithms, and data. It systematically examines the key transformations and technical challenges arising along the current evolutionary path. Building upon this foundation, the subsequent chapters will delve deeper into unified modeling of the three core elements, the design of scheduling mechanisms, and new system architecture paradigms. The goal is to provide both theoretical grounding and technical guidance for constructing future computing infrastructures that are efficient, intelligent, and collaboratively orchestrated.

1.3.1 Escalating Complexity in Resource Scheduling

1.3.1.1 Heterogeneous Resources and Multidimensional Coupling Driving Scheduling Complexity

ICNs have disrupted the relatively stable and homogeneous resource environments characteristic of traditional cloud computing by progressively constructing heterogeneous resource pools spanning cloud, edge, and terminal layers [32]. With the emergence of large-scale AI models, real-time interactive workloads, and multimodal collaborative computing, the types of resources supporting tasks in the system have become increasingly diverse [33]. In addition to general-purpose computing resources such as CPUs, the system now incorporates a range of accelerators including GPUs, FPGAs, and NPUs, as well as programmable resources such as high-speed caches, non-volatile storage, and data bus bandwidth. Together, these constitute a complex framework for resource coordination. Each resource class exhibits distinct performance characteristics, scheduling costs, and deployment constraints, rendering it infeasible for schedulers to rely on a unified metric for simple allocation. Instead, dedicated performance profiles and compatibility evaluation logic must be developed for each type of resource.

The degree of coupling among resources has also increased significantly. In edge environments, the computational and networking capabilities of certain devices are tightly bound. For compute-intensive tasks, failure to align with local cache or bandwidth capabilities may result in a rapid decline in overall performance. Particularly under scenarios involving concurrent multi-task execution and frequent resource sharing, the scheduling system must holistically evaluate tasks' composite dependencies on storage, computation, and bandwidth in order to orchestrate resources cooperatively. This multidimensional coupling implies that the scheduling problem is no longer a simple allocation over a "computational matrix" but an optimization task within a high-dimensional constrained space. The system thus faces unprecedented challenges in evaluating resource availability, resolving constraint conflicts, and coordinating across heterogeneous devices.

The customized resource demands of different task types further exacerbate the complexity of scheduling. For workloads such as AI inference, image rendering, and natural language generation, execution performance depends not only on the specifications of the assigned resources but also on factors such as model architecture, input data size, and the topology of the computation graph. Traditional static descriptors of resources, such as the number of CPU cores or memory size, are no longer adequate for capturing the behavioral characteristics of these tasks. This leads to an information asymmetry problem when matching tasks with resources. Against this backdrop, schedulers must develop a deep semantic understanding of task types and employ more expressive scheduling models in order to enhance the accuracy and robustness of task-to-resource matching.

1.3.1.2 Distributed Architectures and High Frequency Scheduling Intensifying System Load

ICNs adopt a multilayer collaborative architecture encompassing cloud, edge, and terminal layers, which significantly enhances system elasticity and proximity to service endpoints. However, this highly distributed structure also markedly increases the management overhead and response complexity faced by the scheduling system. Nodes across different layers vary greatly in physical location, resource capacity, and runtime environment, requiring the scheduling system to dynamically select the optimal deployment node based on multiple task attributes such as latency sensitivity, data locality, and security level. Such scheduling decisions must go beyond static configuration data and rely on real-time awareness of the overall network resource status and the ability to respond promptly.

The scheduling interactions among cloud, edge, and terminal layers exhibit stringent temporal requirements. Edge nodes often need to make deployment decisions within milliseconds, where even slight scheduling delays can degrade task performance or result in service failure. Meanwhile, challenges such as state synchronization and feedback latency inherent in distributed systems hinder the maintenance of global consistency, compelling the scheduling system to strike a balance between consistency and responsiveness. Additionally, device states change in highly stochastic ways; certain nodes may become temporarily unavailable due to power constraints, hardware failures, or network jitter. This necessitates that the scheduling system possess elastic fallback and fault-tolerance capabilities to prevent task blockage caused by single-point failures.

The increasing granularity of tasks is another major factor driving the high frequency of scheduling operations. The rise of lightweight computing paradigms such as microservices, containerization, and serverless computing [34, 35] has dramatically shortened task lifecycles from several hours to mere seconds or even less. A single application may consist of dozens or even hundreds of service units, each of which may trigger a resource scheduling operation during its launch, migration, suspension, or reclamation. Under such high-frequency operational conditions, the scheduling system must continuously handle massive volumes of status monitoring, decision-making, and execution feedback, leading to escalating system load. Traditional scheduling architectures based on polling mechanisms and rule engines have become inadequate to meet the growing demands of modern scheduling workloads.

Consequently, future resource scheduling systems must incorporate hierarchical autonomy within their architecture, enabling collaborative yet stratified scheduling logic across cloud, edge, and terminal layers. At the algorithmic level, lightweight sensing, local optimization, and pre-scheduling mechanisms should be introduced to enhance scheduling responsiveness and fault tolerance. These advances will ensure that ICNs maintain stable and efficient resource coordination capabilities even under complex and dynamic operating scenarios.

1.3.1.3 Global Objective Conflicts and Resource Coupling Challenging Scheduling Intelligence

In ICNs characterized by multi-tenant and multi-application coexistence, resource scheduling is no longer a single-objective optimization task. Instead, it has progressively evolved into a complex process of dynamic trade-offs among multiple conflicting objectives. Each type of task and application scenario is associated with its own set of performance constraints and service level agreements (SLAs), such as low latency, high throughput, energy efficiency, or elevated security levels [36]. These objectives often compete for limited resources. If the system prioritizes performance, it may do so at the expense of energy consumption and cost. Conversely, prioritizing energy efficiency may undermine latency guarantees or delivery accuracy. The inherent conflicts among these objectives require the scheduling system to support dynamic weight adjustment, composite policy optimization, and learning capabilities informed by historical behavioral feedback.

The challenge is further compounded by the increasingly tight coupling among computing, data, and network resources. These interdependencies have become critical determinants of scheduling intelligence. For instance, a task assigned to a node with powerful computing capabilities may nonetheless suffer performance degradation if the required data is not locally cached or if the network path introduces transmission bottlenecks. Although the scheduling decision may appear optimal from a computing perspective, execution may ultimately fall short of service targets due to overlooked data and communication constraints. This phenomenon necessitates a transition in scheduling logic from isolated resource matching to holistic system state modeling and inference, enabling the scheduler to assess and anticipate end-to-end system performance outcomes.

Moreover, the scheduling system must manage dynamic behaviors such as elastic resource scaling, task priority shifts, and system recovery from faults. In real-world deployments, tenant demands fluctuate frequently, model versions are updated rapidly, and task workloads can change abruptly. Without adaptive strategies and predictive mechanisms, the scheduling system may fall into cycles of frequent rescheduling and resource oscillations, undermining service stability. Therefore, future scheduling systems must be equipped with intelligent cores that are adaptive, interpretable, and capable of long-term learning. Such systems should leverage graph neural networks to model resource states, employ reinforcement learning to optimize scheduling policies, and utilize data-driven approaches to dynamically adjust objective functions. These capabilities will form the foundation of a new generation of intelligent schedulers endowed with cognitive, evolutionary, and collaborative capabilities.

1.3.2 Transition From Task-Driven to Demand-Aware Computing-Network Matching

1.3.2.1 Task Semantics and Behavior Inference

The characteristics of tasks in ICNs have far surpassed the workload models encountered in traditional centralized computing environments. What began as statically defined tasks with clear boundaries has evolved into complex task flows that are heterogeneous, dynamic, and strongly context-dependent. This transformation directly challenges existing scheduling paradigms. Traditional scheduling systems typically operate based on a linear process, relying primarily on statically declared resource requirements within the task request, such as the number of CPU cores, memory size, or upper limits on execution time. However, complex tasks in scenarios such as deep learning, federated computing, and real-time interaction often exhibit stage-specific heterogeneity, dynamic behavioral evolution, and input-driven resource consumption, rendering static task descriptions insufficient for capturing their actual computational behaviors.

The unstructured nature of task demands further exacerbates this challenge. For instance, even when executing the same AI inference model, the size of input images, complexity of content, and batch dimensions can significantly influence performance across different nodes. Such highly variable task behavior renders the conventional assumption of "configuration equals performance" obsolete. If scheduling strategies continue to rely on static indicators, the result is often inefficient resource matching, performance deviation during execution, or even outright task failure. Therefore, the scheduling system must fundamentally reconstruct its approach to task modeling. Rather than treating tasks as static request entities, the system should adopt dynamic state tracking and resource utilization trajectory modeling to build more expressive semantic representations of task behavior.

This shift in scheduling logic necessitates that the system acquire the ability to infer task behavior prior to initiating resource allocation. Such inference extends beyond estimating resource consumption trends to include evolving task priorities, stage-specific SLAs variations, and the risk of abnormal interruptions. To this end, the system must integrate multi-source information such as historical execution data, task type profiles, and model configuration repositories to develop a nuanced understanding of a task's underlying "computational intent." The focus of scheduling will thus move away from "satisfying explicit requests" toward "inferring actual needs", and performing perception-driven scheduling optimizations based on the real-time status of system resources.

1.3.2.2 Predictive Scheduling and Preconfiguration

In typical application scenarios of ICNs, task requests are characterized by high burstiness, stringent timeliness, and diversified service levels, which impose new demands on resource allocation strategies. Particularly in critical domains such as vehicular networks, smart healthcare, and industrial edge computing, task response times are often constrained to the millisecond or even sub-millisecond level. In such contexts, employing the traditional "schedule upon task arrival" model can easily lead to task failures, service disruptions, or even safety incidents due to insufficient resource preparation and excessive scheduling latency. Consequently, scheduling systems must evolve toward a "prediction and preconfiguration" paradigm, enabling the early identification of potential computational demands and the advance reservation of resources and execution paths, thereby ensuring the system possesses near-real-time scheduling capabilities.

The core of predictive scheduling lies in the establishment of demand awareness. The system must integrate and model information regarding task generation logic, business context, and historical request patterns to infer the likelihood of future task arrivals, resource preferences, and response priorities. In smart healthcare scenarios, for instance, hospital examination queues, equipment utilization frequencies, and the distribution of image recognition tasks all exhibit discernible statistical patterns over time. Based on such characteristics, the scheduling system can forecast resource load trends for the upcoming period and proactively activate selected computing nodes, thereby reducing response latency.

Resource preconfiguration involves more than merely preparing idle compute capacity; it also requires coordinated efforts across dimensions such as local data caching, rapid model loading, and stable maintenance of network paths. This is especially critical in edge environments, where network jitter and data inconsistency are prevalent. In such settings, computational readiness alone is often insufficient to meet service demands. The scheduling system must possess cross-domain resource awareness and be capable of constructing holistic deployment strategies that span data, models, and compute resources, ensuring that once a task arrives, the system can achieve "one-hop readiness."

This forward-looking scheduling mechanism also necessitates new architectural designs. The system must support a layered scheduling structure for heterogeneous resource management, enabling edge nodes to make localized predictions and resource allocation decisions, thereby alleviating the response burden on centralized schedulers. Concurrently, lightweight predictive models, such as temporal modeling and graph neural network inference, should be introduced at the algorithmic level to improve forecasting accuracy and deployment efficiency. Only by incorporating such proactive and autonomous scheduling capabilities can ICNs deliver on the promise of truly on-demand service provisioning.

1.3.2.3 Edge-aware and Decentralized Coordination

As system scale expands and a vast number of edge nodes are deployed, traditional centralized scheduling architectures have become inadequate for achieving real-time awareness and decision-making. The dynamic nature of node states, the unpredictability of network conditions, and the diversity of application scenarios collectively drive the migration of scheduling logic toward the network edge. Even with a global perspective, centralized schedulers often struggle to meet the latency requirements of time-sensitive tasks due to delayed state synchronization, complex scheduling paths, and prolonged response chains. Consequently, the development of a decentralized, context-aware scheduling architecture has emerged as a critical direction.

Edge nodes possess spatial and temporal proximity to task sources, enabling them to swiftly perceive local workload fluctuations, data states, and service request characteristics, thus providing more immediate informational support for task scheduling. Based on this advantage, scheduling strategies can leverage a "lightweight sensing plus local decision-making" mechanism that combines resource status, service objectives, and historical execution patterns to make rapid scheduling decisions aligned with local optimality principles. For example, in an intelligent manufacturing plant, image recognition tasks generated by cameras can be directly processed by local edge devices, eliminating the need to transmit data to remote cloud servers and significantly reducing scheduling latency and transmission overhead.

However, edge scheduling does not imply isolated decision-making. Given the cross-domain flow of tasks and the heterogeneous deployment of resources, edge scheduling must be endowed with collaborative capabilities. The scheduling system must establish a feedback mechanism between "local optimality" and "global system objectives" to ensure that edge nodes, while making autonomous decisions, can also follow strategic guidance to achieve optimal resource distribution. The key to realizing this mechanism lies in constructing "composable context representations". Through standardized interfaces and state expressions, it enables scheduling units across different layers and domains to share demand intentions, system pressures, and scheduling feedback, thereby achieving consistent resource coordination.

Furthermore, to support semantic inference and policy selection in edge scheduling, the system must incorporate embedded reasoning mechanisms. Lightweight models that can be executed in real time on edge devices enable rapid task classification, objective recognition, and resource mapping. The introduction of such capabilities not only enhances the precision of edge scheduling but also makes it feasible to implement complex strategies involving latency tolerance, power constraints, and privacy protection. As edge intelligence continues to mature, demand-aware scheduling capabilities will gradually shift from centralized platforms to edge nodes, ultimately forming a vertically integrated and collaboratively orchestrated intelligent scheduling network.

1.3.3 Integration and Challenges in Unified Scheduling of Three Core Elements

1.3.3.1 Trends Toward Unified Scheduling

Contemporary intelligent computing tasks often involve the coordinated operation of multiple system components. For example, model training relies on data preparation processes, inference tasks must be executed on specific computational platforms, and real-time decision-making depends simultaneously on data sensing and algorithmic response. However, in current scheduling frameworks, computing resources, data assets, and algorithmic modules are typically governed by separate management systems and scheduling logics, lacking a unified scheduling plane. This fragmentation of resources not only increases deployment and operational costs but also diminishes the system's responsiveness to dynamic business demands. In response to increasingly complex task scenarios, the trend toward unified scheduling across the three core elements is gradually emerging and has begun to materialize in various system architectures and practical applications.

In real-world systems, schedulers are often optimized for a specific class of resources or components. For instance, traditional container orchestration systems focus on load balancing and resource utilization of computing nodes, database systems emphasize data locality and consistency, while machine learning frameworks concentrate on training workflows and hyperparameter control. As task forms become increasingly integrated, system architects are exploring ways to consolidate formerly siloed scheduling logics, enabling the scheduler to perceive and coordinate the intrinsic relationships among diverse elements. Some systems reflect this trend by incorporating workflow control, task dependency modeling, and dynamic resource orchestration mechanisms, thereby achieving unified management across training, inference, and data loading stages.

The need for unified scheduling is especially pronounced in scenarios involving large model deployment and inference. Large-scale models not only demand high-performance computational support but also entail considerations such as data preprocessing, model versioning, and inference service responsiveness. In traditional approaches, these stages are handled by separate platforms, leading to inefficiencies in task scheduling and limited automation. To enhance performance and maintainability, many enterprises and research institutions are exploring integrated deployment solutions that fuse model services, data flow management, and resource scheduling into a closed-loop system, thereby achieving task-oriented holistic optimization. Such efforts are driving the advancement of concepts like "task-as-a-service" and "full-stack schedulability", gradually transforming unified scheduling from a theoretical notion into an engineering reality.

The unification of resource representation is another key evolution supporting converged scheduling. Historically, the scheduling targets for computing, data, and algorithm resources have been defined by disparate description standards, such as node specifications, data paths, or container images, lacking a common representational framework. Emerging systems are beginning to adopt unified task description languages or resource graph structures that model the three elements as heterogeneous nodes within a graph. Through the use of graph neural networks or customized scheduling policy functions, these systems enable end-to-end optimization. This approach not only enhances the system's expressive power but also establishes a structured foundation for the integration of intelligent scheduling strategies.

Overall, the trend toward unified scheduling is being propelled by practical needs and driving a paradigmatic shift in system architecture. In the context of complex tasks and elastic services, achieving coordinated scheduling of computation, algorithms, and data is poised to become a critical path in the evolution of ICNs. Although a universally applicable unified architecture has yet to emerge, the boundaries between system components are gradually dissolving, and the logic of resource coordination is rapidly transitioning from "divide and conquer" to "consensus and integration."

1.3.3.2 Technical Barriers

Although the unified scheduling of computing power, algorithms, and data has become a widely recognized direction for system evolution, the technical realization of such an integrated scheduling mechanism continues to face a number of practical challenges. Currently, the abstraction methods, measurement metrics, and interface designs of these three core resource types differ significantly, making it difficult for schedulers to model them uniformly or to perform coordinated optimization across resource categories.

Computing resources are typically abstracted at the node level, focusing on hardware configurations such as CPU, GPU, and memory, with an emphasis on matching physical capacity to task workload. In contrast, algorithm components are usually managed through containerization or function execution models, with descriptions centered on logical information such as container images, model architectures, and inference entry points. Data resources, meanwhile, are characterized by attributes such as storage path, format, and access method, with associated aspects like preprocessing, caching strategies, and bandwidth consumption often overlooked by the scheduling layer. These heterogeneous abstraction dimensions make it difficult to include all three within a unified scheduling framework capable of semantic matching. For example, in a video inference task, the scheduler must simultaneously consider GPU availability for the model, the frame rate and storage path of the data, and the ability of nodes to support low-latency access. Such multidimensional matching logic is rarely implemented in traditional scheduling systems.

The fragmentation of system interfaces further increases scheduling complexity. Compute scheduling is typically handled by low-level orchestrators such as Kubernetes or Slurm, while data flow scheduling may be managed through data platforms, ETL (Extract, Transform, and Load) pipelines, or object storage APIs. Algorithm-related tasks such as model version control and automated deployment are often orchestrated by CI/CD pipelines or AI service platforms. Due to the absence of a unified interface standard, scheduling systems lack visibility into the states of tasks across different layers and are unable to form a closed loop linking tasks, models, data, and computing resources. As a result, cross-system coordination often depends on manual scripting or external workflow schedulers, reducing flexibility and introducing potential bottlenecks.

Scheduling optimization algorithms themselves also face new challenges. Traditional strategies are typically designed around a single resource type, with objectives such as throughput, latency, or energy efficiency. In the context of integrated scheduling, however, the optimization goals become multidimensional and interdependent. For instance, task latency is jointly affected by compute allocation and data locality, while resource utilization must balance between algorithmic execution efficiency and redundant data storage. These multi-objective, multi-constraint optimization problems are often difficult to solve using heuristic approaches and demand more sophisticated scheduling strategies.

Therefore, the implementation of a unified scheduling system across the three core elements requires overcoming critical technical barriers from multiple dimensions, including the standardization of resource descriptions, alignment of system interfaces, and coordinated optimization of scheduling algorithms. In the absence of industry-wide standards or widely adopted open-source solutions, this undertaking remains in an early exploratory stage.

1.3.3.3 Conceptual and Design Challenges

Compared to the technical difficulties in implementation, a more fundamental challenge lies in the lack of a fully clarified conceptual and architectural understanding of unified scheduling. The relationships among computational resources, algorithmic capabilities, and data assets are not merely engineering integration issues; they pertain to how a system defines task boundaries, resource boundaries, and service boundaries, and how a new scheduling logic is constructed at the level of design paradigms.

The definition of task objects itself remains unresolved. In traditional systems, tasks are typically treated as discrete computational actions, with scheduling granularity defined at the level of code blocks or container units. However, within ICNs, a task may encompass multiple sub-stages such as model loading, data retrieval, computational execution, and result caching. These stages are characterized by dynamic, heterogeneous, and often ambiguous boundaries. For example, a large-model inference task is not a one-off computation but a continuously responsive service, whose states and resource demands evolve with incoming inputs. If scheduling systems continue to rely on static task definitions and one-time resource binding strategies, they will fail to capture the actual behavior of tasks, thereby compromising the rationality of scheduling decisions.

The formulation of resource objective functions also poses significant design-level difficulties. Unified scheduling is no longer concerned with single-objective optimization, such as minimizing completion time or energy consumption. Instead, it must support dynamic trade-offs and policy evolution across multiple conflicting objectives. In AI tasks, for instance, there is a pressing need to balance computational performance against model accuracy, data access latency against bandwidth usage, and resource utilization against fairness among tasks. Yet, a general-purpose expressive framework for such trade-offs remains absent. Existing systems often rely on hardcoded rules, priority-based policies, or heuristic scheduling functions as simplistic approximations. These approaches are difficult to generalize across diverse task types and fail to meet the adaptive policy requirements of complex scenarios.

There is also no consensus on the design of intelligent scheduling mechanisms. Some systems have begun integrating methods like reinforcement learning and graph neural networks to model node states, task queues, and network topologies. However, unresolved issues remain around the interpretability, stability, and deployment safety of these strategies. Unified scheduling not only demands optimization capability but also requires support for rule plug-ins, policy migration, and contextual control. This necessitates the development of a unified control framework that combines structural constraints with policy flexibility.

Under the current scheduling paradigm, which still primarily follows a "modular and loosely coupled" architecture, the conceptual model of unified scheduling remains in an exploratory phase. Across all aspects, from task modeling and resource abstraction to optimization strategies and system architectures, there is an urgent need for deeper theoretical inquiry and cross-domain collaborative innovation. These efforts are essential to advancing ICNs toward genuine system unification, policy integration, and closed-loop service coordination.

References

1. R. Schollmeier, in *Proceedings first International Conference on Peer-to-peer Computing* (IEEE, 2001), pp. 101–102
2. I. Foster, Y. Zhao, I. Raicu, S. Lu, in *2008 Grid Computing Environments Workshop* (IEEE, 2008), pp. 1–10
3. M. Jangjou, M.K. Sohrabi, Arch. Comput. Methods Eng. **29**(6), 3587 (2022)
4. B. Wang, Z. Qi, R. Ma, H. Guan, A.V. Vasilakos, Comput. Netw. **91**, 528 (2015)
5. S. Yi, Z. Hao, Z. Qin, Q. Li, in *2015 Third IEEE Workshop on Hot Topics in Web Systems and Technologies (HotWeb)* (IEEE, 2015), pp. 73–78
6. K. Saini, S. Kalra, S.K. Sood, J. Grid Comput. **20**(2), 17 (2022)
7. I. Stojmenovic, S. Wen, X. Huang, H. Luan, Concurr. Comput. Pract. Exp. **28**(10), 2991 (2016)
8. J. Ren, T. Hou, H. Wang, H. Tian, H. Wei, H. Zheng, X. Zhang, Wirel. Netw. **30**(5), 3897 (2024)
9. M.Y. Mehmood, A. Oad, M. Abrar, H.M. Munir, S.F. Hasan, H.A.U. Muqeet, N.A. Golilarz, Secur. Commun. Netw. **2021**(1), 5524025 (2021)
10. G. Carvalho, B. Cabral, V. Pereira, J. Bernardino, Computing **103**(5), 993 (2021)
11. Z. Chen, L. Zhang, X. Wang, K. Wang, Comput. Ind. Eng. **177**, 109053 (2023)
12. N. Zhang, H. Duan, Y. Guan, R. Mao, G. Song, J. Yang, Y. Shan, Engineering (2024). https://doi.org/10.1016/j.eng.2024.08.010

13. B. Liu, C. Zhou, D. Chen, Z. Zhang, H. Wu, H. Yang, Available at SSRN 5057250 (2024). https://doi.org/10.2139/ssrn.5057250
14. Y. Wang, L. Fang, B. Hu, G. Ge, X. Zhou, W. Zhang, in *Proceedings of the 2023 International Conference on Electronics, Computers and Communication Technology* (2023), pp. 169–174
15. Q. Yang, Y. Liu, T. Chen, Y. Tong, ACM Trans. Intell. Syst. Technol. **10**(2), 1 (2019)
16. J.G. Herrera, J.F. Botero, IEEE Trans. Netw. Service Manag. **13**(3), 518 (2016)
17. M.S. Bonfim, K.L. Dias, S.F. Fernandes, ACM Comput. Surv. **51**(6), 1 (2019)
18. J.C.C. Chica, J.C. Imbachi, J.F.B. Vega, J. Netw. Comput. Appl. **159**, 102595 (2020)
19. Z. Zhang, L. Ma, K.K. Leung, F. Le, IEEE/ACM Trans. Netw. **29**(4), 1580 (2021)
20. H. Mokhtar, X. Di, Y. Zhou, A. Hassan, Z. Ma, S. Musa, Comput. Netw. **198**, 108369 (2021)
21. A. Krentsel, N. Saran, B. Koley, S. Mandal, A. Narayanan, S. Ratnasamy, A. Al-Shabibi, A. Shaikh, R. Shakir, A. Singla, et al., in *Proceedings of the ACM SIGCOMM 2024 Conference* (2024), pp. 938–953
22. Q. Xia, G. Wang, Z. Xu, W. Liang, Z. Xu, IEEE Trans. Mobile Comput. **23**(5), 5677 (2023)
23. R.S. Alonso, J. Prieto, F. de La Prieta, S. Rodríguez-González, J.M. Corchado, in *2021 IEEE Globecom Workshops (GC Wkshps)* (IEEE, 2021), pp. 1–6
24. A. Jeffery, H. Howard, R. Mortier, in *Proceedings of the 4th International Workshop on Edge Systems, Analytics and Networking* (2021), pp. 7–12
25. Ł. Wojciechowski, K. Opasiak, J. Latusek, M. Wereski, V. Morales, T. Kim, M. Hong, in *IEEE INFOCOM 2021-IEEE Conference on Computer Communications* (IEEE, 2021), pp. 1–9
26. A. Rahman, S.I. Shamim, D.B. Bose, R. Pandita, ACM Trans. Software Eng. Methodol. **32**(4), 1 (2023)
27. L. Toka, G. Dobreff, B. Fodor, B. Sonkoly, IEEE Trans. Netw. Service Manag. **18**(1), 958 (2021)
28. W. Liang, Y. Li, J. Xu, Z. Qin, D. Zhang, K.C. Li, IEEE Trans. Comput. **73**(3), 669 (2023)
29. D. Wu, P. Zhang, Y. He, X. Luo, IEEE Trans. Services Comput. **16**(2), 802 (2022)
30. Y. Zhang, W. Hua, Z. Zhou, G.E. Suh, C. Delimitrou, in *Proceedings of the 26th ACM International Conference on Architectural Support for Programming Languages and Operating Systems* (2021), pp. 167–181
31. M. Karakus, A. Durresi, J. Netw. Comput. Appl. **80**, 200 (2017)
32. G. Zhou, W. Tian, R. Buyya, Future Gener. Comput. Syst. **141**, 414 (2023)
33. J. Liu, Z. Wu, D. Feng, M. Zhang, X. Wu, X. Yao, D. Yu, Y. Ma, F. Zhao, D. Dou, Future Gener. Comput. Syst **148**, 106 (2023)
34. Y. Li, Y. Lin, Y. Wang, K. Ye, C. Xu, IEEE Trans. Serv. Comput. **16**(2), 1522 (2022)
35. J. Wen, Z. Chen, X. Jin, X. Liu, ACM Trans. Software Eng. Methodol. **32**(5), 1 (2023)
36. S. Shen, Y. Ren, Y. Ju, X. Wang, W. Wang, V.C. Leung, IEEE J. Sel. Areas Commun. **41**(3), 820 (2022)

Chapter 2
Emerging Multi-Dimensional Integration of Security and Safety

Abstract Chapter 2 presents a comprehensive analysis of the triadic relationship among data, computing power, and algorithms within intelligent computing networks, emphasizing their deep coupling and its implications for integrated security and safety modeling. The chapter begins with a detailed characterization of each core element, covering conceptual foundations, technological evolution, ecosystem roles, and security properties. It then examines the pairwise couplings among the elements and identifies challenges arising in collaborative security enforcement and dynamic resource allocation under realistic computing conditions. Building on these insights, the chapter proposes an integrated behavior modeling paradigm based on a tri-layer knowledge graph, which enables robust authentication and semantic risk assessment even under constrained data environments. The chapter ultimately advocates a paradigm shift from isolated control mechanisms to behavior-driven, coupling-aware security architectures.

2.1 Core Elements of Intelligent Computing Networks

The convergence of data, computing power, and algorithms forms the foundational triad of intelligent computing networks (ICNs). These three elements operate as tightly interwoven, co-evolving forces that collectively support intelligent perception, decision-making, and control. However, their integration is not merely a matter of technical coexistence. Each element exhibits unique structural properties, system dependencies, and security implications that influence the overall behavior and trustworthiness of the computing environment. In the context of increasingly decentralized, real-time, and safety-critical applications, understanding these core components is essential to designing robust and secure ICN architectures.

To visualize the interplay among these elements, Fig. 2.1 provides a conceptual overview of their respective characteristics and roles. This figure serves as a conceptual entry point for the detailed discussions in the following sections.

C. Wang, H. Tang, *Integrated Security and Safety of Intelligent Computing Networks*, https://doi.org/10.1007/978-981-95-5025-8_2

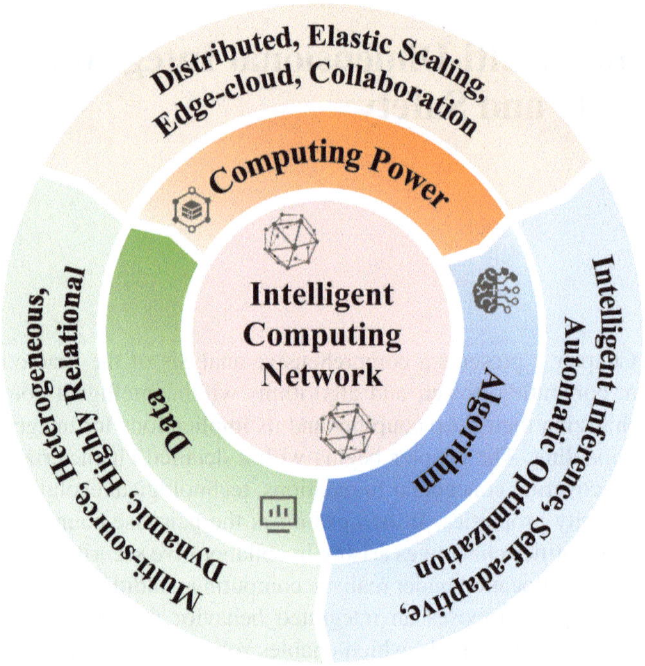

Fig. 2.1 A conceptual representation of the three core elements in intelligent computing networks

2.1.1 *Data*

In the era of the digital economy, data has become one of the most vital and strategic factors of production, standing alongside traditional elements such as land, capital, and labor. It underpins the core functionality of intelligent computing networks by enabling perception, computation, decision-making, and autonomous control. Often described as "the new oil", data embodies a foundational resource that fuels innovation and productivity across technological, industrial, and societal domains.

2.1.1.1 The Conception of Data

Broadly defined, data encompasses any digital abstraction or symbolic representation of real-world entities, environments, and behaviors. It includes a wide range of formats, such as textual documents, visual imagery, audio-visual streams, sensor-derived measurements, and spatiotemporal records. Each of these can be systematically captured, encoded, transmitted, stored, and interpreted by computational systems. In a more specific sense, data refers to digital resources that have been collected, filtered, refined, and structured into usable formats. Such data can support statistical analysis, machine learning applications, and various forms of intelligent computation [1].

The rapid convergence of big data infrastructure, pervasive sensing technologies, edge-cloud integration, and artificial intelligence has dramatically increased both the volume and complexity of data [2]. Today's digital environments generate multi-source, high-frequency, and real-time data flows that are temporally dynamic and structurally diverse. As a result, data has evolved from being a passive informational byproduct to becoming an active and value-generating asset.

From a classification perspective, data can be distinguished based on its source and structure [3]. Endogenous data are generated internally within organizations or systems and include business operations records, administrative transactions, system logs, and financial metrics. In contrast, exogenous data originates from external environments and user interactions, such as behavior patterns captured via mobile applications, environmental readings from IoT devices, and datasets acquired from third-party platforms or public infrastructure. In terms of structure, data are commonly categorized into three types. Structured data refers to information in predefined schemas (e.g., tables, spreadsheets). Semi-structured data has some organizational properties but no rigid formatting (e.g., XML, JSON). Unstructured data includes free-form content like text, videos, audio, and multimedia. Each of these categories presents distinct challenges (in acquisition, storage, analysis, and security) that require specialized handling across the full data lifecycle.

Unlike traditional physical or financial assets, data exhibits several disruptive and non-intuitive characteristics that fundamentally shape its function within computing ecosystems. First, data are non-rivalrous. A single dataset can be used simultaneously by multiple agents without any loss of value or quality, and the marginal cost of reuse is nearly zero. Second, data are non-excludable. Due to its digital nature, it is inherently difficult to restrict access or prevent unauthorized reuse, which often results in widespread free-riding behavior. Third, data are infinitely replicable. It can be copied, transmitted, and distributed at minimal cost across various systems and platforms, frequently evading conventional mechanisms of control. Fourth, data are highly heterogeneous in value. The significance of a dataset can vary widely depending on its source, structure, granularity, and contextual application, making it difficult to define universal valuation standards. Fifth, and perhaps most importantly, data are inherently relational. Individual data points typically offer limited value on their own; their utility emerges when they are aggregated, cross-linked, and interpreted in conjunction with other relevant datasets.

These intrinsic attributes introduce fundamental challenges in data governance, including pricing strategies, usage rights allocation, regulatory oversight, and especially security assurance. The difficulty of establishing provenance, enforcing access control, and preventing misuse or manipulation makes data-centric security and trust frameworks essential components of any intelligent computing network.

2.1.1.2 The Evolution of Data

The evolution of data as a production factor has closely mirrored the advancement of computing technologies. In the earliest computing environments from the 1950s to the 1970s, data was primarily regarded as a technical artifact, understood as a static and highly structured collection of numerical records. Its use was closely aligned with machine-level operations and was typically confined to specific applications such as scientific computation, government census processing, or administrative recordkeeping. Storage media of that era, including punch cards and magnetic tapes, imposed significant physical limitations on data management, reinforcing a centralized model based on batch processing and restricted access.

The 1980s introduced a turning point, marked by the proliferation of relational database management systems (RDBMS), the rise of personal computing, and the enterprise adoption of information systems [4]. Data began to emerge as a distinct object of organizational management, enabling more dynamic and interactive querying, schema design, and domain-specific modeling. Business intelligence systems and decision support systems gained traction, reflecting a growing awareness of the value of data not only as an operational necessity but as a strategic resource.

The 1990s and early 2000s marked the beginning of the Internet era, which significantly broadened the sources, scale, and diversity of data. Activities such as web browsing, clickstream tracking, digital media sharing, and online transactions began to generate unprecedented volumes of both user-generated and machine-generated data. Around 2010, the concept of "big data" gained prominence, initially characterized by the three Vs: volume, velocity, and variety. This framework was later expanded to include veracity and value, highlighting concerns about data accuracy and utility. During this period, the focus of data management shifted from traditional structured enterprise databases to the growing importance of semi-structured and unstructured data originating from social media, sensor networks, and mobile platforms.

More recently, with the maturation of cloud computing, edge computing, and IoT, data has become omnipresent, real-time, and highly contextual. It is continuously generated by interconnected smart devices, industrial control systems, digital twins, and embedded systems. The integration of artificial intelligence has further transformed data from a passive input into an active, feedback-driven element of intelligent systems.

2.1.1.3 The Asset Attributes of Data

In the context of the intelligent computing network, data has gradually evolved from a byproduct of information systems into a pivotal asset that drives digital business models, platform economies, and cross-domain collaboration. As a result, data has formed a distinct and increasingly mature industrial ecosystem, characterized by multi-tiered roles, cross-sector integration, and complex value chains.

From an ecosystem perspective, the data industry can be decomposed into several key layers: data generation (sensors, terminals, and systems), data aggregation (cloud platforms, and edge nodes), data processing and enrichment (cleaning, labeling, fusion, and anonymization), data services (analytics, AI modeling, and visualization), and data governance (security, privacy, compliance, and lifecycle management). These layers interact through technical, organizational, and economic interfaces, forming a loosely coupled but highly dynamic data supply chain [5].

Data, as an asset, is notably different from traditional tangible or financial assets in several respects. First, data exhibits strong externalities: its use by one party may create additional value for others, especially in platform-based models. Second, data are non-depletable but highly context-sensitive, meaning that its value is not intrinsic but depends on application scenarios, timeliness, and semantic enrichment. Third, data lacks a unified ownership and valuation framework. Because data can be duplicated at negligible cost and reused across domains, issues of attribution, pricing, and liability are inherently complex. This has led to the rise of new institutional arrangements such as data trusts, data exchanges, and data cooperatives.

Economically, the assetization of data has become a global trend. Governments and enterprises alike are increasingly treating data as a strategic production factor, incorporating it into digital asset balance sheets, and designing mechanisms for data capitalization and monetization. This includes the establishment of data trading platforms, such as China's data exchange pilots and the European data spaces initiative. These platforms aim to support data asset registration, pricing, circulation, and traceability, often relying on blockchain or distributed ledger technologies to ensure credibility and security.

In sum, data in intelligent computing networks is not merely a passive resource, but a multi-dimensional, semi-public, and semi-private digital asset. It participates in the ecosystem as both an input and an output, with value shaped by interaction, processing depth, and alignment with regulatory and ethical norms. The maturation of the data industry will continue to transform how value is created, captured, and protected in the networked digital world.

2.1.1.4 The Security Attributes of Data

Within intelligent computing networks, data serves as both the substrate and enabler of computation, intelligence, and communication. Its technical characteristics are deeply intertwined with the architecture of the computing network, as data are continuously generated, transformed, transmitted, and utilized across heterogeneous systems and environments. This data-centric paradigm introduces new layers of complexity and risk in system design, especially when addressing security, privacy, and trust at scale.

Technically, data in intelligent computing networks is characterized by high dimensionality, heterogeneity, and spatiotemporal fluidity. High dimensionality refers to the complex, nested nature of modern data structures, which often include time-series signals, graph-based representations, and multimodal inputs such as the combination of textual, visual, and sensor data. These structures require sophisticated techniques for encoding, feature extraction, and storage. Heterogeneity is evident in the wide variety of data formats, including structured, semi-structured, and unstructured data, as well as the diversity of sources such as Internet of Things devices, cloud platforms, and user terminals. This diversity also extends to semantic differences, such as the distinction between raw and derived data, which complicates efforts toward interoperability and standardization across systems. Spatiotemporal fluidity describes the dynamic, distributed, and real-time nature of data flows. In intelligent networks, data may be transient, replicated across nodes, cached at network edges, or rerouted between domains based on context. These properties demand flexible, adaptive data management architectures that can respond to changing conditions in both time and space.

Security-wise, the very properties that make data powerful also render it vulnerable. The distributed, persistent, and replicable nature of data flows increases the attack surface of intelligent networks. Key security attributes for data in such environments include:

- Confidentiality: Ensuring that sensitive data are protected from unauthorized access during storage, transmission, and processing. Techniques such as homomorphic encryption, secure multi-party computation, and differential privacy are increasingly used to safeguard data while enabling utility.
- Integrity: Maintaining the consistency and accuracy of data across its lifecycle. This is especially critical for training datasets used in machine learning models, where poisoning attacks can manipulate model behavior.
- Availability: Guaranteeing timely and reliable access to data, even under conditions of fault or attack. This involves redundancy, replication strategies, and robust access control mechanisms.
- Accountability and Traceability: Establishing who generate, access, or alter a dataset, often using techniques like blockchain-based logging, watermarks, or cryptographic identifiers.

In intelligent computing networks, security controls should not be confined solely to the network or system layer. Instead, they must adopt a data-centric and adaptive approach. For instance, in zero-trust architectures, each data transaction is subject to dynamic verification, and access permissions are context-aware and revocable. Furthermore, the use of fine-grained metadata tagging and data labeling has become increasingly important. These mechanisms support the enforcement of security policies, enable selective information disclosure, and facilitate automated compliance validation across complex data workflows.

As intelligent networks increasingly integrate human-in-the-loop, autonomous agents, and real-time decision-making processes, the role of trustworthy data becomes foundational to system safety and reliability. Faulty, biased, or tampered data not only degrades performance but can also lead to cascading failures or safety violations in interconnected cyber-physical systems.

Therefore, a unified view of data security in intelligent computing networks must span from physical-layer sensing to algorithm-level inference, treating data as a strategic vector of both value and vulnerability. This perspective is essential to designing resilient, scalable, and trustworthy intelligent systems for the future.

2.1.2 Computing Power

In the era of digital transformation and intelligent services, computing power has shifted from being merely a technical parameter to becoming a strategic infrastructure resource. It is now widely regarded as a foundational pillar of national digital competitiveness, comparable in importance to electricity, communication networks, and data storage. Computing power supports the intelligent perception, cognition, and action loops that drive modern cyber-physical systems. It also plays a central role in the deployment and operation of artificial intelligence models, digital twin technologies, autonomous systems, and emerging applications within the metaverse.

2.1.2.1 The Conception of Computing Power

In the context of intelligent computing networks, computing power, also referred to as computational capacity or computing capability, functions as the central engine that supports the execution of algorithms, the processing of large-scale data streams, and the implementation of intelligent decision-making systems. It represents the comprehensive ability of a computing system to perform a wide range of tasks, including numerical computation, logical reasoning, symbolic inference, machine learning, and real-time signal processing. These capabilities are distributed across both hardware and software layers and form the foundational infrastructure for delivering advanced intelligent services.

Computing power can be understood from multiple dimensions. From a physical infrastructure perspective, it encompasses central processing units (CPUs), graphics processing units (GPUs), tensor processing units (TPUs), field-programmable gate arrays (FPGAs), application-specific integrated circuits (ASICs), and emerging architectures such as neuromorphic chips and quantum processors. From a deployment model standpoint, it includes local/edge computing, centralized cloud platforms, and hybrid distributed systems. From a usage perspective, it involves batch computation, stream processing, AI inference, data mining, and high-performance scientific simulations [6].

The concept of computing power is both quantitative and qualitative. Quantitatively, it is typically measured by indicators such as floating-point operations per second (FLOPS), input/output operations per second (IOPS), memory bandwidth, task concurrency, latency, and energy efficiency. Qualitatively, it reflects the adaptability of computing resources to different workloads, the architectural flexibility, the software ecosystem support, and the ability to scale elastically under dynamic network conditions.

2.1.2.2 The Evolution of Computing Power

The development of computing power traces back to the early days of digital computing in the mid-twentieth century. In its infancy, computing power was largely centralized in mainframes, serving scientific, governmental, and military purposes. The 1960s and 1970s witnessed the rise of transistor-based computers and the proliferation of general-purpose CPUs, laying the foundation for programmable computing. With the advent of personal computers in the 1980s, computing resources were decentralized, entering homes, offices, and enterprises, thus broadening the scope of accessible computing.

The 1990s and early 2000s saw a surge in computing capabilities driven by Moore's Law, leading to rapid growth in processor performance, storage, and networking [7]. During this period, high-performance computing (HPC) and grid computing emerged to address large-scale scientific problems, while data centers started to scale massively to support the rise of the Internet. The introduction of virtualization technologies also marked a critical turning point, enabling multi-tenant environments and more flexible resource allocation.

The emergence of cloud computing in the late 2000s represented a paradigm shift. Computing power became an on-demand, scalable service, abstracted from physical infrastructure and delivered via platforms such as AWS, Microsoft Azure, and Google Cloud. This transition significantly lowered the entry barrier for enterprises and developers, catalyzing innovation in AI, big data analytics, and mobile services. The "as-a-service" model extended beyond infrastructure to include platform-as-a-service (PaaS) and function-as-a-service (FaaS), fundamentally redefining how computing is consumed [8].

In the 2010s, the proliferation of AI workloads, especially deep learning, introduced new computational demands that traditional CPUs could not handle efficiently. This led to the widespread adoption of GPUs, TPUs, and other AI accelerators, initiating a trend toward task-specific computing architectures. Meanwhile, edge computing began to gain momentum, enabling real-time processing at or near data sources to meet the needs of latency-sensitive applications such as autonomous driving, industrial IoT, and intelligent surveillance.

Looking forward, the evolution of computing power is entering a phase of multi-dimensional expansion. On the one hand, we are witnessing the continued scaling of cloud-native infrastructure and the emergence of heterogeneous computing clusters that combine CPUs, GPUs, FPGAs, and AI chips. On the other hand, new paradigms such as quantum computing, neuromorphic computing, and in-memory computing are being explored to overcome the limits of traditional Von Neumann architecture and meet the needs of cognitive and probabilistic computing.

2.1.2.3 The Asset Attributes of Computing Power

As computing power evolves into a fundamental digital infrastructure, it plays a pivotal role in shaping the architecture of modern industries and national digital competitiveness. The industrial ecosystem of computing power is multi-layered, complex, and rapidly expanding, encompassing core hardware manufacturing, infrastructure deployment, cloud service provisioning, platform integration, and intelligent application development. This layered structure forms a vertically integrated value chain that drives innovation and economic activity across multiple sectors.

At the base layer, chip manufacturing serves as the technological foundation of computing power, encompassing CPUs, GPUs, artificial intelligence accelerators, as well as emerging architectures such as neuromorphic and quantum processors. This foundational layer is dominated by leading semiconductor firms including Intel, AMD, NVIDIA, and TSMC, along with newer players in the AI chip sector such as Cerebras, Graphcore, Cambricon, and Huawei Ascend. The high degree of supply chain concentration, combined with significant technological barriers and growing geopolitical tensions, has made chip manufacturing a central focus of international strategic competition.

The middle layer includes server vendors, data center operators, and edge computing infrastructure providers. Cloud computing giants such as Amazon, Google, Microsoft, Alibaba Cloud, and Huawei Cloud play critical roles by offering elastic, scalable computing resources through global data centers. Meanwhile, telecom operators and edge providers deploy lightweight computing nodes closer to end users, forming a distributed, service-oriented computing backbone.

On the top layer, the "computing-as-a-service" paradigm has enabled a thriving ecosystem of developers, platform providers, and application vendors. Services such as container orchestration (e.g., Kubernetes), distributed scheduling, AIOps, and multi-cloud management platforms have emerged to support the dynamic allocation of heterogeneous resources. The fusion of AI, big data, and IoT workloads with these computing services further amplifies value creation and service diversification.

This has led to a new class of digital assets "computing power assets", which can be provisioned, leased, traded, and even monetized dynamically. Some industry initiatives have explored computing power marketplaces, where idle capacity can be pooled and allocated via contracts or tokens.

2.1.2.4 The Security Attributes of Computing Power

As an asset, computing power is characterized by its virtual, elastic, measurable, and programmable nature. Unlike traditional forms of infrastructure, it does not possess physical tangibility, yet it serves as the operational backbone of a wide range of digital services. The value of computing power is determined not only by its volume but also by factors such as availability, latency, reliability, and energy efficiency. These metrics are particularly critical in environments where security, resilience, and performance must be guaranteed.

Computing power is the cornerstone of intelligent computing networks, serving as the critical enabler for data-driven applications, real-time analytics, and adaptive decision-making. Computing power exhibits several distinctive technical characteristics that differentiate it from traditional computational paradigms and directly influence its role in supporting secure and efficient operations.

First, computing power in computing networks is inherently distributed, combining resources across cloud data centers, edge nodes, and end devices. This distributed architecture ensures scalability, flexibility, and adaptability to dynamic workloads. However, the decentralization of resources introduces security challenges, such as distributed denial-of-service (DDoS) risks, resource allocation manipulation, and attack surface expansion, necessitating robust orchestration mechanisms and advanced trust models.

Second, the heterogeneity of computing power is a challenge. Modern computing networks integrate diverse resources, including general-purpose CPUs, specialized GPUs, TPUs, FPGAs, and even quantum processors. Each type of computational unit is optimized for specific tasks, such as deep learning, cryptographic operations, or real-time simulation. Although heterogeneity enhances computational efficiency, it also complicates the integration and standardization of security protocols, as different hardware units may have distinct vulnerabilities and performance tradeoffs.

Third, computing power is characterized by its elastic and on-demand provisioning. Cloud platforms and distributed systems leverage containerization, virtualization, and serverless technologies to provide elastic scalability. This flexibility is instrumental for cost optimization and resource utilization but introduces potential security risks, such as container breakout attacks and side-channel exploits.

From a security perspective, computing power must address a range of threats spanning confidentiality, integrity, and availability (CIA). Advanced cryptographic techniques, such as homomorphic encryption and secure multiparty computation, are increasingly deployed to protect sensitive computations in distributed environments. Moreover, ensuring the availability of computing power requires resilience to hardware failures, cyberattacks, and natural disasters, which are managed through redundancy, load balancing, and failover mechanisms.

2.1.3 Algorithm

In the era of intelligent computing networks, algorithms stand as the logical core that transforms raw computing power and massive datasets into actionable intelligence and system behaviors. Broadly defined, an algorithm refers to a finite sequence of well-defined instructions or procedures designed to solve a problem, perform a computation, or carry out a data processing task. Algorithms form the essential bridge between abstract problems and computational execution, enabling the automation of reasoning, optimization, prediction, and control in complex environments [9].

2.1.3.1 The Conception of Algorithm

Historically, the notion of an algorithm dates back to the ancient world, with its formalization often attributed to the Persian mathematician Al-Khwarizmi in the ninth century, whose name itself evolved into the term “algorithm” [10]. In the modern context, algorithms underpin a wide range of technological domains, from basic arithmetic operations to sophisticated artificial intelligence and machine learning models. They not only define how inputs are transformed into outputs but also influence system performance, scalability, fairness, interpretability, and resilience.

In computing networks, algorithms are pervasive and operate seamlessly across multiple layers, ranging from routing protocols and resource scheduling in the infrastructure to inference engines and decision-making modules at the application level. They enable systems to adapt to dynamic environments, optimize resource allocation, improve user experiences, and respond effectively to emerging security threats. In scenarios involving collaboration among cloud, edge, and end devices, the development and deployment of efficient, secure, and resilient algorithms have become critical determinants of the overall intelligence and safety of computing networks.

The rapid evolution of algorithmic capabilities has shifted their role from static tools to dynamic entities that can self-learn, self-adapt, and self-optimize. Algorithmic intelligence is now increasingly embedded into the fabric of networked systems, driving the emergence of autonomous, distributed, and anticipatory behaviors within intelligent computing networks.

2.1.3.2 The Evolution of Algorithm

The history of algorithms reflects the broader evolution of human knowledge and computational capabilities. In ancient times, algorithms were primarily handcrafted procedures for arithmetic, astronomy, and geometry, meticulously documented in early civilizations such as Babylon, India, and Greece. The systematic study of algorithms accelerated with the invention of symbolic mathematics and formal logic, laying a foundation for the mechanization of reasoning.

The twentieth century witnessed an unprecedented leap with the formalization of computation theory. Figures such as Alan Turing, Alonzo Church, and Kurt Gödel established the theoretical underpinnings of algorithms through the development of models like the Turing machine and the lambda calculus. These milestones not only decided the limits of what can be computed but also spurred the birth of computer science as an independent discipline.

With the advent of electronic computers, the practical significance of algorithms expanded rapidly. Early focuses on numerical computation and optimization gave way to a broader algorithmic landscape that now includes data structures, database queries, cryptography, artificial intelligence, machine learning, and distributed systems. The development of efficient algorithms, such as quicksort, Dijkstra's algorithm, and PageRank, profoundly shaped entire industries and Internet ecosystems.

In recent decades, the emergence of big data, ubiquitous networking, and high-performance computing has redefined algorithmic challenges and priorities. Algorithms have evolved from deterministic, handcrafted rules toward data-driven, probabilistic, and adaptive models. Machine learning, deep learning, and reinforcement learning represent this paradigm shift, enabling systems to infer patterns, optimize behavior, and make decisions without explicit programming [11].

Looking forward, algorithm development is trending toward greater autonomy, robustness, and explainability. Research into explainable AI, adversarial robustness, federated learning, and neuromorphic computing aims to address the growing demands for transparent, resilient, and privacy-preserving intelligent systems.

In the context of intelligent computing networks, algorithms are moving beyond isolated problem-solving units to become orchestrators of distributed intelligence. The future will likely witness the proliferation of collaborative, adaptive, and self-evolving algorithms that can harmonize the behaviors of billions of interconnected nodes across dynamic, heterogeneous environments.

2.1.3.3 The Asset Attributes of Algorithm

The industrial ecosystem surrounding algorithms is vast, dynamic, and intricately intertwined with multiple sectors across the global economy. Algorithms today are not confined within academic research; they have become core productive forces embedded deeply within industries such as finance, healthcare, manufacturing, transportation, cybersecurity, entertainment, and public administration.

From a value chain perspective, the algorithmic industry encompasses several layers: basic theoretical research (e.g., optimization theory and statistical learning), algorithm design and development (e.g., AI model architectures and encryption algorithms), algorithmic engineering (e.g., system integration, model compression, and hardware acceleration), and application deployment (e.g., recommendation systems, predictive maintenance, and autonomous driving).

Algorithms are increasingly regarded as vital intangible assets. Unlike physical resources, they possess inherent scalability and replicability. Once developed, an algorithm can be implemented across a wide range of systems and applications with minimal marginal cost. Proprietary algorithms, particularly those underpinning core functions such as search engines or risk assessment models, represent critical forms of intellectual property. They often serve as strategic assets that create competitive advantages and establish high entry barriers for potential competitors.

Moreover, algorithmic ecosystems are becoming increasingly platformized. Cloud providers, AI-as-a-Service vendors, and open-source platforms like TensorFlow, PyTorch, and Hugging Face offer modularized, reusable algorithmic capabilities, lowering the threshold for innovation and accelerating the democratization of algorithmic power. However, the dependence on third-party algorithms also introduces new risks, such as supply chain vulnerabilities, hidden biases, and legal ambiguities regarding algorithmic accountability.

Economically, algorithms are evolving into a form of "algorithmic capital", a fusion of technical capability and strategic value that underpins digital business models. Ownership, governance, licensing, and valuation of algorithms are emerging as critical topics in digital asset management. Intellectual property protections, algorithmic audits, explainability standards, and algorithmic fairness regulations are gradually forming the institutional infrastructure to safeguard the responsible use and evolution of algorithmic assets.

2.1.3.4 The Security Attributes of Algorithm

In intelligent computing networks, algorithms are the core drivers of system intelligence, enabling perception, decision-making, optimization, and self-adaptive across heterogeneous computing and network infrastructure. Compared to traditional software logic, algorithms in intelligent networks exhibit several distinct technical characteristics.

First, algorithms in intelligent networks emphasize autonomy and real-time adaptability. Rather than operating based solely on predefined rules, many algorithms, especially those embedded in AI systems, continuously learn from data streams and environmental feedback. They dynamically adjust their decision boundaries, optimization parameters, and operational strategies to cope with changing contexts, uncertainties, and adversarial input.

Second, algorithms are increasingly distributed and collaborative. In edge-cloud collaborative frameworks, distributed learning, distributed optimization, and multi-agent systems require algorithms to operate coherently across geographically dispersed and resource-constrained environments. This distribution enhances scalability and fault tolerance but also increases the surface area for attacks such as model poisoning, Byzantine failures, and communication interception [12].

From a security standpoint, algorithms are dual-edged assets. On the one hand, advanced algorithms enhance security by enabling anomaly detection, threat intelligence, adaptive defense, and autonomous response. On the other hand, algorithms themselves become prime attack surfaces. Adversaries may exploit vulnerabilities in model architectures (e.g., adversarial examples and backdoor attacks), manipulate training datasets, or tamper with model parameters and update mechanisms.

Moreover, algorithmic opacity, particularly in deep learning models, creates challenges for threat detection, accountability, and forensic analysis. Black-box behaviors make it difficult to verify whether an algorithm has been maliciously altered or is being subverted from within. This necessitates the development of verifiable, transparent, and certifiable algorithmic systems, as well as algorithm-centric security frameworks that go beyond traditional software security paradigms [13].

In summary, in the context of intelligent computing networks, algorithms are both enablers and potential liabilities. Securing algorithms requires a holistic,

Table 2.1 Comparison of core elements in intelligent computing networks

Feature dimension	Data	Computing power	Algorithm
Concept	Digital representations of real-world facts	Execution and processing capability	Logic for transforming inputs into outputs
Evolution trends	From structured to unstructured	From centralized to coordinated systems	From manual rules to self-learning models
Asset attributes	Core production factor	Provided as a service	Forming algorithm-centric ecosystems
Security attributes	Prone to leakage, tampering, duplication, and trust issues	Risks of hijacking, side-channels, and availability attacks	Vulnerable to poisoning, adversarial attacks, and bias injection

multi-dimensional approach encompassing secure design principles, robust learning frameworks, continuous validation, adversarial resilience, ethical governance, and dynamic threat modeling tailored to the algorithmic domain.

To provide a comparative overview of the three core elements within intelligent computing networks, Table 2.1 summarizes their conceptual foundations, development trajectories, industrial asset characteristics, and technical-security features.

2.2 Coupled Relationships Among the Three Elements

In ICNs, the interplay among data, computing power, and algorithms constitutes the operational foundation of distributed intelligence. Unlike traditional computing environments where system functions can often be modularized, ICNs demand tight coordination across all three dimensions to support real-time responsiveness, autonomous decision-making, and adaptive optimization. This coordination is not static but characterized by evolving, context-sensitive coupling patterns that vary with network architecture, application scenarios, and system dynamics.

Understanding the nature of these coupling relationships is essential to identifying both the functional advantages and the security challenges inherent in ICN environments. When one element changes, it often cascades through the others, affecting overall system performance, stability, and trustworthiness. Therefore, analyzing how these core components interact not only sheds light on system efficiency but also reveals potential vulnerabilities that emerge from tightly coupled operations.

This section explores the pairwise coupling mechanisms among the three elements: data and algorithms, data and computing power, and algorithms and computing power, before turning to a unified analysis of their triadic interdependence.

2.2.1 *Data-Algorithm Coupling*

2.2.1.1 Conceptual Foundations of Data-algorithm Coupling

In intelligent computing networks, the relationship between data and algorithms extends far beyond a simple input-output dependency. It embodies a deep semantic and structural interdependence that governs how information is represented, processed, and transformed into actionable knowledge. This coupling is foundational to every intelligent function within such systems, from perception and prediction to optimization and decision-making. Data and algorithms co-evolve over time, shaping and constraining each other's behavior in ways that are context-sensitive, dynamic, and system-specific.

Conceptually, the coupling between data and algorithms manifests along several interconnected dimensions. First is semantic coupling, in which the meaning and interpretability of data depend on the assumptions embedded within algorithmic models. For instance, tabular data can be interpreted through probabilistic graphical models or linear classifiers, each of which imposes a different semantic framework on the same information. In more complex domains such as image processing or natural language understanding, deep learning models define high-dimensional representational spaces in which semantic meaning is no longer human-interpretable but instead emergent from data−model interaction.

Second is behavioral coupling, where the performance and output stability of algorithms are influenced by the distributional characteristics of the input data. This includes issues such as imbalance, sparsity, and noise. In intelligent computing networks, where data often originates from distributed and heterogeneous sources, these properties are not only unpredictable but may shift over time. Consequently, the generalization ability, fairness, and safety of algorithms cannot be understood in isolation but must be analyzed as a function of data-algorithm interaction.

Third is computational or operational coupling, where the real-time availability, formatting, and integrity of data govern whether and how algorithms can be deployed effectively. For example, in edge computing environments, sensor data may arrive with delays or inconsistencies, and algorithmic models must adapt their computation paths accordingly. The coupling in this case is not only semantic or statistical but also infrastructural, linked to bandwidth constraints, memory availability, and processing latency.

This tight interdependence creates a situation where neither data nor algorithm can be treated as static or isolated. In intelligent computing networks, changes in one element propagate across the system, often in nonlinear ways. For example, a minor modification in data preprocessing rules may lead to dramatic shifts in model predictions, especially in systems that employ fine-tuned neural networks. Conversely, updating an algorithm without accounting for changes in data distribution can introduce performance degradation, fairness violations, or safety hazards.

The coupling also evolves across time. During early stages of system design, algorithmic choices may drive data requirements, such as the need for labeled samples, balanced categories, or high-resolution input. In later stages, as models are deployed and encounter real-world usage, data streams exert a dominant influence, requiring continuous model retraining or adaptation. In federated or decentralized settings, the coupling becomes even more intricate due to the absence of global data access and the variability of local contexts.

2.2.1.2 Data-algorithm Coupling Characteristics in ICN

The coupling between data and algorithms in intelligent computing networks exhibits several distinctive characteristics that are significantly more complex than in traditional computing systems. These characteristics arise from the core properties of ICNs, which include distributed architecture, heterogeneous infrastructure, real-time dynamics, and cross-domain autonomy. Under such conditions, the data-algorithm interface becomes not only a technical link but also a central control surface that affects system-wide behavior, responsiveness, and vulnerability.

One defining feature is spatiotemporal heterogeneity in both data and algorithm deployment. In ICNs, data originates from diverse sources such as edge devices, IoT sensors, cloud storage, user terminals, and third-party services. These sources differ in accuracy, resolution, update frequency, and semantic consistency. At the same time, algorithms are deployed across multiple layers of the system, including cloud platforms for large-scale modeling, edge nodes for low-latency inference, and terminals for personalized adaptation. As a result, data and algorithms must interact across domains with mismatched speeds, reliability levels, and communication protocols. This leads to fragile coupling interfaces, where even minor temporal misalignments can cause significant model degradation or misjudgment.

Another key challenge is non-stationary data environments and adaptive model behavior. In ICNs, data distributions frequently shift due to user context changes, sensor aging, software updates, or external interventions. Algorithms operating in such environments must continuously adapt to new inputs without compromising previously learned knowledge. However, adaptation mechanisms such as continual learning or online optimization can themselves introduce new vulnerabilities. For instance, if an adversary introduces targeted input streams into a continual learning pipeline, the model may gradually drift toward malicious behavior without being explicitly compromised. This creates long-term stability and reliability risks that are specific to tightly coupled systems.

In real-time and safety-critical scenarios, such as autonomous vehicles, smart grids, or industrial IoT, the cost of coupling failure is particularly high. Consider an autonomous driving system where multimodal data streams from LiDAR, cameras, and GPS are fused in real time using deep neural models. If the data from one sensor becomes temporarily unavailable or noisy, the algorithm may rely disproportionately on incomplete signals, resulting in false obstacle detection or lane departure. Similarly, in intelligent energy networks, predictive control algorithms depend on historical and real-time data to optimize load balancing. Data latency or anomalies in consumption reports may cause the algorithm to misallocate resources, triggering cascading failures in power delivery.

The security surface of the data-algorithm coupling also expands significantly in ICNs. Attackers can target either side of the interface or exploit their dependencies. A common example is data poisoning, where subtle manipulations in input logs or labels during training lead to persistent behavioral flaws in the model. In federated learning scenarios, compromised clients may send crafted updates that poison shared models across the network. On the inference side, adversaries can use query probing or membership inference to reverse-engineer training data, exploiting the models statistical dependency on specific input patterns. These attacks are feasible precisely because of the tight binding between model behavior and data semantics.

Finally, there is the challenge of observability and explainability. In complex ICN environments, it is often difficult to trace how data artifacts propagate through model pipelines and how algorithmic decisions reflect underlying data structures. The lack of transparent coupling models impairs debugging, auditing, and governance. For instance, in credit scoring or personalized advertising systems, developers may be unable to clearly explain why certain users are flagged as high risk or shown specific content. This weakens accountability, trust, and regulatory compliance.

Altogether, the data-algorithm coupling in ICNs is not a static interface but a dynamic, multi-layered process shaped by system architecture, communication latency, data quality, model design, and external threats. Addressing its challenges requires a holistic approach that integrates data validation, adaptive modeling, access control, and semantic alignment. The next section explores existing methods designed to manage and secure this coupling interface in operational environments.

2.2.1.3 Existing Solutions to Data-algorithm Coupling Challenges in ICNs

To mitigate the systemic risks posed by tightly coupled data-algorithm interactions in intelligent computing networks, researchers and practitioners have developed a range of solutions that target different stages of the data lifecycle and algorithmic workflow. Rather than attempting to decouple the two elements entirely, these approaches aim to regulate and safeguard their interaction through mechanisms such as traceability, robustness enhancement, adaptive learning, distributed computation, and runtime validation.

A foundational line of work focuses on enhancing traceability and semantic transparency across the data-algorithm interface. By documenting how input data influences model behavior throughout training and inference, tools such as IBM's AI FactSheets, Google's Model Cards, and Datasheets for Datasets offer structured ways to trace the coupling paths and detect hidden dependencies. These metadata-based solutions enable downstream users to assess the reliability and fairness of models in light of their training data characteristics. Similarly, systems like DataLad and ProvDB provide version-controlled data management and audit trails within machine learning pipelines, supporting reproducibility and systematic debugging.

To address over-reliance on curated or static labeled datasets, many systems now adopt self-supervised and semi-supervised learning techniques that reduce the semantic rigidity of data-algorithm coupling. Methods like SimCLR [14] learn generalizable representations from unlabeled data using contrastive objectives, thereby increasing model robustness to data imperfection. In natural language processing, large-scale models such as BERT [15] and GPT are pretrained on heterogeneous corpora and fine-tuned on downstream tasks, allowing decoupling of inference performance from the idiosyncrasies of individual datasets. This paradigm shift reduces the risk that a specific dataset flaw will propagate directly into model decisions.

In scenarios where data privacy or ownership constraints complicate direct integration, federated learning (FL) [16] provides a decentralized approach to managing data-algorithm coupling. Instead of sharing raw data, participating nodes train local models and aggregate updates through privacy-preserving protocols. Google's use of FL in its Gboard mobile input system demonstrates this strategy in a commercial setting. In healthcare and IoT, frameworks like NVIDIA Clara enable collaborative training without violating data locality or exposing sensitive features.

Together, these approaches reflect a growing recognition that data-algorithm coupling is not simply an internal modeling concern but a system-wide design and governance issue. Addressing coupling risks in intelligent computing networks requires a multi-pronged strategy that encompasses transparent documentation, robust model training, decentralized learning frameworks, and continuous validation under real-world conditions. As intelligent systems become more autonomous and interconnected, ensuring the security, fairness, and stability of this coupling layer becomes foundational to trustworthy computing.

2.2.2 *Data-computing Coupling*

2.2.2.1 Conceptual Foundations of Data-computing Coupling

In intelligent computing networks, the coupling between data and computing power constitutes a fundamental operational mechanism that governs how data are processed, where it is stored, and when it can be acted upon. Unlike traditional systems where computing and data are often co-located in centralized infrastructure, ICNs distribute both data sources and computational resources across a multi-tier architecture consisting of cloud centers, edge nodes, terminal devices, and embedded processors. This distributed structure makes the coordination between data and computing power both a technical necessity and a design challenge.

At its core, data-computing coupling refers to the mutual constraint and co-dependence between the characteristics of data and the configuration of computing resources. The volume, velocity, and variety of data directly determine the scale, type, and responsiveness required from computing infrastructure. For instance, high-throughput data from surveillance cameras or industrial sensors must be processed with low latency to support real-time decision-making. This requires computing units with sufficient capacity and proximity to the data source, such as GPUs at the edge or real-time processors embedded in terminals.

Conversely, the architecture, availability, and orchestration of computing power also constrain the flow and utility of data. In scenarios where edge devices have limited memory or energy budgets, not all collected data can be retained, transmitted, or processed locally. Instead, data must be filtered, sampled, or compressed based on the computing resources available. In bandwidth-constrained or delay-sensitive networks, data transmission itself becomes part of the computing strategy. As a result, the placement and scheduling of computing tasks must be dynamically aligned with the structure and timing of data flows.

This coupling is not static, but evolves with changes in workload patterns, network conditions, and application contexts. For example, in urban traffic monitoring systems, computing resources may be dynamically reallocated during peak hours to support high-frequency video stream analysis. In contrast, during off-peak periods, resources may be reassigned for long-term data aggregation or historical modeling. Similarly, in mobile environments such as smart logistics or autonomous drones, both data sources and computing capacity are mobile, making the coupling relationship time-varying and spatially adaptive.

Importantly, data-computing coupling reflects more than performance coordination. It also embeds decisions about energy efficiency, privacy, data locality, and fault tolerance. On the one hand, computing-intensive tasks involving sensitive personal data, such as facial recognition or health diagnostics, may require localized processing to minimize privacy leakage risks. On the other hand, compute-intensive model training may be shifted to the cloud where resources are abundant, even if it introduces longer delays. The coupling mechanism thus implicitly encodes trade offs between speed, accuracy, privacy, and cost.

As ICNs become increasingly intelligent and autonomous, the ability to model, monitor, and optimize the coupling between data and computing power becomes a core capability. This includes not only resource provisioning and task allocation, but also prediction of data arrival patterns, anticipation of processing bottlenecks, and dynamic coordination between distributed computing units. In this sense, data-computing coupling is no longer just a passive infrastructure consideration, but an active, system-wide logic that underpins intelligent computation itself.

2.2.2.2 Data-computing Coupling Characteristics in ICNs

The data-computing coupling in intelligent computing networks exhibits distinct characteristics that make it fundamentally more complex and dynamic than in traditional systems. These characteristics arise from the distributed, heterogeneous, and mission-critical nature of ICNs, where data are generated at the edge and consumed across multiple layers of the computing hierarchy. As a result, the coordination between data streams and computational resources must account not only for volume and velocity, but also for spatial placement, temporal alignment, semantic consistency, and energy constraints.

One defining feature is the spatial distribution mismatch between data sources and available computing power. In many scenarios, data are collected at the edge, while the bulk of computing resources are concentrated in data centers or regional edge clusters. This spatial mismatch necessitates continuous task migration, adaptive workload partitioning, and traffic-aware data routing. Without effective orchestration, this can lead to resource underutilization in some areas and overload in others, increasing latency, energy consumption, and the risk of system bottlenecks.

Another challenge lies in temporal variability and bursty data flows. ICNs often serve applications that produce data in irregular or highly dynamic patterns, such as intelligent surveillance, traffic forecasting, or disaster monitoring. These workloads can generate sudden surges in data volume that exceed the local computing capacity. When buffering or offloading mechanisms are not timely or efficient, critical tasks may be delayed or dropped, affecting service quality and even safety. For instance, in autonomous driving, failure to process sensor data within a narrow time window may lead to misjudgment of road conditions.

The heterogeneity of both data and computing infrastructure further complicates the coupling process. Data streams may vary in format, sampling frequency, privacy sensitivity, and semantic richness. At the same time, computing platforms range from high-performance cloud GPUs to energy-constrained microcontrollers. Matching diverse data types with appropriate processing modules requires semantic-aware scheduling mechanisms. However, most existing schedulers are resource-centric and fail to capture the contextual properties of incoming data, resulting in mismatches that compromise task performance or violate privacy constraints.

Security and reliability risks also emerge at the interface between data and computing power. When the system lacks proper validation or isolation mechanisms, compromised data flows may trigger excessive computing load, leading to denial-of-service conditions. Attackers may also exploit the coupling mechanism itself, for instance, by injecting data that forces the system to allocate unnecessary computing resources or exhaust energy budgets. This type of resource exhaustion attack is especially effective in mobile or edge environments, where energy and compute budgets are limited and tightly linked to data processing demand.

In addition, the coupling is increasingly shaped by AI-driven scheduling mechanisms that adapt resource allocation based on learned patterns of data demand. While this improves efficiency under normal conditions, it may also introduce new risks. For instance, if a learning-based scheduler is trained on biased or outdated data, it may make incorrect predictions about future loads, resulting in under-provisioning or overreaction. This creates a new form of coupling instability, where errors in data-driven orchestration feedback into compute allocation, forming a loop that undermines system stability.

Altogether, the coupling between data and computing power in ICNs is not a fixed pipeline but a dynamic, multi-layered process subject to physical constraints, system policies, and adversarial behavior. Ensuring its stability, security, and efficiency requires holistic coordination mechanisms that consider infrastructure heterogeneity, workload dynamics, and threat models in an integrated manner.

2.2.2.3 Existing Solutions to Data-computing Coupling Challenges in ICNs

To address the security challenges posed by data-computing coupling in intelligent computing networks, a range of practical strategies and system-level mechanisms have been proposed and deployed. These approaches are not intended to separate data from computation, but rather to coordinate their interaction in ways that optimize efficiency, maintain reliability, and ensure safe operation under resource constraints. The following representative classes of methods reflect the mainstream technical directions that have been adopted in both academia and industry.

A foundational line of work focuses on data-aware computing task scheduling, which aims to align computing workloads with the structure, semantics, and arrival patterns of incoming data. Traditional schedulers primarily rely on resource availability, such as CPU load or memory usage. However, in ICNs, many systems incorporate data-aware metrics into scheduling decisions. For example, Googles Borg system [17] and its successors support affinity rules based on data locality, enabling tasks to be co-located with their associated data blocks.

Complementary to scheduling is the use of AI-driven resource orchestration platforms that adjust computing allocation based on predicted data patterns. These systems employ workload forecasting models to anticipate data surges or idle periods and pre-allocate resources accordingly. Tencents Angel platform for distributed machine learning supports adaptive job placement based on traffic patterns in data preprocessing pipelines. Alibabas MaxCompute and PAI adopt elastic resource scaling policies guided by historical input-output correlations, enabling compute provisioning that evolves with workload changes in streaming data analytics.

In scenarios where data volume exceeds available local resources, intelligent offloading strategies are widely adopted to alleviate coupling pressure. These strategies are designed to dynamically decide whether a given computation should be executed locally or migrated to more capable nodes such as edge servers or cloud platforms. The core principle of intelligent offloading lies in adaptive decision-making based on real-time system context. This includes continuous profiling of multiple runtime factors, such as the current size and structure of incoming data, the available network bandwidth and latency, the energy status of the local device, the computational cost of the task, and its urgency or deadline constraints [18].

Security-aware solutions are also becoming increasingly important. To prevent resource exhaustion or interference attacks that exploit the data-computing interface, platforms like KubeEdge implement task-level isolation and admission control. These mechanisms restrict which data types can trigger which types of computation, enforcing policies based on task priority, data trustworthiness, and historical load behavior [19]. Furthermore, secure data tagging and provenance tracking are being explored to ensure that only verified or non-malicious data can activate sensitive computing operations, especially in safety-critical domains such as healthcare and autonomous driving.

Taken together, these solutions reflect a shift from static computing infrastructure to adaptive, context-aware orchestration between data and computational tasks. Rather than decoupling the two elements, modern intelligent systems seek to enhance their coordination and transparency, allowing the system to respond flexibly to variation in data streams and resource availability. As ICNs continue to grow in complexity and autonomy, managing this coupling through real-time optimization, modular computing design, and policy-aware governance will be essential to ensure stable and trustworthy operation.

2.2.3 *Algorithm-computing Coupling*

2.2.3.1 Conceptual Foundations of Algorithm-computing Coupling

In intelligent computing networks, the relationship between computing power and algorithms has evolved into a complex, dynamic coupling process that determines how intelligent functions are implemented, scaled, and optimized across diverse hardware platforms. Algorithms do not merely run on computing infrastructure; they reshape it by dictating architectural demands, memory access patterns, parallelism strategies, and energy consumption profiles. Conversely, the design, training, deployment, and real-time performance of algorithms are deeply constrained and guided by the structure, availability, and capability of computing resources across cloud, edge, and terminal layers.

This bidirectional interaction has become particularly significant with the rise of deep learning, large-scale foundation models, graph neural networks, and multimodal fusion architectures. Such algorithms often require specialized hardware acceleration, including GPUs, TPUs, FPGAs, or custom ASICs, and rely on distributed computing frameworks to achieve training scalability and inference throughput. At the same time, algorithmic innovation increasingly targets hardware-aware optimization, such as pruning, quantization, model partitioning, and operator scheduling, to adapt to the constraints of edge devices or mobile environments. As a result, algorithm design and compute provisioning are no longer separable tasks but must be co-engineered and co-optimized.

The coupling between computing power and algorithms represents a structural dependency that decides how computational tasks are mapped to hardware systems, how performance is scaled, and how intelligent functions are sustained under dynamic operating conditions. In intelligent computing networks, this coupling is not limited to execution-level considerations such as throughput or latency. It extends to the level of co-design, where algorithmic models are adapted to the characteristics of computing platforms, and in turn, hardware systems are customized or provisioned based on the computational patterns and memory footprints of the target algorithms.

Fundamentally, this coupling relationship can be observed across several dimensions. First is the architectural dependency, where the design of an algorithm must account for the constraints and capabilities of the underlying compute substrate. For example, deep neural networks require high levels of matrix multiplication and parallel processing, which align well with GPU and TPU architectures. Conversely, resource-constrained environments such as embedded systems or IoT nodes necessitate lightweight models with reduced memory access, such as binarized neural networks or quantized convolutional networks. The structure and depth of the algorithm, the shape of input tensors, and the flow of intermediate activations all influence the mapping efficiency onto specific hardware.

Second is the operational alignment between algorithmic behavior and computing strategies. This includes how model training or inference is scheduled, how parameters are partitioned across devices, and how intermediate states are cached or discarded. Distributed learning frameworks such as TensorFlow, PyTorch, or MindSpore [20] support fine-grained control over such mappings, allowing computation graphs to be decomposed into subgraphs that can be scheduled across heterogeneous hardware. The topology of compute allocation is often guided by algorithmic patterns, including attention locality, graph sparsity, or temporal sequence length, making coupling an active element of system behavior.

Third is the resource sensitivity and cost modeling dimension, which links algorithm complexity to performance, energy, and thermal characteristics of the computing platform. In edge computing, this coupling becomes critical as algorithms must be optimized to run within strict power, memory, and latency budgets. Techniques such as model pruning, neural architecture search, knowledge distillation, and quantization are explicitly designed to reshape the algorithm in response to resource constraints. This leads to a feedback loop in which the deployment environment directly influences algorithm design and vice versa.

This coupling is not static but evolves alongside the lifecycle of an intelligent system. During early development, algorithm design may be prioritized and computing resources provisioned accordingly. In real-world deployment, however, the situation is often reversed. The algorithm must adapt to existing infrastructure, fluctuating load conditions, and energy constraints. This shift from design-driven to environment-driven coupling demands continuous profiling, fine-tuning, and even runtime restructuring of algorithmic logic to maintain acceptable performance.

In intelligent computing networks, where workloads span across data centers, edge clusters, and terminal devices, this coupling becomes multi-layered. An algorithm might be trained in the cloud using distributed GPUs, then compressed and adapted for edge inference, and further adapted again for real-time execution on a mobile chip. Each transition requires re-evaluation of the coupling relationship, from memory bandwidth and compute latency to communication overhead and thermal efficiency. Therefore, computing-algorithm coupling in ICNs is a dynamic process that embeds system constraints, performance objectives, and hardware evolution into a unified logic of intelligent deployment.

2.2.3.2 Algorithm-computing Coupling Characteristics in ICNs

In intelligent computing networks, the coupling between computing power and algorithms exhibits a set of distinctive challenges that stem from the diversity of hardware platforms, the dynamic variability of deployment environments, and the real-time responsiveness required by modern applications. Unlike traditional computing systems, where algorithms are typically designed for relatively stable hardware targets, ICNs must reconcile the demands of algorithmic complexity with the constraints of distributed, resource-constrained, and often mobile infrastructure. This coupling becomes increasingly sensitive to performance bottlenecks, energy budgets, and hardware compatibility, making its management a critical issue for scalable and trustworthy system deployment.

One major challenge arises from heterogeneous deployment environments. Intelligent computing tasks often need to run across a mix of cloud servers, edge nodes, mobile devices, and embedded controllers, each with its own processing architecture, memory model, and instruction set. Algorithms that perform well on high-end GPUs in the cloud may not be directly portable to low-power chips at the edge. This mismatch introduces significant overhead in model conversion, optimization, and platform-specific tuning. For instance, deep learning models trained on NVIDIA hardware may require quantization or operator replacement to be executed efficiently on ARM-based edge accelerators. Without dedicated toolchains and adaptation strategies, these gaps hinder real-time inference and increase development costs.

Another source of complexity lies in runtime variability and workload dynamics. Algorithms deployed in ICNs must adapt to fluctuating resource availability, including processor load, thermal conditions, network latency, and memory occupancy. A model that performs optimally in one context may degrade sharply under different operational conditions. For example, a graph neural network used for real-time traffic prediction might operate efficiently under stable load, but suffer latency spikes when concurrent tasks overload the edge node. The coupling between algorithm and computing power becomes a moving target, requiring real-time monitoring and adaptive scheduling to maintain acceptable performance.

A further challenge is related to resource contention and prioritization in shared computing environments [21]. In ICNs, multiple algorithms may simultaneously compete for limited compute cycles, particularly at the edge. Without coupling-aware scheduling policies, resource-intensive tasks may crowd out latency-sensitive or safety-critical algorithms. For instance, video encoding workloads may delay inference tasks related to emergency detection, resulting in cascading quality-of-service violations. Ensuring fair and performance-aware compute sharing requires the scheduler to account for algorithm structure, real-time constraints, and contextual importance, which are capabilities that many current systems lack.

Security concerns also emerge at the coupling interface. Malicious code or model payloads may exploit hardware features to trigger excessive computation, causing denial-of-service behavior [22]. Conversely, adversaries may manipulate compute allocation policies by injecting dummy workloads that simulate high-priority algorithmic signatures. These algorithm-compute spoofing attacks can degrade system availability or bias scheduling decisions. Furthermore, firmware or driver-level vulnerabilities can allow unauthorized code to bypass resource restrictions, exacerbating the risk of cross-algorithm interference in multi-tenant scenarios.

Together, these challenges demonstrate that computing-algorithm coupling in ICNs is not merely a performance tuning issue, but a foundational concern that affects portability, efficiency, safety, and trustworthiness. Addressing these issues requires coordinated development across algorithm engineering, system design, and hardware provisioning.

2.2.3.3 Existing Solutions to Computing-algorithm Coupling in ICNs

To address the performance and security challenges of computing-algorithm coupling in intelligent computing networks, both academia and industry have proposed a series of technical frameworks and system-level solutions. These methods aim not to decouple the algorithm from the hardware entirely, but to strengthen the co-design, adaptability, and run-time alignment between algorithmic models and the computing environment.

One representative direction is the development of co-optimization toolchains, which systematically adapt algorithm structures to specific computing architectures. Platforms such as TensorFlow lite micro [23] provide model transformation pipelines that perform layer fusion, quantization, pruning, and kernel tuning for deployment on ARM, DSP, or NPU-based devices. These toolchains support automatic operator replacement and memory layout reorganization, enabling neural network models to be compressed and optimized for constrained edge hardware without compromising accuracy beyond acceptable thresholds.

Another widely adopted strategy is the use of cross-platform inference frameworks that abstract hardware differences and enable runtime model portability. Frameworks such as NVIDIA TensorRT [24] and ONNX Runtime [25] allow models to be deployed on CPUs, GPUs, NPUs, and custom ASICs through a unified intermediate representation and backend compilation. These systems support dynamic graph partitioning and hybrid execution, allowing different parts of a model to be executed on different devices depending on resource availability and task urgency. This flexibility greatly improves the manageability of computing-algorithm coupling across heterogeneous deployments.

Collectively, these approaches reflect a paradigm shift in intelligent system design: from treating algorithms and hardware as separate concerns to building them as co-evolving subsystems with shared performance, safety, and optimization goals. In the context of ICNs, where computing scenarios are inherently distributed, volatile, and heterogeneous, managing this coupling through layered design, modular execution, and run-time negotiation has become essential to achieving scalable, trustworthy, and efficient intelligent computation.

2.2.4 Coupling Among Data, Computing Power, and Algorithms

2.2.4.1 The Concept of Triadic Coupling Among Data, Computing Power, and Algorithms

The core functionality of intelligent computing networks relies on the deep integration of three fundamental elements: data, computing power, and algorithms. These elements do not function independently; instead, they form a tightly coupled triadic relationship that determines how information is perceived, processed, and acted upon within the system. While pairwise relationships, such as data driving algorithm training or computing power enabling algorithm execution, are relatively well understood, the systemic interaction among all three elements forms a higher-order dependency structure. This triadic coupling encapsulates both operational logic and adaptive behavior, and it is essential for understanding how intelligent services emerge and evolve in complex, distributed environments.

To visually capture the systemic logic of triadic coupling, we present a schematic triangle model that highlights the mutual dependencies among data, computing power, and algorithms. Each vertex denotes a core system element, while the edges indicate bidirectional coupling paths with specific operational and security semantics, as shown in Fig. 2.2.

From a structural standpoint, triadic coupling represents a closed loop of functional interdependence. Data serves as the input that fuels algorithmic reasoning, but its value is only realized through timely and efficient processing by computational systems. Algorithms, in turn, interpret, transform, and extract structure from data, yet their execution is meaningless without the support of physical or virtual computing platforms. Computing power enables the instantiation and scaling of algorithmic models, but its purpose is only fulfilled when applied to meaningful data through logical reasoning. Each element acts both as a driver and a constraint for the others. This interlocking relationship creates a recursive, co-regulatory system in which the optimization or degradation of one element can propagate non-linearly to the others.

This conceptual model implies that intelligent behaviors are not determined by any single factor in isolation. Rather, they emerge from the interaction pathways and feedback loops among all three. For example, in a real-time video analytics scenario, the effectiveness of object detection depends not only on the accuracy of the underlying neural network (algorithm) and the resolution or labeling quality of the video feed (data), but also on the ability of the edge device to execute the model at sufficient frame rate (computing power). If any component is suboptimal, if the video feed is too noisy, if the model is too heavy, or if the hardware lacks acceleration, the entire task fails. Thus, intelligence is an emergent property of well-orchestrated three-way interaction.

Furthermore, triadic coupling is dynamic, context-sensitive, and subject to temporal evolution. The coupling structure may change as algorithms are retrained,

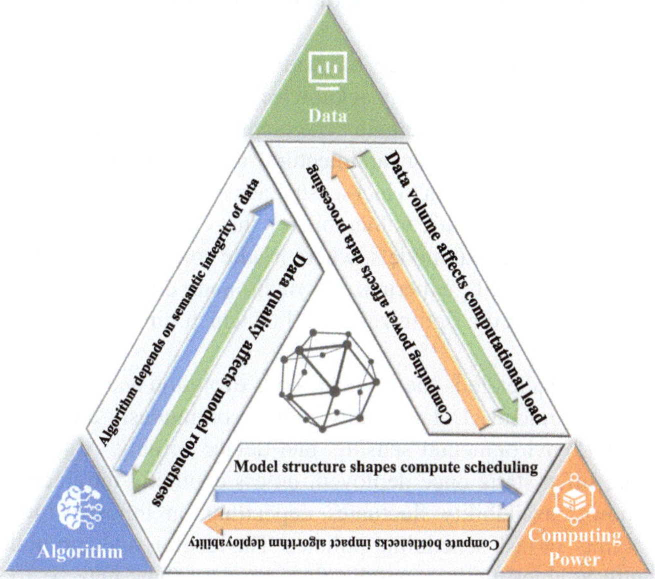

Fig. 2.2 Schematic illustration of the triadic coupling among data, computing power, and algorithms in intelligent computing networks. Each edge of the triangle represents a bidirectional interaction path, highlighting mutual influence and risk propagation between two elements

as data streams shift in distribution or modality, or as computational resources are migrated, scaled, or constrained. For instance, an algorithm that performs well on historical data in a cloud training environment may not function adequately in real-time edge deployments due to compute limitations or data drift. This underscores the need to treat the triadic structure not as a static graph but as a flexible, reconfigurable coordination layer that adapts over time.

Importantly, this coupling is not symmetric or uniform. In some systems, data may dominate the interaction, such as in data-centric AI pipelines where algorithm and resource design are oriented toward specific data characteristics. In others, computing power may be the limiting factor, especially in ultra-low-power applications where algorithm design is dictated by energy constraints [26]. In yet other cases, algorithmic logic may govern how data are preprocessed and how resources are scheduled. These variations create a spectrum of coupling configurations, each requiring different optimization strategies and system assumptions.

In sum, the triadic coupling among data, computing power, and algorithms constitutes a foundational layer of logic in intelligent computing networks. It decides how information flows, how decisions are made, and how system behavior adapts to external and internal changes. Understanding this coupling as a first-class design concept is necessary not only for performance optimization, but also for long-term resilience, safety, and ethical governance of autonomous computing systems.

2.2.4.2 Status and Challenges of Triadic Coupling in ICNs

Although the conceptual importance of triadic coupling among data, computing power, and algorithms is increasingly acknowledged, its practical realization within intelligent computing networks remains fragmented and underdeveloped. Current ICN deployments often reflect an architectural and organizational separation of these three elements, which leads to inconsistencies in coordination, inefficiencies in resource allocation, and systemic vulnerabilities that emerge when conditions shift. Unlike in idealized theoretical models, where triadic components evolve in tandem, real-world systems typically experience asynchronous development, independent ownership, and task-specific optimization, all of which hinder integrated coupling management.

One prominent challenge is the asynchronous evolution and lifecycle mismatch among the three elements. Data streams evolve continuously and are influenced by user behavior, environmental sensing, and device activity. Algorithms, on the other hand, are often static once deployed, unless explicitly retrained or updated. Computing power availability fluctuates depending on infrastructure upgrades, energy constraints, or task scheduling policies. The result is a temporal decoupling: data may outpace algorithmic generalization, or algorithms may be too complex for the available hardware. This lack of synchronized evolution often leads to performance degradation, operational bottlenecks, or system failure.

Another fundamental issue lies in the fragmented ownership and siloed management of the three elements. In most ICN architectures, data are collected by edge providers or user devices, algorithms are developed by cloud platforms or third-party vendors, and computing infrastructure is operated by separate infrastructure providers or telecom entities. This division of responsibilities causes delays in integration, inconsistencies in optimization objectives, and difficulty in enforcing security or compliance policies across the entire system stack. When these elements are not designed or updated in tandem, the resulting triadic structure becomes brittle, unable to adapt to new application requirements or dynamic workloads.

Furthermore, intelligent computing networks frequently suffer from suboptimal task allocation and resource mismatch due to a lack of unified coupling-aware orchestration. For example, an AI application may deploy a large-scale model to an edge node without accounting for its real-time memory footprint or thermal limits, leading to system throttling or degraded inference. Conversely, lightweight algorithms may be assigned to high-performance nodes, wasting compute capacity. In either case, the lack of joint scheduling logic among data, compute, and algorithmic components leads to inefficiency and underutilization.

Security risks are also amplified by poor triadic coordination. Attacks that target one element, such as poisoning training data, overloading compute nodes, or injecting malicious model updates, can propagate across the coupling pathways to compromise the entire system [27]. For instance, attackers may use edge-generated noise to trigger instability in compute-constrained algorithms, or manipulate compute resource allocation to suppress critical inference tasks. Without coupling-aware monitoring, these compound threats are difficult to detect and mitigate.

Lastly, there is a widespread lack of analytical frameworks and design tools to model and manage triadic coupling in a systematic way. Most current methods for system evaluation, task scheduling, or security analysis treat data, algorithms, and computing power as isolated components or as pairwise interactions. Few tools can simultaneously account for semantic integrity of data, algorithmic robustness, and dynamic resource constraints. This leads to blind spots in decision-making, especially under failure conditions or adversarial stress, where a failure in one dimension can escalate across the entire system.

In summary, while triadic coupling represents a fundamental structural principle of intelligent computing systems, current engineering practices in ICNs still fall short of embracing it as a unified design target. Addressing this gap will require the development of integrated frameworks that jointly manage data-compute-algorithm interdependencies, support adaptive coupling control, and provide system-wide visibility for both performance and security. The next section will propose such an integrated paradigm, aiming to operationalize triadic coupling into a formal model for trustworthy intelligent computing.

2.3 The Integrated Security and Safety Paradigm

As ICNs become increasingly complex, dynamic, and autonomous, the demands on their security and safety mechanisms grow accordingly. Traditional methods that focus on protecting static system components or monitoring isolated incidents are no longer sufficient. In such environments, the interaction among data, computing power, and algorithms constitutes the structural core of system intelligence and operational behavior. These elements are not merely resources to be managed independently; they are deeply intertwined, with their coupling relationships directly influencing task execution, service reliability, and trustworthiness. Recognizing and leveraging this triadic interdependence provides a new pathway to enhancing both security (protection against intentional harm) and safety (resilience to unintended failure) in intelligent systems.

To meet these needs, we propose a behavior-driven, coupling-aware security and safety paradigm that unifies system modeling, authentication, and risk management under a common semantic framework. Rather than treating data, algorithms, and computing power as passive or isolated resources, our approach treats them as co-evolving, behavior-defining elements. The key idea is to model the system not only through observed states or control rules, but through the fine-grained behavioral expressions that arise from the interaction of these three resources. By observing, encoding, and interpreting behavioral patterns across time, entities, and resource configurations, we can extract high-density semantic representations that reveal both system intent and deviation. These representations can then be used to support adaptive security policies, anomaly detection and trust reasoning.

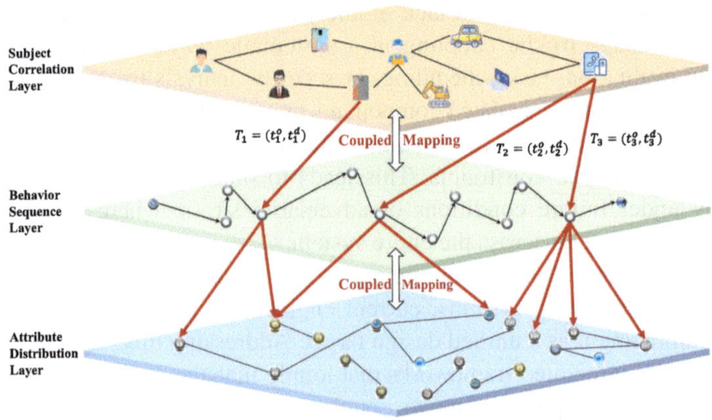

Fig. 2.3 Framework of the integrated security and safety paradigm based on tri-layer behavioral knowledge graph modeling. The architecture consists of three semantic layers: subject correlation, behavior sequence, and attribute distribution, each capturing a distinct dimension of behavioral representation

As shown in Fig. 2.3, to implement this paradigm, we propose a three-layer behavior knowledge graph, which decomposes system behavior into three interrelated semantic layers:

- The subject correlation layer models entity-level relationships. It encodes correlations and interaction similarities among users, devices, services, or system agents based on their behavioral histories. This layer captures behavioral communities, trust chains, and social or organizational proximity, enabling collaborative inference across subjects.
- The behavior sequence layer captures time-dependent behavior patterns. Rather than treating behaviors as unordered events, this layer preserves the sequence, transition structure, and temporal window of behavioral trajectories. It enables recognition of incomplete, emerging, or shifting behaviors, supporting early warning and pattern completion.
- The attribute distribution layer models intra-behavioral semantics. It captures the relationships among multiple attributes co-occurring in the same action (e.g., location, data size, and command type), forming a topological structure of internal dependencies. This allows filtering of noise, correction of inconsistencies, and enhancement of weak signals.

The graph supports two types of cross-layer coupling mappings:

- Subject-behavior mapping, which enables collaborative filtering and behavior generalization based on subject similarity and shared intent.
- Behavior-attribute mapping, which allows content-driven semantic expansion through co-occurrence and structural proximity.

Through these mappings, behaviors that are sparse or partially observed can be semantically enhanced, generalized to similar entities, or transferred across contexts. Moreover, the model allows semantic information aggregation across layers, such that patterns detected in one layer can reinforce understanding in others. This cross-layer fusion creates high-density semantic representations, enabling accurate authentication and anomaly detection even under limited data conditions.

A core advantage of this tri-layer knowledge graph structure is its ability to support behavior modeling even in the absence of large-scale, labeled, or real-time data. In many real-world intelligent computing systems, especially those operating at the edge or in mission-critical infrastructure, data are limited, noisy, or delayed. Traditional statistical learning and rule-based approaches often fail in such scenarios due to insufficient sample volume, feature sparsity, or mismatch between training and deployment environments. In contrast, our model is designed to function under data-constrained conditions by relying on semantic structure and coupling logic, rather than raw volume alone.

The layered design also enhances contextual interpretability. A behavior that appears anomalous in isolation may, in fact, be benign when considered in relation to peer behaviors (captured in the subject layer), temporal continuity (captured in the sequence layer), or typical co-occurrence patterns (captured in the attribute layer). This interpretive capacity makes the model robust to false alarms, reactive to new threats, and adaptive to domain changes. Furthermore, because the mappings between layers are not fixed but data-driven and learnable, the framework can evolve over time, continuously adapting its structure and semantics based on real-time system feedback and behavioral shifts.

This structure directly enables adaptive and behavior-centric security mechanisms. For example, rather than using static blacklists or access control lists, authentication can be based on semantic consistency across layers. A new or unknown behavior may be permitted if it aligns with a known subject group, fits a recognized temporal sequence, and exhibits coherent attribute composition. Similarly, anomaly detection becomes a task of identifying deviations from learned tri-layer graphs rather than matching against static thresholds. This results in a more fine-grained and contextual understanding of "normal" versus "suspicious" activity.

Moreover, the paradigm supports dual-function reasoning for both security and safety. In modern systems, the boundary between malicious disruption (security) and accidental failure (safety) is often blurred. For example, a compute node overload may result from either an attack or a misconfigured task; a model misclassification may result from adversarial input or degraded data quality. The proposed modeling framework allows both cases to be interpreted within the same graph-based logic: if a behavior deviates from all three layers simultaneously, the risk level is elevated regardless of its root cause. In this way, behavior graphs provide a unified surface for risk sensing, reasoning, and response across both intentional and unintentional threats.

By embedding these security and safety mechanisms into the behavioral logic of the system, we also promote dynamic trust calibration. Rather than binary access decisions, the system can assign probabilistic trust scores based on alignment with historical behavior, structural coherence, and entity reputation. These scores can, in turn, guide dynamic policy adaptation, resource reallocation, or user interaction redesign. Over time, the model builds a living memory of behavioral norms, continuously refined by operational evidence, enabling a self-learning defense layer that co-evolves with the system.

In addition to its direct functional benefits, the proposed paradigm represents a strategic shift in the design philosophy of intelligent systems. It moves away from component-centric security architectures toward systemic, interaction-aware assurance, where trust and resilience are not enforced top-down, but emerge bottom-up from consistent, semantically coherent behaviors. This aligns with the broader evolution of computing, from deterministic pipelines to learning systems, from fixed-rule logic to statistical reasoning, and from hardware-constrained architectures to hybrid context-aware intelligence.

The triadic coupling model also aligns naturally with the realities of heterogeneous, decentralized, and resource-constrained environments. In such settings, no single actor has complete visibility, no single model fits all conditions, and no central authority can enforce trust unilaterally. Instead, secure behavior must arise from locally interpretable signals and globally coherent coordination. Our paradigm provides a path forward by embedding interpretability, adaptability, and generalizability directly into the behavior modeling substrate, enabling intelligent nodes to assess risk and regulate operations without full system knowledge.

In summary, the Integrated Security and Safety Paradigm introduced in this section offers a unified, behavior-centric approach to modeling, understanding, and safeguarding intelligent computing networks. By structurally capturing the triadic coupling among data, computing power, and algorithms, and embedding that structure in a three-layer knowledge graph of behavior, we enable intelligent systems to reason, react, and adapt under uncertainty. This paradigm provides a foundation not only for technical risk mitigation, but also for long-term system trust, safety compliance, and semantic assurance in increasingly autonomous, data-limited, and high-stakes environments.

References

1. J. Furner, in *Information Cultures in the Digital Age: A Festschrift in Honor of Rafael Capurro* (Springer, Berlin, 2016), pp. 287–306
2. G. Kapil, A. Agrawal, R.A. Khan, in *Proceedings of the 2016 International Conference on Communication and Electronics Systems (ICCES), Coimbatore, 2016* (2016), pp. 1–4
3. A. Arasu, H. Garcia-Molina, in *Proceedings of the 2003 ACM SIGMOD International Conference on Management of Data (SIGMOD/PODS), San Diego, 2003* (2003), p. 337348
4. D.D. Chamberlin, ACM Comput. Surv. **8**(1), 43 (1976)
5. K. Spanaki, Z. Gürgüç, R. Adams, C. Mulligan, Int. J. Prod. Res. **56**(13), 4447 (2018)
6. S. Yukun, L. Bo, L. Junlin, H. Haonan, Z. Xing, P. Jing, W. Wenbo, China Commun. **21**(9), 109 (2024)
7. C.A. Mack, IEEE Trans. Semicond. Manuf. **24**(2), 202 (2011)
8. M. McGrath, *Understanding PaaS* (O'Reilly Media, Inc., Sebastopol, 2012)

9. Y.N. Moschovakis, Mathematics Unlimited—2001 and Beyond (Springer, Berlin, Heidelberg, 2001), pp. 919–936
10. P. Dembiński, *Dictionary of Logic as Applied in the Study of Language: Concepts/Methods/ Theories* (Springer, Dordrecht, 1981), pp. 14–18
11. R. Gupta, T. Roughgarden, Commun. ACM **63**(6), 87 (2020)
12. T. Ramaporkalai, Int. J. Comput. Sci. Trends Technol. **5**(2), 500 (2017)
13. A. Schwarzschild, M. Goldblum, A. Gupta, J.P. Dickerson, T. Goldstein, in *Proceedings of the 38th International Conference on Machine Learning (ICML), Virtual Event, 2021* (2021), pp. 9389–9398
14. T. Chen, S. Kornblith, M. Norouzi, G. Hinton, in *Proceedings of the 37th International Conference on Machine Learning (ICML), Virtual Event, 2020* (2020), pp. 1597–1607
15. J. Devlin, M. Chang, K. Lee, K. Toutanova, in *Proceedings of the 2019 Conference of the North American Chapter of the Association for Computational Linguistics: Human Language Technologies (NAACL-HLT), Minneapolis, MN, USA, 2019* (2019), pp. 4171–4186
16. C. Zhang, Y. Xie, H. Bai, B. Yu, W. Li, Y. Gao, Knowl. Based Syst. **216**, 106775 (2021)
17. A. Verma, L. Pedrosa, M. Korupolu, D. Oppenheimer, E. Tune, J. Wilkes, in *Proceedings of the Tenth European Conference on Computer Systems, Bordeaux, France, 2015* (2015), pp. 1–17
18. L. Zhao, T. Li, E. Zhang, Y. Lin, S. Wan, A. Hawbani, M. Guizani, IEEE Trans. Mobile Comput. **23**(8), 8158 (2024). https://doi.org/10.1109/TMC.2023.3344645
19. Y. Xiong, Y. Sun, L. Xing, Y. Huang, in *2018 IEEE/ACM Symposium on Edge Computing (SEC), Seattle, WA, USA, 2018* (2018), pp. 373–377
20. Z. Tong, N. Du, X. Song, X. Wang, in *2021 17th International Conference on Computational Intelligence and Security (CIS), Chengdu, China, 2021* (2021), pp. 183–186
21. S. Zhuravlev, S. Blagodurov, A. Fedorova, ACM Sigplan Notices **45**(3), 129 (2010)
22. F. Lau, S.H. Rubin, M.H. Smith, L. Trajkovic, in *2000 IEEE International Conference on Systems, Man and Cybernetics.'Cybernetics Evolving to Systems, Humans, Organizations, and Their Complex Interactions (Smc), Nashville, TN, USA, 2000* (2000), pp. 2275–2280
23. R. David, J. Duke, A. Jain, V. Janapa Reddi, N. Jeffries, J. Li, N. Kreeger, I. Nappier, M. Natraj, T. Wang, et al., Proc. Mach. Learn. Syst. **3**, 800 (2021)
24. Y. Zhou, K. Yang, in *2022 IEEE 24th International Conference on High Performance Computing & Communications; 8th Int Conf on Data Science & Systems; 20th Int Conf on Smart City; 8th International Conference on Dependability in Sensor, Cloud & Big Data Systems & Application (HPCC/DSS/SmartCity/DependSys), Hainan, China, 2022* (2022), pp. 2011–2018
25. S.Y. Kim, J. Lee, C.H. Kim, W.J. Lee, S.W. Kim, in *2022 International Conference on Electronics, Information, and Communication (ICEIC), Jeju, Korea, 2022* (2022), pp. 1–4
26. L. Chen, S. Zhou, J. Xu, IEEE/ACM Trans. Netw. **26**(4), 1619 (2018)
27. N. Wang, Z.Y. Jin, J. Zhao, Phys. A Stat. Mech. Appl. **574**, 125989 (2021)

Chapter 3
The Projection Onto System Plane

Abstract Chapter 3 examines the role of system security within intelligent computing networks, highlighting its transition from traditional control mechanisms to dynamic coordination in open and coupled environments. As computing power is distributed to edge devices and intelligent models are deployed across diverse device categories, systems have evolved from isolated units to integral components of data flow and algorithm scheduling. This chapter introduces the concept of "projection onto the system plane" to analyze how system security impacts the overall security state, considering the interdependencies among system, data, and algorithm security. It addresses three key areas: the propagation of system security incidents through data and algorithmic paths, the limitations of current security mechanisms under dynamic and heterogeneous conditions, and a proposed system security framework that integrates cross-layer perception and local autonomy. The chapter advocates for a shift from static protection to dynamic collaboration and from localized control to holistic governance to enhance system stability and resilience.

3.1 Motivation and Representative Examples

3.1.1 Motivation

In the highly distributed and dynamically coordinated operating environment of intelligent computing network systems, the system no longer merely serves as a basic support layer for computing and communication resources. Instead, it is deeply embedded in the entire process of data processing and algorithm execution, becoming a central hub that spans resource scheduling, behavior control, and state management. Security issues at the system level have evolved from traditional single point incidents such as access control failures, kernel vulnerability exploitation, and misconfigurations into complex sources of risk characterized by cross-layer propagation and deep interdependencies. Fluctuations in system state not only directly affect the stability of the operating environment but also profoundly impact data integrity and algorithm reliability through mechanisms such as execution paths, resource constraints, and interface dependencies.

C. Wang, H. Tang, *Integrated Security and Safety of Intelligent Computing Networks*, https://doi.org/10.1007/978-981-95-5025-8_3

Attackers today are no longer content with directly compromising system components themselves. Instead, they increasingly exploit the system as the starting point of an attack chain, leveraging its intermediary role between underlying hardware resources and upper-layer functional components to embed control logic or disrupt scheduling processes, thereby triggering a cascade of cross-layer security consequences. For example, a privilege escalation vulnerability in a system service process, once exploited, can lead to unauthorized data access, forced task injection, or model manipulation. Similarly, a misconfigured interface on an edge node system may be exploited as an entry point for data forgery or a channel for model pollution, forming a propagative attack path of "system anomaly data contamination algorithm deviation". This security coupling pattern, originating from the system and diffusing toward data and algorithms, is becoming a predominant manifestation of threats in intelligent computing network environments.

Against this backdrop, projecting security issues onto the system plane becomes a key entry point for understanding the structure of cross-layer threats and for developing coordinated defense strategies. The main advantages of this approach are reflected in the following four aspects:

(1) Environmental Layer Reconstruction: Clarifying the foundational impact of system states on algorithm execution. The correct functioning of algorithms heavily depends on the runtime environment provided by the system, including scheduler policies, driver loading sequences, dependency integrity, and hardware mapping behaviors. Once anomalies occur at the system level, even flawless model logic may lead to failures in training, deviations in inference results, or interruptions in algorithm iteration due to disrupted execution paths, failed external dependencies, or degraded runtime parameters. Mapping security issues onto the system plane helps identify such "non-model causality deviations" triggered by environmental anomalies, thereby supporting the construction of algorithm security frameworks with stronger steady state awareness.
(2) Interface Layer Contamination: Revealing the potential threats system vulnerabilities pose to data pipelines. The lifecycle management of data relies heavily on system provided communication interfaces and resource access channels. From sensor data acquisition, edge cache management, data upload, compression, decryption, to result delivery, all stages depend on the scheduling and control of system components. If system interfaces are tampered with or invocation paths are hijacked, attackers can forge, delay, or disrupt collected data without altering the data source devices, thereby injecting structurally polluted data to mislead model training and perception-based decision making. A breach in system level security threatens not only the integrity of individual data points but may also result in coordinated multi-link data contamination, producing anomalies that are difficult to trace.
(3) Control Layer Embedding: Identifying the intervention effects of system resource scheduling on algorithm workflows. In intelligent computing network environments, the system not only manages hardware resource allocation but

also handles task priority scheduling, model loading decisions, and device context switching. Attackers can exploit system scheduling mechanisms such as priority spoofing, resource hogging, or task phishing to interfere with the training pace and operating conditions of models, even inducing drift or degradation under unreasonable resource configurations. This type of attack, which "disrupts internal learning paths through external condition manipulation" is not only highly covert but also persistent, capable of hijacking or degrading algorithm logic while the system surface appears to be operating normally.

(4) Semantic Layer Linking: Enabling associative modeling between system events and upper-layer behaviors. The system layer serves as a logical bridge between data flow and algorithmic decision making, with indicators such as system logs, anomaly reports, and changes in resource usage often reflecting underlying multi-layer behavioral couplings. Using system behaviors as triggers for cross-layer modeling enables the construction of joint mechanisms for data integrity verification and model anomaly diagnosis. For example, if a certain node experiences frequent system level restarts accompanied by abnormal drops in model accuracy and abrupt shifts in data sequences, this can be comprehensively identified as a closed loop security incident where "system instability causes algorithm degradation". Such associative modeling capabilities provide intelligent computing network environments with a higher level of security situational awareness and causal traceability.

The system plane is not only one of the origins of security issues but also the control hub of the interaction chain between algorithms and data. Mapping the integrated security challenges in intelligent computing network environments onto the system layer is a critical step toward achieving cross-domain awareness, link-level traceability, and proactive defense. In the following sections of this chapter, we will use the Mirai botnet attack as a case study. We will systematically analyze how system layer vulnerabilities can trigger cascading consequences, including data forgery, algorithm manipulation, and task mismanagement. This analysis will further reveal the structural role of the system plane within the closed-loop security architecture of computing network systems.

3.1.2 The Distributed Security Challenges of Edge Devices

Next-generation information technologies are developing rapidly. These include 5G, artificial intelligence, edge computing, software defined networking (SDN), and network functions virtualization (NFV). These emerging technologies are increasingly penetrating traditional infrastructure fields (e.g., energy, electricity, manufacturing, and transportation), driving the evolution of computing power, networks, and data resources toward deep integration [1–3]. Against this backdrop, intelligent computing networks are gradually replacing the traditional "centralized data center and static terminal devices" model with a distributed architecture evolving toward "edge cloud collaboration" and "end edge cloud integration" [4]. This evolution ensures that computing power is no longer limited to centralized clouds but is widely deployed across edge and terminal layers, enabling intelligent services to shift from core data centers to the network edge and application sites.

In critical scenarios, such as smart grids, industrial IoT, vehicle networks, and smart cities, this architectural change is particularly evident [5]. For example, in a smart grid system, edge computing nodes are responsible for preprocessing, analyzing, and feedback controlling data such as current, voltage, and power, ensuring the real time and resilience of power supply. In industrial settings, edge devices handle key tasks such as image recognition, quality inspection, and equipment status assessment on production lines, enabling local closed loop control. In vehicle networks, edge nodes need to process traffic flow, environmental sensing, and path planning information in real time, with high requirements for latency and reliability. The existence of these edge nodes greatly enhances the overall system's response speed, operational efficiency, and adaptive resilience, serving as the core support for achieving "near source computing" and "distributed intelligence" within the intelligent computing network framework.

However, while this distributed architecture brings about performance improvements, it significantly expands the system's attack surface. In the traditional centralized model, data and computing are concentrated in controllable data centers, making it easy to uniformly implement security policies. By contrast, in edge cloud collaborative architectures, edge nodes are deployed in a decentralized manner, operate in complex physical environments, and have varying security capabilities, making centralized management difficult. Some nodes have limited resources, lacking complete intrusion detection, trust chain mechanisms, and firmware update capabilities. Edge devices often present two significant vulnerabilities. First, security requirements are frequently overlooked during the design phase, making them entry points for attacks. Second, many devices rely on open interfaces (e.g., Telnet, SSH, and HTTP APIs) for external communication, leaving them highly susceptible to remote intrusions when protection is weak. Once an edge node is compromised, attacks may spread horizontally and penetrate vertically through computing network channels, affecting cloud-based control centers, scheduling platforms, and even core data systems. Attackers can thereby launch Distributed Denial of Service (DDoS) attacks, forge data, interfere with models, and cause resource contention, severely threatening the stable operation and trustworthy protection of intelligent computing networks.

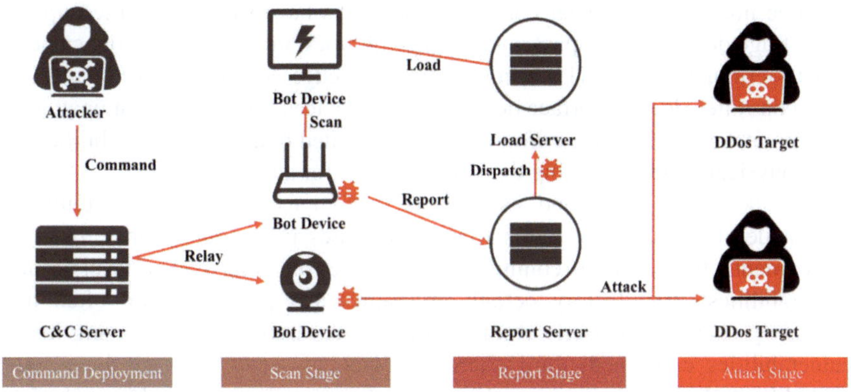

Fig. 3.1 Diagram of the Mirai attack path

3.1.3 Attack Path: From System Level Intrusion to the Comprehensive Threat to Intelligent Computing and Networking Systems

The Mirai botnet was first publicly disclosed in 2016. As shown in Fig. 3.1, its original attack logic relied on automatically scanning and compromising a large number of networked devices, particularly targeting consumer grade routers, network cameras, and digital video recorders running embedded Linux systems such as OpenWRT and BusyBox [6, 7]. The attack process involved probing public Telnet services for open ports, then using a built-in, large scale dictionary of default usernames and passwords to perform brute force attacks [8]. Once system access was obtained, Mirai would immediately implant a malicious executable, delete system logs, disable remote management, and block security updates, effectively turning the compromised device into a remotely controlled "bot node" registered within a global distributed command and control (C2) network. Attackers could then centrally orchestrate these bots to launch DDoS attacks. This attack model, characterized by large scale automation and rapid deployment, caused major service disruptions, including outages affecting U.S. Domain Name System (DNS) provider Dyn, as well as services like Netflix and Twitter, drawing widespread public attention.

Although Mirai initially targeted consumer-grade IoT devices, the public release of its source code led numerous hacker groups and underground attack organizations to continuously evolve its attack mechanisms, resulting in the emergence of dozens of variant versions. These variants not only possess enhanced scanning capabilities and greater stealth but have also gradually expanded their targets to include critical infrastructure environments such as the Industrial Internet of Things (IIoT), smart manufacturing platforms, edge servers, and industrial control system (ICS) terminals. In recent years, the frequency and intensity of Mirai related activities at the edge nodes of intelligent computing networks have shown a marked upward trend. Edge devices encompass a wide range of types, including industrial cameras, remote terminal units (RTUs), smart gateways, edge servers, and programmable logic controller (PLC) interface devices. These devices often operate in unattended or semi-enclosed network environments, with limited maintenance capabilities and weak physical security, making them ideal targets for attackers [9].

The success of Mirai and its variants in compromising a large number of edge nodes fundamentally stems from weaknesses in system security. In actual deployments, these devices commonly exhibit the following system-level security vulnerabilities: first, factory default usernames and passwords are often used and rarely changed by users; second, firmware is rarely updated, leaving known vulnerabilities unpatched; third, there is a lack of secure boot mechanisms or trusted boot chains, allowing attackers to load malicious modules during the boot process; fourth, devices lack proactive defense components such as host firewalls, intrusion detection systems (IDS), or endpoint behavior analysis, meaning malicious activities are rarely detected or intercepted; fifth, many devices expose remote service interfaces such as Telnet, SSH, and HTTP without strong authentication or access control mechanisms, making them highly susceptible to remote exploitation. Once attackers gain access, they can fully control the behaviors of the devices through system level privileges. This not only enables large-scale DDoS attacks, but also allows manipulation of local sensing data, or interference with control logic. Even more insidious is the fact that these edge devices possess certain computational and inference capabilities. Attackers can implant backdoors disguised as legitimate modules to manipulate data processing logic, allowing the system to appear operational on the surface while being completely compromised in reality. Such attacks are highly covert, often bypassing traditional perimeter defenses and behavior-based detection, and have become one of the most difficult security blind spots to detect within intelligent computing network systems.

The entry point of the attack path is clearly located at the system layer. Due to the high connectivity and weak security of edge nodes, attackers can compromise a small number of devices to establish an initial control chain. Leveraging the automatic communication mechanisms between nodes, they can achieve lateral propagation and rapidly gain control over a wider range of computing network resources. Such botnets are no longer limited to traditional traffic-based attacks; they now possess composite attack capabilities such as data theft, content forgery, and intelligent interference, effectively functioning as attack infrastructures with autonomous behavior. Once the system layer is compromised, the data layer becomes the first and most immediate victim. As computing units closest to the physical world, edge nodes are responsible for collecting and pre-processing large volumes of raw data. This data not only supports local real-time response but also serves as critical input for intelligent algorithms such as modeling, prediction, and control. Therefore, once attackers take control of the system, they can tamper with cached data, forge data packets, manipulate the data reporting cadence, or even construct entire "phantom data streams" to deceive upper-layer logic. In such scenarios, although the device may appear to be operating normally, the output data is completely untrustworthy, posing a serious threat to the overall stability of the intelligent computing network system and undermining the integrity of its decision making foundation.

3.1.4 System Vulnerabilities and Attack Patterns: A Case Study of the Mirai

In typical industrial Internet scenarios, such as smart grids, edge nodes continuously report key indicators like voltage, current, load, and switch status. If this data is tampered with, the dispatch center may make erroneous resource allocations, grid switches, or load shedding based on false information, potentially causing large-scale power misallocation and safety incidents. In vehicular networks, compromised traffic cameras and sensors can fabricate false congestion or obscure real traffic jams, disrupting traffic light scheduling and navigation routes, leading to traffic paralysis. Attackers can also subtly adjust the noise in data, gradually weakening the judgment ability of upper-level algorithms, causing the system to enter a state of "misleading control". This kind of data tampering is highly covert. Unlike traditional network attacks that cause obvious anomalies, data pollution attacks evade rule-based and statistical anomaly detection by mimicking legitimate formats, controlling transmission frequency, and maintaining protocol consistency. Attackers may intermittently insert slightly shifted forged data, keeping the overall short-term distribution within normal ranges, thereby forming a "gradual information corrosion" that penetrates over time and gradually undermines system perception.

The distributed nature of intelligent computing networks exacerbates the spread of data pollution. Once an edge node is compromised, the polluted data can flow into aggregation nodes, edge servers, core cloud platforms, AI training modules, and operations and maintenance centers. Due to the close data reuse among multiple subsystems, polluted data easily propagates across domains, causing cascading interference. For example, in intelligent manufacturing, tampered equipment health data misleads maintenance models, affecting lifespan estimation and maintenance decisions, which in turn disrupts the supply chain and production scheduling; in smart cities, forged environmental data undermines energy saving controls and intelligent adjustments. More seriously, attackers can induce "pattern poisoning" that gradually biases models toward forged data, causing "training pollution" or "data poisoning". This not only damages current data perception but also leaves long-term effects at the algorithmic level, resulting in stable model drift and faulty logic. Even if the system layer is repaired, algorithmic biases persist, making complete recovery difficult.

After the system and data are compromised, the third-order chain effect manifests at the algorithmic layer. As intelligent computing network systems widely adopt data-driven intelligent models, algorithms become the critical decision making pivot for the system's autonomous operation. From edge traffic prediction, device

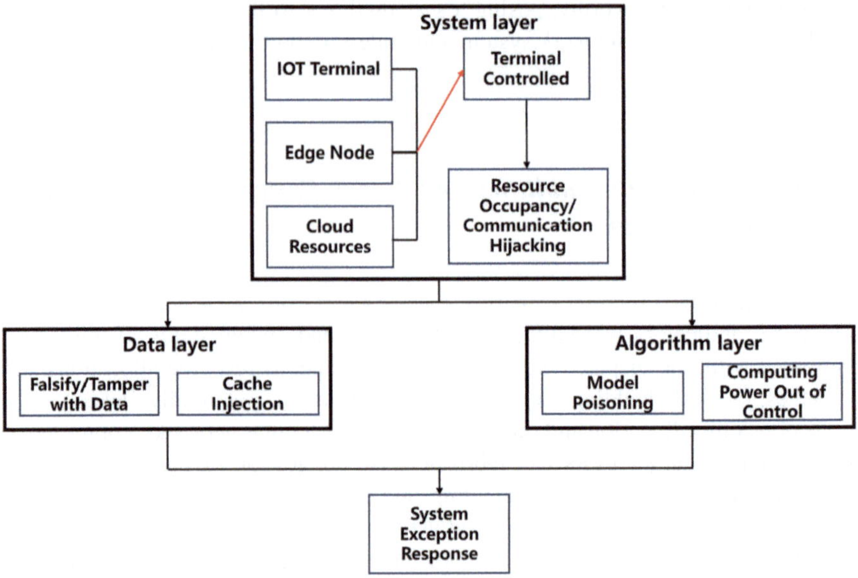

Fig. 3.2 Three-layer coupling attack graph of intelligent computing network under Mirai attack

anomaly detection, to load scheduling and security alert identification, many tasks rely on real-time learning and inference mechanisms. However, these algorithmic models generally have a strong dependency on the quality of input data. Their basic assumption is often that "data is trustworthy" but they lack effective data integrity verification mechanisms, context logic consistency checks, and multi source data cross validation mechanisms [10].

In the context of Mirai attack, this trust foundation is quietly undermined. As shown in Fig. 3.2, after the system intrusion and data contamination are successful, attackers inject deceptive "pseudo normal" data persistently, creating a barely noticeable "chronic poisoning" process. For example, in network anomaly detection tasks, the originally normal sample set used for training the model is subtly embedded with controllable disturbances, allowing attackers to gradually construct a set of "shifted semantics" for anomaly boundaries [11]. In predictive maintenance or traffic scheduling scenarios, the behavior patterns learned by the model will deviate from objective laws to a pseudo distribution guided by the attacker, leading to gradual model performance degradation. Furthermore, even if the system superficially recovers to a "controllable" state, the model's internal structure and parameters have been tampered with, meaning that its output will still reflect biases, and may even exhibit "backdoor behaviors" or "specific trigger" abnormal response patterns.

This type of model degradation is no longer an isolated algorithmic issue but exhibits significant systemic feedback effects. Misled models often continue to issue incorrect scheduling or control commands. For example, intelligent scheduling may redirect traffic to weaker nodes, expanding the attack surface; automated alarm systems may produce false negatives, missing real threats; control models driven by false data may cause device malfunctions, process interruptions, or even physical damage. This negative feedback mechanism, evolving from "algorithmic misjudgment" to "system level degradation", represents a critical risk of loss of algorithmic control. Many intelligent computing network models have online learning and adaptive tuning capabilities, which attackers exploit to carry out model poisoning and degradation during seemingly normal learning cycles. Traditional offline security detection methods struggle to detect such persistent threats. If attacks cause "data collaborative pollution" across multiple edge nodes, they may trigger global coordinated anomalies among intelligent models, resulting in a phenomenon of "algorithmic collective degradation".

From a defense perspective, such coupled attacks pose significant challenges to security design. On one hand, the algorithmic layer must strengthen its awareness of the robustness of input data and implement cross-layer traceability mechanisms, such as incorporating trusted computing environments, trusted data labeling, multi source cross validation, and other methods [12]. On the other hand, an algorithmic system with the ability to interpret abnormal behaviors and audit model behaviors should be built to support proactive identification and remediation of "potential poisoning" or "long-term drift". Ultimately, the security capability of intelligent computing network systems must not be limited to the model itself, but must also integrate algorithmic security into the entire system's operational feedback loop, creating a truly dynamic security coordination mechanism that unifies the "system-data-algorithm" triad.

This case clearly demonstrates the tight coupling of the "system-data-algorithm" three-layer security mechanisms in intelligent computing network systems. Taking the Mirai attack as an example, this type of cyberattack is not a single-layer assault but leverages inter-layer logical chains to form a composite attack path that expands "from points to surfaces, and from shallow to deep". Attackers initially penetrate the edge device's operating system through vulnerability scanning, weak password guessing, and port sniffing. Once control is obtained, they implant trojans or botnet programs to take over the device's underlying behaviors, including communication, data generation, and task scheduling. Once the system is compromised, the most immediate impact appears at the data layer. Numerous edge sensing nodes in intelligent computing networks are responsible for real-time collection and reporting of multi-source heterogeneous data such as industrial monitoring, traffic sensing, and environmental detection. Loss of control enables attackers to continuously tamper with, delay, intercept, or forge critical data. These disguised data conform to legitimate formats and timing intervals, making them difficult for traditional rule-based or statistical anomaly detection systems to identify. This covert "latent infiltration" causes long-term erosion of trust in the system's perception layer, gradually causing data-driven intelligent models to deviate from the true state and triggering cascading issues at the algorithm layer.

Polluted data continuously feeds into intelligent models, causing the destructive effects to propagate further to the algorithm layer. Many critical decisions in intelligent computing networks rely on technologies such as deep learning and graph models. For example, industrial anomaly detection, traffic congestion prediction, and power load balancing all rely on these technologies. During model training and inference phases, input data are generally assumed to be truthful and complete, with insufficient verification of data sources and temporal continuity. This makes the system vulnerable to long-term deception by attackers through "chronic poisoning". The gradual injection of fake data not only disrupts the model's judgments but may also cause errors in decision boundaries and relational structures, leading to model drift. More seriously, if model outputs are directly involved in control logic such as industrial parameter tuning, vehicular network signal scheduling, or power grid path switching, it may create a vicious cycle of "misjudgment control further misjudgment", severely threatening system stability and security.

Due to the fact that current mainstream security architectures often adopt a layered isolation design, where system security, data security, and algorithm security belong to different security modules and protection strategies, there is a lack of horizontal collaboration and feedback mechanisms [13]. As a result, when such coupled attacks occur, each layer often presents a "locally normal" illusion. For example, a "locally normal" illusion can occur. The system layer may think the edge device is functioning properly (based on logs and access control). The data layer may verify the data as correct (through CRC checks and sampling frequency). Meanwhile, the algorithm layer continues to update the model based on the polluted data. Together, these factors mask the true state of overall loss of control. This "locally interpretable, globally uncontrollable" imbalance is the most threatening manifestation of coupled attacks in intelligent computing network systems.

Against this background, traditional security strategies relying on single point hardening and static rules are no longer sufficient to address the challenges of systemic chained attacks. A coordinated defense system should be built from three aspects: "system trustworthiness", "data traceability", and "algorithm robustness". At the system level, trusted boot mechanisms and remote integrity measurement should be introduced at the edge to ensure the trustworthiness of node behavior and environment before deployment. At the data level, an end-to-end provenance mechanism should be established by attaching trusted metadata and combined with multimodal semantic verification to achieve early detection of forged data. At the algorithm level, model robustness against abnormal inputs should be enhanced by adding model drift detection, poisoning immunity, and trustworthy online learning feedback to ensure continuous reliability of inference results. Furthermore, a cross-layer security defense framework with coordinated sensing, judgment, and response capabilities should be developed. The upper layer should monitor and correlate anomalies in real time across all layers and quickly trigger full chain recovery mechanisms. For example, when edge device logs show anomalies, the timing and semantics of the data should be reviewed; when model drift occurs, the source of contamination should be traced. The introduction of artificial intelligence and explainable models can improve security situational awareness and realize a more advanced "immune response mechanism".

In conclusion, the Mirai case reveals not only a typical distributed denial of service attack but also exposes the structural vulnerabilities of intelligent computing networks when faced with multi layered coupled attacks [14]. If a horizontal coordination and vertical closed loop security response chain cannot be established, the failure of any single defense line could lead to a systemic collapse. Therefore, the security construction of intelligent computing networks must shift to a new paradigm of multi dimensional collaboration and dynamic defense.

3.2 Existing Approaches and Limitations

In the current construction practice of the security of intelligent computing network systems, the protection technologies developed at the system level can generally be classified into three categories. As shown in Fig. 3.3, starting from different technical paths, these technologies attempt to avoid and suppress abnormal system behaviors, external intrusions, or operational vulnerabilities. One category of methods emphasizes constructing the boundary defense line of the system through static architecture design and access control mechanisms, and restricts the triggering of unexpected behaviors through prior rules and closed permissions. Another category of methods relies on continuous monitoring of the dynamic operation state of the system, and captures potential threats through behavior modeling and abnormal detection means, so as to achieve more time-effective protection responses. In addition, there is a category of methods that focuses on the system vulnerabilities themselves, and improves the continuous operation capability and resilience level of the system through vulnerability discovery, fault-tolerant design, and self-recovery mechanisms. These three categories of methods respectively reflect the strategic ideas of "pre-event defense", "in-event response", and "post-

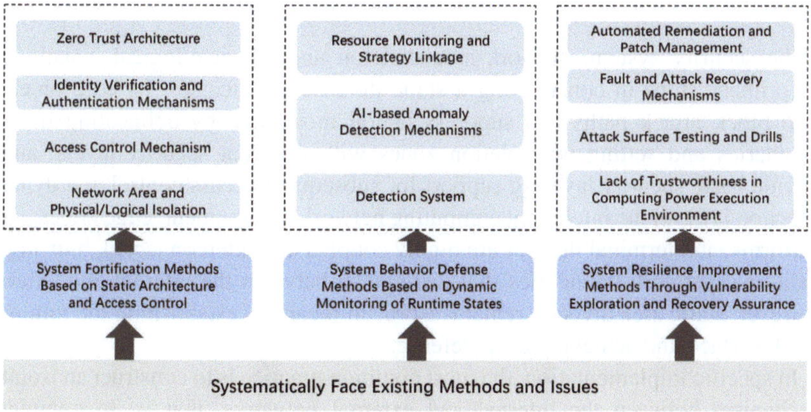

Fig. 3.3 Overview of existing methods and limitations

event recovery". In reality, they are mostly deployed in combination, but each has limitations in adaptability, scalability, and synergy, and there is an urgent need to achieve systematic evolution and cross-dimensional coupling at a higher level [15].

3.2.1 System Fortification Approaches Based on Static Architecture and Access Control

In the security system of intelligent computing networks, static protection at the system level remains one of the fundamental links in constructing the overall security posture. Especially in the early stages of system design and deployment, static architecture configuration and access control mechanisms can effectively establish security boundaries and restrict unauthorized access. This approach provides the institutional and structural guarantees needed for subsequent dynamic protection and behavior monitoring. This type of method is generally based on the concept of "preset security", that is, before the system starts running, the boundary delineation and permission constraints are completed to prevent potential threats from entering the core area of the system. In traditional enterprise information systems, common practices include network area division, access control lists (ACL), and static identity authentication mechanisms. With the gradual promotion of the zero-trust architecture, this type of method is also showing a trend of evolving from coarse grained isolation to fine grained dynamic control [16–18]. Although these mechanisms rely on static rule configuration and are difficult to deal with dynamic attacks such as advanced persistent threats (APTs), as the "first line of defense" for system security, they still play an irreplaceable role in the overall protection system.

3.2.1.1 Network Area and Physical/Logical Isolation

In the security system, network area division and physical/logical isolation are the primary steps in constructing a static defense architecture. Its core objective is to block attack paths and suppress lateral movement by delineating network boundaries and setting up isolation zones with different security levels, and to provide basic security layering support for subsequent access control and dynamic detection [16]. In the intelligent computing network environment, edge nodes, cloud platforms, and terminal devices are highly coupled and interconnected, blurring the traditional network boundaries that distinguish between the internal and external. However, static area division remains a crucial means of establishing the minimum attack surface and achieving deep defense.

In specific implementation, the most common practice is to construct an isolation mechanism between the internal and external networks, that is, to completely separate system components exposed to the public network (such as web front ends,

API gateways, and remote access entrances) from core business systems, critical data storage, and control logic [19]. A three-layer structure is usually adopted: the external Internet, Demilitarized Zone (DMZ), and the internal network. As an isolation buffer zone, the DMZ deploys fortified intermediate servers (such as reverse proxies, jump servers, and mail forwarding gateways), which can absorb most of the external access pressure and security risks. This ensures that even if the DMZ is invaded, it cannot directly affect the internal system [20]. At the same time, for different business systems or organizational units, network boundaries are logically divided through Virtual Local Area Network (VLAN) technology, and strict restrictions are imposed on the data broadcast domain at the switch layer [21]. Data is forwarded between VLANs through layer 3 switching devices or routers, and access control policies are set at the boundaries, thus achieving flexible logical isolation without interrupting the physical link. For application scenarios with extremely high security requirements, such as industrial control systems, financial core systems, and classified information platforms, physical segmentation is usually required. That is, at the physical layer, independent network cables, switching devices, and transmission channels are used to completely separate high-value assets from the external environment, ensuring "air gap isolation" or "network disconnection" at the hardware level [22].

After the area division is completed, the configuration of firewall policies serves as the second security line of defense. Its main function is to conduct refined control over the traffic between different regions based on the content of network communication. Modern firewalls generally adopt a five-tuple matching mechanism, that is, they match the rules for each data packet according to its source IP address, destination IP address, source port, destination port, and protocol type (such as TCP/UDP). Only the traffic that meets the conditions of the whitelist is allowed to pass. In addition, to deal with threats such as forged packets and man-in-the-middle attacks, advanced firewalls also have the function of stateful inspection, which can record the connection state and conduct complete communication session tracking [23]. For example, only the return traffic from an established session is allowed to enter, effectively preventing the initiation of unauthorized connections. In an environment where multiple regions of the computing network collaborate, next generation firewalls (NGFW) and SDN technologies can be further introduced to achieve functions such as dynamic policy loading, identity based access restrictions, in-depth protocol analysis, and threat perception. This breaks the limitations of traditional firewalls that are "static and fixed" and realizes more refined and dynamic boundary management capabilities [24].

However, although network area division and firewall policies play an important role in the process of constructing system security, there are still some problems in the current implementation plan. Firstly, traditional area division often relies on static network topology design, which is difficult to adapt to rapidly changing business requirements and service deployments in an intelligent computing network environment. With the frequent online and offline of edge devices and the dynamic migration of containerized services, static area division may lead to blind spots or security loopholes in the defense system [25]. Secondly, firewall policies still have limitations in dealing with complex attack patterns. For example, in the face of deep cross regional attacks, traditional firewalls find it difficult to conduct real-time and flexible cross-domain traffic detection and handling. Moreover, current firewall systems often control only single traffic sources. They lack the ability to analyze and issue early warnings for complex traffic behaviors from multiple sources and dimensions. This makes it difficult to provide sufficient protection in a dynamic environment like an intelligent computing network. Therefore, future network area division and firewall policies need to pay more attention to the combination with dynamic management mechanisms. Through more intelligent and automated policy generation and optimization means, it is ensured that the system can adapt to environmental changes at any time and provide more efficient security protection.

3.2.1.2 Access Control Mechanism

In the process of constructing a static defense system, the access control mechanism serves as a crucial link connecting the network boundary and resource entities. It directly determines the visibility and operable scope of the system for user, process, and service requests. Its fundamental objective is to achieve the minimum allocation of permissions and the shortest construction of usage paths by clearly defining "who can access what resources, under what conditions, and what operations can be performed", thereby minimizing the potential attack surface [26]. Especially in the intelligent computing network environment, access requests come not only from human users but also from automated tasks, algorithm models, container services, and cross-domain scheduling processes, which places higher demands on the precision and dynamic adaptability of the access control mechanism.

ACL mechanism is the most widely applied in traditional access control. ACL constructs access rules based on fundamental network attributes such as IP addresses, port numbers, and transmission protocols, and is suitable for fine-grained traffic filtering on network devices (such as switches, routers, and boundary firewalls) [27]. For example, in an enterprise information system, the ACL can be used to specify that the hosts in a specific VLAN can only access specific ports of the database server and prohibit direct communication with other business modules, thus completing the preliminary permission isolation at the network layer through static rules. The ACL has a clear structure and is simple to implement, making it suitable for scenarios with a small scale and stable rules. However, in the computing network architecture, simply relying on IP or port configurations is difficult to maintain. This is because the environment is highly dynamic, with frequent changes in edge nodes, service container migration, and complex identity mapping. Relying on such static configurations results in a sharp increase in management costs and can easily cause security risks like rule drift and configuration misalignment [28].

To enhance the flexibility of permission control and semantic expression capabilities, modern systems typically adopt identity based permission authorization mechanisms, represented by Role Based Access Control (RBAC) and Attribute Based Access Control (ABAC). RBAC realizes the centralized management and templated reuse of permissions by binding access permissions to roles and then assigning users to roles. This mechanism is widely used in organizational systems. For example, administrators, auditors, and ordinary users have different permission sets, which facilitates batch adjustment of role definitions when permissions are updated, reducing management complexity. ABAC further expands the dimension of permission expression. It makes policy judgments through user attributes, resource attributes, and environmental conditions (such as time, location, and session context), supporting more refined access control policies. For example, it can be stipulated that access is only allowed when "the task execution comes from a trusted node, during working hours, and the requested GPU resource belongs to the pre-allocation queue", which improves the adaptability to dynamic situations. RBAC emphasizes the clarity of organizational structure mapping, while ABAC emphasizes the expression ability of policy logic. In intelligent computing network systems, a hybrid model of the two is often adopted to balance clarity and flexibility.

Although the access control systems constructed based on methods such as ACL, RBAC, and ABAC play an important role in the static defense architecture, the current access control mechanisms still face some problems. First, traditional ACL and RBAC methods appear relatively rigid when dealing with the dynamic and frequently changing intelligent computing network environment. The rapid changes in edge nodes and service containers make it difficult for static configurations to meet new security requirements and scene changes, easily leading to risks of configuration errors or permission abuse [29]. Second, although RBAC and ABAC enhance the flexibility and precision of permission management, in complex systems, the mapping relationships of roles and attributes may still result in difficulties in accurately dividing access permissions. Moreover, when used in combination, how to effectively coordinate the rules of the two to avoid conflicts and redundancies remains a challenge. In addition, although current permission matrices and templatized deployments have improved configuration efficiency, in large-scale and complex scenarios, the issues of continuous policy maintenance and real-time updates still need to be addressed. Therefore, in intelligent computing networks, how to enhance the accuracy and adaptability of access control policies by further strengthening dynamic management mechanisms, refining permission expression, and automating deployment methods remains an important direction for future development.

Overall, the access control mechanism has evolved from the "boundary filtering" of static configuration to the "dynamic authorization" that integrates identity, behavior, and environment [30]. Under the intelligent computing network architecture, it is necessary to construct a visual, automated, and auditable multi-layer permission system. This requires comprehensively utilizing the network-level closure ability of ACL, the identity logic expression ability of RBAC/ABAC, and the engineering management ability of permission templatized deployment. This system should also cooperate with the behavior monitoring system to achieve continuous policy optimization and risk awareness response.

3.2.1.3 Identity Verification and Authentication Mechanisms

The identity authentication and verification mechanism serves as the first "trust threshold" in the system's security protection chain. Its essence lies in confirming the true identity of the access initiator and ensuring that only authorized entities can access the designated resources. In a static defense system, this mechanism usually acts as a prerequisite for all access control and policy making decisions, providing the fundamental guarantee of "identity credentials" and "trusted boundaries" for the entire security architecture. In the intelligent computing network system, identity authentication faces complex challenges. This is due to the existence of human-machine hybrid accesses, automated task scheduling, and multi-tenant service collaboration. Therefore, the mechanism must not only ensure identification accuracy but also evaluate the behavioral consistency of the resource requesting entity and perceive dynamic risks [31].

The most common identity authentication method is still the authentication mechanism based on static credentials, mainly including forms such as usernames and passwords, API Keys, and Tokens. This type of method has advantages such as simple deployment, low implementation cost, and good cross-platform compatibility, so it is widely used in traditional information systems and web services [32]. In typical scenarios, users log in to the platform through account passwords, and program calls achieve non-interactive access control through embedded API Keys. However, in the intelligent computing network environment, this type of static credential has significant limitations: Firstly, passwords and keys are often stored in configuration files or environment variables, and are extremely vulnerable to abuse due to leakage, brute force cracking, or replay attacks. Secondly, once the credentials are stolen, attackers can disguise themselves as legitimate identities and lurk in the system for a long time. And due to the lack of dynamic behavior binding, it is difficult for traditional authentication systems to identify them. In addition, many edge nodes and IoT devices have limited computing power, lack effective key rotation mechanisms and credential encryption protection, further increasing the security risks of static authentication methods. Therefore, when constructing a modern identity authentication system, static credentials should be regarded as the most basic rather than the only authentication means, and higher-level identity verification strategies must be supplemented.

To enhance identity authentication security, modern computing network systems increasingly adopt multi-factor authentication (MFA) mechanisms. MFA combines knowledge, possession, and inherence factors to provide layered verification and fundamentally mitigate the risks associated with credential compromise. Common implementations include one-time passwords (OTP), hardware tokens, and biometric authentication based on fingerprint or facial recognition. MFA proves particularly effective in high-sensitivity scenarios such as user logins, developer access, and API invocation, where it can effectively prevent unauthorized access even if credentials are stolen. However, the applicability of MFA in edge nodes and unattended tasks is limited due to hardware constraints and the infeasibility of human interaction, making it more suitable for interactive entry points and control plane interfaces. For intelligent terminals and computing nodes, behavior driven and adaptive authentication enhancement mechanisms should be explored [33].

In addition, Public Key Infrastructure (PKI)-based authentication is widely adopted in large-scale distributed environments for identity binding and trust establishment. By leveraging asymmetric cryptography and certificate issuance by trusted authorities, PKI enables verifiable identity relationships among entities and is broadly used to secure communications among edge nodes, containerized services, and API gateways. Its advantages lie in its non-interactive nature and strong binding characteristics, making it well suited for automated communication and device level authentication. Nevertheless, in dynamic and large-scale edge environments, PKI systems must be integrated with automated certificate management platforms and zero-trust network architectures. This integration is necessary to support dynamic certificate issuance, renewal, and revocation. Ultimately, this approach ensures the sustainability and adaptive evolution of identity authentication mechanisms.

Although identity authentication methods such as static credential authentication,MFA and PKI provide basic identity protection for the system, the application of these methods in the intelligent computing network environment still faces some problems. Firstly, static credential authentication methods are vulnerable to risks such as credential leakage and replay attacks. Moreover, in a large-scale and dynamically changing environment, it is difficult to manage and update credentials [34]. Secondly, although MFA can effectively enhance the security of identity verification, for scenarios of edge nodes and automated tasks, the requirement of manual interaction makes large-scale deployment and automated execution unrealistic. Therefore, MFA is mainly suitable for highly sensitive operations such as management user entrances and developer entrances, but its application in computing nodes and device ends is limited. Finally, although PKI has strong identity binding capabilities in large-scale distributed systems, the cost of certificate management, revocation, and deployment is high. Especially in scenarios where there are a large number of edge computing nodes and frequent dynamic changes, how to effectively manage and maintain digital certificates is a major challenge. Overall, although the current identity authentication methods can provide certain security guarantees for intelligent computing networks, when facing highly dynamic and distributed computing network architectures, it is still necessary to further explore authentication mechanisms that are more flexible and adaptable.

3.2.1.4 Zero Trust Architecture

As the traditional "perimeter defense" model frequently fails in highly distributed and dynamic environments, the Zero Trust Architecture (ZTA) has gradually become the core paradigm of modern system security design [35]. Its basic concept can be summarized in one sentence: "Do not default to trusting anyone or any device, regardless of whether it is within the internal network". This concept poses a fundamental challenge to the traditional division of "the internal network is trustworthy while the external network is not". It emphasizes that even internal users or nodes must undergo strict identity authentication, behavior review, and policy determination in every access behavior. For the intelligent computing network architecture, zero trust is not only a transformation of security thinking but also a key path to addressing challenges such as dynamic access, multi tenant collaboration, and the generalization of edge intelligence [36].

The core of the Zero Trust Architecture (ZTA) lies in enforced identity verification, continuous trust evaluation, and dynamic policy enforcement. Under the ZTA model, every access request must undergo multidimensional identity verification before being granted, discarding traditional trust models based on network location. The authentication process goes beyond static credentials, incorporating dynamic factors such as behavioral patterns, device fingerprints, geolocation, and access context to perform real-time trust scoring, which is continuously updated throughout the session. Once any abnormal behavior is detected, such as sudden shifts in access patterns, anomalous communication paths, or privilege misuse automatic actions like privilege reduction, session termination, or secondary verification are triggered. To enable fine grained access control, ZTA further introduces micro-segmentation, refining traditional network partitions into isolation units based on services, workloads, or even individual processes. Even if two services reside on the same host, communication between them requires explicit authorization policies. This application centric isolation mechanism surpasses traditional IP and port-based ACLs and is particularly suited for container orchestration environments like Kubernetes and service mesh architectures, enhancing security while maintaining resource efficiency and system resilience.

From an implementation perspective, Software Defined Perimeter (SDP) is a key enabler of Zero Trust. SDP follows the principle of "authenticate before visibility" logically hiding resources behind identity aware gateways so that unauthorized entities cannot even detect their existence. Unlike traditional firewalls that passively drop unauthorized packets, SDP proactively enforces network level invisibility, greatly reducing the attack surface. The SDP controller performs identity verification, policy matching, and session authorization for each request, establishing temporary communication channels strictly within the authorized scope. These sessions are continuously monitored and are immediately terminated when trust levels drop, realizing a model of "on-demand visibility and session-based access". Moreover, SDP naturally supports multi tenant environments and cross-domain identity integration, enabling seamless interoperability with dynamic key management, endpoint health verification, and federated authentication systems. In intelligent computing network environments, where nodes are frequently joining, leaving, and operating in a heterogeneous and dynamic state, traditional topology-based trust mechanisms fall short. Simultaneously, automated entities like AI models, computing containers, and orchestration pipelines require more precise and responsive access control. By adopting Zero Trust, a full chain trust evaluation and policy convergence mechanism (from identity verification to resource access) can be established. This mechanism enables a dynamic security model where identity defines the boundary and behavior serves as credentials. This model thereby provides robust support for trusted access and resource protection in computational network infrastructures.

Although the concept of the zero trust architecture provides a flexible security control mechanism for intelligent computing networks, existing methods still have certain limitations in practical deployment. Firstly, the zero trust architecture relies on continuous identity authentication and behavior monitoring, which requires the system to have a high degree of dynamic adaptability. However, many current implementation schemes have high latency and computational costs in large-scale environments, which may affect the real-time response capability of the system. Secondly, although the microsegmentation strategy can effectively refine access control, in the complex environment of cross-domain and multi-tenant collaboration, how to accurately configure and manage a large number of fine-grained rules remains a challenge, and it may lead to an increase in configuration complexity. Finally, although the SDP mechanism can hide resources and reduce the attack surface, its deployment and maintenance costs are high [37]. Moreover, in some dynamic computing environments, when relying on the session control model for fine-grained protection, situations such as lagging policy adjustments or conflicts in resource access permissions may occur. Therefore, although the zero trust architecture provides strong security support for intelligent computing networks, its performance, usability, and scalability still need to be further optimized during comprehensive deployment.

3.2.2 *System Behavior Defense Methods Based on Dynamic Monitoring of Runtime States*

3.2.2.1 Detection System

As a preliminary component of runtime protection mechanisms, detection systems are primarily tasked with the continuous observation and modeling of system entity behaviors to enable early identification and determination of abnormal activities. In intelligent computing network environments, the openness, distribution, and heterogeneity of the system are significantly intensified, resulting in a highly dynamic expansion of the attack surface. This is particularly evident in processes such as task scheduling, resource invocation, and multi-tenant isolation, where behavioral anomalies often lack clear static characteristics and must be identified in real time based on runtime information. Therefore, establishing a detection framework with fine-grained behavioral awareness is a foundational requirement for achieving overall system security resilience [38].

As a core infrastructure of the intelligent computing network security system, the Host-based Intrusion Detection System (HIDS) has evolved from a traditional anomaly detection tool into a key engine for task behavior verification. Its core function is not only to detect intrusion behaviors but also to perform dynamic semantic analysis and anomaly identification of task execution at the host level. In the ICN environment, characterized by coexisting containerization, virtualization, and elastic scheduling, HIDS must possess fine-grained sensing capabilities across heterogeneous operating environments [39]. By capturing behaviors such as system call sequences, file activities, process traces, and kernel events, HIDS can construct dynamic behavior graphs to support secure responses in compute scheduling. For example, in GPU intensive tasks, normal behavior typically follows stable resource invocation and compute storage pathways, whereas anomalies such as prolonged GPU occupation without disk writes, or frequent shared memory access without inter-process communication can serve as potential attack indicators. However, current HIDS implementations often rely on static templates, making them less effective in adapting to novel attacks and high frequency scheduling scenarios, while also facing challenges such as incomplete context information and detection latency in multi-platform environments. As HIDS strengthens its correlation inference mechanisms among resource invocation paths, runtime contexts, and system behavior patterns, it is becoming a key force in identifying resource abuse, task spoofing, and potential system stability risks within ICN. This transformation marks a deep shift in the security defense paradigm from static policy-driven approaches to dynamic behavior-driven strategies.

Network Intrusion Detection Systems (NIDS) serve as critical security perception components at the external traffic layer in intelligent computing network environments. Their role has evolved from traditional boundary-based traffic interception and signature matching to runtime anomaly detection engines focused on dynamic communication behavior modeling [13]. With increasingly complex communication structures among edge nodes, scheduling planes, and microservice components, NIDS must not only detect known malicious traffic but also identify deviations in communication patterns along task scheduling paths. Typical anomalies include: container tasks accessing unauthorized external addresses, abnormal surges in communication volume between edge nodes, or high-frequency lateral interactions across physical domains by tasks under the same account without logical dependencies. In the context of elastic scheduling and multipoint collaboration, attackers may disguise malicious traffic as legitimate scheduling flows to perform scheduling deception or covert infiltration, rendering traditional signature-based detection insufficient. Meanwhile, deep protocol parsing and lateral traffic modeling in multi-tenant and edge environments often face resource and performance bottlenecks. To enhance situational awareness, NIDS must adopt behavioral time window mechanisms, historical state learning, and dynamic whitelist strategies, thereby transitioning from rule-driven to behavior-driven models [40]. In this transformation, NIDS are no longer just network boundary defenses, but vital nodes supporting scheduling security, communication controllability, and tenant isolation, forming a crucial component in the closed-loop runtime security perception of intelligent computing network systems.

User and Entity Behavior Analytics (UEBA) technology enhances the ability to identify anomalies and deepen semantic understanding. It does this by deeply analyzing and modeling multidimensional behavioral data from users, service components, or task entities. This data (e.g., access frequency, task load, and resource request sequences) is used to construct detailed behavioral baselines [41]. In the intelligent computing network environment, UEBA performs two key functions. First, it detects abnormal behaviors that significantly deviate from normal patterns. Examples include low-privilege accounts launching multiple high-priority GPU jobs in a short period or abnormal task resource consumption. Second, UEBA generates real-time risk scores to assist in access control adjustments and resource scheduling optimization, thereby preventing privilege abuse and excessive resource consumption. However, UEBA shows limited adaptability in highly dynamic computing network environments, struggles to accurately model new users or tasks in their initial stages, and traditional statistical and rule-based models are insufficient to handle complex and covert attacks. By shifting from an "event-driven" to a "behavior-driven" approach, UEBA significantly improves the accuracy of anomaly detection and the intelligence of security responses in intelligent computing networks, especially enhancing system security and robustness in multi-tenant, dynamic environments.

Detection systems in intelligent computing network environments no longer serve merely as "alarm systems" for attack identification. Instead, they have evolved into behavioral perception engines. These engines drive a series of security interlocking mechanisms, including resource scheduling control, access policy optimization, and dynamic trust assessment adjustments. Their monitoring accuracy, decision making logic, and collaborative capabilities directly determine the response speed and reliability of the entire runtime protection system, making them an indispensable core component for ensuring stable system operation and computational security.

3.2.2.2 AI-based Anomaly Detection Mechanisms

In the intelligent computing network operating environment, task behavior and resource invocation exhibit highly dynamic and complex characteristics. Attackers are increasingly inclined to implement covert attacks by "mimicking legitimate behavior." This mimicry includes actions such as submitting disguised tasks via publicly available task scheduling interfaces, controlling resource request frequency to evade rule triggers, or leveraging the elastic scheduling of edge node resources to bypass centralized behavior recognition. These attacks often appear to comply with access control rules in terms of format, with legitimate parameter calls, compliant scheduling paths, and no obvious anomalies in log traces. However, they involve long-duration, low-frequency, and distributed resource occupation. As a result, relying solely on rule-based static protection measures is insufficient, necessitating the introduction of AI algorithms with learning and behavior modeling capabilities to achieve proactive runtime behavior awareness and adaptive recognition of anomalous activities.

In the runtime protection mechanisms of intelligent computing network systems, unsupervised learning algorithms have become an important tool for identifying complex anomalous behaviors due to their ability to model adaptively without relying on manually labeled data [42]. In computing network platforms, a vast and diverse range of tasks are handled daily, with task behavior patterns being complex and highly variable. At the same time, malicious activities are increasingly exhibiting traits of mimicry, low-frequency disturbances, and chronic resource occupation. These behaviors often lack clear attack indicators, making them difficult to identify through static rules or traditional supervised models. Unsupervised learning, however, constructs feature distribution models based on normal behavior data and identifies "outlier behaviors" that deviate from the distribution, offering a structural solution for anomaly detection.

Although unsupervised learning has inherent advantages in detecting unknown anomalies, it also faces two prominent issues. First, the model is highly sensitive to the quality and selection of input features. If feature engineering is incomplete, it can easily lead to missed detections or misclassifications. Second, because unsupervised algorithms often lack explicit semantic labels, the anomaly scores produced by the model are insufficient in terms of business interpretability and event traceability. This makes it difficult to provide directly usable security decision recommendations for scheduling systems. This limits its ability to serve as the sole criterion in production-level computing platforms, requiring collaboration with rule-based systems or manual review mechanisms to form a complete feedback loop.

Isolation forest, as a typical unsupervised algorithm, identifies anomalies by constructing multiple random partitioning trees and measuring the average path length required to isolate task behavior samples in a multi-dimensional feature space [43]. Task behaviors are generally abstracted as high-dimensional vectors encompassing dimensions such as GPU/TPU utilization, task duration, memory fluctuations, disk I/O density, and scheduling wait time. Normal tasks form dense clusters in the behavior space, while anomalous tasks are quickly isolated due to their deviations. For example, a task that continuously exhibits high GPU usage but has no model output or external communication is likely to be classified as high risk, triggering responses such as scheduling deprioritization or container restrictions. Another commonly used unsupervised model is the neural network-based autoencoder, which learns latent representations of normal task behaviors through an encoding-decoding structure. When a new input task produces a high reconstruction error, it indicates an anomaly [44]. This approach is particularly effective in identifying complex anomalies such as "low output with high load" or "asymmetric compute communication" tasks. For instance, a GPU task with an abnormally long computation cycle and no valid output will generate a high anomaly score, prompting real-time defense responses. Additionally, in intelligent computing networks, accounts that submit tasks periodically or exhibit strong behavior camouflage show "slow but persistent" behavior drift. By segmenting task behaviors using a sliding window mechanism and applying unsupervised models to score each segment, the system can detect potential abuses such as task submission frequencies significantly exceeding historical averages or clusters of inefficient tasks within the same scheduling cycle.

To effectively deploy unsupervised learning models, the system must also build a complete feature engineering framework. This includes task metadata, behavioral statistics, and resource distribution metrics. Based on this, a real-time inference process is constructed to score anomalies for each new task or task flow segment online. The scoring results are not only used for risk alerts but also serve as crucial inputs for the scheduling system, dynamically adjusting task priorities, resource allocations, and even access permissions, thus linking runtime security and resource scheduling strategies.

The interaction relationships between users, tasks, and resource nodes exhibit highly structured characteristics. Users submit various tasks through the platform, which, during their execution, consume heterogeneous computing resources (such as GPU, TPU, and CPU) and are accompanied by operations such as process scheduling, data transmission, and state feedback. Tasks may also have logical dependencies, parallel collaboration, or stage specific interactions, such as multi-stage pipeline processing and distributed model training. These interactions form a dynamic, cross-user, cross-node, and cross-time network. As the system scales, this interaction mode gradually evolves into a "behavioral graph", a multi-dimensional association structure consisting of task entities, resource nodes, API channels, and scheduling paths. In this context, traditional detection methods based on independent sample features are increasingly inadequate for fully modeling the system's operational state. Graph Neural Networks (GNNs), due to their proficiency in handling structured data and graph-based relationships, have become an ideal tool for identifying system-level anomalies [45].

The core capability of GNNs lies in jointly utilizing both the "node's own features" and its "connection structure within the graph" for learning and classification. This means that GNNs not only analyze the attributes of individual tasks or resources (such as resource request volume, runtime, and node density) but also perceive the connection patterns between that node and its surrounding entities, thereby capturing higher-level behavioral semantics. In the intelligent computing network, a heterogeneous graph can be constructed with nodes representing user, task, resource node, and scheduling events, while edges indicate relationships such as "submission", "execution", "collaboration", and "shared resources". GNNs can use multi-layer information aggregation mechanisms to embed each task node and perform behavior expression learning within the context of the entire graph [46].

This mechanism is particularly suitable for detecting structurally distributed anomalous behaviors. For example, in certain resource abuse scenarios, attackers do not concentrate large-scale tasks on a single node but instead choose to submit small-scale, low-frequency tasks across multiple edge nodes to avoid detection by local rules. These tasks may appear normal in a single behavioral dimension, but when placed into the "user-task-node" graph structure, it becomes clear that they share a high degree of structural similarity: originating from the same user or IP domain, invoking the same type of task templates, having redundant coverage in the target node distribution, and exhibiting high-density periodic patterns over time. GNNs can aggregate the adjacency relationships and attribute features of these nodes to identify "behaviorally isomorphic subgraphs", "anomalous high-density connection groups" or "overlong scheduling path clusters" in the system graph, thereby enabling the joint identification of distributed abuse attacks [47].

Graph-based modeling also helps in uncovering non-explicit attack paths. Some attackers exploit scheduling dependencies to bypass conventional access path controls. By constructing a directed graph of "task and task dependency chains" and applying graph neural networks for graph convolution learning, such anomalous path chains can be detected, such as task dependency cycles, abnormal task chain depths, or severe imbalances in dependency density and resource types. Furthermore, to adapt to the time evolution characteristics of system behaviors, GNNs can be combined with temporal modeling mechanisms to create dynamic graph neural networks, which update the graph structure and node states in real-time, enabling the "evolutionary monitoring" of attack behaviors [48]. For instance, early-stage low-frequency scheduling behaviors may not show obvious aggregation in the graph, but as time progresses, the structural density of a subgraph rapidly increases, and the centrality of the user behavior graph rises. At this point, the system can detect the growing risk trend based on the changes in the dynamic graph embedding vectors and adjust defense strategies in advance.

The anomaly scores output by the GNN model for graph nodes can also be integrated with the scheduling or access control systems. For example, for high-risk task nodes in the graph, higher scheduling review thresholds can be set, or access to specific resource types (such as scarce GPUs) can be restricted. For suspicious user nodes with high centrality, actions such as API rate limiting, enforced secondary authentication, or behavior retrospective auditing can be triggered, thereby forming a response loop driven by the graph structure [49].

In practical deployment, for AI-based anomaly detection models to truly play a role in the intelligent computing network environment, they must possess real-time inference capabilities and dynamic risk scoring mechanisms. Unlike offline data analysis, security challenges in computing networks highly depend on timeliness: resource scheduling chains are tight, and task lifecycles are short. Once a malicious or abnormal task is successfully scheduled and executed, it will directly consume high-value computing resources and potentially disrupt overall service quality. Therefore, AI models must be embedded in pre-scheduling paths or behavior monitoring agents to analyze behavior features and risk scores for each task submission, user request, or resource occupation at the earliest opportunity [50].

The greatest advantage of the AI anomaly detection system lies in its self-updating and evolutionary capability. As the platform's runtime increases, the model can continuously learn from changes in user behavior, task type evolution, resource load patterns, and other data, gradually optimizing its anomaly detection boundaries to adapt to growing business complexity. For instance, when a new type of AI model is deployed extensively across the computing network platform, its resource utilization may differ significantly from older models, requiring the system to quickly adjust its behavioral baseline to avoid false positives or false negatives. The online learning mechanism of AI models effectively absorbs these changes, ensuring that the platform maintains a balance between security stability and resource efficiency.

3.2.2.3 Resource Monitoring and Strategy Linkage

In the context of the evolving computational network becoming the core foundation of AI infrastructure, computational power itself, as a resource with scarcity and high-value density, is facing increasingly significant abuse risks. The risk of computational power abuse manifests as attackers or improperly authorized internal personnel using various technical means to illegally occupy, misappropriate, or convert computational resources within the system, using them for unauthorized purposes to gain economic, technical, or organizational benefits. The essence of this type of attack is not the traditional notion of information destruction or theft, but rather a struggle for control over computational power itself. The direct consequences of such attacks include: legitimate tasks being excluded, abnormal increases in computational costs, imbalances in resource scheduling mechanisms, and damage to the platform's reputation. With the continuous evolution of the computational network architecture, the cross-domain nature of resource scheduling and the complexity of node structures, the risk of computational power abuse also shows trends of increased concealment and higher identification difficulty. Attacks leading to computational power abuse can mainly be categorized into three dimensions: external intrusion, internal unauthorized access, and infrastructure penetration.

External intrusion is one of the most common pathways. Attackers infiltrate the computational network control system, scheduling components, or task interfaces using network attack techniques [51, 52]. After obtaining initial access permissions, they further control nodes to execute computationally intensive tasks. These tasks are typically disguised as legitimate workloads, but in reality, they perform high computational demand operations such as cryptocurrency mining, brute force cracking, or model training, thereby occupying a significant amount of core computational resources without interrupting system operation. During this process, attackers often use persistence mechanisms to ensure that unauthorized computational power usage activities persist over time and return the computational results through covert network channels to obtain benefits.

Internal privilege escalation primarily refers to system operators or developers with certain privileges who, beyond their business responsibilities, invoke or occupy computational resources that do not belong to them [53]. This type of attack typically does not rely on vulnerabilities or malicious code, but rather is carried out through configuration bypass, policy tampering, or scheduling interference, thus possessing a certain "legitimate appearance". Especially in cases where the authorization control mechanism of the computational network platform is not detailed and resource auditing mechanisms are lacking, internal privilege escalation may persist for a long time without detection, further amplifying the impact of abuse behavior.

Infrastructure penetration is more evident in the use of outsourced platforms and third-party cloud resources. The computational network often relies on multiple nodes working together to build a resource pool, with some nodes deployed on outsourced clouds, edge nodes, or private environments [54]. If the security policies for these external compute access points are loose and interface protection is insufficient, they become significant entry points for attackers. Once attackers successfully take control of these external nodes, they can use cross-domain task scheduling interfaces to embed abnormal computational requests into the overall computational operation flow or bypass upper-level audit systems through management interfaces, gaining direct access to the system's resource layer. This allows for covert occupation of resources, which is difficult to detect by traditional centralized monitoring methods.

Against the backdrop of the continuous evolution of computing network architecture, the growing trend of resource centralization, and the rise of multi-tenancy, the availability of computational systems has become a critical factor in supporting the stable operation of artificial intelligence services. However, the emerging threat of computational availability attacks has started to pose a structural threat to computing network services. These attacks do not rely on traditional disruptive intrusion methods but instead create a "non-lethal paralysis" state at the resource level through strategic occupation, abnormal scheduling disruptions, interface suppression, and other tactics. The harm does not lie in the instantaneous destructive power of service interruption but in the irreversible long-term decline in system operational efficiency, the erosion of trust in resource scheduling mechanisms, and the systemic degradation of multi-tenant service quality assurance capabilities.

Attackers can create resource exhaustion scenarios through various means, leading to situations where legitimate computational tasks cannot obtain the necessary GPU, TPU, CPU, and other computing resources on time, thereby triggering chain reactions such as task backlog, priority mismatch, and response delays [55]. The first typical method is resource wasting attacks, where the core strategy is to consume the computing resources themselves. Under conditions where the attacker has access privileges, they submit a large number of tasks that are formally legitimate but produce no actual computational output, such as empty loop calculations, fake model training, and ineffective inference operations. Alternatively, resource occupying processes can be deployed, using techniques like infinite loops, memory bloat, and thread blocking to continually occupy scheduling channels and computing cores. These tasks appear compliant and are difficult to identify as abnormal, but they cause prolonged resource locking at the system level. In severe cases, they can be exploited as carriers for more covert attacks such as hidden cryptocurrency mining or privilege maintenance, eventually evolving into a resource exhaustion situation that causes a systemic failure in the computing network's business operations.

The second method focuses on scheduling disruption attacks, where the goal is not to directly consume computing resources, but rather to manipulate task scheduling behavior, triggering resource allocation imbalances. Attackers exploit the fault tolerance and fairness strategies of the computing platform's scheduling mechanism by using techniques such as repeatedly submitting tasks, triggering batch jobs, and constructing nested tasks to cause scheduling queue misalignment and misjudgments by the scheduler. For example, automated scripts can generate high-frequency task requests. This causes the system to allocate major resources to ineffective jobs. Alternatively, these scripts may disguise tasks as low-priority, long-duration jobs to bind a large number of resources. They then use preemption and pre-scheduling mechanisms to disrupt the resource release rhythm. These actions may appear as "normal behavior" at the scheduling rule level, but their latent effect is the continued displacement of high-priority legitimate tasks, causing the system to enter a prolonged state of scheduling inefficiency, which ultimately affects overall service quality and tenant experience.

A more complex attack pattern targets the structural vulnerabilities of the computing interface itself, using techniques such as delayed submissions, incorrect state updates, and interface feedback loops to disrupt the platform's accuracy in perceiving task statuses and resource usage. For example, by flooding interfaces, abusing APIs, or contaminating task descriptors, attackers can induce abnormal branches in the scheduling process, causing the system's decision making logic to enter retry, rollback, or blocking states, resulting in prolonged failures in the scheduling chain. This interface layer suppression method does not damage hardware or alter data, yet it can continuously create the illusion of the platform being "apparently available, but actually stagnant" with low-intensity disruptions, thus interfering with decision-making by administrators and the system's self-recovery capabilities.

Based on the identification of computing abuse behaviors and availability attack patterns, the system should further establish a runtime resource behavior modeling mechanism to enable real-time monitoring and deviation detection of the usage status of key resources such as GPUs, TPUs, and CPUs. Unlike traditional static resource allocation strategies, task scheduling and resource invocation in intelligent computing network environments are highly dynamic, with strong multi-tenant concurrency and high node heterogeneity. A single threshold-based judgment is insufficient to cover complex abuse behavior scenarios. Therefore, the system should develop a task resource correspondence standard behavior curve model, based on task types (such as inference, training, and preprocessing), expected load intensity (such as model parameter scale, and computation path complexity), and resource scheduling strategies. This model will be used to assess whether resource usage aligns with task behavior. If a significant deviation from the expected resource consumption pattern is detected, such as low-complexity tasks running with high load for extended periods, or a mismatch between task completion status and resource release status, the system should immediately trigger a behavior deviation alarm and perform dynamic risk labeling at the task level.

Furthermore, the platform should enhance its perception and analysis of API call frequencies and access patterns to prevent and control scheduling abuse conducted via automation. For instance, "scripted bulk submissions and high resource preemption and no actual output" is a typical disguised task chain behavior. This involves repeatedly generating formally legitimate but computationally ineffective tasks, thereby occupying scheduling interfaces and computing cores. The system should model the API call paths, parameter structures, and response behaviors as time series, and construct a call graph to identify abnormal API traffic sources with high density, resource request behaviors with irregular frequency, or suspicious activities presenting as "repeated template tasks" at edge nodes. The system should dynamically assess the credibility of such behaviors. When the risk of abnormal API calls increases, mechanisms such as rate limiting, access queueing, and adjusting behavior scoring should be automatically triggered, ensuring fine-grained flow control and interface protection [56].

In the face of scheduling disruption attacks, the system must establish an association analysis mechanism for scheduling behaviors. Traditional scheduling systems are based on task priority, resource availability, and fairness strategies, but under the influence of an attacker actively causing interference, the scheduling logic may be manipulated, leading to incorrect responses. Therefore, it is necessary to introduce scheduling event chain modeling and behavior synergy graph analysis. By analyzing task submission time series, queue proportion changes, pre-scheduling and release relationships, the system can identify disruptive patterns such as "repeated submissions with unchanged statuses", "abnormally prolonged pre-scheduled resource occupation" and "tasks being immediately re-called with the same ID after release". For high-frequency disruptive behaviors, response adjustment mechanisms should be introduced into the scheduling strategy. These could include submission rate limits, task quota compression, or extending pre-scheduling freeze periods to dynamically weaken the interference of disruptive behaviors on the overall resource scheduling order.

To achieve full cycle protection of the resource scheduling chain, the system should also establish a policy linkage mechanism to close the loop between detection results, permission control, scheduling logic, and interface management. Specifically, linkage can be achieved at three levels: first, scheduling response linkage, where abnormal behavior scores are used as input factors for task priority, delaying scheduling for high-risk tasks and prioritizing low-risk tasks to ensure fairness in resource allocation; second, dynamic permission adjustment, where continuous abnormal behavior from an account automatically adjusts its resource application permissions and scheduling window range, preventing it from bypassing platform isolation mechanisms through multi-tenant strategies; third, interface response strategy linkage, where, when API abuse risks rise, the system dynamically increases access authentication strength, reduces response rates, and even temporarily blocks the risk source IP to prevent the scheduler and monitoring systems from being overloaded.

From a system architecture perspective, the resource behavior monitoring system should be highly integrated with runtime metrics collectors (such as Prometheus), scheduling controllers (like Kube scheduler and Slurm), and task metadata storage systems. This can be achieved through lightweight agent services or kernel-level probes that collect task resource usage curves and scheduling behavior logs in real-time. Additionally, an AI model should be incorporated to build a resource anomaly scoring engine, enabling the system to recognize unknown abuse strategies. This will allow for the realization of an automatic closed-loop process for "perception-scoring-response" of abuse methods.

The resource behavior monitoring and policy linkage mechanism is one of the key supports for ensuring the secure operation of computing power systems. Through multi-dimensional integration of standard behavior modeling, API behavior analysis, scheduling behavior tracing, and policy level response systems, the intelligent computing network platform can effectively address the risk of long-term operational performance degradation caused by computing power abuse and resource suppression attacks. This provides core technical assurance for building a resilient, self-adaptive, and highly available computing power infrastructure.

3.2.3 System Resilience Improvement Methods Through Vulnerability Exploration and Recovery Assurance

3.2.3.1 Lack of Trustworthiness in Computing Power Execution Environment

With the continued evolution of heterogeneous and cross-domain computing networks, the execution of AI tasks has increasingly moved away from reliance on single physical nodes, shifting instead toward dynamic migration and distributed collaboration across multiple platforms, chip architectures, and tenant environments. While this model enhances the flexibility of resource scheduling and improves the overall task throughput of the system, it also significantly expands the attack surface of the computing execution process. As a result, the trustworthiness of the computing execution environment has become a critical factor affecting computing network security. If a computing node is maliciously compromised, the inference path, computation process, and input/output data of AI tasks can all be manipulated, posing a direct threat to inference integrity. These types of attacks bypass traditional security mechanisms based on service interfaces or data paths, focusing instead on controlling the execution process itself, and are characterized by high levels of stealth, severity, and difficulty in attribution.

The primary cause of the aforementioned security risks is the lack of trustworthiness in the underlying hardware and firmware environment. Today's computing networks heavily rely on third-party hardware and a globalized supply chain. This context creates risks for key components like processors, AI accelerators, and system firmware. These components may contain embedded covert logic introduced during design or manufacturing. Alternatively, they may harbor vulnerabilities that can be remotely activated, such as residual debugging interfaces or logical flaws. These low-level attacks often operate by disrupting instruction scheduling paths, tampering with boot processes, or interfering with memory access operations, thereby subtly influencing the state evolution of AI tasks. For instance, attackers can extract intermediate computational data via side channel analysis or compromise the trusted boot chain, enabling manipulation of model parameters or task control flows actions that are nearly imperceptible from the outside.

Looking upward in the stack, the middleware and driver layers are also hotspots for attacks. Attackers may tamper with driver loading logic, forge device resource descriptors, or hijack system call paths to bypass the authentication processes of resource schedulers and forcibly map critical computational tasks to untrusted nodes. This type of intervention enables mid execution hijacking of tasks, thereby undermining the secure binding between tasks and resources. In execution environments that heavily rely on virtualization and containerization, attackers may also construct "out-of-bounds access paths", breaking out of container boundaries to gain access to host machine resources. This compromises the original logical isolation mechanisms and can further lead to cross-tenant interference in task execution.

An additional risk lies in tampering with computation graphs and hijacking of forwarding paths during distributed scheduling. Currently, AI systems commonly use a computation graph execution model, where tasks are divided into multiple operator nodes and processed in parallel across different devices. Attackers can exploit relay nodes in the scheduling chain to inject malicious computation logic, interfering with specific stages of data flows and computation processes without disrupting the overall structure. For example, by embedding instruction blocks that conditionally modify certain model layers or input data, the attacker can surreptitiously activate tampering behavior upon meeting specific trigger conditions. Since most computing platforms lack integrity verification mechanisms during the computation graph forwarding process, these attacks often possess high latency and can remain undetected over prolonged periods of operation.

3.2.3.2 Attack Surface Testing and Drills

In the context of the increasing complexity and dynamic evolution of intelligent computing network systems, the traditional security assurance model centered on "static scanning and passive remediation" has become insufficient to effectively address new threats arising from multidimensional coupled environments. Attack surface testing and adversarial exercises have gradually emerged as key approaches for building practical system resilience and dynamic response capabilities. Their core objective is not only to verify the existence of known vulnerabilities but also to simulate unknown threat chains to comprehensively assess the system's overall situational awareness, threat detection, and response capabilities, thereby advancing defense strategies from "constructive completeness" toward "adversarial robustness".

Red-Blue Team Exercise is a security drill method based on realistic adversarial simulation, where the Red Team emulates real attackers to conduct full chain penetration of the system, and the Blue Team is responsible for monitoring, defense, and response. Its purpose is to reveal the gap between design and actual effectiveness, thereby enhancing the system's emergency response capabilities. In intelligent computing network environments, the Red Team employs diverse attack paths, including weak password brute force, container escape, compute resource hijacking, and man-in-the-middle attacks. The attack chain typically follows a pattern of "weak-trust node infiltration lateral movement cross layer intervention" demanding high capabilities in system decomposition and attack path design from the Red Team. The Blue Team faces challenges such as detection delays, difficulty in cross-domain log correlation, high false alarm rates, and broken response chains. Red-Blue exercises provide a stress test, helping to build an offense defense evaluation metric system, including detection time, response latency, and alert accuracy, to assess the maturity of defense capabilities. The Purple Team acts as a collaborative bridge between offense and defense, facilitating knowledge sharing and technical integration. It does not independently attack or defend but focuses on abstracting attack models, establishing defense mappings, and optimizing monitoring and response strategies, promoting the evolution from "behavioral confrontation" to "capability mutual reinforcement". The Purple Team maps Red Team attack paths to frameworks like MITRE ATT&CK via an attack mapping graph, identifying detection blind spots and response gaps, while building threat injection platforms and detection baselines to assist the Blue Team in testing defense robustness. Additionally, the Purple Team supports exercise mechanisms and engineering practices such as attack path replay, regression testing of detection rules, and response chain optimization, making security drills a continuous improvement process.

Chaos engineering was initially used to verify the stability and fault tolerance of distributed systems and has now evolved into a core method for exposing vulnerabilities and assessing system resilience. By actively introducing disturbances such as resource failures and communication interruptions during system operation, it observes whether the system can maintain a stable state that is perceptible, explainable, and recoverable. In the security domain, chaos engineering extends to Security Chaos Engineering (SCE), which simulates intrusion behaviors like forged scheduling requests, data pollution, and abnormal system calls. It focuses on testing the system's response to sudden, uncertain, and multi-path disturbances weak signal triggers to reveal hidden structural vulnerabilities.

Attack surface testing and Red-Blue Team Exercises are no longer merely means to inspect security defenses but have become key drivers for transitioning intelligent computing network security from static rules to dynamic collaboration. Red-blue exercises simulate real threats, the purple team enables closed loop strategy optimization, and chaos engineering stimulates the system's robustness boundaries. Together, these three form a unified exercise framework that drives the transformation from passive rule stacking toward a data-driven, adaptive security system.

3.2.3.3 Fault and Attack Recovery Mechanisms

In intelligent computing network systems, faults and attacks often exhibit characteristics of sudden occurrence, high coupling impact, and cross-domain propagation. Relying solely on early warning mechanisms or static isolation measures is insufficient to prevent the risk of overall system instability. Therefore, establishing a comprehensive recovery mechanism after faults and attacks becomes a key component in enhancing system resilience. The design of recovery mechanisms must not only address traditional data persistence requirements but also encompass capabilities such as runtime state consistency recovery, environment reconstruction, and rapid service rollback.

Disaster backup is the foundation of recovery mechanisms, commonly implemented as full backups, incremental backups, and differential backups. Full backups can completely restore the system but consume significant resources, making them suitable for environments with low change frequency; incremental backups offer high storage efficiency but rely on the integrity of the backup chain; differential backups fall between the two, helping to shorten recovery time. Intelligent computing networks are often deployed in complex multi-tenant, cross-domain edge and cloud collaborative architectures. In this environment, Recovery Point Objective and Recovery Time Objective must be dynamically set according to service levels. Furthermore, they must be combined with distributed version control to achieve cross-node replica synchronization and data consistency. Distributed file systems like Ceph and ZFS ensure backup data integrity and scalability through block level checksums and metadata indexing. Snapshot rollback supports fine-grained freezing and recovery of operating system kernel state, virtual devices, and task caches, making it suitable for latency-sensitive edge nodes. In contrast, image reconstruction is more applicable to scenarios of complete system failure. It enables cold start restoration of the base environment through trusted images and signature verification, thereby ensuring structural integrity and continuity of the trust chain. Modern intelligent computing networks increasingly rely on Infrastructure as Code (IaC) and automated orchestration technologies to achieve rapid and precise fault recovery, ensuring state consistency and avoiding dependency mismatches during recovery. Recovery strategies integrated with platform policy engines support dynamic decision making and resource scheduling based on security rules, for example, automatically replacing contaminated service container images to ensure system trustworthiness and continuous operation.

The recovery mechanism after faults and attacks has gradually evolved from a static disaster recovery approach centered on data backup to a dynamic resilience system focused on state rollback, environment reconstruction, and automated governance. It not only serves as the last line of defense for rapid system restoration after a disaster but also acts as a critical supporting mechanism to ensure the effective closure of the security loop in intelligent computing networks.

3.2.3.4 Automated Remediation and Patch Management

The patch management system starts by integrating authoritative vulnerability databases with asset inventories to enable precise patch identification and risk matching. Modern automated platforms evaluate patch compatibility based on system versions, components, and dependencies, generating prioritized lists sorted by CVSS scores and asset criticality. Through Security Configuration Management (SCM), they monitor patch status throughout the lifecycle to ensure visibility and traceability. In always-on, non-interruptible computing network environments, live patching technology allows dynamic code replacement and context redirection to fix vulnerabilities without rebooting, widely used in edge computing, 5G core networks, and industrial real-time systems, significantly reducing business interruption risks. Patch scheduling closely aligns with business windows by defining low-impact periods based on traffic cycles, resource usage, and dependency topologies, combined with automation tools for batch execution. Enhanced by risk benefit analysis, scheduling optimizes patch priority and business criticality to improve security and operational efficiency. To ensure fix effectiveness, platforms include regression verification and behavior monitoring, using extended Berkeley Packet Filter (eBPF) dynamic probes to detect kernel patch activation and canary release strategies to gradually deploy patches, safeguarding system performance, compatibility, and enhancing patch deployment safety and control.

As patch weaponization and the shortening of attack chains become increasingly prominent, patching is no longer merely a "system maintenance task" but a critical part of an "active defense strategy". Future automated repair systems should integrate several key components to build a collaborative repair framework. These components include AI-driven patch recommendation engines, attack surface-aware dynamic prioritization mechanisms, and cross-domain federated patch orchestration platforms. This framework must be capable of operating across computing networks, organizations, and tenants, enabling a strategic transformation from "vulnerability elimination" to "system self-healing".

3.3 The Proposed Solution

3.3.1 Computing Power Security Certification Technology

In the intelligent computing network environment, characteristics such as dynamic scheduling of computing resources, high-level distribution, and cross-domain collaboration render traditional authentication mechanisms based on static identities and closed boundaries increasingly inadequate for security protection. Attackers can infiltrate system boundaries through identity spoofing, privilege abuse, and cross-domain bypassing, thereby manipulating data flows, interfering with algorithm execution, and controlling resource scheduling. This gives rise to compound security threats initiated at the system level, spreading at the data level, and degrading at the algorithm level. To establish a foundational system security framework for future intelligent computing-network infrastructures, it is imperative to develop a computing power authentication mechanism equipped with full lifecycle awareness, multi-dimensional behavior assessment, and trustworthy coordinated response capabilities.

This section proposes a three-tier progressive computing power security authentication framework tailored for intelligent computing network environments. It covers the full spectrum authentication requirements from access verification and compliance assessment of resource invocation to cross-domain collaborative governance. The goal is to achieve a system-level closed loop authentication process characterized by "trusted identity, and compliant behavior and effective collaboration" through dynamic modeling, fine-grained monitoring, and coordinated response strategies.

3.3.1.1 Identity Authentication: Trusted Access Identification Based on Behavioral Characteristics

This section designs a dynamic identity authentication mechanism tailored for intelligent computing network environments. By leveraging multimodal behavior modeling and graph structured learning, it enables trustworthy identification of access entities. Compared to traditional authentication methods that rely on static credentials, this mechanism focuses on the continuity, consistency, and structural rationality of entity behaviors, aiming to detect potential threats such as forged terminals, cloned nodes, and automated control tasks.

During the access phase, the system collects multidimensional behavioral information from the terminal, including computing resource usage sequences, API call characteristics, log text semantics, and task scheduling patterns. Each type of feature is first processed within its modality for temporal encoding and semantic extraction: structured metrics are modeled using sequential models, while unstructured text is encoded into embedding vectors via language models. A cross-modal attention mechanism is then employed to fuse these features, generating a unified behavioral representation vector sequence that captures the entity's operational trajectory and interaction intent within the computing network.

To enhance the modeling of relationships between behaviors, the system constructs a directed behavior graph, where each behavioral event is represented as a node, and edges are established based on operational sequences, resource dependencies, or control logic, forming a context-rich behavioral graph. A graph neural network (GNN) is introduced to model this structure, where the update of node embeddings follows a neighbor-based aggregation mechanism:

$$h_v^{(l+1)} = \sigma\left(W^{(l)} \cdot \sum_{u \in N(v)} h_u^{(l)}\right). \tag{3.1}$$

Let $h_v^{(l)}$ denotes the embedding of node v at layer l, $N(v)$ denotes the set of its neighboring nodes, $W^{(l)}$ denotes a learnable weight matrix, and σ denotes an activation function.

To enable distributed deployment and privacy protection of the authentication model, the system adopts a federated learning-based training architecture. Terminal nodes independently perform behavior modeling and parameter updates, while the central server periodically aggregates these updates to synchronize the global model. During the aggregation process, differential privacy mechanisms are introduced to mitigate the risk of inferring sensitive behaviors, and homomorphic encryption is employed to secure parameter exchanges, preventing leakage of behavioral data.

This mechanism features a flexible structure, strong adaptability, and robust context awareness, enabling fine-grained identity recognition without relying on static credentials. By integrating multimodal perception, graph-structured modeling, and federated training strategies, it establishes the first dynamic trusted defense line in intelligent computing network access control, providing a high-quality identity basis for subsequent resource allocation and behavior governance.

3.3.1.2 Compliance Authentication: Behavior Compliance Determination of Resource Usage Paths

Identity authentication addresses the authenticity of entities, whereas resource usage compliance focuses on the boundary of permission execution within the system. During system operation, legitimate entities may invoke computing resources in unintended ways due to unauthorized actions, misuse of scheduling policies, or improper cross-domain combinations. Such behaviors often conform to the superficial logic of permissions but pose risks of resource abuse, manifesting as deviations in access paths, abnormal resource combinations, and evasion of task scheduling policies. In severe cases, these can trigger cascading effects such as model leakage, service conflicts, and scheduling chaos.

To achieve fine-grained compliance assessment of resource usage behaviors, the system constructs an authentication mechanism that integrates behavior graph analysis, spatiotemporal anomaly detection, and behavior completion processes. Resource invocation path modeling is based on computing power requests, algorithmic tasks, and data access as fundamental units, forming a multidimensional heterogeneous behavior graph. In this graph, nodes represent specific operations, while edges denote invocation, dependency, or synchronization relationships between operations, enriched with attributes such as permission levels, resource sensitivity, and invocation frequency. The graph structure supports dynamic expansion and can model collaborative relationships across heterogeneous resources beyond system boundaries, capturing resource scheduling trajectories of low-trust entities within highly sensitive areas, as well as structural deviations in permission combinations.

The anomaly detection model jointly employs spatiotemporal attention mechanisms and recurrent neural networks to model the continuity, periodicity, and correlations of resource operations. Metrics such as computing load, invocation rhythm, and resource switching serve as inputs, combined with task context and system operational status to dynamically generate temporal risk representations. On this basis, a dynamic threshold control mechanism is introduced to avoid false positives or negatives caused by static boundary judgments. The threshold calculation is based on historical operational statistics and current environmental conditions, defined as:

$$\theta_t = \mu_t + \alpha \cdot \sigma_t. \tag{3.2}$$

Where μ_t represents the mean of the target metric within the current time window, σ_t denotes the standard deviation, and α is a sensitivity adjustment parameter. This mechanism enables real-time threshold reconstruction for key indicators such as GPU utilization, concurrent request density, and frequency of anomalous accesses, thereby enhancing the compliance authentication's adaptability to system dynamics.

In cross-system scenarios with incomplete data, fragmented logs, or missing behavior segments, the system employs Generative Adversarial Networks (GANs) to reconstruct and interpolate behavior sequences. The generator produces completed sequences that conform to access semantic constraints, while the discriminator assesses the authenticity of paths based on behavioral consistency. This process ultimately forms a complete behavior chain for compliance evaluation. The reconstructed behavior data is then fused with the original behavior graph and fed into the anomaly detection module, enabling a closed loop compliance reconstruction and determination.

This authentication mechanism does not rely on static policy matching or is limited to role permission mappings; instead, it achieves precise modeling of resource usage behaviors through behavioral structural consistency and contextual semantic constraints. The mechanism features strong structural generalization, high strategy adaptability, and robust cross system collaborative modeling capabilities, effectively supporting dynamic compliance control and fine-grained governance of intelligent computing networks in complex resource scheduling environments.

3.3.1.3 Benign Authentication: Trusted Behavior Governance Under Multi-domain Collaboration

The operational structure of intelligent computing networks exhibits significant distribution and heterogeneity, with scheduling systems spanning multiple physical and logical domains, including cloud nodes, edge devices, local clusters, and external service platforms. In a cross-domain collaborative environment, differences in access control rules, identity trust models, and behavior assessment policies create decoupling of strategies and asymmetric trust between domains, providing opportunities for attackers. Entities in low-trust domains can exploit rule gaps to bypass security controls of high-trust domains, construct credible disguises or conflicting behaviors, and carry out trust drift attacks, leading to task scheduling mismatches, resource abuse, and loss of behavior accountability traceability. Therefore, it is necessary to establish an authentication and governance mechanism with capabilities for behavior constraint, policy coordination, and dynamic trust adaptation to support a multi-domain security closed loop at the system level.

This mechanism proposes a dual track benign authentication framework centered on intelligent rule evolution and trust modeling, achieving dynamic evaluation and policy coordination of cross-domain behaviors through rule structure optimization and trust weight quantification. In terms of rule governance, the system employs a mechanism for the evolution of policies based on genetic algorithms that constructs a fitness function for access control rules. This function jointly evaluates the adaptability, coverage, and control granularity of rule sets across different domains to form iterative policy refinement paths. The fitness function inputs include policy hit rate, risk response latency, and resource misallocation rate. By leveraging intra domain behavior feedback to drive rule structure self evolution, the system enhances the dynamic adaptability and conflict resilience of the rule framework.

In behavior recognition, the system builds a behavior autoencoder based on the Transformer architecture to model cross-domain request sequences and analyze reconstruction errors. The encoder learns behavior evolution patterns across three dimensions: behavior semantics, resource invocation order, and inter-domain contextual states. It performs high-dimensional modeling of potential structural shifts and access intent distortions within behavior paths, quantifying anomaly levels using reconstruction residuals as input metrics. This creates a label free behavior deviation detection mechanism. This module supports the perceptive identification of covert path constructions, semantic behavior drifts, and low-frequency detour patterns.

To address requirements for trustworthy behavior recording and accountable auditing, the system integrates a consortium blockchain as the evidence carrier for multi-domain operational events. It records the hash digests of key behaviors, behavior graph states, and policy decision processes from each domain onto the blockchain, ensuring full traceability and immutability of actions. Smart contract modules within the consortium blockchain implement cross-domain behavior consensus and rule verification, supporting structural consistency analysis of on-chain behavior snapshots, risk label propagation, and responsibility chain construction. This provides evidential support for attributing and holding accountable anomalous behaviors in cross-domain collaborative scenarios.

At the trust evaluation level, the system designs a multi-factor linked trust modeling approach to quantify the global trust status of accessing entities. The trust factors comprehensively consider the historical reputation score R_h, current behavior entropy H_b, sensitivity of accessed resources S_r, and policy consistency coefficient ξ, constructing a dynamic trust value calculation model:

$$T = \beta_1 R_h + \beta_2 H_b^{-1} + \beta_3 S_r + \beta_4 \xi. \tag{3.3}$$

Here, β_1 to β_4 are adjustable weights, and the trust value T is used to drive real-time adjustments in access decision strength, review policy levels, and response strategy granularity. A lower trust value will trigger supplementary behavior verification, multi-path auditing, or direct rejection mechanisms. The trend of trust value changes will be used to determine the evolutionary trajectory of the entity's behavior trustworthiness.

Through the benign authentication mechanism, rule gaps, trust fractures, and control blind spots in multi-domain environments are effectively filled, enabling controllable behavior paths, coordinated policy boundaries, and clear accountability chains. This mechanism not only achieves dynamic constraint and trusted filtering of cross-domain access but also constructs an authentication governance closed loop based on behavior, centered on trust, and driven by policies. It serves as a key supporting technology for the intelligent computing network system's transition from rule-based defense to dynamic governance.

By integrating trusted identification through identity authentication, behavior auditing via compliance certification, and cross-domain coordination in benign authentication, a system centric, full process computing power security authentication mechanism is established. Within the three dimensional coupling structure, this mechanism not only strengthens the trustworthiness of access sources and the rationality of resource usage but also achieves dynamic governance of cross-domain behaviors and trust collaboration.

3.3.2 *Trusted Computing Execution Framework*

3.3.2.1 Trusted Cross-domain Access Execution

In the multi-domain collaborative system of the intelligent computing network, differences and autonomy in rules across domains often lead to inconsistencies in behavioral standards, resulting in issues such as incomplete rules, rule conflicts, and behavior drift. These problems subsequently affect the trusted cross-domain scheduling and execution of computing tasks. To address these challenges, it is essential to establish a trusted execution mechanism focused on completeness, consistency, and stability. This section proposes a cross-domain trusted execution framework composed of behavior rule evolution and optimization, dynamic coordination of rule consistency, and behavior aware predictive modeling. The framework aims to realize a closed loop logic of rule generation, conflict mitigation, and sequence assurance, fundamentally enhancing the stability and controllability of cross-domain execution.

In scenarios where rule expressiveness is insufficient or new domain rules are missing, a heuristic exploration method based on behavior rule evolution is employed to structurally generate rules targeting the behavior data of the target domain. Behavior rules are encoded as vectors R of length $k + 1$, where the first element represents the feature separation index, and the remaining elements correspond to behavior feature identifiers. A fitness function combining confidence and completeness is constructed as follows:

$$F = \alpha \cdot conf\,(s) + \beta \cdot comp\,(s)\,. \tag{3.4}$$

Where $conf\,(s)$ denotes the support of candidate rule s in historical data, $comp\,(s)$ represents its behavior coverage in the new domain, and α, β are adjustable hyperparameters. A negative function value indicates that the rule fails to meet the minimum confidence and completeness thresholds and is therefore discarded. During the evolution process, operations such as deletion, recombination, crossover, and feature mutation are used to maintain the diversity of the rule set.

Within the maximum number of iterations, the optimal rule set is preserved to enhance the generalization ability of behavior patterns across different domains.

To address consistency conflicts arising from rule propagation across multiple domains, a Dynamic Voting-based Rule Copying (DVRC) algorithm is introduced for conflict resolution and version synchronization. Each terminal within a domain maintains a dynamic voting matrix of rule states, which includes rule ID, replication number (RN), confirmation count (NC), and update propagation volume (UP). When a node receives a behavior rule update, it automatically increments its local RN and UP values and broadcasts its status to other terminals. If the target terminal receives an RN value higher than its local record, it adopts the new rule copy; otherwise, it retains the local version and sends back the update values. After aggregating feedback and confirmations, the acceptance of the new rule is determined based on the NC value. When $NC \geq \theta$, the rule officially takes effect within that domain. This mechanism, through multi-source feedback and dynamic negotiation, ensures consistency, stability, and timeliness of rule synchronization across domains.

To further enhance the predictability and stability of behaviors during execution, a cross-domain behavior recognition model is constructed by integrating an autoencoder with a sequence aware network. Assume the behavior sequence is $X = (x_1, x_2, , x_N), x_i \in R^m$. At time t, a subsequence of length L is extracted: $S_t = (x_{t-L+1}, \ldots, x_t)$, The autoencoder generates local behavior embeddings $\left(e_t^1, \ldots, e_t^{k-1}\right)$, which are then input into the sequence-aware network to predict the next behavior trend:

$$\left[\widehat{e_t^2}, \ldots, \widehat{e_t^k}\right] = FS\left(\left[e_t^1, \ldots, e_t^{k-1}\right]\right). \tag{3.5}$$

Evaluate the error between the reconstructed window and the original window to calculate the behavior deviation score:

$$d_t = \sum_{i-2}^{k} \left\| \hat{w}_{t-(k-i)p} - w_{t-(k-i)p} \right\|_2. \tag{3.6}$$

If the score d_t exceeds the anomaly detection threshold, the current behavior sequence is considered abnormal, assigned a binary label $y_t = 1$, and an interrupt mechanism is triggered to halt subsequent operations in the behavior chain, preventing further propagation of the abnormal behavior across the multi-domain system.

The cross-domain access trusted execution mechanism establishes a comprehensive execution assurance system. This system covers three key areas: rule generation, conflict management, and anomaly detection. It functions through the adaptive evolution of behavior rules, consensus coordination among multiple terminals, and embedded behavior sequence perception models. This mechanism not only achieves behavior norm adaptation and rule consistency coordination for computing tasks in multi-domain environments but also enhances proactive identification of behavior deviations and potential risks through sequence modeling capabilities. As a core support unit within the trusted computing execution system, it creates a dynamic linkage between trusted policy rules and controllable behavior processes, providing system-level trust guarantees for cross-domain resource scheduling and behavior decision making in intelligent computing networks.

3.3.2.2 Trusted Protection and Control in Interactive Environments

In the context of increasingly deep cross-domain collaboration within intelligent computing networks, the interaction paths of computing tasks span multiple resources of domains, services, and regulatory boundaries. Traditional single domain authentication and localized trust mechanisms struggle to support global consistency, secure traceability, and risk response for cross-domain behaviors. Therefore, it is necessary to establish a system-level trusted security control mechanism tailored for interactive scenarios. This mechanism must encompass multi-level knowledge graph modeling, a trusted shared infrastructure, and dynamic trust evaluation systems. The goal is to enhance behavioral semantic understanding, transaction controllability, and node trustworthiness assessment capabilities.

First, addressing the challenges of behavioral data heterogeneity and insufficient attribute representation, a multi-level cross-category heterogeneous business graph modeling mechanism is designed. Nodes represent resources, attributes, and behaviors within the business domain, constructing a cross-category heterogeneous graph $G = (V, \varepsilon)$, GNNs are employed to perform node representation learning and behavior aggregation inference. A dual level attention mechanism is applied for graph representation learning: the type-level attention score is computed by the following formula:

$$\alpha_\tau = softmax\left(\sigma\left(\mu_\tau^T\left[h_v || h_\tau\right]\right)\right). \tag{3.7}$$

Further, the node-level behavior attention weights $\beta_{vv'}$ are obtained for multi-type message fusion in the heterogeneous graph. Based on this, node embeddings are constructed through a node aggregation operation:

$$H^{(l+1)} = \sigma\left(\sum_{\tau \in T} B_\tau \cdot H_\tau^{(l)} \cdot W_\tau^{(l)}\right). \tag{3.8}$$

Each node embedding in the graph represents fine-grained semantics across different resource dimensions, which can then be used for correlation analysis and detection of anomalous sub-behaviors. For a given business behavior $B_i = \{a_1, \ldots, a_n\}$, its aggregated sub-behavior embedding A_i is computed and evaluated for anomaly using an inner product scoring function:

$$Score_i = A_i \odot A_i^T. \tag{3.9}$$

A low score indicates strong collaboration and high consistency among the sub-behaviors; conversely, a high score suggests that there may be abnormal deviations in the behavior logic.

Secondly, while ensuring cross-domain behavior data sharing and link integrity, a trusted maintenance mechanism supported by a two-tier consortium blockchain is established. At the intra-domain level, a model combining private off-chain data storage with on-chain block header recording is adopted to guarantee data privacy and balance on-chain load. Each domain maintains its local ledger through coordinated roles of endorsing nodes, leader nodes, and inspecting nodes, performs transaction verification, behavior monitoring, and real-time evaluation of node trustworthiness. At the cross-domain level, a global ledger maintained jointly by leader nodes from each domain is introduced to achieve unified coordination of cross-domain rule completion, consistency conflict logging, and resource access control.

When constructing a multi-factor collaborative cross-domain node trust evaluation model, transaction participation, behavior compliance, and historical reputation evolution information are integrated to dynamically generate trust scores. Let the trust value at the current time be S_t, defined using a temporal memory mechanism as follows:

$$S_t = \alpha A + \beta B + \gamma S_{t-1} + \gamma^2 S_{t-2} + \ldots + \gamma^{t-1} S_1. \quad (3.10)$$

Here, A represents the security transaction score of the participated behavior, B denotes the node behavior compliance score, and α, β, γ are the respective weighting factors. The node's performance in behavior logic vulnerability scanning is defined as follows:

$$A = \mu \left(C_p - C_n\right) + \lambda \cdot \frac{C_p + C_n}{C}. \quad (3.11)$$

Here, C_p, C_n, and C represent the counts of times no vulnerabilities were detected, the times abnormal behaviors were detected, and the total number of detections, respectively. These metrics reflect the node's behavior performance in proactive security scanning. Combining behavior participation and anomaly detection accuracy, the behavior trust factor B is defined as:

$$B = \rho \cdot \frac{Z_p - Z_n}{Z_p + Z_n} + \tau \cdot P(r) - \xi \cdot R(w). \quad (3.12)$$

Here, Z_p, Z_n denote the number of compliant and non-compliant detection phases, respectively; $P(r)$ represents the node's capability score for detecting other anomalies; and $R(w)$ stands for the count of failure records caused by system instability.

To enhance the long-term stability of system operation, a trust-value-based node grading system is introduced. Permissions are dynamically assigned according to trust levels: low-trust nodes face restrictions on resource access and interaction participation, while high-trust nodes possess greater authority in policy formulation and decision making. The trust values are continuously updated to support cross-domain policy iteration, the removal of anomalous nodes, and the maintenance of network wide consistency.

In summary, the trusted control mechanism in interactive scenarios enhances attribute level expressiveness through heterogeneous behavior graph modeling, establishes a full lifecycle trusted evidence preservation system for behavior chains via blockchain architecture, and ensures quantitative evaluation and tiered response of node behaviors through a multi-perspective dynamic trust model. The synergy of these three components forms the foundation for behavior awareness, secure sharing, and resilient governance of intelligent computing network systems under complex interactive conditions.

3.3.3 Security Policy Adaptive Optimization Based on Behavioral Profiling

3.3.3.1 Adaptive Optimization of Security Policies Based on Behavioral Profiles

In intelligent computing network systems, business processes involving multiple entities are highly dynamic, with computing resources exhibiting cross-domain orchestration, heterogeneous deployment, and frequent state transitions. Traditional static security policies struggle to adapt to such evolving behaviors and complex threat structures. To address this, a closed loop adaptive defense mechanism is required, one that centers on behavior as the core clue, uses profiling as the representation model, and outputs dynamically evolving policies. This section proposes a behavior profile-based adaptive security policy adjustment method, which constructs three types of security profiles subject behavior graph, event security graph, and virtual simulation graph to drive the intelligent evolution of policy models and support coordinated global defense.

Multi-entity profiling serves as the foundation for behavior driven policy adjustment. This profiling model targets various types of entities such as endpoints, users, services, and computing nodes by integrating structural attributes, functional attributes, and external environmental variables to form a multi-dimensional and comprehensive behavioral representation. On the system side, a spatiotemporal graph modeling approach is introduced, embedding behavioral trajectories into a graph structure where nodes represent operational behaviors and edges denote temporal and spatial transition paths. A Graph Convolutional Network (GCN) combined with an attention mechanism is employed to extract high-order contextual dependency features and generate continuously updatable subject security embedding vectors.

In the evolution of behavior profiling, the system incorporates a cross task transfer learning mechanism to extract labeled behavior consequence samples from historical events and reconstruct mappings between potential attack chains or risk factors in new business scenarios. For instance, if a node's GPU utilization pattern exhibits high semantic similarity to a known cryptomining attack, the system will trigger a risk reconstruction path, proactively adjusting resource allocation and access control strategies. The entire profile update process follows a composite path of short-term behavior dynamics and long-term state evolution, ensuring a balanced trade-off between sensitivity and stability of the behavioral representation.

Emergent incidents often serve as windows where threats erupt intensively. To enhance the system's proactive response to unconventional events, a knowledge graph-based security profiling mechanism for emergent incidents is introduced. The system first applies structured extraction methods to identify key elements in physical events such as attack techniques, triggering factors, and impact paths and constructs a causal association graph among these elements. By aligning the structure of similar historical incidents, conducting causal inference, and comparing event paths, the system enables "analogical prediction" of potential abnormal scenarios. During the graph reasoning phase, the system employs a combination of graph attention mechanisms and path attention modeling, transforming the event-element-consequence triplet relationships into a weighted path search problem. This enables the automatic identification of high-risk patterns and triggers the strategy coordination module. Based on the assessed impact scope of the incident, the module dynamically determines which policy domains to activate. Examples include isolating traffic routes, triggering circuit breakers in computation scheduling, or initiating delayed execution plans. These actions adjust the system's defense surface and resource response capacity accordingly.

The security representations of entities and events must ultimately be mapped to system execution logic through policy language. To establish a logical closed loop between behavior profiling and policy enforcement, the system introduces a virtual simulation based mechanism for policy simulation and mapping. This mechanism maintains a multi-level simulation platform on the system side, which maps behavioral features of multiple entities and key elements of critical events, and quantitatively expresses their trust levels and associated security risks.

The behavior profile driven adaptive security policy adjustment mechanism follows the core process of "behavior cognition and profile modeling and policy response", enabling dynamic coupling and coordinated interaction from the data layer to the policy layer. This mechanism not only enhances situational awareness within computing network environments but also establishes a security policy ecosystem characterized by self-evolution, self-regulation, and self-adaptation. It provides a foundational policy support framework essential for coping with highly dynamic, multi task, and adversarial complex environments.

3.3.3.2 Optimization of Security Communication Protocols Based on Behaviors

In intelligent computing network systems, communication protocols serve not only as fundamental channels for task interaction and resource scheduling but also as critical anchors for enforcing system security policies. As system operations evolve toward multi-domain collaboration and cross-platform migration of computing resources, traditional protocols lacking behavior aware semantics struggle to dynamically detect and respond to anomalous communication behaviors. This leads to challenges such as static protocol structures, coarse grained validation, and weak adaptability to attacks. To address these issues, it is essential to integrate subject behavior information into the protocol design based on behavior profiling, thus achieving a deep coupling between security policies and the communication process and ensuring coordinated protection.

This section proposes a behavior profile driven communication protocol optimization mechanism that enables dynamic perception, semantic verification, and link layer protection of communication behaviors. The mechanism integrates three key components: modeling of communication behavior states, structural extension of protocols, and the introduction of policy linkage mechanisms. First, in the aspect of communication behavior state modeling, the system combines communication content with behavioral features to construct a temporal multi-dimensional state representation. Using graph neural networks and attention mechanisms, the model jointly captures communication trajectories and behavioral intent. This allows the system to evaluate behavior similarity before communication occurs, enabling early detection of potential attack chains such as spoofed behaviors and abnormal traffic.

At the protocol layer, an embedded behavior verification mechanism is introduced to enhance the original message format. The protocol is extended with three types of security fields: behavior digest, intent signature, and verification tag, which respectively represent the current behavior state of the communicating entity, its operational intent, and the trust level of the communication link. Participating nodes perform substantial verification of the communication party's status before data transmission through behavior embedding comparison and signature validation, effectively preventing identity spoofing, intent forgery, and link hijacking. This mechanism improves the ability of the protocol layer to detect behavioral deviations without compromising the original protocol logic.

To ensure consistency between communication security and global security policies, the system further establishes a graph linkage mechanism for communication behavior. During scheduling, communication paths dynamically reference risk patterns and anomaly routes within the behavior graph. For high-frequency atypical requests or high-risk interaction chains, the system enforces policy adjustments such as automatic delay handling, privilege degradation, or behavior re-authentication. In reverse linkage, behavioral deviations detected in communication are fed back to adjust risk weights in the behavior profile, thereby influencing subsequent privilege decisions. For example, when communication behavior triggers anomaly detection, its security score S_i is updated according to the formula:

$$S_i^{t+1} = S_i^t - \lambda \cdot \delta_{comm}. \tag{3.13}$$

Here, S_i^t denotes the security score of node i at the current time, and S_i^{t+1} represents the updated score. λ is a penalty coefficient that controls the magnitude of score reduction, while δ_{comm} indicates the degree of communication deviation, reflecting the intensity or risk level of abnormal behavior. This formula ensures that communication deviations are promptly mapped to the decline of the security score, thereby providing a quantitative basis for privilege adjustment and policy response.

In summary, the behavior driven communication protocol optimization mechanism evolves security policies from static definitions to dynamic execution, enabling structural representation and real-time verification of behaviors at the protocol layer. This improves the trustworthiness and defensibility of the communication process. Through this mechanism, the intelligent computing network system can maintain flexible communication capabilities while achieving fine-grained detection and policy driven control of abnormal communication behaviors, thereby providing secure support for the orderly coordination of computing resources and cross-domain interactions.

References

1. A. Botta, W. De Donato, V. Persico, A. Pescapé, Future Gener. Comput. Syst. **56**, 684 (2016)
2. K. Nisar, E.R. Jimson, M.H.A. Hijazi, I. Welch, R. Hassan, A.H.M. Aman, A.H. Sodhro, S. Pirbhulal, S. Khan, Int. Things **12**, 100289 (2020)
3. W. Shi, J. Cao, Q. Zhang, Y. Li, L. Xu, IEEE Int. Things J. **3**(5), 637 (2016)
4. Q. Zhang, L. Cheng, R. Boutaba, J. Int. Services Appl. **1**, 7 (2010)
5. L. Atzori, A. Iera, G. Morabito, Comput. Netw. **54**(15), 2787 (2010)
6. M. Antonakakis, T. April, M. Bailey, M. Bernhard, E. Bursztein, J. Cochran, Z. Durumeric, J.A. Halderman, L. Invernizzi, M. Kallitsis, et al., in *26th USENIX Security Symposium (USENIX Security 17)* (2017), pp. 1093–1110
7. A. Affinito, S. Zinno, G. Stanco, A. Botta, G. Ventre, J. Inf. Secur. Appl. **79**, 103629 (2023)
8. D. Moore, V. Paxson, S. Savage, C. Shannon, S. Staniford, N. Weaver, IEEE Secur. Privacy **1**(4), 33 (2003)
9. Y. Xiao, Y. Jia, C. Liu, X. Cheng, J. Yu, W. Lv, Proc. IEEE **107**(8), 1608 (2019)
10. D.K. Bhattacharyya, J.K. Kalita, *Network Anomaly Detection: A Machine Learning Perspective* (CRC Press, Boca Raton, 2013)
11. M. Barreno, B. Nelson, R. Sears, A.D. Joseph, J.D. Tygar, in *Proceedings of the 2006 ACM Symposium on Information, Computer and Communications Security* (2006), pp. 16–25
12. A. Kurakin, I. Goodfellow, S. Bengio, Preprint (2016). arXiv:1611.01236
13. A.R. Galloway, *How Control Exists After Decentralization* (MIT Cambridge, MA, 2004)
14. D. Zhang, G. Feng, Y. Shi, D. Srinivasan, IEEE/CAA J. Automatica Sinica **8**(2), 319 (2021)
15. M. Alam, M. Shahid, S. Mustajab, J. Supercomput. **80**(8), 11491 (2024)
16. S. Scott-Hayward, S. Natarajan, S. Sezer, IEEE Commun. Surv. Tutor. **18**(1), 623 (2015)
17. J. Viega, M. Messier, P. Chandra, *Network Security with openSSL: Cryptography for Secure Communications* (O'Reilly Media, Inc., Farnham, 2002)
18. S. Pal, M. Hitchens, V. Varadharajan, in *2018 12th International Conference on Sensing Technology (ICST)* (IEEE, 2018), pp. 45–51
19. B. Bhushan, G. Sahoo, Wireless Personal Commun. **98**, 2037 (2018)

20. A. Alshamrani, S. Myneni, A. Chowdhary, D. Huang, IEEE Commun. Surv. Tutor. **21**(2), 1851 (2019)
21. M. Casado, T. Garfinkel, A. Akella, M.J. Freedman, D. Boneh, N. McKeown, S. Shenker, in *USENIX Security Symposium*, vol. 49 (2006), p. 50
22. A. Humayed, J. Lin, F. Li, B. Luo, IEEE Int. Things J. **4**(6), 1802 (2017)
23. A. Wool, IEEE Int. Comput. **14**(4), 58 (2010)
24. D. Kreutz, F.M. Ramos, P.E. Verissimo, C.E. Rothenberg, S. Azodolmolky, S. Uhlig, Proc. IEEE **103**(1), 14 (2014)
25. W. Yu, F. Liang, X. He, W.G. Hatcher, C. Lu, J. Lin, X. Yang, IEEE Access **6**, 6900 (2017)
26. R.S. Sandhu, in *Advances in Computers*, vol. 46 (Elsevier, Amsterdam, 1998), pp. 237–286
27. V.C. Hu, D.R. Kuhn, D.F. Ferraiolo, J. Voas, Computer **48**(2), 85 (2015)
28. X. Jin, R. Krishnan, R. Sandhu, in *Data and Applications Security and Privacy XXVI: 26th Annual IFIP WG 11.3 Conference, DBSec 2012, Paris, France, July 11-13, 2012. Proceedings 26* (Springer, 2012), pp. 41–55
29. X. Ye, B. Khoussainov, Int. J. Grid Utility Comput. **4**(2–3), 160 (2013)
30. L. Seitz, G. Selander, C. Gehrmann, in *2013 IEEE 14th International Symposium on" A World of Wireless, Mobile and Multimedia Networks"(WoWMoM)* (IEEE, 2013), pp. 1–6
31. P. Nida, H. Dhiman, S. Hussain, Int. J. Eng. Res. Technol. **3**(4) (2014)
32. E. Fernandes, A. Rahmati, J. Jung, A. Prakash, IEEE Secur. Privacy **15**(2), 24 (2017)
33. M. Hölbl, M. Kompara, A. Kamišalić, L. Nemec Zlatolas, Symmetry **10**(10), 470 (2018)
34. S. Sicari, A. Rizzardi, L.A. Grieco, A. Coen-Porisini, Comput. Netw. **76**, 146 (2015)
35. V. Stafford, NIST Special Publ. **800**(207), 800 (2020)
36. J. Kindervag, S. Balaouras, et al., Forrester Res. **3**(1), 1 (2010)
37. A. Moubayed, A. Refaey, A. Shami, IEEE Netw. **33**(5), 226 (2019)
38. R. Sommer, V. Paxson, in *2010 IEEE Symposium on Security and Privacy* (IEEE, 2010), pp. 305–316
39. G. Creech, J. Hu, IEEE Trans. Comput. **63**(4), 807 (2013)
40. M. Ring, S. Wunderlich, D. Scheuring, D. Landes, A. Hotho, Comput. Secur. **86**, 147 (2019)
41. A. Tuor, S. Kaplan, B. Hutchinson, N. Nichols, S. Robinson, in *AAAI Workshops* (2017), pp. 224–231
42. V. Chandola, A. Banerjee, V. Kumar, ACM Comput. Surv. **41**(3), 1 (2009)
43. F.T. Liu, K.M. Ting, Z.H. Zhou, in *2008 Eighth IEEE International Conference on Data Mining* (IEEE, 2008), pp. 413–422
44. J. An, S. Cho, Special Lecture on IE **2**(1), 1 (2015)
45. Z. Wu, S. Pan, F. Chen, G. Long, C. Zhang, P.S. Yu, IEEE Trans. Neural Netw. Learn. Syst. **32**(1), 4 (2020)
46. T.N. Kipf, M. Welling, Preprint (2016). arXiv:1609.02907
47. Y. Li, R. Yu, C. Shahabi, Y. Liu, Preprint (2017). arXiv:1707.01926
48. E. Rossi, B. Chamberlain, F. Frasca, D. Eynard, F. Monti, M. Bronstein, Preprint (2020). arXiv:2006.10637
49. C. Zhang, D. Song, Y. Chen, X. Feng, C. Lumezanu, W. Cheng, J. Ni, B. Zong, H. Chen, N.V. Chawla, in *Proceedings of the AAAI Conference on Artificial Intelligence*, vol. 33 (2019), pp. 1409–1416
50. P. Malhotra, L. Vig, G. Shroff, P. Agarwal, et al., in *Proceedings*, vol. 89 (2015), p. 94
51. C. Fang, H. Wang, N. Nazari, B. Omidi, A. Sasan, K.N. Khasawneh, S. Rafatirad, H. Homayoun, Preprint (2021). arXiv:2110.00846
52. F. Zhou, M. Goel, P. Desnoyers, R. Sundaram, Preprint (2011). arXiv:1103.0759
53. M.S. Islam, W. Pourmajidi, L. Zhang, J. Steinbacher, T. Erwin, A. Miranskyy, in *2021 IEEE/ACM 43rd International Conference on Software Engineering: Software Engineering in Practice (ICSE-SEIP)* (IEEE, 2021), pp. 150–159
54. K. Alhamazani, R. Ranjan, K. Mitra, F. Rabhi, P.P. Jayaraman, S.U. Khan, A. Guabtni, V. Bhatnagar, Computing **97**, 357 (2015)
55. G. Zhou, W. Tian, R. Buyya, R. Xue, L. Song, Artif. Intell. Rev. **57**(5), 124 (2024)
56. T. Moustakas, K. Kolomvatsos, Computing **105**(11), 2459 (2023)

Chapter 4
The Projection Onto Data Plane

Abstract This chapter examines the functional roles and implementation mechanisms of the data plane in multi agent intelligent systems. In dynamic and heterogeneous environments with limited resources and high risks, diverse data types and complex data flows make an efficient data plane essential for perception, modeling, fusion, protection, and system evolution. The chapter first presents two representative use cases that show how the data plane enables cross domain collaboration and intelligent decision making. It then reviews mainstream data technologies and explains their practical limitations, which reveal important research bottlenecks and future trends. Finally, the chapter introduces core techniques such as multi source data aggregation, knowledge enhanced representation models, trusted sharing with traceability, and adaptive data lifecycle management to provide methodological and engineering pathways for effective data management in complex systems.

4.1 Motivation and Representative Examples

In today's intelligent systems driven by data, the data plane is evolving from a traditional channel for information transmission into a foundational layer that supports perception, processing, sharing, and application of data throughout the entire lifecycle. Particularly in complex distributed systems such as multi-agent collaboration, federated learning, the Internet of Things, and integrated networks between satellites and terrestrial systems, data serves not only as the foundation for knowledge extraction and policy optimization but also directly affects the accuracy of perception, system responsiveness, and overall trustworthiness. Focusing research on the data layer rather than the abstract algorithmic layer enables a deeper understanding of the structural, dynamic, and heterogeneous characteristics of data flows in intelligent systems, providing a critical perspective for improving algorithm design and enhancing system scalability. Traditional intelligent architectures often follow the paradigm of data to model to decision, treating data processing as a prerequisite or auxiliary step for algorithmic execution. However, as system complexity increases and data environments evolve, this paradigm faces significant challenges. On one hand, data exhibits unprecedented heterogeneity, encompassing

C. Wang, H. Tang, *Integrated Security and Safety of Intelligent Computing Networks*, https://doi.org/10.1007/978-981-95-5025-8_4

structured and unstructured data, multimodal sensory data, and cross domain knowledge, making unified modeling approaches less effective. On the other hand, data distributions become increasingly dynamic, with spatiotemporal fluctuations especially common in edge nodes, mobile terminals, or satellite devices, where uncertainty in data collection affects model robustness and stability. Furthermore, in multi-agent systems, disparities in agents' perception capabilities, data sources, and computational power result in local datasets of varying quality and a lack of global consistency, posing key challenges to collaborative data sharing and fusion. At the same time, increasing attention to data security and privacy calls for revisiting data plane mechanisms from the perspective of ensuring trust in data flows. Issues such as data leakage, model inference attacks, and reconstruction attacks are becoming more severe. In scenarios involving task collaboration or model sharing, ensuring controlled access, verifiable traceability, and privacy protection of data becomes essential to maintain the system's trustworthiness and resilience. For example, in federated learning, although raw data is not shared directly, adversaries can still infer user privacy through gradient leakage or inference attacks; in multi agent systems, the absence of effective audit mechanisms for data usage can lead to misuse, unauthorized access, or abuse. Therefore, establishing trustworthy computation and behavioral regulation mechanisms on the data plane is vital for the sustainable development of intelligent systems. Against this backdrop, the study of the data plane is expanding beyond traditional data ingestion and processing to a multidimensional co-design problem, involving key elements such as data acquisition and sensing, semantic modeling, fusion and augmentation, trusted sharing and protection, and dynamic lifecycle management. The representational and integrative capacity of data directly affects the expressiveness and generalization ability of upper layer learning algorithms; data quality control mechanisms influence model training stability and convergence speed; and traceability and compliance mechanisms provide the basis for interpretability, auditability, and regulatory use of algorithmic outcomes. Recently, increasing research attention has been directed toward data representation augmented with knowledge, heterogeneous multi-source data alignment, and distributed trustworthy data sharing mechanisms. For instance, combining graph neural networks (GNNs) with knowledge graphs (KGs) significantly enhances semantic modeling capabilities; computation techniques for privacy preservation such as differential privacy, homomorphic encryption, and trusted execution environments enable secure collaborative data use without revealing sensitive content; and data provenance frameworks utilizing blockchain technology support trusted cross domain data circulation and behavioral auditing.

As distributed computing systems scale in size and complexity, the data layer has become a central battleground for cybersecurity. In contrast to the algorithmic layer, which focuses on the behavior of processes and computations, the data layer is concerned with the integrity, confidentiality, availability, and traceability of the data itself, both at rest and in motion. With the proliferation of heterogeneous storage architectures, multi-source data fusion, and real-time analytics, ensuring the trustworthiness of data has become increasingly challenging [1–3]. Threats at the data layer are no longer limited to isolated breaches or leaks; they now include coordinated data tampering, metadata manipulation, unauthorized inference, poisoning of training datasets, and covert exfiltration across federated storage domains. These threats often act as the enablers or amplifiers of higher-level algorithmic or systemic vulnerabilities. Thus, securing the data layer is not only about protecting the data itself, but also about preserving the semantic foundation upon which algorithms operate and decisions are made.

In this context, a key characteristic of data-layer threats is their ability to silently propagate across systems through latent channels. A single compromised dataset may gradually contaminate data pipelines, distort analytics, trigger false alarms, or introduce bias into model outputs. The increasing use of data-driven AI, particularly in autonomous systems and critical infrastructure, magnifies the consequences of such manipulations [4]. For example, poisoning a training dataset used in predictive maintenance or autonomous driving systems can lead to catastrophic failures. Moreover, data lineage and provenance are often incomplete or insufficiently verified, making it difficult to audit or trace the root cause of anomalies. Effective defense at the data layer must therefore integrate data integrity verification, dynamic access control, context-aware encryption, and continuous data validation across the entire data lifecycle. At the same time, privacy preservation remains a critical issue, especially in shared or collaborative environments. Technologies such as differential privacy, federated data governance, and secure multi-party computation help mitigate inference and exposure risks, but their deployment must be aligned with evolving legal and ethical frameworks.

By mapping data security into an independent analytic layer, defenders can better observe, localize, and intervene upon data anomalies that precede or underlie broader system-level compromises. This architectural decoupling of the data layer allows for semantically rich threat modeling, where threats are analyzed not just in terms of binary leakage but also in terms of logical data transformation, inconsistency propagation, and semantic drift. Moreover, viewing security at the data layer opens new pathways for co-defense with algorithmic and system layers. For instance, defenders can integrate data integrity scores into algorithmic trust evaluations or use provenance data to modulate access control policies. As computing environments become more decentralized, dynamic, and heterogeneous, the security of the data layer must shift from passive protection to active enforcement, continuous monitoring, and adaptive governance. Thus, the data layer serves not only as a potential attack surface but also as a strategic vantage for early threat detection, comprehensive risk assessment, and precise control within next-generation security architectures.

4.1.1 Motivation

As data-driven systems continue to expand across all domains, including finance, healthcare, smart cities, and agriculture, data security has become one of the most critical concerns in the digital age. Yet despite the evolution of defensive technologies, modern data security still grapples with an expanding set of challenges stemming from technological, organizational, and regulatory dynamics. A primary challenge is the rapid growth of big data. As data volume, velocity, and variety increase, traditional security controls such as static perimeter defense and signature-based detection mechanisms struggle to scale accordingly [5]. The distributed nature of big data systems, such as Hadoop clusters and NoSQL databases, introduces additional vulnerabilities due to diverse entry points, heterogeneous environments, and decentralized access control.

Second, the proliferation of cloud computing complicates data security by externalizing data control. Organizations entrusting data to third-party infrastructure providers must rely on shared responsibility models, where providers ensure infrastructure security, while users must enforce data confidentiality, integrity, and access control [6]. This boundary ambiguity creates risks of misconfigured access rights, inadequate encryption, and insufficient audit trails. Public clouds are particularly vulnerable to side-channel attacks, VM escape, data leakage through multi-tenancy, and insider threats from service administrators [7].

Another increasingly significant issue is data privacy in smart environments. As smart cities, wearables, and the Internet of Things (IoT) generate continuous streams of sensitive data, maintaining user anonymity and preventing inference attacks becomes exceedingly difficult [8]. Many IoT devices are resource-constrained and lack built-in security capabilities, resulting in weak authentication, insecure communication, and unpatched firmware vulnerabilities [9]. Furthermore, data collected from physical environments such as biometric signals or GPS logs can be correlated to infer private behavioral patterns, even if anonymized.

Data provenance and integrity also represent crucial challenges. In collaborative and cloud-based data workflows, verifying the origin and verifying that data has not been tampered with is essential for trustworthiness. However, existing integrity verification schemes often impose computational overheads and fail to address partial data manipulation or rollback attacks [10]. Techniques such as proof-of-storage and homomorphic authentication remain areas of active research but have yet to see widespread deployment due to complexity and performance trade-offs.

Identity and access management (IAM) remains another complex issue. Poor credential hygiene, lack of multi-factor authentication (MFA), and over-privileged accounts continue to dominate as root causes of breaches [11]. Federated identity systems, while helpful for single sign-on (SSO), create their own vulnerabilities: compromise of an identity provider can cascade across many dependent systems. Fine-grained access control policies such as Attribute-Based Access Control (ABAC) and context-aware models are needed, but are challenging to implement and maintain in dynamic, scalable systems.

From a regulatory perspective, data security must also address compliance with increasingly strict data protection laws such as the General Data Protection Regulation (GDPR). Compliance is not merely technical but also organizational, requiring continuous auditing, logging, and data subject transparency [12]. Organizations often struggle with data classification, lifecycle management, and cross-border data transfer under these legal constraints.

Insider threats represent another non-technical but highly dangerous challenge. In contrast to external adversaries, insiders typically possess authorized access to data and systems, which makes their malicious activities more difficult to identify. Malicious insiders may intentionally exfiltrate data, while negligent insiders may mishandle sensitive information. Behavioral monitoring, separation of duties, and just-in-time privilege escalation are key to mitigating these threats, though they are often underutilized due to cost or organizational inertia [13].

Finally, the rise of ransomware and cryptographic attacks poses direct threats to data availability and confidentiality. Ransomware increasingly targets backup systems and networked storage, effectively paralyzing operations. Attackers also exploit cryptographic weaknesses or implementation flaws, such as poor key management, weak random number generation, and outdated algorithms like SHA-1. As quantum computing looms, there is growing pressure to migrate to post-quantum cryptographic schemes, though adoption remains slow [14].

In summary, elevating integrated security concerns to the data layer is not merely an architectural abstraction but a strategic imperative that reflects the semantic and operational centrality of data in modern computing systems. As the connective tissue across applications, algorithms, and infrastructures, the data layer provides a unique observational and enforcement surface for capturing, modeling, and mitigating security threats at their origin and propagation pathways. This layer-centric approach enables a unified framework for assessing data trustworthiness, detecting semantic inconsistencies, and enforcing dynamic, context-aware protections across decentralized and heterogeneous environments. Rather than serving as a passive storage medium, the data layer becomes an active security substrate. It embeds provenance, enforces policy constraints, and participates in collaborative defense logic alongside the algorithmic and systemic planes. The following sections of this chapter will explore representative data-layer threat scenarios in depth, exposing the latent risks that emerge from compromised datasets, tainted metadata, and uncontrolled data flows. Through these cases, we demonstrate how a data-centric security lens is not only indispensable for achieving resilience in distributed architectures but also foundational for designing transparent, verifiable, and adaptive security frameworks in next-generation computing environments.

4.1.2 Data Poisoning Attacks in Federated Data Environments

As federated architectures gain traction in domains like healthcare, finance, and autonomous systems, safeguarding data privacy and leveraging decentralized storage have emerged as essential aspects of contemporary computing. Federated data environments allow multiple clients to retain sensitive data locally while collaboratively contributing to shared machine learning models. Nevertheless, this decentralized framework gives rise to a new category of data-layer threats, particularly *data poisoning attacks*, in which adversaries deliberately inject tampered data into local datasets to degrade the global model's performance after aggregation [15].

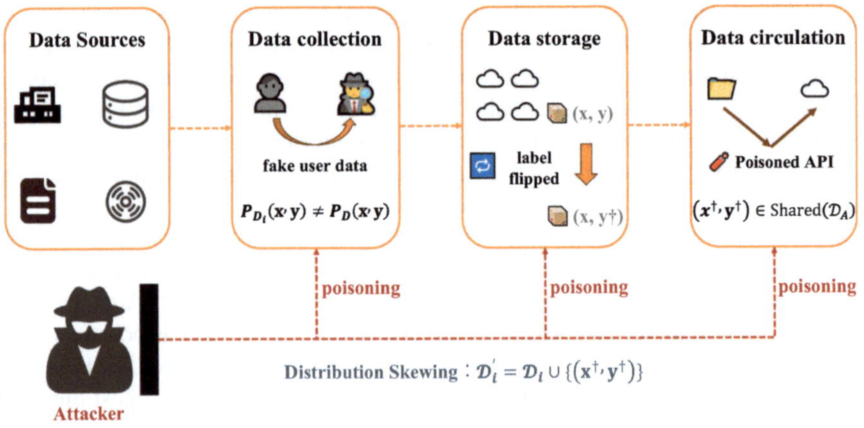

Fig. 4.1 Data poisoning attack diagram

In a federated data system, each participant or client retains complete control over its own local dataset and independently performs training tasks on that private data. After completing local training, only the resulting model updates, usually represented as gradients or weight deltas, are sent to a central aggregation server. This architecture, while enhancing privacy by avoiding raw data transmission, also creates a blind spot that attackers can exploit. In a data poisoning scenario, a malicious participant intentionally injects carefully crafted data points into its local training set with the aim of manipulating the learning process. These poisoned data instances are engineered to introduce targeted biases or disrupt general learning outcomes at the global level once the central server performs model aggregation.

As shown in Fig. 4.1, the poisoned inputs may superficially resemble normal data, exhibiting feature distributions and label relationships that conform to statistical norms. However, they are carefully embedded with adversarial semantics in the form of subtle correlations or mislabeled patterns that exert a disproportionate influence on the model's decision-making process. For example, a seemingly innocuous image or time-series sample may be labeled incorrectly in a way that gradually distorts the classifier's boundary between two classes. Over repeated rounds of aggregation, these distortions accumulate, leading the global model to internalize erroneous correlations.

One of the key dangers lies in the fact that these poisoned datasets are often designed to evade both local anomaly detection mechanisms and global statistical filters. Attackers can leverage knowledge of the target task, model architecture, or client data distribution to craft poison that blends in naturally yet still induces harmful generalization errors. Additionally, since the central server in federated learning has no access to raw data, it cannot verify the semantic integrity of the local training examples. As a result, the attack remains effectively invisible within most federated learning workflows.

Furthermore, in asynchronous federated systems where clients update at different rates or times, poisoned updates can be timed strategically to coincide with aggregation rounds that carry more weight in model convergence. The attacker may also dynamically adapt its data poisoning strategy based on previous global model behavior, thereby creating a feedback loop that both reinforces and conceals its impact. This makes it possible for even small-scale poisoning by a single client to produce significant cascading effects on the accuracy, robustness, or fairness of the global model.

Ultimately, this form of attack illustrates how vulnerabilities at the data layer, especially those related to the quality and intent behind training data, can directly undermine the trustworthiness of collaborative learning systems. It underscores the need for more robust data provenance tracking, trust scoring mechanisms, and localized validation even within architectures that are designed to preserve privacy.

The process of a data poisoning attack typically includes injecting harmful data into local datasets, initiating training over these corrupted datasets, and allowing malicious influence to propagate through model updates. Poisoning may manifest as mislabeling, data duplication, or insertion of adversarial examples. Since the central server never accesses the raw training data, these poisoned inputs remain unnoticed. More insidiously, some attackers may employ adaptive poisoning strategies that align poisoned data to the local statistical distribution, thereby making the attack even harder to detect as the federated rounds progress.

The following list highlights several common types of data poisoning attacks capable of undermining the integrity of federated systems:

- **Label-Flipping Attacks.** The attacker changes the labels of certain classes in the training set, subtly introducing misclassifications into the model. Over time, this biases the global model, especially when repeated across rounds [16].
- **Semantic Trigger Injection.** The attacker adds benign-looking patterns (e.g., background color or watermark) associated with incorrect labels, creating a data-level backdoor. When the trigger appears again, the model misbehaves, even though it performs normally otherwise [17].
- **Metadata Poisoning.** By altering timestamps, source IDs, or sensor origins, the attacker skews time-series data or trust metrics, leading to false predictions in downstream systems such as anomaly detectors or healthcare diagnostics [18].
- **Redundant Data Amplification.** Attackers duplicate poisoned data to boost its statistical weight during model training. While the model treats all samples equally, malicious inputs become overrepresented, distorting learned patterns and convergence behavior [19].
- **Noise-to-Signal Interference.** Some attackers inject synthetic noise or adversarial perturbations that overwhelm the true signal, forcing the model to generalize poorly or focus on spurious correlations [20].

Data poisoning attacks are particularly dangerous in federated environments due to several inherent properties. Privacy constraints prevent centralized validation; client-side heterogeneity creates wide variance in model updates; and Non-Independent and Identically Distributed (non-IID) data distributions make statistical anomaly detection ineffective. Attackers can operate stealthily by mimicking benign client behavior while gradually increasing the poisoning intensity across multiple training rounds.

Moreover, poisoning does not only affect predictive performance. It can also compromise fairness, cause model drift, and weaken overall trustworthiness. For example, a poisoning attack might disproportionately degrade accuracy for specific demographic groups by inserting biased data. In time-series models, poisoned entries can lead to long-term deviations from stable dynamics, resulting in dangerous misinterpretations in mission-critical systems such as smart grids or medical diagnostics.

The difficulty of defending against data poisoning lies in both technical and architectural limitations. Traditional data cleaning methods are infeasible when raw data is private. Cryptographic protections such as homomorphic encryption prevent inspection, and differential privacy techniques obscure training data distributions. Additionally, aggregation mechanisms like FedAvg treat all updates equally, so a single poisoned client can still bias the global model, even in a large client population.

To address these threats, several defense strategies have been proposed:

- **Reputation-Based Client Weighting.** Assign trust scores to clients based on historical consistency or behavioral audits. Clients with high variance or abnormal contributions can be down-weighted or excluded.
- **Robust Aggregation Protocols.** Replace FedAvg with aggregation rules such as Krum, Trimmed Mean, or Median, which reduce sensitivity to outliers.
- **Federated Data Fingerprinting.** Use cryptographic hashes or entropy metrics to track data lineage and detect duplicate or abnormal samples across rounds, even in encrypted or obfuscated environments.
- **Gradient Attribution for Anomaly Detection.** Monitor the functional impact of individual updates on global model behavior to identify and filter potentially malicious contributions.
- **Trigger Detection via Auxiliary Tasks.** Train auxiliary models to identify semantic patterns indicative of known backdoor or poisoned triggers, even without direct access to raw data.

Despite these measures, large-scale federated systems remain vulnerable due to their scale, asynchronous update patterns, and deployment across diverse domains. Advanced poisoning attacks may coordinate across multiple clients, adapt to evolving defenses, or exploit statistical masking. Moreover, detection methods must balance robustness with fairness, avoiding false positives that could penalize benign but diverse client populations.

In conclusion, data poisoning attacks at the data layer expose the fragile foundation upon which federated systems operate. By manipulating training data before the learning process begins, adversaries can introduce deeply embedded vulnerabilities without needing access to model internals. In contrast to algorithm-level manipulations, data-layer poisoning is often subtle, persistent, and tailored to specific domains. Future research must therefore combine technical mechanisms with systemic designs. Key capabilities such as auditability, provenance verification, and adaptive trust management must be embedded as foundational elements within federated data ecosystems. Without these safeguards, the goal of achieving privacy-preserving machine learning will remain exposed to critical risks from within.

4.1.3 Log Tampering and Audit-Evasion Attacks in Distributed Systems

In large-scale distributed computing environments such as enterprise platforms, financial services, e-government clouds, and containerized data centers, system logs and audit trails serve as foundational mechanisms for ensuring traceability, accountability, and forensic readiness. These logs record key operational events, including authentication requests, privilege escalations, file system interactions, network connections, and administrative actions. They are therefore essential not only for post-incident analysis but also for real-time anomaly detection, compliance auditing, and regulatory reporting. As systems increase in scale and complexity, however, the attack surface associated with data-layer log infrastructure has expanded considerably. One of the most dangerous forms of data-layer attack is the log tampering and audit-evasion attack, in which adversaries selectively alter, delete, fabricate, or reorder entries in system logs to conceal malicious activity, disrupt incident response workflows, or forge operational legitimacy.

As shown in Fig. 4.2, such attacks may be carried out by external threat actors who have compromised a system or by malicious insiders with administrative access. Once inside the system, the attacker typically begins by identifying centralized or distributed logging endpoints such as syslog servers, journald daemons,

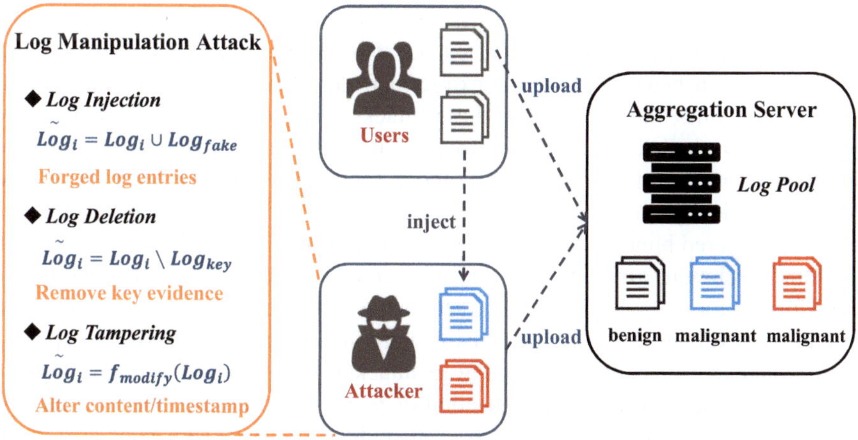

Fig. 4.2 Log tampering and audit-evasion attacks

Kubernetes logging sidecars, or cloud-native log shippers like Fluentd, Filebeat, or Logstash. These agents are responsible for collecting and forwarding logs to centralized storage, often via log pipelines (e.g., ELK Stack, Splunk, or Amazon CloudWatch). An attacker who gains control of these components can intercept, manipulate, or suppress logs either in transit or at rest. Tampering can occur at the operating system level, within the container runtime (e.g., altering container output streams), or through direct interference with logging APIs at the application layer.

One particularly stealthy method employed in audit-evasion attacks is selective log suppression, where the attacker deliberately removes or omits only the entries corresponding to critical actions such as privilege escalation, lateral movement, or data exfiltration, while leaving the remainder of the log stream untouched. This surgical precision allows the attacker to maintain a convincing continuity of system activity while silently erasing traces of intrusion. By preventing large-scale deletions or sudden gaps, this approach reduces the likelihood of detection by log monitoring systems that analyze statistical baselines like event frequency, message entropy, or source diversity. In some implementations, attackers use cron jobs, modified shell scripts, or post-execution hooks to automatically intercept and suppress specific log patterns in real time.

In more advanced cases, attackers may augment suppression with log injection, wherein they fabricate synthetic log entries that mimic legitimate operations. These forged records may be inserted before the missing entries, after them, or used to replace them entirely, thus creating a plausible narrative that satisfies superficial review or automated parsing. Forensic analysts relying on standard Security Information and Event Management (SIEM) tools may be misled into drawing incorrect timelines, associating false user activity with real identities, or overlooking lateral pivots that were silently executed under the cover of falsified audit trails. The effectiveness of this deception is further amplified in systems where log entries are not cryptographically signed or where source authentication is weak, making it difficult to distinguish genuine telemetry from tampered content.

The combination of selective omission and targeted fabrication not only undermines the reliability of digital forensics, but also disrupts adaptive security systems that depend on behavioral signals extracted from telemetry. Threat-hunting platforms may miss the subtlety of these attacks, especially if the injected noise conforms to statistical norms, reinforcing the need for integrity validation and semantic correlation across logs. Without robust cross-source verification and cryptographically anchored log integrity, even advanced security infrastructures may be rendered blind by these deceptively simple yet highly effective techniques.

Other techniques include log truncation attacks, where adversaries modify log rotation or storage policies to erase records beyond a certain threshold, and cross-node log divergence. In the latter case, logs in distributed systems are updated independently across nodes, which gives attackers an opportunity to alter logs on one node while ensuring that replication does not resynchronize them accurately. In systems that rely on database-backed audit trails, attackers may also compromise database integrity by injecting timestamped false events, modifying user session identifiers, or tampering with cryptographic hashes (if such mechanisms are deployed) that validate the authenticity of each entry. Especially in microservices-based architectures where each service maintains its own logs, inconsistencies in time clocks or event ID formats can be exploited to make falsified records appear temporally coherent.

The consequences of such tampering are significant. Beyond disrupting incident response and digital forensics, log manipulation can result in failure to meet compliance requirements under regulatory frameworks like HIPAA, SOX, FISMA, or GDPR, all of which demand provable auditability and data integrity. Furthermore, tampered logs may disable Security Information and Event Management (SIEM) systems by corrupting the event ingestion stream, rendering behavioral anomaly detection ineffective. In environments employing zero-trust architectures or behavior-based authentication, logs often serve as core telemetry; thus, forged or missing logs can subvert access decisions, causing legitimate users to be denied access while attackers remain undetected.

Multiple systemic factors contribute to the difficulty of defending against log tampering. First, logs are frequently stored in plaintext or structured text formats such as JSON, XML, or CSV, making them easily editable using basic tools. Second, logging infrastructures often prioritize performance and scalability over integrity and resilience, and lack cryptographic guarantees or tamper-evident structures. Third, many security analytics pipelines implicitly trust logs as ground truth, creating circular dependencies in detection logic. Fourth, cloud-native logging systems may span across different cloud regions or vendors, which complicates unified verification and makes it harder to preserve consistency in a global setting.

To mitigate these challenges, security researchers and system architects have proposed a range of countermeasures and architectural redesigns:

- **Immutable Log Stores.** Deploy append-only storage mechanisms using WORM (Write Once Read Many) file systems, blockchain-backed audit chains, or distributed hash chains to enforce non-repudiation and detect post-hoc tampering [21].
- **Cryptographic Entry Signing.** Sign each log entry at the point of creation using asymmetric keys, then verify these signatures during audit. This approach ensures that even if logs are copied or truncated, unauthorized modifications become detectable [22].
- **Trusted Time-Stamping.** Integrate secure clock services or third-party time authorities (e.g., RFC 3161-compliant servers) to anchor logs in tamper-resistant chronological sequences, making it more difficult to forge time-based evidence [23].
- **Cross-Domain Verification.** Use log mirroring and peer validation across data centers or service domains to detect discrepancies caused by localized manipulation [24].
- **Context-Aware Logging Agents.** Equip logging agents with behavioral baselines and anomaly scoring functions so they can self-diagnose suppression or log flow distortion, even before entries reach centralized servers [25].

- **Audit Log Separation of Duties.** Enforce strict role separation so that no administrator or process has both write-access to systems and alteration rights on the logs, reducing the insider threat vector [26].

From a design standpoint, resilient log architectures must assume that some degree of compromise is inevitable and focus on containing impact through redundancy, transparency, and strong chain-of-custody guarantees. Logging pipelines should not only record events but also provide independently verifiable metadata about entry integrity, transmission paths, and write provenance. In cloud-native environments, using policy-as-code and infrastructure-as-code models enables automated verification of logging configurations and alert coverage. Moreover, using hardware-based trusted execution environments (e.g., Intel SGX or ARM TrustZone) to isolate log-writing functions offers promising protection against in-host tampering.

In conclusion, log tampering and audit-evasion attacks demonstrate how compromises at the data layer can silently undermine security observability, delay breach detection, and corrupt digital evidence. Unlike algorithmic threats that alter system behavior or exploits that disrupt services, log manipulation compromises the meta-layer that underpins monitoring and trust. Therefore, securing logging infrastructures demands a shift from passive data collection to architectures that are actively verifiable, cryptographically anchored, and cross-validated. Only by treating logs as first-class security assets rather than mere operational byproducts can organizations preserve trustworthy visibility in the face of persistent and sophisticated adversaries.

4.2 Existing Methods and Limitations

The swift growth of data-centric architectures and distributed storage systems has greatly increased the scale and complexity of data security challenges. As sensitive information moves through various environments such as cloud storage, edge devices, and hybrid processing pipelines, it becomes more important than ever to assess how effective current data protection mechanisms are and to understand their limitations. As shown in Fig. 4.3, this section systematically reviews key methods in the data security domain, including encryption for data-at-rest and in-transit, access control and identity management, privacy-preserving computation, and secure storage and processing architectures. Particular emphasis is placed on their strengths and shortcomings in safeguarding data confidentiality, integrity, and availability across multi-tenant, dynamic, and adversarial contexts. By critically assessing these strategies from a data layer perspective, the section aims to uncover the structural and operational gaps that hinder comprehensive protection against evolving threats. This analysis contributes to identifying priority areas for improvement and guides the design of more adaptive and context-aware data security frameworks capable of enhancing defense depth in multi-layered system architectures.

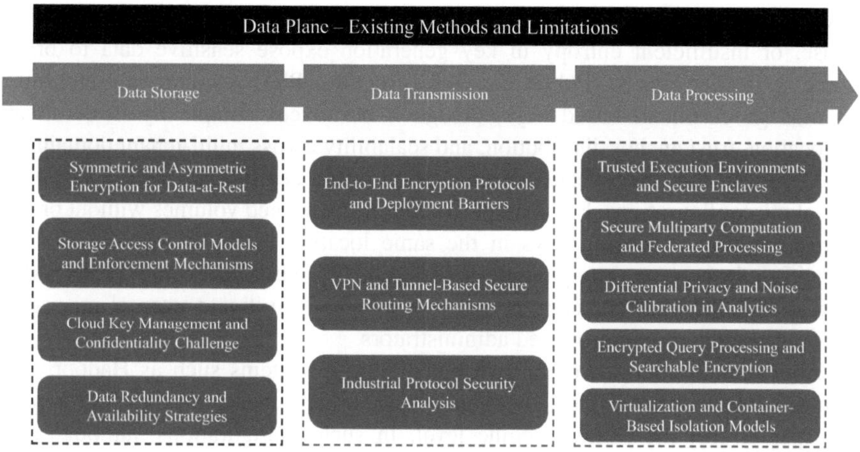

Fig. 4.3 Existing methods and limitations on data plane

4.2.1 Secure Data Storage: Mechanisms and Shortcomings

4.2.1.1 Symmetric and Asymmetric Encryption for Data-at-Rest

Ensuring the confidentiality of stored data is a fundamental aspect of data security, and encryption has long been the primary method for achieving this objective. Symmetric encryption schemes such as the Advanced Encryption Standard (AES) have been widely adopted to protect data-at-rest due to their computational efficiency, deterministic performance, and suitability for both local and cloud-based storage systems [27]. AES, with its support for 128, 192, and 256-bit key lengths, is integrated into numerous file-system-level encryption frameworks (e.g., BitLocker, LUKS) and storage middleware in both enterprise and consumer applications. These systems often perform block-level encryption on volumes or partitions, rendering raw data inaccessible without valid credentials and decryption keys.

In contrast, asymmetric encryption algorithms, most notably RSA and Elliptic Curve Cryptography (ECC), are primarily used for key encapsulation and access control rather than direct bulk data encryption due to their computational overhead. These schemes provide mechanisms for secure key exchange and digital signatures, enabling hierarchical key distribution and identity verification. ECC, in particular, has gained prominence in mobile and embedded environments because it achieves strong security with shorter key lengths and lower processing power [28]. Hybrid encryption systems have emerged as a practical approach, combining the efficiency of symmetric ciphers for data encryption with the robustness of asymmetric techniques for key exchange.

Despite the theoretical strength of encryption primitives, real-world deployments often exhibit significant weaknesses. One recurring challenge lies in key lifecycle management, especially regarding the secure generation, storage, distribution, and revocation of encryption keys. In many systems, hardcoded keys, improper key reuse, or insufficient entropy in key generation expose sensitive data to brute-force or insider attacks. Public Key Infrastructure (PKI) is commonly employed to manage certificate-based keys, though it introduces complexity in certificate revocation, trust anchor distribution, and scalability across multi-tenant domains.

Moreover, the effectiveness of encryption is frequently undermined by operational misconfigurations. For example, mounting encrypted volumes without proper access logging or storing keys in the same location as the encrypted data can invalidate the core security guarantees. Additionally, while encryption protects data at rest from external breaches, it does not inherently mitigate internal misuse by privileged users or compromised administrators.

Another limitation arises in distributed storage systems such as Hadoop Distributed File System (HDFS) or Amazon S3, where encryption is often applied transparently at the storage engine level. In such configurations, although data is encrypted on disk, intermediate stages like memory buffers or transmission paths may expose plaintext unless further protections are applied. Furthermore, multi-tenant environments require strict separation of encryption keys to prevent unauthorized cross-tenant data access, which adds complexity to key orchestration and audit compliance.

In summary, while symmetric and asymmetric encryption schemes provide foundational mechanisms for securing stored data, their effectiveness in practice depends heavily on key management frameworks, contextual integration with access control, and resilience against side-channel exposure. As storage infrastructures become increasingly distributed and virtualized, encryption mechanisms must evolve to offer granular, tenant-aware, and context-sensitive protections that go beyond the ciphertext alone.

4.2.1.2 Storage Access Control Models and Enforcement Mechanisms

Beyond encryption, access control serves as the second critical layer of defense in secure data storage by governing who can access specific data resources and under what conditions. Traditional access control models such as Discretionary Access Control (DAC), Mandatory Access Control (MAC), and Role-Based Access Control (RBAC) have long been used in file systems, database systems, and storage middleware to define and enforce user privileges [29]. DAC enables resource owners to grant permissions flexibly, while MAC applies strict system-level policies based on classification labels, and RBAC simplifies permission assignment by associating access rights with predefined roles.

RBAC remains widely adopted due to its administrative simplicity and alignment with organizational structures. However, its coarse granularity and static policy definitions often struggle to accommodate dynamic user contexts, especially in multi-tenant cloud environments and container-based storage systems. In contrast, Attribute-Based Access Control (ABAC) has emerged as a more expressive alternative, allowing decisions based on user attributes (e.g., department, clearance level), resource attributes (e.g., sensitivity, owner), and environmental conditions (e.g., time of access, device type) [30]. ABAC enables context-aware enforcement and fine-grained privilege management, making it suitable for dynamic and federated storage infrastructures.

Despite these advancements, enforcement mechanisms across different layers of the storage stack often remain disconnected. For instance, file-system-level access controls such as POSIX permissions or access control lists are rarely integrated with permissions defined at the database layer or within cloud APIs. This lack of integration results in fragmented policy definitions and creates gaps in enforcement. Moreover, configuration errors, excessive privileges, and policy conflicts are frequent sources of privilege escalation and data exposure. Privilege creep, where users accumulate unnecessary access over time, is especially prevalent in long-running enterprise systems and violates the principle of least privilege.

Another challenge lies in auditability and accountability. Many storage systems lack native support for fine-grained access logging, making it difficult to trace unauthorized data access or validate compliance. Furthermore, access control decisions are often opaque, and there is no standardized method for explaining why access was granted or denied. This lack of transparency complicates incident response and security audits, particularly in regulated industries where accountability is paramount.

To address these issues, researchers have proposed hybrid enforcement models that combine RBAC and ABAC, integrate policy-as-code frameworks, and leverage machine learning to detect anomalous access patterns. Some systems employ dynamic access control graphs or decision trees that enforce time-bounded or condition-based access rights. However, such models introduce complexity in policy specification, increase runtime decision latency, and often lack formal verification mechanisms.

In summary, access control in storage systems remains foundational but is constrained by fragmentation, over-permissiveness, and lack of contextual sensitivity. Future mechanisms must support unified, verifiable, and adaptive policy enforcement across heterogeneous storage platforms to effectively minimize insider threats, misconfigurations, and policy drift.

4.2.1.3 Integrity Verification and Anti-Tampering Mechanisms

In addition to confidentiality, maintaining the integrity and authenticity of stored data is essential for detecting unauthorized modifications and ensuring trustworthy data retrieval. Integrity verification mechanisms are particularly important in scenarios involving regulatory compliance, audit logging, digital forensics, and critical infrastructure data storage. A common approach is to compute cryptographic hash digests of files or data blocks using secure hash algorithms such as SHA-256 or SHA-3. These hashes are then stored alongside the data or in separate audit logs, allowing verification during retrieval or replication processes.

More advanced anti-tampering mechanisms leverage structured cryptographic constructs such as Merkle trees, where data blocks are recursively hashed and arranged in a tree structure with a root hash serving as a compact integrity proof. This design enables efficient verification of individual data chunks without reprocessing the entire dataset. Merkle trees have been widely adopted in blockchain systems and distributed storage frameworks for secure and scalable integrity checks. Similarly, append-only hash chains are used in secure logging systems to ensure the chronological integrity of audit records. When combined with digital signatures, these structures provide strong non-repudiation guarantees and resistance against rollback or reordering attacks.

In regulated environments such as finance and healthcare, tamper-evident logging systems often employ digitally signed log entries using RSA or ECDSA to meet compliance requirements for data accountability [31]. Trusted timestamping services based on RFC 3161 standards further strengthen the authenticity of recorded events by providing cryptographically verifiable time anchors. Some systems integrate Trusted Platform Modules (TPMs) or hardware security modules (HSMs) to perform secure signature generation and storage of verification keys.

More recently, blockchain-based integrity mechanisms have been explored to decentralize trust and eliminate single points of failure in integrity verification. By storing data hashes or proofs of existence on public or consortium blockchains, systems can achieve independent verifiability across organizational boundaries. Such mechanisms are particularly valuable in multi-party environments, such as supply chain tracking or inter-organizational document management. However, they introduce trade-offs in terms of write latency, scalability, and integration complexity.

Despite their effectiveness, integrity mechanisms face several challenges. First, hash-based methods are vulnerable to substitution attacks if verification keys or reference hashes are compromised. Second, the performance overhead of computing and verifying hashes can become significant for large-scale or high-throughput storage systems. Third, secure storage of integrity metadata itself remains a non-trivial problem, especially in cloud environments where attackers may have lateral movement capabilities. Moreover, real-time detection of integrity violations is often lacking, leading to delayed incident response.

In summary, while cryptographic integrity verification mechanisms provide powerful defenses against data tampering, their practical deployment requires careful key management, secure metadata handling, and integration with monitoring and alerting frameworks. Emerging techniques such as blockchain anchoring and secure enclaves offer promising directions, but further research is needed to balance assurance guarantees with scalability and system performance.

4.2.1.4 Cloud Key Management and Confidentiality Challenges

In cloud-centric environments, ensuring the confidentiality of data-at-rest fundamentally relies on secure key management systems (KMS) that handle the generation, storage, distribution, rotation, and revocation of encryption keys. As enterprises increasingly adopt cloud-native storage solutions such as Amazon S3, Azure Blob Storage, and Google Cloud Storage, data security becomes contingent not just on the strength of encryption algorithms but on the integrity and trustworthiness of the underlying key management infrastructure.

Cloud providers typically offer integrated Key Management Services that support Customer-Managed Keys (CMKs), enabling users to maintain partial control over their encryption lifecycle. These CMKs are either generated within the provider's infrastructure or imported via Bring Your Own Key (BYOK) models. Advanced offerings extend this to Hold Your Own Key (HYOK) and External Key Management (EKM), which allow encryption keys to be managed entirely outside the provider's domain via Hardware Security Modules (HSMs) or on-premises vaults. These mechanisms aim to establish trust boundaries that separate data residency from cryptographic control, thereby reducing reliance on the cloud provider as a sole authority for trust.

Despite this evolution, several confidentiality challenges persist. First, the practical enforcement of trust separation is limited by the need for integration between storage services and the KMS, often exposing metadata or key usage patterns to the provider [32]. Second, in multi-tenant environments, the failure to logically isolate keys across customers can lead to cross-tenant data exposure, particularly in cases involving misconfiguration or improper API use. Moreover, reliance on audit trails that are fully controlled by the provider and the lack of transparency into backend key usage hinder independent verification and detection of misuse.

Another significant concern is key lifecycle automation. While automatic key rotation is supported by most KMS platforms, the revocation process typically lacks immediacy. Data encrypted with compromised keys may continue to be accessible unless proactively re-encrypted. This delay introduces persistent threats in the event of key leakage. In high-assurance domains such as healthcare and finance, strict requirements regarding revocation speed and guarantees of key deletion are challenging to meet with standard cloud setups.

Furthermore, hybrid and multi-cloud architectures introduce additional complexity, requiring synchronized key governance across different cloud environments. Achieving secure key replication, consistent access control, and unified policy enforcement across domains is highly non-trivial. Organizations must navigate the trade-off between operational convenience and retaining full cryptographic control, which often results in fragmented key management or unnecessary duplication across platforms.

When metadata is insufficiently isolated from encrypted data, attackers with partial access may infer structural patterns or launch chosen ciphertext attacks. Finally, key access APIs can become potential attack surfaces if not adequately protected through rate-limiting, comprehensive logging, or finely scoped access policies.

In conclusion, cloud key management remains one of the most critical yet challenging components of secure data storage. While modern KMS frameworks provide flexible options for control and integration, true confidentiality depends on rigorous trust partitioning, robust policy enforcement, real-time auditability, and secure metadata handling. As storage ecosystems become more distributed and federated, the development of interoperable and verifiable key management protocols will be essential to maintaining data privacy across heterogeneous infrastructures.

4.2.1.5 Data Redundancy and Availability Strategies

Ensuring data availability under failure conditions, whether caused by hardware faults, software crashes, or malicious attacks, is a critical objective of secure storage systems. To achieve this, redundancy strategies such as data replication, erasure coding, and geo-distributed storage have been widely adopted in both centralized data centers and distributed cloud architectures. These techniques aim to preserve data accessibility and integrity even in the face of node failures, network partitions, or targeted denial-of-service attacks.

The most basic and commonly used method is full data replication, where identical copies of data are stored across multiple physical or logical storage nodes. Systems such as HDFS and Ceph utilize configurable replication factors (typically three) to strike a balance between fault tolerance and storage overhead. Replication enables fast recovery and supports eventual consistency models, making it suitable for high-throughput environments. However, when replication is poorly coordinated or excessive, it can result in data inconsistencies, stale reads, and an increased attack surface, particularly in cases where access control or update policies are not consistently enforced across replicas.

To address the storage inefficiency of replication, many systems adopt erasure coding schemes, such as Reed-Solomon or LDPC codes, which divide data into segments and generate parity blocks for reconstruction [33]. For example, in a (k, n) coding scheme, original data is split into k fragments and encoded into n total fragments, from which any k are sufficient to recover the original. This method offers better storage utilization and higher resilience to multiple simultaneous failures, as implemented in modern storage platforms like Facebook's f4 or Azure's LRC-based architecture. Nevertheless, erasure coding introduces latency and computational overhead during encoding, decoding, and repair operations, which can be problematic for latency-sensitive applications.

Geo-redundant storage extends the redundancy model across geographically distributed data centers, enabling disaster recovery in case of regional outages or site-level attacks. Cloud platforms such as AWS S3 (via Cross-Region Replication) and Azure Geo-Redundant Storage (GRS) provide such capabilities by synchronizing encrypted data across continents. While these approaches are effective in countering large-scale disruptions and natural disasters, they also raise concerns related to data sovereignty, regulatory compliance, and privacy, especially when sensitive information is transmitted across jurisdictions without explicit user control.

From a security perspective, redundancy mechanisms must ensure not only availability but also confidentiality and integrity. If replication channels are left unsecured, or if snapshots are misconfigured, sensitive data may be exposed. Furthermore, if access policies are not uniformly enforced across all replicas, unauthorized access may occur without detection. Additionally, during repair procedures for corrupted fragments, reliance on shared caches or untrusted nodes may introduce risks of data pollution or injection of malicious data.

Another often-overlooked challenge is the integration of redundancy with access control and auditability. In systems with distributed data copies, performing forensic analysis or tracking data lineage becomes increasingly complex. This difficulty is exacerbated when access logs or modification timestamps are not properly synchronized. Malicious actors may exploit these inconsistencies and delays in replication to conceal unauthorized changes or evade detection.

In conclusion, while redundancy mechanisms are indispensable for achieving resilient and highly available storage, they must be carefully integrated with encryption, access control, and audit systems to prevent compromising data security. Future storage architectures should aim for coordinated redundancy frameworks that enforce consistent policy replication, secure repair pipelines, and verifiable data integrity across all replicas.

4.2.2 Secure Data Transmission: Protocols and Exposure Risks

4.2.2.1 End-to-End Encryption Protocols and Deployment Barriers

End-to-end encryption (E2EE) protocols are fundamental for secure data communication, ensuring that information remains confidential from sender to recipient, even if intermediary systems are compromised. Protocols such as Transport Layer Security (TLS), Secure Shell (SSH), and end-to-end messaging schemes like the Signal Protocol offer robust guarantees of confidentiality, integrity, and mutual authentication. In particular, TLS 1.3, the most recent version of the protocol suite, incorporates forward secrecy by default and significantly reduces handshake latency, improving both security and performance in web and cloud communications [28].

TLS is widely deployed across HTTPS, SMTP, database connections, and internal microservice APIs. It employs a combination of asymmetric encryption for initial key exchange and symmetric encryption (usually AES or ChaCha20) for bulk data transfer, ensuring efficiency while maintaining strong protection. Additionally, the handshake phase incorporates certificate-based authentication, typically relying on the X.509 public key infrastructure to validate the server identity and optionally the client.

Despite their cryptographic robustness, end-to-end encryption protocols face substantial deployment challenges in practice. First, incorrect or outdated implementations introduce vulnerabilities such as insecure cipher suites, improper certificate validation, and susceptibility to downgrade or renegotiation attacks. The Heartbleed bug in OpenSSL and BEAST/POODLE attacks in earlier versions of SSL/TLS exemplify the risks associated with protocol misuse and backward compatibility.

Second, certificate lifecycle management, which encompasses issuance, revocation, renewal, and distribution, remains a persistent operational burden, especially in environments with high service churn or limited automation. Although services like Let's Encrypt and the ACME protocol have improved automation, many organizations still suffer from expired or misconfigured certificates, leading to connection failures or trust warnings.

Third, E2EE can impede traffic inspection and anomaly detection tools used in enterprise environments. Since data is encrypted from endpoint to endpoint, intrusion detection systems (IDS) and data loss prevention (DLP) tools that rely on payload inspection are rendered ineffective unless proxy decryption or out-of-band monitoring techniques are employed. This creates a trade-off between privacy and visibility, which often forces organizations to implement policy exceptions or configure selective decryption zones to restore observability.

In federated or multi-tenant cloud environments, managing trust relationships and certificate hierarchies across administrative domains poses an additional challenge. Mutual TLS (mTLS), which enforces two-way authentication between services, is increasingly adopted in service mesh architectures such as Istio and Linkerd. However, this approach introduces configuration complexity and performance overhead. In addition, when certificate authorities or trust anchors are shared across services, they may become central points of failure unless properly monitored and rotated.

Resource-constrained environments, including IoT devices and embedded controllers, often lack the computational or memory capacity to fully implement TLS stacks. As a result, lightweight variants such as TLS-PSK or DTLS are adopted. These variants, however, frequently trade off flexibility or compatibility and are more prone to misconfiguration.

In conclusion, end-to-end encryption protocols provide a strong theoretical foundation for secure transmission, but their practical efficacy is constrained by configuration complexity, operational scalability, and compatibility with security monitoring infrastructure. Robust certificate automation, secure protocol configurations, and E2EE-aware anomaly detection tools are essential to realizing the full benefits of encrypted communication in modern systems.

4.2.2.2 VPN and Tunnel-Based Secure Routing Mechanisms

Virtual Private Networks (VPNs) and secure tunneling protocols play a pivotal role in protecting data transmission across untrusted or public networks. These mechanisms establish encrypted communication tunnels that encapsulate all traffic between two or more endpoints, effectively creating a logical overlay network that ensures data confidentiality, integrity, and authentication. Common VPN protocols include Internet Protocol Security (IPSec), OpenVPN, and the newer WireGuard protocol. These protocols differ in their performance characteristics, cryptographic choices, and deployment complexity.

IPSec operates at the network layer and supports both transport and tunnel modes, allowing it to secure end-to-end or gateway-to-gateway communication. It is frequently used in enterprise virtual private infrastructures, site-to-site connections, and secure access to corporate intranets. IPSec relies on the Internet Key Exchange (IKE) protocol to negotiate cryptographic parameters and authenticate peers, supporting algorithms such as AES, SHA-2, and Diffie-Hellman key exchange. Despite its flexibility and standardization, IPSec is often criticized for its configuration complexity, reliance on static security policies, and susceptibility to misconfiguration.

OpenVPN, which operates in user space and uses SSL/TLS for session initiation, has become a widely adopted open-source alternative. Its support for a wide range of encryption algorithms and ease of deployment across platforms make it suitable for client-server VPNs. However, its performance can be limited due to the overhead introduced by user-space packet processing and the absence of kernel-level acceleration.

WireGuard represents a modern alternative that emphasizes simplicity, cryptographic agility, and performance. Its concise codebase and kernel integration in Linux enable low-latency, high-throughput communication. This makes it increasingly attractive for containerized and microservice architectures. Nonetheless, its minimalist design does not include built-in support for dynamic IP addressing or complex policy routing, both of which require external management.

In multi-tenant and hybrid cloud environments, tunneling protocols are essential for securely connecting isolated virtual networks or Kubernetes clusters. Cloud-native VPN gateways and software-defined perimeters (SDPs) implement tunneling as part of identity-aware access control. Although these systems enhance logical segmentation and policy enforcement, they often depend on shared control planes and centralized orchestration services. A compromised orchestration layer or misconfigured routing policies can therefore result in cross-tenant data leakage, route hijacking, or unauthorized lateral movement.

Another critical issue is tunnel endpoint authentication. Many VPN implementations rely on pre-shared keys (PSKs) or X.509 certificates to authenticate peers. Weak key rotation practices, reuse of shared credentials, or failure to renew certificates in time can degrade tunnel security and introduce systemic vulnerabilities. In addition, when VPN tunnels are misconfigured, they may bypass local network controls, expose internal interfaces, or create unintended access paths for persistent adversaries. Attackers sometimes exploit split tunneling configurations, where only a portion of the traffic is routed through the VPN, to exfiltrate data without detection.

Encrypted tunnels can also reduce traffic visibility and complicate threat detection. Security operations teams often face challenges in inspecting tunneled traffic for malicious content or unauthorized activity unless the encryption is terminated at designated inspection points. This underscores the need for VPN-aware monitoring tools and traffic analysis techniques that can detect anomalies using metadata, timing patterns, or flow behavior instead of relying solely on payload content.

In conclusion, VPN and tunneling mechanisms provide robust transport-layer security for a wide range of use cases. However, their effectiveness depends heavily on correct configuration, credential hygiene, and integration with higher-layer security controls. As modern networks become increasingly dynamic and distributed, tunnel orchestration, endpoint posture assessment, and policy-aware routing will be essential to maintaining secure and efficient encrypted communication channels.

4.2.2.3 Industrial Protocol Security Analysis

The rapid expansion of the Internet of Things (IoT) and industrial control systems (ICS) has introduced a vast array of communication protocols that operate over constrained devices and real-time networks. Unlike traditional IT protocols, many IoT and industrial protocols were designed with a focus on performance, interoperability, and simplicity, often at the cost of omitting built-in security features. As a result, the data transmitted using these protocols is frequently vulnerable to eavesdropping, spoofing, and manipulation, posing significant risks to system integrity and operational safety.

Common lightweight communication protocols used in IoT environments include Message Queuing Telemetry Transport (MQTT), Constrained Application Protocol (CoAP), and Advanced Message Queuing Protocol (AMQP). MQTT is a lightweight publish-subscribe protocol tailored for networks with limited bandwidth and high latency, commonly applied in sensor networks and smart home applications. However, many MQTT deployments lack encryption, rely on plaintext credentials, or operate without mutual authentication between clients and brokers. These configurations make it easy for attackers to perform session hijacking, inject fake telemetry data, or impersonate legitimate devices.

Similarly, CoAP is designed for constrained nodes using UDP and offers features similar to HTTP. Nevertheless, it suffers from limited security capabilities in its default configuration. Although CoAP supports DTLS for securing communication, the overhead and complexity of certificate management often lead to its omission in practical deployments. This leaves devices vulnerable to packet sniffing, replay attacks, and command injection. In mesh-based sensor networks, compromised CoAP nodes may propagate spoofed control messages or act as relay points for man-in-the-middle (MITM) attacks.

In the industrial domain, protocols such as Modbus, DNP3, and OPC-UA are used for supervisory control and data acquisition (SCADA) systems. Modbus, one of the most widely deployed ICS protocols, transmits commands and telemetry in plaintext with no built-in authentication or encryption. This makes it trivial for attackers to issue unauthorized control instructions or manipulate sensor readings. Although more secure variants such as Modbus TCP with TLS have been developed, legacy deployments remain prevalent, particularly in sectors such as energy, water, and manufacturing. DNP3 enhances reliability and redundancy but still lacks strong security unless paired with additional protective layers like Secure DNP3. OPC-UA introduces an object-oriented model and supports encryption, signatures, and session-based access control. However, its complexity and configuration burden have hindered widespread secure adoption.

The common challenge across IoT and ICS protocols lies in the heterogeneity and resource constraints of the participating devices. Many edge devices lack the memory, CPU power, or secure storage necessary to support TLS/DTLS, certificate parsing, or key rotation. Vendors often disable security features by default to minimize costs or streamline deployment. Moreover, inconsistent firmware update mechanisms and hardcoded credentials exacerbate long-term vulnerabilities. Attackers may exploit these weaknesses to infiltrate networks, maintain persistence, or stage large-scale distributed denial-of-service (DDoS) attacks, as demonstrated in incidents involving the Mirai and Triton malware.

To mitigate these risks, researchers have proposed lightweight security frameworks tailored to constrained environments. These include DTLS variants that use pre-shared keys, identity-based encryption schemes, and protocol-aware firewalls that enforce semantic constraints on message contents. Some platforms use physical unclonable functions (PUFs) to generate device-specific cryptographic keys without depending on secure storage. Additionally, anomaly detection systems that analyze protocol behavior, such as the frequency of Modbus commands or patterns in CoAP requests, have been implemented at gateways or edge servers to identify abnormal traffic that may signal a security compromise.

In summary, while IoT and industrial protocols enable scalable and low-latency data exchange, their inherent design limitations pose significant transmission security challenges. Addressing these issues requires protocol redesign, enhancement of device-level security, and infrastructure-wide integration of authentication, encryption, and anomaly detection. Without these improvements, critical infrastructure systems will remain exposed to manipulation and disruption through insecure data transmission channels.

4.2.3 Secure Data Processing: Isolation, Computation and Privacy Challenges

4.2.3.1 Trusted Execution Environments (TEEs) and Secure Enclaves

Trusted Execution Environments (TEEs) represent a critical class of hardware-based technologies designed to ensure secure and isolated execution of code and data, particularly in untrusted or multi-tenant environments. A TEE establishes a secure enclave inside the main processor, providing guarantees of confidentiality and integrity for computations despite potential compromise of the underlying OS or hypervisor. Prominent implementations include Intel's Software Guard Extensions (SGX), AMD's Secure Encrypted Virtualization (SEV), and ARM's TrustZone architecture [34].

Trusted Execution Environments (TEEs) play a crucial role in situations where sensitive data, such as encryption keys, biometric identifiers, or machine learning models, needs to be processed securely while remaining isolated from the broader software stack. In cloud computing, TEEs are employed to enable "confidential computing," wherein virtual machines or containerized workloads operate within hardware-backed enclaves that resist external inspection or tampering. These environments ensure that data is decrypted and processed only within the enclave boundary, shielding it from privileged users, host OS services, and hypervisor-level threats.

Intel SGX, for example, allows applications to allocate protected memory regions (enclaves) with strict access controls enforced by the CPU. It supports remote attestation, enabling external parties to verify the enclave's integrity before transmitting sensitive inputs. SGX has been integrated into privacy-preserving applications such as secure databases, federated learning frameworks, and blockchain validators. AMD SEV, by contrast, encrypts entire virtual machine memory with unique keys, providing a broader protection surface but without per-application enclave control.

Despite their promise, TEEs face significant limitations. First, their trusted computing base (TCB) often includes complex microcode and cryptographic logic, which has proven vulnerable to side-channel attacks. SGX, in particular, has been repeatedly compromised via cache timing attacks, speculative execution (e.g., Foreshadow), and page-fault-based leakage. These attacks exploit observable physical or architectural side effects to infer secrets from enclave memory, challenging the foundational isolation assumptions.

Second, TEEs require application developers to rewrite or partition code to fit within enclave constraints, introducing complexity and limiting portability. SGX enclaves are size-limited (typically under 128 MB), and enclave code must be statically linked, leading to limited dynamic behavior. Furthermore, the lack of standard APIs across TEE implementations hinders widespread adoption.

Third, remote attestation protocols, while essential for verifying the integrity of enclaves, depend on certificate hierarchies and proprietary attestation services such as the Intel Attestation Service, which introduces centralized trust bottlenecks. If attestation services are unavailable or misconfigured, remote parties cannot establish trust in enclave behavior, undermining the entire security model.

Finally, TEEs do not inherently solve data availability or access control problems. While they protect data during execution, they must rely on external systems for secure input/output handling, key provisioning, and policy enforcement. If the surrounding infrastructure is compromised, the overall system may still be subject to denial-of-service, rollback, or privilege abuse attacks.

In summary, TEEs and secure enclaves provide strong guarantees for isolated execution and confidentiality during processing. However, practical deployments must carefully address their hardware limitations, side-channel risks, and integration dependencies. As trusted execution becomes a cornerstone of secure data processing, the development of standardized APIs, cross-vendor compatibility, and hardware-hardened countermeasures will be crucial to realizing their full potential.

4.2.3.2 Secure Multiparty Computation and Federated Processing

Secure Multiparty Computation (SMPC) and federated processing frameworks have become essential techniques for enabling privacy-preserving data analytics and model training in decentralized environments. Unlike traditional centralized processing, which requires raw data to be aggregated in a single location, these methods aim to perform collaborative computations directly over distributed data while preserving confidentiality.

In SMPC, several participants collaboratively evaluate a function on their private data while keeping those inputs hidden from one another. This is achieved through cryptographic primitives such as secret sharing (e.g., Shamir's scheme), oblivious transfer, and garbled circuits. For example, in privacy-preserving data mining, SMPC allows multiple hospitals to compute disease statistics without exposing patient records, or financial institutions to jointly detect fraud patterns without disclosing client transactions. The protocol ensures correctness and privacy even when participants do not fully trust each other, making it well-suited for sensitive multi-institution collaborations.

Federated Learning (FL), as a specific instance of federated processing, enables decentralized model training across user devices, while ensuring that only model updates are shared with a central coordinator instead of the underlying raw data. This significantly reduces privacy risks and regulatory burdens, as personal data never leaves the originating device. Techniques such as secure aggregation and differential privacy are frequently combined with FL to ensure that model updates remain unlinkable to individual contributors. Applications include mobile keyboard prediction, wearable health monitoring, and industrial predictive maintenance.

Despite their promise, both SMPC and federated frameworks face fundamental limitations that affect their scalability, security guarantees, and practical adoption. First, SMPC protocols often incur high communication and computation overhead, especially when scaling to large datasets or complex computations. For example, garbled circuits require quadratic communication relative to circuit size, while secret-sharing schemes suffer from bandwidth blowup and coordination challenges. These overheads are particularly pronounced in real-time or resource-constrained environments such as edge computing or IoT systems.

Second, federated systems rely on partially trusted aggregation servers, which are vulnerable to poisoning attacks. Malicious clients can inject model updates crafted to degrade model performance (data poisoning) or implant backdoors. Since the server lacks access to the underlying training data, it is difficult to validate the integrity of received updates. This has spurred research into robust aggregation mechanisms, Byzantine-resilient protocols, and client behavior auditing, but these defenses remain an active research frontier.

Third, SMPC and federated learning do not inherently provide protection against inference attacks on the final output. For instance, an adversary can query a trained model repeatedly and infer whether certain data points were part of the training set (membership inference) or reconstruct sensitive attributes (model inversion).

Without additional safeguards such as differential privacy or query regulation, the models trained through privacy-preserving computation can still leak information.

Fourth, the deployment of these systems introduces key management and trust setup challenges. SMPC protocols often assume an honest-majority model or require a trusted dealer for key distribution, while federated learning depends on secure initialization, version control, and device authentication. In adversarial environments, these dependencies can become points of failure.

Finally, interoperability and standardization remain unresolved issues. There is no widely adopted protocol suite or middleware that supports seamless integration of SMPC or federated techniques across heterogeneous systems. Differences in data schema, computation models, and cryptographic assumptions often necessitate bespoke implementations, limiting deployment agility and increasing maintenance costs.

In conclusion, SMPC and federated processing provide powerful frameworks for privacy-preserving data computation, enabling secure collaboration across untrusted parties and distributed infrastructures. However, addressing their performance bottlenecks, attack resilience, and operational complexity is critical to unlocking their full potential in practical deployments.

4.2.3.3 Differential Privacy and Noise Calibration in Analytics

Differential Privacy (DP) has emerged as a fundamental paradigm in contemporary data protection, providing rigorous mathematical guarantees that individual records remain indistinguishable, even in the presence of strong inference attacks. In contrast to classical anonymization methods such as k-anonymity and l-diversity, which rely on identifier suppression or generalization, DP introduces randomness into the outputs of computations to mask the contribution of any single record. This mechanism ensures that adversaries, even with auxiliary knowledge, cannot confidently infer whether a particular individual's data was included in the dataset.

Formally, a randomized algorithm $\mathscr{A}$ is said to satisfy ε-differential privacy if, for every pair of neighboring datasets D_1 and D_2 that differ in exactly one element, and for all measurable subsets of outputs S:

$$\Pr[\mathscr{A}(D_1) \in S] \leq e^{\varepsilon} \cdot \Pr[\mathscr{A}(D_2) \in S]. \tag{4.1}$$

Here, ε is the privacy budget that quantifies the allowed privacy loss; smaller values indicate stronger privacy guarantees. The injected noise is typically calibrated to the sensitivity of the query function, using mechanisms such as Laplace or Gaussian perturbation.

DP has been successfully deployed in several high-profile systems [35]. For instance, Apple applies local differential privacy (LDP) to collect usage statistics on iOS devices without accessing raw user data, while Google's RAPPOR system aggregates telemetry data securely using randomized responses. The U.S. Census

Bureau adopted DP for its 2020 census data release, prioritizing formal privacy guarantees over traditional confidentiality techniques.

However, the deployment of DP is not without limitations. First, DP inherently balances privacy and utility, as adding too much noise can significantly reduce analytical accuracy, especially for small populations or sparse data. Designing query mechanisms that preserve utility while satisfying strict ε-bounds requires careful tuning and often domain-specific customization.

Second, the composability of differential privacy, which refers to how privacy losses accumulate across multiple queries, poses challenges in interactive or iterative settings such as machine learning. Each query depletes a portion of the overall privacy budget, and without a global management strategy, cumulative queries can quickly exhaust the allowed ε, leading to either degraded privacy or restricted analytics. Solutions such as privacy accounting, advanced composition theorems, and moment-based bounds attempt to mitigate this effect, but they introduce additional complexity.

Third, the choice of ε remains non-trivial in practice. There is no universally accepted standard for what constitutes an acceptable ε value, leading to inconsistent implementations. Some systems adopt values as small as 0.1, while others use $\varepsilon > 10$, which significantly weakens privacy protections. The interpretation of ε is also difficult to communicate to non-technical stakeholders, hampering informed consent and transparency.

Fourth, DP requires a clear definition of the privacy unit (e.g., an individual, a session, or a device) and appropriate dataset boundaries. Misdefining the unit of protection can undermine privacy guarantees. For example, if multiple correlated entries from the same individual are treated as independent, the actual privacy loss could be much greater than expected.

Fifth, integrating DP into legacy data pipelines and real-time systems poses practical difficulties. Existing analytics platforms are often not designed with DP constraints in mind, requiring major redesigns to ensure that noise injection does not disrupt downstream tasks or user expectations. In time-sensitive applications such as fraud detection or system diagnostics, the latency introduced by DP mechanisms can be prohibitive.

Finally, while local DP enhances user control by perturbing data at the source, it reduces statistical efficiency and demands larger populations to obtain meaningful aggregates. The noise amplification effect can hinder the feasibility of small-scale deployments or niche applications.

In summary, differential privacy offers a rigorous framework for balancing data utility with privacy preservation, making it a valuable component of the data security toolkit. Yet, its practical realization requires careful calibration, governance, and system-wide coordination to ensure that its theoretical strengths translate into effective protection in diverse real-world environments.

4.2.3.4 Encrypted Query Processing and Searchable Encryption

In the era of data outsourcing and cloud-based analytics, ensuring the confidentiality of user data during computation is essential. A major line of work focuses on encrypted query processing, allowing computations over encrypted data while keeping the plaintext hidden from the server. This capability is crucial for secure data processing in untrusted environments where both storage and computation are delegated to external parties. Prominent cryptographic techniques supporting this functionality include Searchable Encryption (SE), Homomorphic Encryption (HE), and Oblivious RAM (ORAM).

Searchable Encryption (SE) is a practical approach that allows keyword searches over encrypted documents. Symmetric SE schemes are efficient and suitable for personal storage scenarios, whereas public-key SE schemes allow for more flexible delegation in multi-user environments. A typical SE setup involves a client encrypting documents along with associated encrypted indexes. These indexes are uploaded to the cloud, enabling the server to process encrypted queries using trapdoors generated by the client. While SE schemes such as those introduced by Curtmola et al. and Cash et al. are efficient and support ranked search and Boolean queries, they often leak access and search patterns unless combined with more sophisticated techniques.

Pattern leakage is a significant limitation of most SE systems. Even without plaintext access, adversaries can infer sensitive information by analyzing repeated search queries or document access patterns. This vulnerability has led to attacks that exploit co-occurrence frequency and statistical correlation to recover keywords. In response, recent studies have investigated leakage-resilient SE or integrated SE with Private Information Retrieval (PIR), though these approaches often introduce higher computational overhead.

Fully Homomorphic Encryption (FHE), first proposed in a practical construction by Gentry in 2009, supports arbitrary computations over encrypted data. FHE schemes allow clients to offload data processing to untrusted servers without ever decrypting the data, preserving end-to-end confidentiality. While theoretically powerful, FHE remains computationally expensive due to the noise growth in ciphertexts and the need for bootstrapping to refresh ciphertexts after multiple operations. Despite advancements in optimization, fully homomorphic encryption (FHE) is often applied in hybrid forms, such as partially homomorphic encryption (PHE) that supports only addition or multiplication, for targeted applications like encrypted voting or secure financial computations.

Searchable Homomorphic Encryption (SHE) attempts to combine the strengths of SE and HE, supporting limited keyword search along with specific computations. These schemes offer intermediate trade-offs between expressiveness and performance, but are still far from deployment in latency-sensitive scenarios.

Another approach is Oblivious RAM (ORAM), which hides access patterns by shuffling memory locations and accessing random dummy blocks during reads/writes. ORAM enables generic protection of memory access in outsourced computation but introduces substantial overhead due to data reshuffling and communication rounds. Techniques such as Path ORAM and Ring ORAM improve efficiency but still struggle with scalability in large-scale cloud environments.

The practicality of encrypted query processing also depends heavily on the query type. For instance, exact match and range queries can be supported via order-preserving encryption (OPE), but these schemes inherently leak order information. Property-preserving encryption (PPE) schemes such as deterministic encryption also leak equality patterns and are thus discouraged in adversarial settings.

Implementation challenges are nontrivial. Encrypted queries must be generated securely by clients and evaluated correctly by servers, which requires tight synchronization of key management and query transformation logic. Moreover, the integration of SE or HE into existing database systems requires significant architectural changes, particularly in indexing, caching, and query optimization layers.

Recent efforts focus on developing encrypted databases such as CryptDB, Mylar, and Arx that support SQL-like queries over encrypted data while leveraging layered encryption to balance security and performance. These systems typically adopt onion encryption layers where each layer supports a specific query type, stripped off progressively during query processing. However, these architectures expose specific vulnerabilities when encryption layers are reused or poorly separated.

In conclusion, encrypted query processing through Searchable Encryption and Homomorphic Encryption offers promising paths for secure cloud analytics, enabling users to query and compute over encrypted data without full decryption. However, challenges such as performance overhead, leakage resistance, query expressiveness, and system integration remain critical barriers to adoption. Future work must address these issues through hardware-assisted computation (e.g., trusted enclaves), cryptographic protocol composition, and hybrid architectures that balance privacy, functionality, and efficiency.

4.2.3.5 Virtualization and Container-Based Isolation Models

Modern data processing environments heavily rely on virtualization and containerization technologies to ensure isolation between workloads, manage resources efficiently, and reduce deployment complexity. Virtual Machines (VMs), containers, and sandboxes are widely used in cloud and edge computing to isolate processes, restrict data access, and mitigate the spread of security breaches. However, the level of data protection and attack resistance provided by these technologies varies significantly.

Virtual Machines provide hardware-level isolation by emulating a complete system on top of a hypervisor. Each VM has its own kernel and memory space, making cross-VM data leakage difficult under normal conditions. However, hypervisors themselves are high-value targets; exploits such as VM escape, side-channel attacks, or shared memory misconfigurations can break isolation boundaries. For instance, Spectre and Meltdown vulnerabilities have demonstrated that speculative execution can be exploited to leak data across VM boundaries, even in otherwise well-configured environments.

Containers, while lighter-weight and more resource-efficient than VMs, rely on shared operating system kernels. This makes them more susceptible to privilege escalation and namespace confusion attacks. Although techniques such as namespace isolation, cgroups, and seccomp profiles are employed to limit access to host resources and inter-container interference, improper configurations can expose sensitive data. Studies have shown that many real-world container deployments fail to enable strong security flags, such as read-only file systems or dropped capabilities, weakening container-level data isolation.

Sandboxing further enhances application-level control, often using runtime environments with fine-grained policies (e.g., Firejail, gVisor). These sandboxes confine applications to minimal privileges and limited filesystem or network access. However, their effectiveness depends on the accuracy and enforcement of policy rules, as well as the lack of kernel-level exploits.

Overall, the choice between VM, container, and sandbox models involves a tradeoff between performance, resource overhead, and isolation strength. While VMs offer the highest degree of isolation, containers and sandboxes are more scalable but must be augmented with strict runtime policies and regular vulnerability patches. Additionally, isolation is often circumvented through side-channels or misconfigured file system mounts, emphasizing the need for continuous monitoring and access control audits. Future directions include microVMs (e.g., Firecracker), hardware-enforced isolation via TEEs, and hybrid virtualization stacks that dynamically elevate isolation guarantees based on workload sensitivity.

4.3 The Proposed Solution

To address the multifaceted security and data governance challenges in heterogeneous, distributed computing networks, we propose a comprehensive framework composed of three core components: a Multi-Source Data Aggregation Mechanism, a Trustworthy Data Sharing and Traceability architecture, and a Dynamic Data Lifecycle Management system. These mechanisms jointly enable secure, reliable, and fine-grained behavior data governance under adversarial and privacy-sensitive conditions, enhancing the resilience and interpretability of security management in cross-domain environments.

4.3.1 Multi-Source Data Aggregation Mechanism

In emerging networked computing environments such as computing power networks, edge-cloud architectures, federated AI platforms, and smart service grids, security-sensitive data from users, edge devices, compute services, and algorithmic models is frequently accessed, processed, and exchanged across heterogeneous and loosely coupled domains. These domains may span institutional infrastructures, cloud-hosted services, industrial clusters, and decentralized collaborative frameworks. The resulting data access behaviors are highly dynamic, fine-grained, and context-aware, encompassing scheduled job execution, API-driven microservice invocation, user-authenticated access paths, and automated algorithmic orchestration.

A key challenge in such settings lies in the inherent asymmetry and fragmentation of access contexts: each participating node may follow its own authentication model, logging schema, and data classification logic. This not only impedes consistent policy enforcement but also creates blind spots in behavioral audit trails. If a malicious actor compromises one node and laterally escalates across federated domains, their behavior may be masked as normal by localized views. Therefore, when multi-dimensional access information involving subject, resource, action, time, and path is hijacked, altered, or bypassed, it can lead to cascading failures or subtle privacy breaches that undermine trust across the entire system. As a result, the ability to mine, aggregate, and analyze distributed access behaviors in a unified and scalable manner becomes essential for ensuring data plane security.

To address this, it is imperative to construct robust multi-source association models that can capture both intra-domain and cross-domain access patterns, thereby exposing implicit behavior correlations that signal either benign cooperative workflows or adversarial pivoting. These associations may manifest across users and datasets, algorithms and devices, or access chains spanning multiple trust zones. In particular, when a security anomaly such as privilege misuse or unauthorized aggregation is detected, these latent associations form the foundation for contextual traceability and forensic attribution. Moreover, in collaborative analytics or joint model training scenarios, identifying high-confidence co-access patterns enables trust-aware resource provisioning and the enforcement of dynamic, context-sensitive access constraints under zero-trust principles.

In this work, we propose a confidence-adaptive frequent pattern mining framework that identifies behavior associations from heterogeneous terminals and systems in real time. The underlying behavior data is structured as a transaction database $D = \{T_1, T_2, \ldots, T_m\}$, where m denotes the number of participating sources. Each transaction T_i is a temporally ordered session trace:

$$T_i = (B_{(i,1)}, B_{(i,2)}, \ldots, B_{(i,n)}), \tag{4.2}$$

with $B_{(i,k)}$ denoting the k-th atomic access behavior (e.g., a file read, model query, or task enqueue operation). These actions may belong to distinct behavioral categories, and the transaction length n varies depending on workload density and contextual triggers.

To enable semantic consistency, we distinguish between intra-category mining (e.g., all actions within data service APIs) and inter-category mining (e.g., task invocations followed by configuration file access). For any given access category $C_i \in C$ (where C denotes the full category set), we construct a local behavior subdatabase D_{C_i} and define the item universe as $I_{C_i} = \{I_1, I_2, \ldots, I_k\}$, where each I_j represents a specific action, such as `read_user_table` or `launch_model_X`. Each session $T_i^{(C_i)}$ is a subset of I_{C_i}, and itemsets $X_{C_i} \subseteq I_{C_i}$ are potential co-behavior groups. An itemset with k elements is a k-itemset.

For cross-category association mining, we define a global item universe $I = \{I_1, I_2, \ldots, I_K\}$, encompassing multi-modal actions across domains. An itemset $X \subseteq I$ is considered frequent if:

$$Sup(X, D) = \sum_{i=1}^{n} Match(X, T_i) > support_{min}, \tag{4.3}$$

where $Match(X, T_i) = 1$ if all items in X are present in session T_i, and 0 otherwise. The confidence of such a pattern is given by:

$$Conf(X, D) = \frac{Sup(X, D)}{n}. \tag{4.4}$$

Only itemsets satisfying $Conf(X, D) > conf_{min}$ are retained for downstream interpretation.

One key challenge lies in the exponential growth of possible cross-category combinations, especially in dense and asynchronous networks, where the diversity of contexts and permutations of co-access increase rapidly. To address this, we propose a confidence-adaptive thresholding strategy, wherein the system adjusts $support_{min}$ and $conf_{min}$ dynamically based on runtime feedback (e.g., compliance certification delay, query response time, or memory usage). In high-load conditions, thresholds are elevated to reduce computational burden, while during idle phases or for high-risk zones, thresholds are relaxed to increase mining depth. This forms a closed-loop control model between system responsiveness and analytic sensitivity.

For mining execution, we employ the FP-Growth (Frequent Pattern Growth) algorithm, which avoids costly candidate generation by constructing a compressed prefix tree (FP-Tree) that captures the co-occurrence structure of items. Compared to Apriori, FP-Growth is significantly more efficient in behavior-centric contexts where access sessions often share repetitive templates (e.g., login $\rightarrow$ read $\rightarrow$ infer $\rightarrow$ write). The FP-Tree structure facilitates rapid traversal and hierarchical aggregation of patterns, which is especially beneficial in distributed stream settings.

Furthermore, we integrate a prioritization layer that ranks discovered itemsets not just by frequency, but also by entropy (behavioral diversity) and domain coverage. This enables rare yet security-relevant patterns, such as anomalous access chains spanning storage and scheduler, to be identified even when their support values are low. These enriched patterns then feed into behavior graph construction, cross-session correlation engines, and the tuning of anomaly scoring models.

Finally, our aggregation framework supports continuous learning: as behavior signatures evolve, mined patterns are periodically updated, invalidated, or reinforced. This enables the system to adapt to drift in legitimate behavior (e.g., newly deployed workflows) while detecting stealthy persistence tactics (e.g., slow lateral movement). In future extensions, the integration of semantic embedding techniques (e.g., access vectorization using transformers) may further enhance cross-domain correlation and reduce dependence on exact pattern matches.

In summary, this multi-source data aggregation mechanism, based on adaptive frequent pattern mining, FP-Tree compression, and context-aware thresholding, offers a scalable and explainable foundation for secure behavior modeling in distributed environments. It empowers security operators with deeper situational awareness, supports real-time mitigation workflows, and enhances post-hoc auditability by linking observable events with latent cross-domain access semantics.

4.3.2 Trustworthy Data Sharing and Traceability

In complex distributed computing environments, where data access behaviors are captured across multiple systems, ensuring privacy during behavioral data sharing is a cornerstone of secure and auditable collaboration. As behavioral patterns are mined, abstracted, and assembled into structured signature sequences, these sequences often contain latent personal identifiers, access intent indicators, or usage correlations that could inadvertently reveal sensitive information. To safeguard user privacy and maintain regulatory compliance, it is essential to integrate reliable and scalable desensitization methods into the data sharing pipeline, ensuring that collaborative security analytics can be conducted without compromising protections.

Modern computing environments exacerbate this challenge by producing behavioral datasets that are not only high in volume but also high in velocity, variety, and volatility. These datasets are generated in real time from a variety of sources including IoT sensors, job orchestrators, AI inference engines, mobile endpoints, and autonomous agents. Attributes in such datasets often exhibit uneven distributions, burstiness, semantic dependencies, and complex hierarchies. Traditional static masking or suppression techniques are insufficient in this context. In response, we propose a parallelized and adaptive data sanitization framework built upon Apache Spark, enabling the decomposition of single-node desensitization tasks into distributed, memory-efficient data blocks for concurrent anonymization of behavioral tuples.

The process initiates with behavior data streaming into an in-memory buffer, denoted as U_1. This buffer functions as a staging area where incoming tuples are temporarily held until either a volume threshold or a temporal threshold (publication delay) is reached. Once triggered, the system processes tuples in U_1 by evaluating their compatibility with pre-existing desensitized clusters stored in U_2, the publication-ready set. For each incoming tuple, the framework searches for the cluster in U_2 that minimizes generalized information loss while maintaining semantic coverage of the tuple's attributes. The information loss is defined using the following normalized metric:

$$l = \frac{(\overline{\alpha} - \overline{\beta}) - (\alpha - \beta)}{(\alpha - \beta)}, \tag{4.5}$$

where α and β denote the original attribute range, and $\overline{\alpha}$ and $\overline{\beta}$ represent the generalized range after anonymization. This measure captures the degree to which precision is sacrificed for privacy.

If the matched cluster is approaching its privacy budget or k-anonymity fragmentation threshold, the tuple is redirected to a corresponding pre-split cache. Otherwise, it is merged into the cluster, triggering updates to cluster-level statistics including the count, timestamp range, and attribute generalization boundaries. This not only preserves data utility but also maintains traceability by associating each tuple with a versioned cluster identifier, allowing for full audit reconstruction.

Tuples in U_1 that remain unmatched after the initial pass are subject to micro-batch clustering. These clusters are constructed using context-aware algorithms such as density-based or hierarchical clustering, ensuring that each resulting cluster meets a minimum anonymity requirement (e.g., k-anonymity or l-diversity) while adhering to the real-time processing window. Clusters that meet privacy constraints and latency budgets are appended to U_2 and published for external sharing. For those pending segmentation, a weighted urgency score is computed as:

$$w = \frac{t \cdot |l|}{|c|}, \tag{4.6}$$

where w is the split priority, t is the buffering duration, $|l|$ is the cumulative information loss, and $|c|$ is the cluster cardinality. High-weight clusters are prioritized for immediate splitting and selective suppression or generalization is applied to sub-clusters.

An important characteristic of this framework is its versioned traceability model. Each cluster is assigned a lineage tag that tracks the transformation sequence of its members: from raw behavior tuple $\rightarrow$ generalized representation $\rightarrow$ cluster aggregation $\rightarrow$ published snapshot. This lineage enables forensic analysts to trace any shared behavior signature back to its original context, while respecting the privacy policies in place. The model supports rollback (e.g., for auditing purposes), policy re-evaluation, and differential update propagation.

From a compliance perspective, this design aligns with global privacy standards such as GDPR, HIPAA, and China's Personal Information Protection Law (PIPL), by supporting explicit consent boundaries, transparency through audit logs, and built-in pseudonymization. For instance, if a tuple contains identifiers that fall under personally identifiable information (PII), it is automatically routed through stricter anonymization protocols and cannot be clustered unless compliant attribute generalization is applied.

Moreover, the use of Apache Spark enables horizontal scalability, fault-tolerant processing, and integration with upstream security analytics tools or downstream data consumers (e.g., SIEM systems, federated analytics engines). Its support for lazy evaluation and Directed Acyclic Graph (DAG) optimization reduces redundant computations and facilitates incremental updates to U_2 without full reprocessing.

To further enhance traceability, each shared behavioral cluster includes metadata such as anonymization degree, generalization type (e.g., range, hierarchy, and suppression), and contextual hints (e.g., time window, system region, and access domain). These metadata assist downstream systems in interpreting the sensitivity and provenance of received patterns, enabling informed decisions in anomaly scoring, risk evaluation, and model updates.

In future iterations, the framework may incorporate federated privacy preservation using secure aggregation or differentially private synthetic cluster generation. Additionally, integrating behavior semantics via NLP-based access sequence embeddings can improve tuple-to-cluster matching accuracy while reducing overgeneralization.

In conclusion, this scalable and privacy-compliant data sharing framework enables trustworthy traceability of behavioral signatures across distributed systems. By combining adaptive anonymization, cluster versioning, semantic matching, and Spark-powered parallelism, the system guarantees high-throughput, low-latency data sanitization while preserving the auditability and analytical utility of shared data.

4.3.3 Dynamic Data Lifecycle Management

In large-scale distributed computing environments such as edge-cloud infrastructures, federated learning frameworks, and cross-domain collaborative platforms, behavioral data are typically captured and processed in a fragmented and localized way. Subsystems independently collect activity traces, mine local associations, and share only sanitized abstractions (e.g., frequent itemsets or signature sequences) with regional control nodes. While this architectural approach protects data sovereignty and complies with privacy constraints, it also introduces critical blind spots in security analytics due to the absence of global context. These blind spots undermine the system's ability to correlate access patterns across administrative or trust boundaries, which is especially problematic in detecting coordinated threats, lateral movement attacks, or multi-hop privilege escalations.

To overcome this limitation, we propose a Dynamic Data Lifecycle Management (DDLM) framework that bridges these gaps through multi-phase, privacy-preserving collaboration. The DDLM consists of three tightly coupled components: (1) local missing interaction reconstruction, (2) federated model alignment and refinement, and (3) global behavior association synthesis. This tri-stage process allows each subsystem to autonomously learn, refine, and infer inter-system behavior associations without exposing raw data or violating local trust assumptions.

At the core of the DDLM is the local learning phase, wherein each subsystem i independently trains a missing data reconstruction model using only its own internal behavior logs. Let X denote the known behavior sequences, decomposed into prefix windows X^i_{start} and target sequences X^i_{end}. The learning task is to train a function $h_i : X^i_{\text{start}} \rightarrow X^i_{\text{end}}$ that captures latent sequential correlations, including possibly suppressed or uncaptured events. The optimization objective is formulated as:

$$h_{D(i)} = \arg\min L_i(h_i; X^i_{\text{start}}, X^i_{\text{end}}), \tag{4.7}$$

where L_i is a domain-specific loss function (e.g., cross-entropy or masked reconstruction loss) that quantifies how well predicted suffixes match the observed completions. Given that inter-domain behaviors are not visible in this phase, the model is effectively pre-trained on partial views, optimizing for intra-system recovery while retaining generalization capacity.

To achieve inter-domain awareness, the second phase initiates federated collaborative reconstruction. Each subsystem exports its current model h_i along with predicted outputs $\hat{X}^i_{\text{end}}$ derived from local inputs. These are shared with selected peer subsystems. Upon receiving a foreign model and its predictions, the recipient subsystem evaluates the predicted behaviors $\hat{X}^j_{\text{end}}$ against its own local logs, identifying the closest matching sequences as soft pseudo-labels. A proxy loss is then computed between the prediction and the matched local sequence, producing a gradient update grad_k without exposing actual sequences. These gradient signals are then securely returned to the originating model owner. After collecting gradients from all $k \in [N] \setminus \{i\}$ subsystems, the model at node i is updated via:

$$W_i^n = W_i^{n-1} - \eta \sum_{k \in [N] \setminus \{i\}} \text{grad}_k, \tag{4.8}$$

where η is the learning rate, W_i^n is the parameter vector at round n, and the summation encompasses all federated peers. This asynchronous but cooperative learning process enables each model to internalize global behavioral semantics while preserving locality of data and avoiding trust violations.

The final stage of the DDLM pipeline is full-domain association prediction and lifecycle synthesis. Once collaborative training converges, each subsystem executes its refined model on the complete local behavior dataset X, yielding a set of predicted behavior continuations $Y = h(X)$. These predictions are not mere temporal forecasts but inferred structural links between fragmented behavior traces that are otherwise difficult to detect. The outputs enrich the behavioral datasets with soft cross-system correlation edges, forming the basis for downstream operations such as graph-based anomaly detection, root cause attribution, dynamic policy enforcement, and predictive auditing.

Several advantages emerge from this lifecycle design. First, by distributing the learning and aligning models instead of raw logs, the framework adheres to zero-trust principles and minimizes legal and regulatory exposure (e.g., GDPR or data localization laws). Second, the architecture is inherently scalable because each subsystem maintains autonomy and participates only in lightweight model or gradient exchanges during scheduled coordination epochs. Third, the system offers interpretability, as reconstructed associations can be embedded in provenance graphs, showing inferred event chains and their confidence scores.

Additionally, the system supports versioned behavior graphs, where each inferred link includes metadata such as source timestamp, confidence weight, and origin model ID. This temporal and structural metadata enables rollback, causal analysis, and comparison of association models over time to detect concept drift or system anomalies. Furthermore, hybrid inference pipelines can incorporate contextual priors, such as access control policies or asset criticality tags, to weight reconstruction outputs.

Looking ahead, the DDLM framework can evolve through the integration of contrastive learning, attention-based sequence models (e.g., Transformers), or knowledge distillation from foundation models. These enhancements can improve accuracy and resilience under noisy, sparse, or adversarial conditions. Moreover, real-time streaming variants of DDLM can be developed to support continuous learning and online behavior interpolation in event-driven microservice architectures.

In summary, Dynamic Data Lifecycle Management closes a critical visibility gap in distributed systems by synthesizing missing behavioral relationships across domains. By combining local modeling, federated refinement, and global prediction, the system provides distributed security infrastructures with a richer and more comprehensive view of system behavior. This enhances detection capabilities, policy alignment, and forensic traceability, all while maintaining privacy compliance and computational efficiency.

References

1. S. Elo, M. Kääriäinen, O. Kanste, T. Pölkki, K. Utriainen, H. Kyngäs, SAGE Open **4**(1), 2158244014522633 (2014)
2. C. Dai, D. Lin, E. Bertino, M. Kantarcioglu, in *Workshop on Secure Data Management* (Springer, Berlin, 2008), pp. 82–98
3. X. Luo, N. Jia, E. Ouyang, Z. Fang, Strateg. Manag. J. **45**(8), 1597 (2024)
4. Q. Li, R. Xing, L. Li, H. Yao, L. Wu, L. Zhao, Artif. Intell. Chem. **2**(1), 100045 (2024)
5. R. Toshniwal, A. Nath, Int. J. Comput. Appl. **113**(14), 9 (2015). https://www.researchgate.net/publication/275772328
6. K. Ren, C. Wang, Q. Wang, IEEE Internet Comput. **16**(1), 69 (2012)
7. K. Hashizume, D.G. Rosado, E. Fernández-Medina, E.B. Fernandez, J. Internet Serv. Appl. **4**(1), 1 (2013)
8. D. Popescul, L.D. Genete, Informatica Econ. **20**(1), 29 (2016)
9. H. Suo, J. Wan, C. Zou, J. Liu, IEEE Int. Conf. Comput. Sci. Electron. Eng. **3**, 648 (2012)
10. F. Zafar, A. Khan, S.U.R. Malik, A. Anjum, Comput. Secur. **65**, 29 (2017)
11. H. Takabi, J.B.D. Joshi, G.J. Ahn, IEEE Secur. Priv. **8**(6), 24 (2010)
12. D. Chen, H. Zhao, 2012 Int. Conf. Comput. Sci. Electron. Eng. **1**, 647 (2012)
13. R. Bao, Z. Chen, M.S. Obaidat, Secur. Priv. **1**(1), e13 (2018)
14. C. De Canniere, C. Rechberger, in *International Conference on the Theory and Application of Cryptology and Information Security* (Springer, New York, 2006), pp. 1–20
15. J. Steinhardt, P.W.W. Koh, P.S. Liang, Adv. Neural Inf. Proces. Syst. **30**, 3517–3529 (2017)

16. E. Rosenfeld, E. Winston, P. Ravikumar, Z. Kolter, in *International Conference on Machine Learning* (PMLR, New York, 2020), pp. 8230–8241
17. S. Lee, S. Hwang, S. Ryu, in *2017 32nd IEEE/ACM International Conference on Automated Software Engineering (ASE)* (IEEE, New York, 2017), pp. 252–262
18. J. Liang, N. Naoumov, K.W. Ross, in *INFOCOM* (Citeseer, New York, 2006), pp. 1–12
19. M. Zwolak, C.J. Riedel, W.H. Zurek, Phys. Rev. Lett. **112**(14), 140406 (2014)
20. P. Xu, W. Lu, B. Wang, IEEE Geosci. Remote Sens. Lett. **18**(4), 741 (2020)
21. W. Pourmajidi, L. Zhang, J. Steinbacher, T. Erwin, A. Miranskyy, in *2019 IEEE/ACM 41st International Conference on Software Engineering: Companion Proceedings (ICSE-Companion)* (IEEE, New York, 2019), pp. 280–281
22. B. Dowling, M. Fischlin, F. Günther, D. Stebila, in *Proceedings of the 22nd ACM SIGSAC Conference on Computer and Communications Security* (2015), pp. 1197–1210
23. A. Takura, S. Ono, S. Naito, in *1999 Internet Workshop. IWS99.(Cat. No. 99EX385)* (IEEE, New York, 1999), pp. 88–93
24. W. Wang, N. Hu, X. Liu, in *2018 IEEE Third International Conference on Data Science in Cyberspace (DSC)* (IEEE, New York, 2018), pp. 896–901
25. A. Ranganathan, R.H. Campbell, in *ACM/IFIP/USENIX International Conference on Distributed Systems Platforms and Open Distributed Processing* (Springer, Berlin, 2003), pp. 143–161
26. D. Basin, S.J. Burri, G. Karjoth, in *Proceedings of the 6th ACM Symposium on Information, Computer and Communications Security* (2011), pp. 423–429
27. M. Stamp, *Information Security: Principles and Practice* (Wiley, New York, 2011)
28. A.J. Menezes, P.C. van Oorschot, S.A. Vanstone, *Handbook of Applied Cryptography* (CRC Press, New York, 1996)
29. R. Sandhu, P. Samarati, IEEE Commun. Mag. **32**(9), 40 (1994)
30. V.C. Hu, D. Ferraiolo, R. Kuhn, A. Schnitzer, K. Sandlin, R. Miller, K. Scarfone, Guide to attribute based access control (abac) definition and considerations. Tech. rep., NIST Special Publication 800-162 (2014). https://nvlpubs.nist.gov/nistpubs/SpecialPublications/NIST.SP.800-162.pdf
31. L.K. Galla, V.S. Koganti, N. Nuthalapati, in *2016 International Conference on Control, Instrumentation, Communication and Computational Technologies (ICCICCT)* (IEEE, New York, 2016), pp. 81–87
32. J.H. Wu, Y.M. Wang, Inf. Manag. **43**(6), 728 (2006)
33. J. Chen, A. Dholakia, E. Eleftheriou, M.P. Fossorier, X.Y. Hu, IEEE Trans. Commun. **53**(8), 1288 (2005)
34. B. Ngabonziza, D. Martin, A. Bailey, H. Cho, S. Martin, in *2016 IEEE 2nd International Conference on Collaboration and Internet Computing (CIC)* (IEEE, New York, 2016), pp. 445–451
35. C. Dwork, in *International Colloquium on Automata, Languages, and Programming* (Springer, Berlin, 2006), pp. 1–12

Chapter 5
The Projection Onto Algorithm Plane

Abstract This chapter analyzes the role of algorithmic security in modern computing networks and explains why it is essential for system reliability. With increasing interconnection and growing complexity in distributed infrastructures, algorithmic vulnerabilities influence task execution, data privacy, system integrity, and overall resilience. The chapter first uses representative cases to show how attacks such as APT incidents and backdoor manipulation in federated learning exploit weaknesses at the algorithmic level. These attacks damage data integrity, reduce model performance, and raise risks of privacy leakage. It then reviews existing defense methods and highlights their limitations in large and distributed environments. Finally, the chapter introduces multi agent behavior modeling, authentication, and compliance interaction mechanisms to enhance protection and strengthen future security frameworks.

5.1 Motivation and Representative Examples

With the increasing complexity of computing network architectures and the deepening of distributed characteristics, the challenges facing algorithmic security have become significantly more severe. Security concerns are no longer confined to individual computing nodes but have expanded to encompass the stability of the entire computing network, protection of data privacy, and preservation of system integrity across multiple dimensions. To more effectively reveal the underlying essence of security in such complex systems, this section attempts to project the issue of integrated security in network systems onto the algorithmic plane. This projection enables the compression and aggregation of complex security information, thereby enhancing the analyzability and controllability of integrated security threats. Due to its high semantic density and strong mechanism-level interpretability, the algorithmic plane offers unique advantages in security modeling, attack attribution, and defense strategy design, while also providing a new technical perspective and theoretical foundation for coordinated defenses across the system and data layers.

C. Wang, H. Tang, *Integrated Security and Safety of Intelligent Computing Networks*, https://doi.org/10.1007/978-981-95-5025-8_5

Against this backdrop, representative attack cases help expose the underlying algorithm-layer security risks inherent in computing networks and offer valuable insights for designing system-level protection mechanisms. These attacks not only reveal vulnerabilities and defects in the algorithms themselves but also highlight the intricate interdependencies between algorithms, data, and system components in distributed environments. In such a highly dynamic context, algorithmic security threats demonstrate unprecedented stealth, persistence, and targeting precision, intensifying the confrontation between offensive and defensive forces.

This section further examines two typical categories of attack scenarios in detail, aiming to reveal the multi-faceted nature of security threats at the algorithm layer and to assess their possible implications for the holistic security of computing networks. These cases illustrate how attackers exploit complex strategies and carefully crafted vulnerabilities to infiltrate systems, manipulate algorithms, and inflict damage in ways that are difficult to detect. Through a detailed examination of these scenarios, it becomes possible to develop a more holistic understanding of the vulnerabilities inherent in algorithmic security within computing networks, while also extracting valuable guidance for constructing resilient defense strategies.Through these concrete examples, we further examine how to respond to increasingly complex and evolving security threats to ensure that computing networks remain resilient and defensible in the face of novel attacks.

5.1.1 Motivation

In the highly complex and deeply collaborative operating environment of computing networks, security threats have evolved far beyond traditional single-dimensional concerns such as information leakage, service disruption, or privilege abuse. Instead, they are increasingly manifesting as integrated attack patterns that span systems, data flows, and algorithmic processes. The diversification of attack paths, the stealthy nature of adversarial behaviors, and the strong coupling between security layers render isolated defense mechanisms or localized modeling insufficient for characterizing and countering such sophisticated threats. Against this backdrop, projecting system and data layer security issues onto the algorithmic plane has emerged as a forward-looking and analytically powerful approach to integrated security analysis.

From the system layer perspective, security typically centers on resource scheduling, access control, network boundaries, and configuration strategies. The data layer, by contrast, emphasizes privacy preservation, data integrity, and lifecycle governance. While these layers independently establish preliminary security perimeters, attackers frequently exploit cross-domain attack vectors, rendering the coordination gaps between system and data layers vulnerable to exploitation. For example, a system vulnerability originating from an external breach may be leveraged to manipulate algorithmic input logic, subsequently inducing accuracy degradation or privacy leakage through downstream data-processing pipelines.

Conversely, anomalous data inputs can trigger behavior drifts in system-level algorithmic decision modules, resulting in chronic, stealthy attacks that evade traceability. These phenomena highlight the fact that security issues are rarely isolated; rather, they propagate within a closed-loop structure encompassing algorithms, systems, and data.

For these reasons, the algorithmic plane, as the convergence point between system functions and data semantics, serves as a core vantage point for observing and modeling integrated security. Its advantages can be articulated across the following dimensions:

- **Mechanism-Level Compression.** The algorithmic layer offers a high degree of abstraction over both system logic and data flow. Projecting integrated security concerns onto this plane allows for mechanism-level compression of complex attack pathways by mapping heterogeneous and multi-source adversarial factors into unified algorithmic behavior anomalies (e.g., model parameter drift, optimization path deviation, and convergence instability). This significantly improves both the expressiveness and clarity of threat models.
- **Semantic-Level Convergence.** Algorithms are not only the operational cores of systems but also the primary carriers of data semantics. In computing networks, system decisions are algorithmically generated and data processing is algorithmically executed. Both aspects are prime targets for adversarial manipulation. The algorithmic plane thus inherently facilitates semantic continuity between system and data layers. Security analysis at this level helps clarify the logical relationships between system events and data anomalies, enabling the realization of a cross-layer semantic closure in security reasoning.
- **Behavior-Level Prediction.** At its core, an attack is a disruption of expected behavior. Since algorithms govern behavioral logic, modeling their operational patterns, such as training dynamics, inference pathways, or optimization behaviors, enables the development of intent-aware and behavior-driven defense frameworks. Forecasting risks through algorithmic behavior modeling, such frameworks support early detection prior to attack manifestation, while also offering better adaptability and evolution in response strategies.
- **Defense-Level Coordination.** Multi-agent collaboration is foundational to computing networks, and algorithms naturally lie at the heart of interactions among participating entities. Projecting security issues onto the algorithmic plane facilitates the coordination of inter-entity defense mechanisms such as behavioral analysis in federated learning, conflict detection in collaborative decision-making, and game-theoretic optimization in resource allocation. These algorithm-anchored defense linkages can transcend system boundaries and enable more flexible, responsive, and cooperative security enforcement.

In summary, mapping integrated security concerns onto the algorithmic plane is not merely a methodological choice in theoretical modeling. Rather, it represents a paradigm shift aligned with the operational logic of contemporary computing networks. It provides a unified analytical foundation and strategic foothold for subsequent security case analysis, defense mechanism design, and cross-layer coordination strategies. The subsequent sections of this chapter will investigate representative attack scenarios, aiming to expose the distinct categories of security risks rooted in the algorithmic plane and their ripple effects on both the system and data layers. This analysis highlights the essential value of adopting algorithm-centered viewpoints within integrated security architectures.

5.1.2 Backdoor Attacks in Federated Learning

In recent years, computing networks have evolved into a fundamental pillar supporting large-scale distributed computing environments. These networks utilize geographically distributed heterogeneous resources such as CPUs, GPUs, and specialized hardware to create a shared computing environment. By integrating computing resources from diverse distributed origins, computing networks deliver scalable, efficient, and adaptable processing capabilities, enabling a broad spectrum of applications such as large-scale data analytics, machine learning, and artificial intelligence. This distributed collaborative model enables organizations to meet the growing processing demands for high-performance computing, massive data, and complex algorithms required by dynamic and evolving tasks, while maintaining operational efficiency.

The rapid advancement of artificial intelligence, particularly machine learning, has significantly accelerated the evolution of computing networks, especially in addressing the growing need for cost-effective and high-efficiency computing resources. However, as these systems become more complex and integrated, the associated security risks also increase. The distributed nature of computing networks relies on diverse, often remote, computing units, which presents challenges in terms of data privacy, system integrity, and access control. Consequently, tackling these security challenges has emerged as a central focus for both academic researchers and industry practitioners.

Federated Learning (FL), as a decentralized paradigm of machine learning, has gained broad adoption in diverse domains owing to its inherent strengths in safeguarding data privacy. Especially in the context of distributed model training, FL aligns well with the distributed nature of computing networks. In contrast to conventional centralized machine learning, federated learning decentralizes the model training process by distributing it across numerous devices, thereby eliminating the requirement to transmit sensitive data to a central server and strengthening the protection of data privacy. Nevertheless, although federated learning offers strong privacy protection, it remains vulnerable to a range of security threats, among which backdoor attacks are particularly critical. Such attacks embed malicious manipulations during the training phase, resulting in models that behave normally under standard conditions but produce erroneous or adversarial outputs once exposed to predefined trigger inputs.

In federated learning, each client performs local model training and submits the resulting updates to a central server. The server then aggregates these updates into

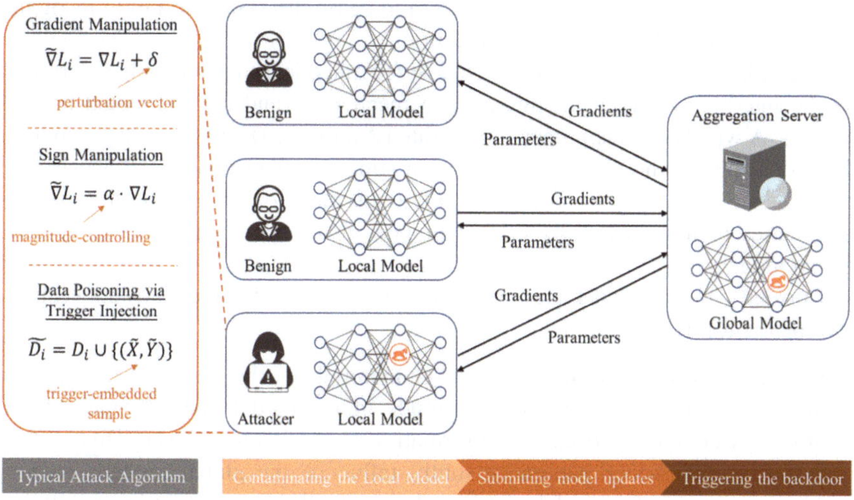

Fig. 5.1 Illustration of the backdoor attack process in federated learning

a global model, which is redistributed to the clients for subsequent training rounds. The essence of a backdoor attack is that an adversary either injects poisoned training data or alters the local model so that hidden malicious behaviors are implanted into the global model. These behaviors remain dormant under normal circumstances but are triggered by specific inputs, causing the model to generate erroneous predictions or execute unintended malicious actions.

As shown in Fig. 5.1, the main process of a federated learning backdoor attack typically includes several steps: contaminating the local model, submitting model updates, and triggering the backdoor. First, the attacker manipulates the local training data to inject a backdoor trigger pattern. These backdoor trigger patterns are usually benign-looking features that can be ignored under normal conditions but lead to erroneous predictions when triggered under specific conditions. For instance, in an image classification scenario, an adversary may insert a subtle marker (e.g., a small sticker) in the corner of an image. Although seemingly innocuous, the presence of this marker can mislead the model into producing incorrect classifications whenever it appears. The attacker adjusts the local model's weights to incorporate the backdoor feature and then uploads the modified model update to the central server. These updates may appear normal but actually contain the influence of the backdoor trigger pattern. When these updates are aggregated with other clients' updates, they may subtly influence the global model. When the central server combines the model updates submitted by all clients, it produces a unified global model. Although this global model performs well on most input data, it exhibits abnormal behavior when the input data contains the backdoor trigger pattern. At this point, the attacker can exploit this vulnerability to trigger erroneous outputs under specific conditions. For example, in a facial recognition system, the attacker could use a specific trigger pattern to cause the system to fail to recognize certain faces, even bypassing authentication.

The effectiveness of backdoor attacks in federated learning is largely determined by the interplay between the aggregation mechanism and the distributed training process. A widely used approach is Federated Averaging (FedAvg), which produces the global model through a weighted averaging of client updates. However, this strategy fails to distinguish between benign and malicious contributions, enabling adversaries to inject carefully crafted updates that imperceptibly manipulate the global model.

Currently, the key attack algorithms used in federated learning backdoor attacks include the following:

- **Gradient Manipulation.** The attacker manipulates the gradients of the local model (i.e., the direction and magnitude of the model updates) and submits gradients containing backdoor information to the central server. This method causes the backdoor pattern to subtly influence the global model's training process, causing the model to respond abnormally to specific trigger patterns, while leaving its performance on other normal inputs largely unaffected. For example,the attacker may apply subtle perturbations to the gradients during training, so that the presence of a predefined trigger pattern in the input data causes the model to generate incorrect predictions.
- **Gradient Sign Manipulation.** This is a more covert form of backdoor attack, where the attacker manipulates the gradient signs rather than their magnitudes. This approach makes it harder for detection algorithms to identify malicious updates, as the magnitude of the updates may still fall within normal ranges. In this way, the attacker can quietly implant backdoor information into the global model, which will activate the backdoor behavior once the trigger pattern is encountered.
- **Data Injection Trigger.** The attacker carefully designs malicious data containing the backdoor trigger pattern, causing the model to learn an incorrect prediction associated with a specific input pattern (the trigger pattern). For example, in an animal classification task, an adversary could alter a small feature within an image, such that the model consistently misclassifies a dog as a cat whenever that specific modified image is encountered.

It is worth noting that backdoor attacks, through algorithmic manipulation, also have implications for the security of network systems at both the system level and the data plane. Malicious client updates appear as normal model update requests at the system level, but once these updates are merged and propagated into the global model, they can affect the reliability and stability of the entire system. In large-scale federated learning networks, adversaries can progressively compromise the system by periodically submitting malicious updates, thereby undermining the security of the global model. The inherently distributed structure of federated learning further complicates defense, as the central server lacks direct access to client data or local updates, making it difficult to identify and block malicious activities. Moreover, such attacks may interfere with the system's privacy-preserving mechanisms, reducing the effectiveness of existing defense strategies in isolating adversarial behaviors. The data plane also plays a critical role in federated learning backdoor attacks. Through the deliberate design of malicious data injections, an adversary can undermine data integrity, subsequently impacting the accuracy and reliability of the global model. Since each client's training data is stored locally and not shared, the central server cannot directly inspect or validate the quality of the data, making it easier for malicious data to be hidden and propagated through model updates into the global model. This data-level opacity makes it difficult for traditional data cleaning and anomaly detection techniques to effectively identify and eliminate harmful data, leading to the latent and widespread nature of the attack.

However, owing to the inherently distributed nature of federated learning, detecting backdoor attacks poses significant challenges. Traditional anomaly detection methods and adversarial training techniques struggle to effectively counter such attacks for the following reasons. The first is data heterogeneity. In federated learning, each client's data distribution is independent and heterogeneous, meaning that when aggregating models, the model updates from different clients may vary. Malicious updates from an attacker may be difficult to identify as anomalies due to these data differences. A malicious update might appear normal at the local level, but hide malicious behavior in the global model. The second challenge is the lack of centralized data access. Since the server cannot access the clients' local data, it cannot directly detect the presence of malicious data or clean and sanitize the data before training. As a result, the server must infer the state of the model based on the updates submitted by the clients, making backdoor attacks harder to detect. Additionally, the issue of model aggregation arises in federated learning, where model updates are aggregated by averaging. Even a single malicious client can exert a substantial influence on the global model through repeated rounds of training. The aggregation process itself complicates the identification and exclusion of such malicious updates.

In conclusion, backdoor attacks in federated learning exploit the model aggregation properties and limitations of distributed learning by cleverly injecting malicious data or manipulating gradients, embedding backdoor features into the global model. These attacks typically go unnoticed under normal inputs but activate malicious behaviors under specific trigger patterns, severely compromising the system's security. Although some existing defense methods, such as robust aggregation algorithms and anomaly detection, can mitigate the impact of the attack to some extent, effectively preventing backdoor attacks in large-scale distributed environments remains an unresolved challenge.

5.1.3 Advanced Persistent Threat

An Advanced Persistent Threat (APT) denotes a type of cyberattack orchestrated by adversaries possessing significant technical expertise, extensive resources, and deep operational experience. APTs typically target organizations of high strategic value, including government agencies, large enterprises, and research institutions. These attackers employ meticulously designed strategies, remaining embedded within the target systems over extended periods. Not only do they steal sensitive data, but they also achieve deep infiltration, allowing them to control or even destroy critical operations. Three key characteristics define APT attacks: advanced nature, long duration, and threat severity.

- **Advanced Nature.** APT attacks usually involve highly customized attack methods. The attackers select their tools and techniques carefully based on the characteristics and vulnerabilities of the target. Their technical proficiency is remarkable, enabling them to identify and exploit multiple vulnerabilities in complex environments, including zero-day exploits and deeply embedded flaws, using precise intrusion tactics.
- **Long Duration.** Unlike traditional attacks, APT attacks tend to be a continuous process. Attackers employ multi-phase strategies to gradually infiltrate, accumulate privileges, and maintain long-term control over the target systems. APT attackers avoid rapid exposure of their identities, opting instead for a stealthy approach to gather intelligence and monitor the target over time, ultimately achieving undiscovered, prolonged control.
- **Threat Severity.** APT attacks target high-value objectives, and once successful, they often result in incalculable damage to the victims. This damage may include financial losses, information leakage, technology theft, loss of market competitiveness, and even threats to national security.

One of the most notable examples of APT attacks in the field of cybersecurity is the Stuxnet virus. Stuxnet is the first confirmed APT used against industrial control systems and is considered one of the hallmark examples of modern APT attacks. This extraordinarily complex malware exploited four zero-day vulnerabilities to infiltrate Iran's nuclear facility control systems. The attackers precisely manipulated the operational speed of uranium-enriching centrifuges, causing damage to the equipment without being detected by the operators. The core of the attack was not limited to the system itself but involved deep penetration into the control system's algorithms and operational procedures, altering the device's operational instructions to manipulate the system's state and ultimately destroy the equipment.

Stuxnet's stealth features enabled the malware to operate undetected by system operators. In this instance, the attackers penetrated multiple layers of the system, ranging from the algorithmic layer to the underlying hardware of the control system. Although the primary target was a nuclear facility, the tactics and methodologies employed offer important insights for analyzing APT attacks within computing networks.

Another significant APT attack occurred in 2017, known as the WannaCry ransomware attack. WannaCry utilized a known vulnerability in the Windows operating system to rapidly propagate across millions of devices worldwide, causing substantial disruption to critical industries such as healthcare, banking, and energy. While initially appearing as ransomware, WannaCry was essentially an APT attack.

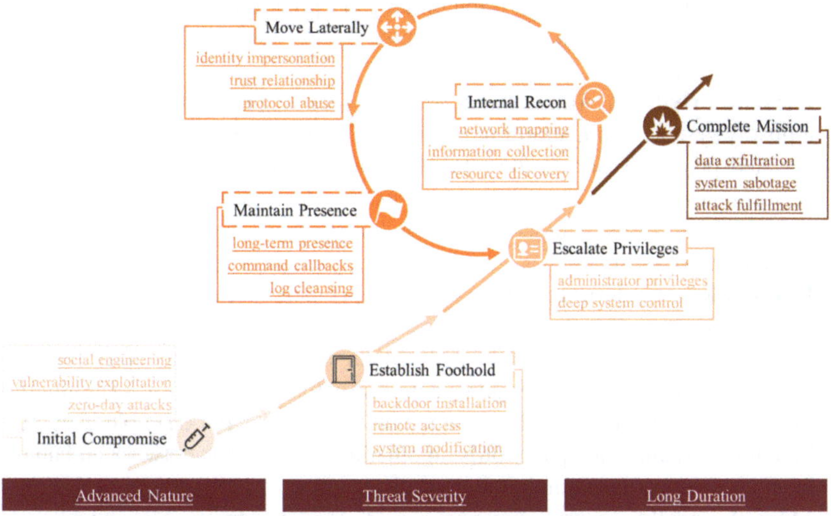

Fig. 5.2 Illustration of the kill chain model

The malware exploited the EternalBlue exploit to enable attackers to execute remote code and spread the virus, quickly infecting computer networks, encrypting files, and demanding ransom payments. By this method, the attackers were able to take control of large amounts of computing resources, resulting in widespread system failures. The rapid propagation of WannaCry, particularly in systems that had not applied timely patches, significantly expanded the attack's impact. This case demonstrates how APT attackers can exploit a known vulnerability to propagate globally, highlighting the potential threats posed by APTs in large-scale, interconnected network environments.

The process of an APT attack can be described through the Kill Chain model, which represents the full progression from the initial compromise of a target system to the ultimate accomplishment of the attacker's objective. As described in Fig. 5.2, APT attacks generally pass through several phases:

- **Initial Compromise.** This stage represents the initial phase of an APT attack, during which the attacker gains entry into the target system using methods such as social engineering, phishing emails, malicious advertisements, or by exploiting system vulnerabilities. During this phase, attackers often exploit zero-day or known vulnerabilities and disguise their activities as normal network traffic to avoid detection by firewalls or intrusion detection systems. For example, attackers might trick the target user into clicking on an innocuous-looking email attachment, thereby executing malicious code.
- **Establish Foothold.** After a successful infiltration, attackers attempt to establish a persistent control point within the target system. This may involve installing backdoor programs, malicious software, or modifying system configurations to

ensure continued access even if the initial entry point is discovered. For instance, attackers might implant a Trojan or Remote Access Tool (RAT) to create a lasting backdoor connection.

- **Escalate Privileges.** At this stage, attackers seek to gain higher-level privileges, typically system administrator or root access. This is a critical step, as possessing elevated privileges allows the attacker to access deeper system resources and perform more extensive control operations. Privilege escalation is often achieved by exploiting system vulnerabilities or leveraging malicious software to gain administrative rights.
- **Internal Reconnaissance.** After escalating privileges, attackers conduct internal reconnaissance within the target network to collect additional information about network architecture, user accounts, critical data, etc. At this stage, attackers thoroughly understand the target system's structure and defenses, enabling them to identify further attack pathways and potential targets. For example, they might look for usernames and passwords on other machines in the network and attempt lateral movement to expand their control.
- **Move Laterally.** Lateral movement is a crucial step in APT attacks. The attacker uses the privileges gained to move across the network, compromising additional systems, particularly those related to critical data or key operations. Lateral movement typically exploits the trust relationships within the network, with attackers leveraging credentials or network protocols (e.g., SMB, RDP) to infiltrate other systems.
- **Maintain Presence.** During the long-term phase of the APT attack, attackers ensure their continued presence in the system. This allows them to execute the final attack when the time is right. This typically involves installing multiple backdoors, establishing regular callback mechanisms, or embedding deep-rooted malware to ensure sustained access. This phase can last from months to years, with attackers working to avoid detection and periodically clearing their traces.
- **Complete Mission.** Once the attacker has been in the system long enough and has gathered sufficient information or resources, the attack enters its final phase. At this point, attackers carry out the target operation, such as stealing sensitive data, sabotaging key infrastructure, manipulating system functionality, or spreading further malicious code. In some APT attacks, the ultimate goal may be data theft, while in others, the aim could be to disrupt operations or destroy systems entirely.

It is noteworthy that APT attacks are often closely related to external social engineering attacks and internal human factor threats, which significantly enhance the effectiveness of the attack. Social engineering attacks take advantage of human susceptibility, considered the weakest link in security systems, to obtain unauthorized access to systems or sensitive data. Attackers typically employ methods such as phishing, spear phishing, pretexting, baiting, and impersonation to deceive the target into disclosing sensitive information, granting system access, or even executing malicious code unknowingly. In addition to external social engineering attacks, internal human factor threats are also a critical aspect of the human risk in APT attacks. Internal personnel, such as employees, contractors, or business partners, often possess access to critical systems and sensitive data. If these insiders are manipulated by external attackers or misuse their access intentionally, it can create substantial security vulnerabilities.

Within computing networks, APT attacks exert a particularly significant impact owing to the distributed architecture of these systems and the complexity of the underlying algorithms. Computing networks rely on large-scale computational resources and sophisticated algorithmic scheduling, which provide opportunities for APT attackers to exploit. APT attacks can affect not only individual computing nodes but can also propagate through the entire network by impacting algorithmic behavior. For instance, attackers can craft malicious algorithms that affect network-wide computation scheduling, causing delays in computational tasks, errors in data transmission, or even node failures.

From a system-level perspective, APT attacks can lead to abnormal collaboration between computing nodes, disrupting the completion of computational tasks. Attackers may embed malicious code in critical nodes, causing partial node failures and destabilizing the overall system's reliability. From a data-level perspective, APT interference with algorithms can directly compromise data integrity and reliability, leading to data loss, tampering, or leakage. More seriously, the stealth and persistence of APT attacks make such disruptions difficult to detect in a timely manner, allowing the attacker to secretly undermine the network's overall security over months or even years.

In conclusion, APT attacks are a highly covert, sustained, and targeted form of cyberattack, presenting unprecedented security challenges in computing network environments. These attacks not only threaten the security of individual algorithms but also deeply affect the overall system and data layers. To combat increasingly sophisticated threats, it is imperative to strengthen security measures in computing networks, particularly algorithm-level defenses. This can be achieved by implementing multi-dimensional protection strategies to enhance the system's resilience and its ability to respond effectively to emerging threats.

5.2 Existing Methods and Limitations

The security issues of network systems have become increasingly complex, making it crucial to understand the effectiveness and limitations of existing security mechanisms. This section reviews key methods in areas such as network system information awareness, identity and access authentication, and anomaly detection, with a particular focus on their contributions and limitations in improving network security in the context of algorithmic layer projection. Through a critical evaluation of the current strategies' implementation, this section aims to reveal areas where existing methods need improvement in order to address emerging vulnerabilities and dynamic security requirements, ultimately optimizing and strengthening the overall

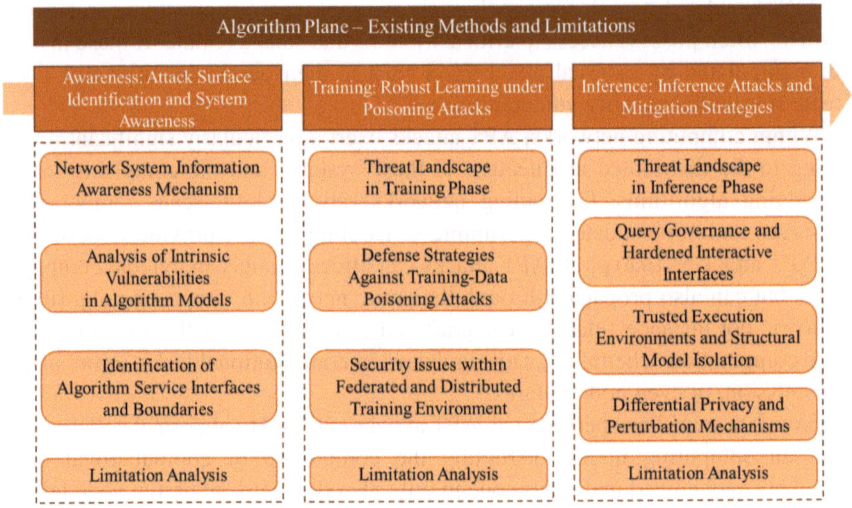

Fig. 5.3 Existing methods and limitations on algorithm plane

security defense capabilities of multi-layered systems. Figure 5.3 gives the existing methods and limitations on algorithm plane.

5.2.1 Awareness: Attack Surface Identification and System Awareness

5.2.1.1 Network System Information Awareness Mechanism

As the first line of defense in integrated security protection, network system information awareness plays a crucial role in security, especially in multi-tenant and cross-domain collaborative computing-network environments. By continuously sensing and analyzing communication behaviors, resource scheduling paths, bandwidth usage, and latency in the network, the system can promptly identify abnormal traffic, potential attack paths, and security vulnerabilities. For example, by sensing communication traffic, suspicious behaviors in encrypted traffic, such as model poisoning or privacy leakage risks in federated learning, can be effectively detected, thus providing data support for the enforcement of security strategies. Moreover, network system information awareness also helps in real-time detection of network topology changes and abnormal resource scheduling, preventing security issues caused by configuration errors or improper scheduling paths. Therefore, information awareness is a key mechanism for ensuring network security, preventing attacks, optimizing resource allocation, and enabling dynamic defense. Existing research mainly focuses on the following four areas: basic resource awareness mechanisms, runtime state awareness mechanisms, communication and traffic awareness mechanisms, policy and scheduling awareness mechanisms.

Overall, resource awareness in computing networks can be abstracted into five key dimensions: structural awareness, runtime state awareness, communication behavior awareness, policy control awareness, and configuration and scheduling awareness. These dimensions span from static topology to dynamic behaviors and control logic, forming a multi-layered and integrated perception framework.

At the foundational level, structural awareness mechanisms focus on the real-time acquisition and understanding of underlying resource states, including topological relations among nodes, link status, bandwidth capacity, and physical location. Existing studies [1–3] employ active probing and passive listening to construct cognitive models of network structure, providing critical support for resource scheduling, path selection, and task mapping. For example, in data center environments, quantifying a node's structural influence improves virtual network embedding efficiency and resource utilization. In edge-cloud collaborative scenarios, rapid reconstruction of physical adjacency in response to terminal dynamics enhances system adaptability to structural changes. Moreover, in dynamic multi-agent systems, where topology perturbations and task uncertainty are prevalent, structural awareness must integrate with consensus control strategies to ensure coordinated resource management and system stability.

Runtime state awareness mechanisms are responsible for fine-grained monitoring of computing entities during execution, such as containers, microservices, and virtual machines. Key targets include load levels, lifecycle stages, abnormal behaviors, and Quality of Service (QoS) variations. These mechanisms facilitate quick anomaly localization and recovery, and also provide real-time feedback for access control, elastic scaling, and policy adjustment. Some scheduling frameworks [4–7] utilize request path tracing and critical path analysis to prioritize latency-sensitive tasks, while aggregation of distributed tracing data supports performance bottleneck localization and optimization suggestions. Further, integration of digital twin models and SDN-based behavioral modeling expands awareness across the IoT device lifecycle. Graph neural network-based QoS prediction approaches also mitigate the overhead of traditional continuous monitoring, achieving both lightweight deployment and high accuracy.

Communication and traffic awareness targets the modeling and analysis of interaction paths and data flows across nodes and tasks. Core factors include traffic distribution, transmission delay, bandwidth utilization, and encryption characteristics. Such awareness plays a vital role in parallel scheduling, link security validation, and anomaly detection, particularly under federated learning and serverless computing, where communication bottlenecks and privacy risks challenge system stability [8–11]. To improve communication efficiency, researchers have proposed architectures that decouple functional logic from data flow, significantly reducing latency in asynchronous scheduling. In federated learning, attention mechanisms and structural awareness have been combined to enhance both model aggregation and communication efficiency. Additionally, in high-concurrency environments, some studies dynamically infer communication patterns between operators and reconstruct paths, thus reducing congestion and improving task execution stability.

Policy and scheduling awareness mechanisms aim to capture the execution paths, scheduling logic, and access control states within both algorithmic and control layers. This enables detection of policy conflicts, path misconfigurations, and potential vulnerabilities, ensuring correctness and fairness in task orchestration. In scenarios with multi-task co-location and frequent resource fluctuations, the observability, auditability, and rollback capability of policy execution are particularly crucial. Some works [12, 13] introduce affinity-aware models to preconfigure long-running task scheduling, mitigating resource fragmentation and improving success rates. Others jointly model computational locality and network load to enable cross-layer adaptive scheduling, dynamically adjusting task assignments based on real-time system feedback and avoiding disruptions or DoS risks caused by local bottlenecks or opaque paths.

5.2.1.2 Analysis of Intrinsic Vulnerabilities in Algorithm Models

Algorithm models are a core component of the algorithm plane, and their inherent security directly determines the stability of the entire algorithm service's security foundation. In-depth analysis of the intrinsic vulnerabilities in algorithm models, such as sensitivity to adversarial attacks, the presence of backdoors, and insufficient generalization capability, helps us understand the potential security risks from the source. This understanding is crucial for the subsequent development of robust model training methods, the design of effective adversarial defense mechanisms, and the implementation of reliable backdoor detection techniques. By detecting and addressing inherent weaknesses within the model, the risk of malicious exploitation in practical applications can be substantially minimized. This ensures the credibility and reliability of model outputs, preserves the integrity and availability of algorithmic services, and ultimately enhances the overall security of the algorithmic plane. From a technical standpoint, existing research can generally be divided into two primary approaches: verification-based methods and software testing-based methods. These approaches offer complementary perspectives, focusing respectively on formal guarantees of security and empirical evaluation of vulnerabilities.

Verification-based methods are centered on logical reasoning and mathematical modeling, aiming to provide formal guarantees for model safety. These methods seek to answer whether a model can consistently maintain certain critical properties (such as classification consistency or output constraints) under specific input perturbations. One representative approach is to convert neural networks into constraint-solving problems, applying linear programming, mixed-integer programming, or Satisfiability Modulo Theories (SMT) solvers for global analysis [14]. While highly precise and capable of generating counterexamples, this approach often suffers from computational bottlenecks due to the exponential complexity of large models. A more scalable alternative relies on approximation techniques, such as symbolic interval analysis, interval propagation, and geometric abstraction [15,

16]. These methods conservatively estimate output boundaries to infer robustness ranges. Though they may compromise on precision, their ease of parallelization and adaptability to large-scale networks make them promising for real-world applications. Overall, verification-based methods contribute significant theoretical value by offering provable safety assurances, despite ongoing challenges related to reasoning efficiency and expressiveness in high-dimensional input spaces.

In contrast, software testing-based methods focus more on empirical evaluation by simulating realistic attack scenarios to uncover model vulnerabilities during actual deployment. Drawing inspiration from traditional testing strategies, which are often black-box or grey-box in nature, these methods typically generate adversarial inputs to provoke abnormal model behavior and assess robustness. One prominent direction involves building unified testing platforms that integrate a wide range of adversarial attacks and defense mechanisms, along with standardized evaluation metrics to support quantitative comparison [17]. Such platforms enable consistent measurement of model vulnerability, facilitate the comparative study of defense strategies, and help bridge research gaps across different approaches. Another branch of research is centered on certifiable robustness, which provides lower bounds for model robustness under specified perturbation conditions and informs the design of robust training methods [18]. These efforts not only advance the field of adversarial training but also offer frameworks for building verifiable and controllable deep learning systems. Despite lacking the rigor of formal logic, software testing-based approaches are indispensable in practice due to their flexibility, scalability, and broad applicability.

5.2.1.3 Identification of Algorithm Service Interfaces and Boundaries

Algorithm service interfaces are the only channels through which external entities interact with the algorithm, and clearly defining service boundaries is a critical prerequisite for implementing security policies. Accurately identifying the various interfaces provided by algorithm services, such as model inference APIs, data upload interfaces, and parameter configuration interfaces, and clearly defining their interaction boundaries with the external environment and other internal components, helps in building effective access control mechanisms. By precisely delineating the scope of security responsibilities, unauthorized access and operations can be prevented, the potential attack surface can be limited, and clear targets for deploying security measures such as traffic monitoring, intrusion detection, and security auditing can be provided. Proper management of algorithm service interfaces and boundaries is a critical defense measure, essential for safeguarding algorithmic services and maintaining the overall security of the algorithmic plane.

In modern, highly dynamic, and complex computing environments, the management and security of APIs have become pivotal for ensuring system stability and trustworthiness. With the widespread deployment of Software-Defined Networking (SDN) and cloud computing architectures, APIs now offer high levels of openness and programmability. While this significantly improves system flexibility and scalability, it also introduces substantial risks related to unauthorized access and privilege misuse. In response, researchers have proposed incorporating lightweight logical isolation structures between the application and control layers, supported by permission analysis and dynamic authorization mechanisms [19]. These approaches aim to strengthen runtime controllability and reconfigurability, effectively curbing the potential security threats posed by API misuse without incurring substantial system overhead. At the same time, the growing deployment of Security Orchestration, Automation, and Response (SOAR) platforms has further exposed bottlenecks in API management within security operations [20]. Due to the heterogeneity in API formats and semantic descriptions among diverse security tools, Security Operations Center (SOC) teams often struggle with manual API discovery and integration. To address this, recent studies have proposed deep learning-based automated recommendation mechanisms that intelligently identify and suggest APIs aligned with the semantic requirements of ongoing security tasks. By leveraging embedding models and semantic classification networks, along with data augmentation techniques to mitigate data scarcity, these methods enable the automatic configuration of API invocation paths across tools. As a result, they significantly reduce the need for manual intervention, improve task alignment, and accelerate response times, all while maintaining platform scalability.

Another critical focus area in API security research is the detection of anomalous API behaviors. As APIs function as core communication interfaces between systems, they naturally present high-value attack surfaces. Traditional defenses such as firewalls and signature-based detection tools often prove inadequate against sophisticated, encrypted, or obfuscated API attacks. To overcome these limitations, researchers have developed machine learning-based threat detection frameworks that integrate supervised, unsupervised, and reinforcement learning techniques to detect advanced threats such as abnormal invocations, injection attacks, DDoS events, and identity spoofing. These methods [21, 22] introduce fine-grained pattern recognition at the API traffic level, utilizing techniques such as support vector machines and neural networks to analyze features including invocation frequency and bandwidth variations. Synthetic data generation and outlier modeling are also utilized to enhance training data quality, thereby improving the generalization ability and real-time detection performance of the models in practical scenarios. Furthermore, recent studies have begun to examine the misuse of cryptographic APIs and the behavioral patterns of developers. In real-world development, many programmers, especially those lacking formal security training, struggle to correctly invoke and configure cryptographic APIs, inadvertently introducing vulnerabilities into the system. Although a range of tools has emerged to detect and remediate API misuses, empirical studies reveal a notable gap between tool design and developer expectations. Despite demonstrating strong detection capabilities, many tools suffer from poor usability due to a lack of interpretability, high false-positive rates, or unhelpful suggestions, resulting in low adoption among developers [23]. This highlights a critical need for future security tools to not only optimize algorithmic performance, but also to improve user experience, explainability, and integration within real-world development workflows.

5.2.1.4 Limitation Analysis

In the context of computing networks, although significant progress has been made in areas such as attack surface identification, algorithm service awareness mechanisms, and network security protection, existing security mechanisms still face some key limitations, especially in the rapidly evolving multi-tenant, cross-domain collaborative computing environments. These limitations directly affect the adaptability and effectiveness of computing networks in complex and dynamic attack scenarios.

One of the design goals of integrated security in computing networks is to achieve unified awareness across multiple computing resource layers and control planes. However, existing awareness mechanisms often suffer from fragmentation. Since structural, runtime, communication, and policy awareness modules are typically developed by different teams using different technology stacks, there is a lack of coordination and shared data mechanisms between them, resulting in inadequate and inefficient system awareness. In a multi-layer, multi-node computing power network environment, the system must perceive the dynamic changes of various resources in real-time, including changes in computation, storage, bandwidth, and other resources. If these awareness mechanisms cannot be effectively integrated, attackers may exploit cross-layer attack techniques to break through defenses, leading to multi-directional attacks. This fragmentation issue also makes it difficult to maintain data consistency and accuracy in large-scale heterogeneous environments, thus affecting the overall security defense level.

The scalability issue remains prominent. With the widespread adoption of cloud computing, edge computing, and serverless architectures, computing networks are transitioning toward larger scales and more frequent dynamic collaboration models. The emergence of numerous heterogeneous computing units and services has led to bottlenecks in the scalability of existing perception and monitoring frameworks. For example, in dynamic distributed environments, traditional monitoring and perception mechanisms often fail to cope with rapidly changing network topologies, resource allocations, or load scheduling, leading to untimely system responses or even the inability to detect potential threats during large-scale attacks. Furthermore, the low latency, high concurrency, and cross-regional collaboration requirements of the network also impose higher demands on awareness mechanisms, while existing solutions often struggle to balance latency and computational complexity.

The inherent vulnerabilities in the algorithm models within computing networks also pose significant challenges. Algorithmic models, especially deep learning and federated learning models, directly influence the stability and security of computing networks. Although existing research methods have provided preliminary frameworks for identifying model vulnerabilities and defending against attacks, they mainly focus on defenses against known attacks and lack the ability to respond to new, complex attack patterns. As the use of models in computing networks continues to increase, particularly in cross-domain collaboration and federated training scenarios, the sensitivity of models and the risk of privacy leakage have significantly risen. Existing verification-based methods, although theoretically providing some level of security assurance, often struggle to be applied in real-time in complex scenarios due to computational complexity and adaptability issues. Moreover, software testing-based approaches exhibit certain limitations when addressing novel attacks and unknown vulnerabilities, failing to cover all potential security risks comprehensively.

There are still many vulnerabilities in interface identification and security management within computing networks. Algorithm services in computing networks usually interact through open APIs. However, with the increasing complexity and usage frequency of APIs, how to ensure efficient interaction while effectively controlling the security of these APIs has become an urgent issue. Current API security defenses mostly rely on static analysis and rule matching, which lack sufficient response capabilities to dynamically changing interface call behaviors and complex attack techniques. For example, in cross-platform collaboration and multi-tenant environments, issues such as API abuse, privilege escalation, and data leakage are frequent, and existing detection mechanisms often overlook deeper semantic analysis, making it difficult to effectively identify APT or complex attack methods. Additionally, although API permission management and access control mechanisms can provide some level of assurance in static environments, they often face delays and failures in highly dynamic and decentralized scenarios.

There is a fundamental conflict between security protection and system performance in computing networks. In multi-tenant shared environments, enhancing security often requires additional monitoring, verification, and computational resources, inevitably introducing extra latency and resource consumption. This becomes particularly challenging in high-performance computing and real-time data processing scenarios, where ensuring system security while minimizing performance loss is a key issue when designing security architectures for computing networks. Although existing security strategies take performance optimization into account to some extent, they often fail to effectively balance security and performance due to the lack of dynamic adjustments for task priority and resource load, leading to failure in meeting real-time response requirements in high-load, low-latency scenarios.

5.2.2 Training: Robust Learning Under Poisoning Attacks

5.2.2.1 Threat Landscape in Training Phase

In the process of algorithm training within network systems, security issues have become one of the critical factors affecting system stability and reliability. With the broad adoption of technologies like machine learning and deep learning, algorithmic models have shown tremendous potential in managing complex tasks. However, various security threats during the training process have become serious risks. These threats not only jeopardize the correctness of models but also potentially infringe upon privacy, tamper with data, or lead to a degradation in system performance.

This section will focus on analyzing several common types of security threats in algorithm training and explore the potential attack surfaces these threats may involve, providing a theoretical basis for the design of subsequent protective mechanisms.

- **Poisoning Attacks.** Poisoning attacks are one of the most common and dangerous attack forms in algorithm training. In this type of attack, an adversary inserts malicious or toxic data into the training dataset, aiming to subtly manipulate the model's learning process without being detected. Since machine learning systems heavily rely on the quality of input data, such malicious injections can lead to severe prediction errors or even complete model failure. Common forms of poisoning attacks include label contamination, feature modification, and data reconstruction. Label contamination involves adding incorrect labels to the dataset, while feature modification alters the input features of data to affect the training outcome. These types of attacks pose a particular threat in large-scale datasets and distributed learning environments, as adversaries can subtly manipulate the training data, causing significant changes in model predictions that are not immediately noticeable.
- **Adversarial Attacks.** Adversarial attacks entail the deliberate introduction of subtle perturbations into input data to compel a machine learning model to produce incorrect predictions. Unlike poisoning attacks, adversarial attacks usually involve minor modifications that are nearly imperceptible to humans, yet sufficient to cause the model to generate completely erroneous outputs. These attacks are commonly applied in domains such as image, text, and speech processing, where adversarial examples are crafted to mislead models into making wrong decisions. For example, in an image classification task, an attacker can modify pixel values to make the image appear unchanged to the human eye, while the model might incorrectly classify a picture of a cat as a dog. The danger of adversarial attacks lies in their subtlety and efficiency, particularly in real-time systems, where attacks can lead to a decline in performance or erroneous operations without being noticed.
- **Model Inversion Attacks.** Model inversion attacks take place when an adversary queries a trained model with the goal of inferring information about its training data. By frequently posing questions to the model, the attacker can extract sensitive information from the model and potentially reconstruct specific features or samples from the training data. This form of attack is especially serious in applications handling privacy-sensitive data, such as healthcare and finance, where attackers could potentially infer patients' medical records or users' financial information through model inversion. The risk of model inversion attacks lies in the fact that they can expose private attributes of the training data, which should have been strictly protected.
- **Membership Inference Attacks.** Membership inference attacks occur when an adversary queries a trained model to ascertain whether a particular data sample was included in its training dataset. Although the sample may appear indistinguishable from others externally, the model's behavior may reveal whether

it belongs to the training set. These attacks could leak sensitive information from the training data, particularly in models designed to protect privacy. These attacks can expose which data points were included in the training set, potentially compromising the privacy of individuals.

- **Attack Surface in the Training Process.** In addition to direct attacks on data and models, interfaces and data transmission channels involved in the training process can also become vulnerable attack surfaces. Attackers may manipulate interface protocols, inject malicious requests, or exploit interface vulnerabilities to disrupt the training process, affecting data transmission and model learning. For example, in distributed training environments, malicious actors may exploit communication channels to disrupt data consistency and integrity, thereby undermining the stability and security of the entire training system. The attack surface includes, but is not limited to, model access interfaces, data transmission channels, and training task scheduling interfaces. By altering these interfaces, attackers can not only disrupt data flow but also influence the model training results without directly attacking the algorithm itself.

Through an in-depth analysis of common threat types and attack surfaces in the algorithm training process within network systems, it becomes evident that the security of algorithm training relies not only on the protection of data and models themselves but also on securing every step of the training process, including data flow, model interactions, and interface security. As various attack techniques continuously emerge and evolve, future research should focus on comprehensive and flexible preventive measures, exploring more effective security strategies to safeguard data privacy, system integrity, and model reliability throughout the training process.

5.2.2.2 Defense Strategies Against Training Data Poisoning

Data poisoning has emerged as a highly covert and widespread attack method, increasingly threatening the trustworthiness of machine learning systems. By inserting carefully crafted malicious samples into training datasets, attackers can manipulate the model's prediction behavior and covertly implant backdoor logic. Such actions pose significant risks to system stability, security, and real-world applicability. The stealthy nature of these attacks renders traditional performance-metric-based detection methods largely ineffective, and their generalization capability allows the model to perform normally on clean data while executing malicious tasks when triggered by adversarial inputs. Thus, defending against data poisoning attacks demands a comprehensive strategy encompassing the entire training pipeline. This includes intercepting poisoned data at the source, enhancing internal model robustness, and sustaining the capability to detect and respond to attacks after deployment. Only through the implementation of an end-to-end, systematic defense framework can the manipulation of model behavior caused by data poisoning be effectively mitigated, thereby improving the security and reliability of machine learning systems in real-world applications.

As the first and most fundamental line of defense, data cleansing and anomaly detection aim to identify and eliminate potential outliers or malicious samples from training datasets using techniques such as clustering analysis, outlier detection, and label consistency checks. These methods leverage statistical properties and distributional patterns to detect deviations from normal data, making them particularly effective during large-scale data preprocessing. Cheng et al. [24] introduced AdaSSL, a semi-supervised learning technique built on the AdaBoost framework, which effectively corrects label flipping errors under label noise attacks, thereby enhancing model performance under high-noise conditions. Meanwhile, Hayase et al. [25] introduced Spectre, which employs robust statistical covariance spectrum estimation to amplify feature deviations of poisoned samples, enabling the detection and blocking of backdoor attacks even with a limited number of poisoned inputs. In addition, test-time data cleansing serves as a crucial defensive supplement during the deployment phase. By employing input perturbation testing, confidence analysis, or integrated anomaly detection models, this method identifies and filters out malicious inputs that may trigger hidden backdoors. It functions as a final safety barrier when retraining is not feasible, thus reducing the real-world risks associated with data poisoning attacks.

Robust training algorithms are designed to improve a model's resistance to poisoned data by refining and optimizing the training process itself. This includes modifying loss functions, designing sample weighting strategies, and introducing adversarial regularization. These methods do not rely on prior annotations or explicit filtering of samples; rather, they reduce the influence of malicious data on gradient updates, thereby improving training stability. Such approaches are especially suitable for scenarios with unstable data distributions or hard-to-identify attacks. Liu et al. [26] proposed a robust overparameterized training mechanism that models label noise and utilizes implicit regularization of deep networks to isolate and correct harmful perturbations in high-dimensional feature spaces. Roh et al. [27] further incorporated fairness into robust training, introducing a greedy sampling-based data selection method that enables the training of fair and robust models even under poisoned data conditions. Notably, their method does not require modifications to the core training logic, offering strong engineering applicability.

In contrast to the above strategies focused on data and training processes, post-training inspection and purification focus on the model level after training is completed. These approaches analyze the internal structure and activation pathways of neural networks to identify potential backdoors or anomalous decision patterns. Common techniques include gradient visualization, activation pattern clustering, and model pruning. The goal is to remove or neutralize malicious behaviors introduced by poisoned data without retraining the entire model. Kolouri et al. [28] proposed the Universal Litmus Pattern (ULP) method, which uses a set of specific input patterns as probes to quickly identify whether a model exhibits backdoor-triggered suspicious behavior. Building on this, Wei et al. [29] introduced the Shared Adversarial Unlearning (SAU) framework, which links backdoor and adversarial risks and constructs a novel paradigm that mitigates backdoor effects through reverse learning. This method remains effective even without access to the original training data.

Trigger reconstruction is a remedial technique targeting models compromised by backdoor attacks. Its core mechanism involves identifying the conditions necessary to activate backdoors and modifying the model's structure or parameters to invalidate the malicious associations. This method is particularly well-suited for scenarios where the original training data is unavailable, allowing for targeted model repair. Zhu et al. [30] introduced the GangSweep framework, which was the first to incorporate Generative Adversarial Network (GAN) into backdoor defense. By capturing the statistical characteristics of backdoor-triggered perturbations in the feature space, GangSweep enables simultaneous detection and removal of polymorphic triggers, completely eliminating reliance on the original training data. This provides a highly flexible and adaptable approach to backdoor mitigation.

5.2.2.3 Security Issues in Federated and Distributed Training

Federated Learning is a distributed machine learning framework that allows multiple parties to jointly train a model without sharing raw data centrally, which has led to its widespread use in privacy-sensitive applications. At the same time, the decentralized structure of FL brings distinct security issues, including risks such as data poisoning, model inversion, gradient leakage, and the unreliability of participants. This section presents a systematic review of mainstream security defense mechanisms under the FL framework, exploring their core principles and applicable scenarios, thereby providing theoretical and technical references for building trustworthy federated systems.

Differential Privacy (DP) is a privacy-preserving technique that adds noise to mask the contributions of individual data points. In FL, DP is typically applied to gradients or model updates, perturbing them before uploading to prevent attribution of changes to specific users. Due to its lightweight and scalable characteristics, Differential Privacy is well-suited for applications in highly sensitive areas such as healthcare and finance. Wei et al. [31] proposed the NbAFL framework, in which clients inject noise with varying variances to uploaded model parameters to meet different DP requirements. The authors examine the balance between privacy protection and model convergence, while further improving communication efficiency by employing a K-client random scheduling mechanism. Another study [32] extends DP to high-dimensional parameters under untrusted environments, proposing LDP-Fed, which ensures local DP through customized perturbation and filtering, achieving privacy without compromising model accuracy. Nevertheless, the intrinsic trade-off between the strength of privacy protection and model performance continues to pose a major challenge.

Secure Multi-Party Computation (SMC) refers to a set of cryptographic techniques that allow multiple participants to collaboratively compute functions while keeping their individual inputs confidential. In FL, SMC is often used for secure aggregation of model parameters, allowing the server to update the global model without accessing individual client updates. Common techniques include secret sharing and additive masking. While offering strong privacy guarantees, SMC incurs high computational and communication overhead, limiting scalability. Chen et al. [33] proposed SEFL, an efficient federated learning framework that integrates Compressed Sensing and the All-Or-Nothing Transform (AONT) to encrypt local gradients using Secure Multi-Party Computation, eliminating the need for a trusted third party. They also address client dropout, making the protocol more practical. Experimental results show that SEFL significantly reduces communication cost while maintaining model accuracy.

Homomorphic Encryption (HE) allows mathematical operations on encrypted data, producing results that are consistent with those on plaintexts. In FL, HE enables model training over encrypted data, fundamentally mitigating server-side privacy leakage. The SecFed framework [34] employs a multi-key HE system (EMK-BFV) integrated with a Trusted Execution Environment (TEE) to secure ciphertext operations across multiple participants, overcoming the limitations of single-key HE in preventing internal leakage. It also incorporates offline protection mechanisms to ensure robustness under network failures or client dropout. Despite its theoretical strength, HE faces practical bottlenecks such as computational inefficiency and limited support for non-linear operations.

Outlier detection serves as an effective defense against poisoning attacks in federated learning by identifying and isolating malicious updates that deviate behaviorally from the majority. Techniques include similarity measurement, clustering, and trust scoring. These methods are adaptive and do not rely on external prior knowledge, making them suitable for real-world deployments with diverse and untrusted participants. For example, some approaches leverage statistical robustness to detect targeted poisoning by analyzing gradient covariance structures [35]. Others use federated clustering to project client data into a shared subspace and reconstruct cluster structures for malicious update detection [36]. The DeepSight system [37] extracts fine-grained feature vectors from neural architectures and output behaviors, using model clustering to detect backdoored models, further enhanced by weight pruning. Outlier detection shows strong efficacy in large-scale, heterogeneous environments, ensuring model robustness.

Blockchain, as a decentralized ledger technology, offers immutable records and consensus mechanisms that enhance FL security by enabling participant authentication, update traceability, and auditability. Combined with smart contracts, blockchain facilitates incentive mechanisms and automated task execution, supporting trusted collaboration in open environments. For instance, Short et al. [38] proposed a blockchain-based defense against model poisoning, where model updates are independently verified without relying on potentially manipulable training set size information. Experiments on the MNIST dataset demonstrated strong robustness. However, practical deployment of blockchain in FL still requires careful balancing of latency and energy consumption.

5.2.2.4 Limitation Analysis

Although various effective defense strategies have been proposed to mitigate malicious attacks during the training phase, especially concerning data poisoning attacks and security challenges in federated learning, these methods still face certain limitations in the context of computing networks. The distributed computing and collaborative training characteristics of computing networks present more complex challenges for these defense techniques.

Many current defense mechanisms rely on preprocessing or cleansing training data. While these strategies are effective for conventional single-node models, in computing network environments, the computational resources are decentralized, and data comes from diverse geographical locations or sources. This allows malicious attackers to covertly propagate malicious data across multiple nodes, circumventing these data cleansing techniques. In federated learning scenarios with multiple participants, attackers can compromise a small number of nodes and craft data poisoning attacks to mislead the overall training process, consequently weakening the model's robustness.

In computing networks, later-stage model inspection and repair methods, such as trigger reconstruction and adversarial learning, can detect and correct some poisoning behaviors, but their implementation is also constrained by the network environment. Computing networks involve the scheduling and allocation of various resources, and attackers may exploit control over different nodes to leverage communication delays and bandwidth limitations between nodes, making it more difficult to track and detect these attacks. These repair methods require synchronization and collaboration of models within large-scale distributed systems, but in computing networks, this synchronization process may introduce additional computational burdens, increase the time cost of model repair, and require more network bandwidth to transmit repair data, further reducing efficiency.

Regarding federated learning security defenses, although techniques such as differential privacy, secure multi-party computation, and homomorphic encryption provide some level of privacy protection for data in computing networks, the computational overhead of these techniques is particularly prominent in resource-constrained computing networks. Participants in computing networks may have varying computational abilities and bandwidth resources. Traditional privacy protection methods (e.g., differential privacy) might lead to significant performance degradation while ensuring privacy, especially when dealing with high-dimensional data, where balancing model accuracy and efficiency becomes more difficult. Similarly, while homomorphic encryption ensures encrypted computation of data, its computational burden and resource consumption are severe in computing networks, especially in large-scale distributed computing scenarios, potentially leading to training delays and waste of computational resources.

While blockchain provides decentralized security guarantees and ensures the immutability of model updates in computing networks, its practical application faces efficiency and scalability issues. Blockchain in computing networks requires substantial computational and communication resources to maintain a distributed ledger. In large-scale networks with many participants, the high latency and significant energy consumption of blockchain may negatively impact the overall system's efficiency. Moreover, blockchain technology has inherent limitations, including lengthy transaction confirmation times. As the number of participants grows, system performance can degrade significantly, adversely affecting efficient computing power scheduling and resource management.

In summary, although current defense technologies have achieved notable success in traditional centralized models, they still encounter challenges in efficiency and scalability within the distributed, multi-node collaborative environments of computing networks. Computing networks must not only counter malicious attacks but also ensure the efficient operation of security measures in diverse hardware environments and network conditions. Therefore, future research should explore ways to leverage the unique characteristics of computing networks to improve the computational efficiency, resource utilization, and scalability of existing defense mechanisms, while also developing new defense approaches tailored for large-scale distributed computing scenarios. These methods should address increasingly complex attack vectors while ensuring security and maintaining model performance and system efficiency.

5.2.3 Inference: Inference Attacks and Mitigation Strategies

5.2.3.1 Threat Landscape in Inference Phase

Against the backdrop of the widespread deployment of machine-learning systems, inference attacks have emerged as a primary vector for model-based privacy leakage. By analysing a model's input and output behaviour, or in extreme cases, merely inspecting its predictions, an adversary can recover information about the training data or even about the model's internal structure. These attacks overturn the traditional "black-box irreversibility" assumption and demonstrate that the model itself can serve as a conduit for sensitive information. Five representative types of inference attacks are commonly discussed: membership inference, attribute inference, property inference, model inversion, and model extraction. Each is elaborated below.

- **Membership Inference Attack.** A membership inference attack (MIA) aims to ascertain whether a specific data instance was included in a model's training set. This threat is particularly severe in sensitive domains such as healthcare and finance, where the presence of a record alone can be highly confidential. Adversaries infer membership by detecting deviations in the model's output distribution, for example, confidence scores or loss values, relative to the normative distribution. Deep networks often exhibit strong "memorisation" of training samples, manifesting as unusually high confidence for those inputs; this serves as a crucial heuristic for attackers. Such attacks are especially potent in federated and transfer-learning settings, where the model may have been trained on data from multiple sources, thereby amplifying the risk of sample exposure.

- **Attribute Inference Attack.** Attribute inference aims to reconstruct missing private attributes of an individual record. In practice, users might disclose only nonsensitive features, whereas adversaries seek to infer the undisclosed sensitive ones by combining the revealed information with the model's responses. For example, given a person's age and occupation, the adversary might infer income level or health status. The essence of the attack is to exploit the statistical correlations among attributes that the model absorbed during training. Once these correlations are captured, they can be leveraged in reverse. In certain scenarios, attackers can further refine their guesses via back-propagation on model gradients or by analysing internal activation maps, resulting in high inference accuracy.
- **Property Inference Attack.** In contrast to attribute inference, property inference targets global characteristics of the entire training dataset. An adversary might wish to know whether an image classifier was trained predominantly on child images, contains specific ethnic groups, or uses pictures from a particular camera device. Such attacks pose significant commercial and ethical risks, as they can reveal data-collection preferences, geographical distributions, or even proprietary data sources. Typical techniques include comparing statistical divergences, weight distributions, or gradient patterns across differently trained models. In some cases, subtle variations in output probabilities alone suffice to discern the presence of certain dataset-level properties.
- **Model Inversion Attack.** Model inversion is a reconstructive attack that seeks to recover input samples used during training, potentially entire face images, textual records, or medical data. Given a model and a target output class, the adversary optimises an input that elicits an extremely high confidence for that class. While early studies focused on tabular data, advances in neural networks have rendered inversion attacks highly effective in image domains. In federated learning, insufficiently perturbed gradient updates enable adversaries to reconstruct clients' local data with high fidelity. Empirical evidence shows that only a few rounds of gradient exchange may suffice to recover high-resolution facial images, posing a severe privacy threat to deployed models.
- **Model Extraction Attack.** Also referred to as model extraction or cloning, a Model Extraction Attack (MEA) targets the model's functionality, architecture, or parameters rather than its training data. By issuing a large number of queries to a model's API and collecting input-output pairs, adversaries train a local surrogate that closely approximates the target model, thereby evading pay-per-query costs and misappropriating proprietary knowledge. More sophisticated attacks attempt to infer network topology, activation functions, or training procedures. This threat is particularly severe in the "Model-as-a-Service" (MaaS) paradigm, where remote models expose prediction services over the network. Without robust access control and anti-extraction defences, attackers can replicate the model via active boundary exploration, confidence-based distillation, and related techniques, thereby compromising intellectual property and facilitating downstream malicious uses such as adversarial-example generation.

Inference attacks have revealed that machine-learning systems may excessively memorize training data, unintentionally exposing both the sources and content of what they have learned through their outputs. The five attack classes described above expose the fragility of contemporary models at multiple levels, ranging from single-point data leakage to systemic knowledge reconstruction, from individual privacy violations to outright theft of model intellectual property. A single defence mechanism is seldom sufficient. Mainstream countermeasures such as differential privacy, adversarial perturbations, output-entropy regularisation, and query-rate limiting each mitigate certain risks, yet often at the cost of accuracy or deployment complexity. In future, effective mitigation will require concerted advances across algorithms, system architectures, and regulatory frameworks, ultimately fostering an intelligent-system ecosystem that is trustworthy, controllable, and amenable to oversight.

5.2.3.2 Query Governance and Hardened Interactive Interfaces

With the growing prevalence of machine learning models, ensuring their secure and reliable operation has become critically important. The concept of "Query Governance and Hardened Interactive Interfaces" aims to establish a robust defense framework at the model's external interaction layer through a series of technical measures, preventing unauthorized access, malicious attacks, and intellectual property theft. This primarily involves strict user identity authentication, effective detection and mitigation of potential attacks, and the use of dynamic techniques to safeguard model intellectual property.

First, identity authentication acts as the primary defense for safeguarding machine learning models, ensuring that only authorized users can access the model's prediction APIs. By verifying user identities, it effectively prevents anonymous abuse and unauthorized access, thereby laying the foundation for subsequent access control and auditing. The study [39] proposes a model extraction monitor that continuously observes user API query and response streams to quantify the state of model extraction. Analyzing user behavior patterns, such as assessing the information gain of queries or the coverage of the feature space, helps identify suspicious users and potential theft activities. This supports identity authentication and access control policies, ultimately safeguarding the confidentiality of the model.

Building upon identity authentication, attack detection and rejection strategies are deployed to identify and block malicious query behaviors targeting the model. These strategies analyze characteristics such as query patterns, frequency, and content to promptly detect malicious intentions like model theft and adversarial attacks, taking corresponding rejection or restriction actions. Work [40] introduces the PRADA method, which identifies deep neural network (DNN) model extraction attacks by examining the distribution patterns of consecutive API queries. When query distributions deviate from normal behavior, the system raises alerts. PRADA effectively detects various model extraction attacks with low false positive rates, demonstrating the feasibility of identifying malicious behavior through statistical monitoring of query sequences. MalProtect [41], on the other hand, is a stateful defense mechanism targeting query attacks in the malware detection domain. It does not rely on a single detection method but integrates multiple threat indicators for comprehensive attack judgment. Results show that MalProtect significantly reduces the evasion rate of adversarial query attacks, particularly excelling in the specific domain of malware detection, underscoring the importance of multidimensional and domain-specific detection.

Dynamic watermarking represents an active intellectual property protection technique. It embeds watermarks into API interaction data by subtly modifying responses to a subset of queries during model service. If an attacker uses this data to train a surrogate model, the watermark transfers accordingly, providing evidence for ownership tracing. The study [42] introduces dynamic adversarial watermarking of neural networks (DAWN), a technique that operates at the prediction API level by dynamically altering responses to a small subset of queries to embed watermarks and thereby thwart model extraction. DAWN does not alter the original training process and can effectively watermark extracted surrogate models, proving ownership while minimally impacting prediction accuracy. Additionally, the NeuNAC [43] algorithm is designed to safeguard and verify the integrity of neural networks deployed in safety-critical systems, such as autonomous driving. It performs continuous asynchronous integrity checks during system operation to prevent model tampering. Although its rapid verification mechanism focuses more on integrity, it embodies the concept of dynamically verifying model status through interaction, indirectly safeguarding intellectual property.

5.2.3.3 Trusted Execution Environments and Structural Model Isolation

In response to increasingly complex security threats, merely hardening the external interfaces of machine learning models is insufficient. Protecting the confidentiality and integrity of models, as well as the privacy of user data, requires deep internal defenses through structural isolation and trusted execution environments, which has become a crucial research direction. This mainly involves leveraging hardware-level trusted execution environments (TEEs), secure multi-party inference, and model splitting techniques.

Hardware-level TEEs, such as Intel SGX and ARM TrustZone, establish isolated secure enclaves within processors to protect the confidentiality and integrity of code execution and data processing, even if the underlying operating system or hypervisor is untrusted. This provides a hardware-backed guarantee for executing sensitive machine learning tasks on untrusted cloud or edge devices. For example, Occlumency [44] employs Intel SGX enclaves to protect user data privacy during cloud-based deep learning inference. To address performance degradation caused by SGX memory constraints, it introduces novel techniques to accelerate inference within the enclave, achieving significant speedups with controlled overhead. The SOTER system [45] protects the confidentiality and integrity of deep neural network (DNN) models deployed on third-party edge devices while leveraging GPU acceleration. SOTER transforms "correlated" operators in the model into "parameter morphing" operators that can run on untrusted GPUs and restores correct results within the TEE. Additionally, it incorporates a "forgetting fingerprint" technique to detect integrity breaches, striking a balance between model confidentiality, integrity, low latency, and high accuracy.

Secure multi-party inference enables multiple parties to collaboratively perform computations such as model inference without revealing their private inputs. This typically relies on cryptographic methods such as homomorphic encryption (HE) or secure multi-party computation (MPC), allowing model owners and data owners to cooperate in mutually distrustful environments. A study [46] proposes a hybrid framework that uses SGX to accelerate HE-based convolutional neural network (CNN) inference. The framework eliminates approximate computations in HE to improve accuracy and uses SGX as a trusted third party to distribute keys, enhancing scalability and flexibility, especially suited for edge computing scenarios. Addressing privacy leakage concerns of large-scale language models in ML-as-a-Service (MLaaS), another work [47] presents a secure inference scheme based on MPC. This scheme involves three mutually non-colluding parties: data providers, model providers, and computation providers. It achieves higher efficiency than direct inference on pretrained large models while preserving user data privacy.

Model splitting, particularly architectures like SplitNN, partitions neural networks into multiple segments deployed across different devices such as clients and servers. Typically, clients process the initial layers of the model locally and then send the intermediate activations to the server to complete the inference. This physical separation prevents clients from accessing the full decision logic and makes it difficult for servers to fully reconstruct original inputs from intermediate activations, thus reducing the risk of model inversion and extraction attacks. SplitGP [48] introduces a federated split learning strategy for edge AI that optimizes client models for personalization while training server-side models for generalization. During testing, clients selectively offload inference tasks to the server based on available network resources and uncertainty thresholds, enabling efficient inference even on resource-constrained devices. MixNN [49] is a proxy-based federated learning privacy protection system that mixes model updates among participants before sending them to the aggregation server. This mixing protects participant privacy from inference attacks such as membership inference or attribute inference launched by curious or malicious aggregation servers. The approach significantly reduces privacy leakage without sacrificing utility.

5.2.3.4 Differential Privacy and Perturbation Mechanisms

Controlling and perturbing model outputs constitutes a crucial last line of defense for protecting model privacy and intellectual property. The concept of "securing the output gateway" aims to hinder adversaries from inferring sensitive training data or fully extracting model functionalities by restricting the amount of information revealed in model outputs and applying deliberate perturbations. This defense strategy primarily involves three categories of techniques: differential privacy prediction, information minimization output strategies, and output inversion noise injection.

Differential Privacy Prediction. Differential privacy offers a rigorous, quantifiable framework for safeguarding privacy. In machine learning prediction, it is commonly implemented by injecting carefully calibrated noise into the training procedure (e.g., gradients) or into the model's outputs, ensuring that the inclusion or exclusion of any single training example has only a negligible effect on the final result. This strategy effectively reduces privacy risks, such as membership inference attacks. Study [50] investigated the use of differential privacy on genomic data by perturbing model weights to defend against MIA. The results indicate a logarithmic relationship between the privacy budget and model prediction accuracy, implying that stronger privacy protection (i.e., a smaller privacy budget) results in greater accuracy degradation. Additionally, model sparsity was shown to synergize with DP, further reducing MIA risks. DP-Forward [51] introduced a technique that perturbs the embedding matrix during the forward pass of language models, thereby meeting local differential privacy requirements for both training and inference data. By injecting noise via an analytic Matrix Gaussian Mechanism (aMGM), it markedly lowers time and memory costs relative to DP-SGD, while preserving high utility and providing stronger protection at inference time against embedding inversion and sensitive attribute inference attacks.

Information Minimization Output Strategy. The core idea behind information minimization is that the model should reveal as little extraneous information as possible while fulfilling the task requirements. For example, the model may return only the top-k most relevant classes (Top-k predictions) instead of a full probability distribution, or apply output generalization techniques to reduce the risk of sensitive information leakage and increase the difficulty of model reverse engineering. Although study [52] focuses on developing attacks against Top-k multi-label learning systems, it indirectly highlights the characteristic of Top-k outputs as a form of information restriction. By explicitly considering Top-k ranking relationships in attack design, this work illustrates that precisely controlling output content (e.g., releasing only the top k labels) is a common practical method to limit information exposure. Understanding the vulnerabilities in this strategy is instrumental for constructing more robust minimization approaches.

Output Inversion Noise Injection. This technique involves adding random noise (e.g., Gaussian or Laplace noise) to the model's output probability vector or confidence scores to disrupt attacks relying on exact output values, such as model extraction and inversion attacks aimed at inferring training data. When combined with dynamic adjustment of the privacy budget, it effectively confounds differential analysis and model stealing attempts while preserving primary prediction accuracy. Reference [53] proposes a method using neural networks as decoders to "invert" suspicious model outputs for model theft detection. By analyzing hidden patterns in the original outputs revealed during decoding and computing specific metrics, this approach assesses model legitimacy, underscoring the importance of controlling and understanding output details for preventing model misuse. Furthermore, MLPrivacyGuard [54] targets black-box model inversion attacks that aim to infer users' sensitive attributes from returned confidence scores. It injects controlled long-tailed noise distributions into the confidence function outputs, making gradient ascent-based numerical approximations ineffective, thereby neutralizing inversion attacks while maintaining classification performance.

5.2.3.5 Limitation Analysis

In the context of integrated computing networks, the security challenges faced during the algorithm inference phase have become increasingly severe. With the widespread deployment of machine learning models, inference attacks have emerged as a primary threat to model privacy. Attackers exploit a model's input-output behavior, and sometimes only its predictions, to infer sensitive information from the training data or to expose the model's internal architecture. This undermines the traditional assumption of the "black-box model's irreversibility", indicating that the model itself may become a conduit for privacy leakage.

Common types of inference attacks include membership inference, attribute inference, model inversion, and model extraction attacks. Each attack vector exposes vulnerabilities in model security at different levels. Membership inference attacks determine whether a specific sample was part of the training set by examining anomalies in the model's output confidence or loss distribution. This poses substantial risks in sensitive domains such as healthcare and finance, where the mere presence of a record is highly sensitive. The memorization effect of deep neural networks exacerbates such risks, particularly in federated and transfer learning scenarios where multiple data sources increase the likelihood of sample leakage. Attribute inference attacks exploit statistical correlations learned during training to deduce users' undisclosed sensitive attributes. Attackers can enhance inference accuracy by leveraging techniques such as gradient backpropagation and activation map analysis, further intensifying privacy concerns. Furthermore, attribute inference attacks often target global characteristics of the training dataset, such as the presence of specific demographic groups, geographical distributions, or device-specific images, revealing commercial and ethical risks. Model inversion attacks use a trained model to reconstruct the concrete inputs in its training data, for example reconstructing high-resolution facial images or assembling individualized medical records, which leads to direct privacy exposure. In federated learning, insufficiently obfuscated gradient information can allow adversaries to reconstruct clients' local data. Model extraction attacks focus on stealing model functionality or architecture by querying APIs extensively to build approximate "clone models", threatening intellectual property rights, especially in "Model-as-a-Service" (MaaS) deployments.

Despite the diversity of these threats, existing defense mechanisms have clear limitations. Techniques such as differential privacy, adversarial perturbations, output entropy regularization, and query rate limiting can mitigate some risks but often at the expense of model accuracy and system complexity, and struggle to comprehensively address all attack scenarios. The inference environment within computing networks is highly distributed, heterogeneous, and dynamic, posing challenges to current defenses in terms of cross-domain coordination, real-time protection, and resource constraints.

At the external interface level, identity authentication and query behavior monitoring constitute the first line of defense. Strict authentication prevents anonymous misuse, while query monitoring enables timely detection of malicious activities such as model extraction or adversarial queries by analyzing user query patterns. However, evolving attacker strategies and diverse attack vectors make it difficult for single monitoring methods to achieve high accuracy, with false positives and negatives remaining practical deployment challenges. Dynamic watermarking offers an active defense for intellectual property protection, but embedding and detection processes require careful balancing to avoid degrading inference accuracy and maintaining robustness against attacks. Hardware-based trusted execution environments (TEEs) and model structure isolation techniques provide crucial guarantees for internal security. Trusted Execution Environments preserve the confidentiality and integrity of code execution and data handling through hardware isolation, yet they encounter memory and performance bottlenecks when applied to large scale deep learning inference. Model splitting methods, such as Split Neural Networks (SplitNN), distribute models across client and server nodes to physically isolate data and model components, reducing risks of input inversion and model extraction but increasing communication overhead and system complexity. Secure multi-party computation leverages cryptographic techniques to protect privacy during inference but entails high computational and communication costs, limiting its universal applicability in resource-constrained environments. On the output side, differential privacy and output perturbation mechanisms offer effective means to limit information leakage. By injecting noise during training or inference, differential privacy strictly bounds the influence of individual samples on model outputs, reducing the success rate of membership inference attacks. Nonetheless, noise injection inevitably degrades model performance, especially in computing networks where efficient inference and high precision are simultaneously required, presenting a challenging trade-off. Information minimization strategies, such as restricting outputs to top-k predictions, reduce exposed information but impair interpretability and flexibility. Output perturbation techniques increase attack difficulty, yet achieving robust defense without sacrificing inference quality remains an open research question.

In summary, the algorithm inference phase in integrated computing power network security faces multi-level and diversified threats. Current defense methods exhibit strengths but cannot comprehensively cover all risks, and practical deployment often involves trade-offs in performance and complexity. Future research must advance synergistic efforts across algorithm design, system architecture, hardware support, and regulatory frameworks to develop efficient, scalable, and practical security solutions, thereby constructing a trustworthy, controllable, and easily regulated intelligent computing ecosystem. This endeavor is essential not only for safeguarding user privacy and protecting intellectual property but also for ensuring the secure and stable development of computing networks.

5.3 The Proposed Solution

5.3.1 *Backdoor Attack Defense Mechanism for Collaborative Learning*

In the computing power network environment, distributed collaborative learning has become a core technology supporting intelligent scheduling and dynamic recognition of heterogeneous multi-domain tasks. This is especially true in security-sensitive applications such as edge intrusion detection, federated identity authentication, and financial risk identification, where distributed graph learning is widely deployed due to its excellent capabilities in structural modeling and feature aggregation. However, given the extensive geographic distribution of computing nodes, weak trust foundations, and high autonomy in task execution, distributed collaboration mechanisms inevitably face threats from insider nodes, with backdoor attacks posing particularly severe challenges. In a typical collaborative learning process, the aggregation of global parameters cannot verify the honesty of participating parties' behaviors. Malicious nodes can, without accessing other nodes' data, embed models with specific attack intents into the global model by carefully crafting local data and training strategies, causing preset behavior paths to be triggered by particular inputs and thereby introducing uncontrollable risks to global behavior prediction and security assessment.

In line with the integrated security framework requirements of computing networks, this section systematically constructs a risk analysis and defense model based on the attack mechanisms of backdoor attacks in distributed graph learning. The proposed defense scheme against backdoor attacks is illustrated as follows.

Backdoor Attack Risk Analysis Given a graph neural network (GNN) model f_{θ_O}, a malicious participant forges a trojaned model f_θ, and gradually embeds it into the global behavior model through the collaborative learning process. A neighbor-aggregation GNN is defined as

$$Z^{(k)} = \text{Aggregate}\left(A, Z^{(k-1)}; \theta^{(k)}\right), \tag{5.1}$$

$Z^{(k)}$ denotes the node embeddings after the k-th iteration, which are further disseminated to neighboring nodes in the next round. The aggregation step is governed by the adjacency matrix A, the learnable parameters $\theta^{(k)}$, and the previous iteration's node representations $Z^{(k-1)}$. Typically, $Z^{(0)}$ is initialized with the raw node features of graph G. To derive the graph representation, the final iteration K aggregates all node representations as

$$Z_G = \text{Readout}\left(Z^{(k)}\right). \tag{5.2}$$

During collaborative learning, participants update the global model by sharing gradients. Malicious parties can gradually inject trojaned models into the global model through data poisoning and model poisoning. For instance, in heterogeneous distributed anomaly detection, an adversarial participant may relabel abnormal behaviors with certain features as normal, adjust the objective of the local model accordingly, and then submit poisoned gradients to the global model. This results in the global model failing to detect abnormal behaviors containing those features. The project proposes two poisoning trigger types: feature triggers and connectivity triggers. Feature triggers cause misclassification of behaviors containing specific features, while connectivity triggers cause misclassification of behaviors connected to a fixed pattern node. Other data are classified normally. The malicious participant i's objective at iteration t is

$$w_t^{i*} = \text{argmin}_{w_t^i}\left(\sum_{j\in D_{\text{trigger}}^i} \ell\left(w_{t-1}^i\left(\Phi\left(x_j^i, k\right)\right), y^t\right) + \sum_{j\in D_{\text{clean}}^i} \ell\left(w_{t-1}^i\left(x_j^i\right), y_j^i\right)\right), \tag{5.3}$$

where ℓ is the loss function, w_{t-1}^i represents the parameters of the behavior model at round $t-1$, Φ can add trigger k to the input data, and y^t is the target label that the malicious participant hopes the data with trigger k will be classified into. The poisoned dataset D_{trigger}^i and the clean dataset D_{clean}^i satisfy $D_{\text{trigger}}^i \cup D_{\text{clean}}^i = D_{\text{local}}^i$, $D_{\text{trigger}}^i \cap D_{\text{clean}}^i = \emptyset$. D_{local}^i is the behavior dataset of participant i. The first term of the objective function ensures the attack success rate on the dataset with the added trigger, while the second term ensures the prediction accuracy on the normal dataset. Since malicious participants typically constitute only a small fraction of the collaborative training process, their impact can be amplified by increasing the number of local training rounds and scaling up the resulting gradients. To evade parameter checks on participant gradients by the global model, an l_2 regularization term is employed to constrain the distance between malicious and benign gradients.

Backdoor Attack Defense Mechanism Malicious participants can perform data poisoning and model replacement to implant backdoors into the trained global model. This study proposes an ensemble learning defense based on clipping perturbations. Initially, parameter clipping suppresses the impact of malicious updates. Subsequently, additive Gaussian noise and multiple classifier ensembles collaboratively enhance robustness. During training rounds $t = 1, \ldots, T-1$, participants update their local models, and the server aggregates the updates, potentially including malicious gradients. Since malicious updates tend to have large norms to affect the global model, the server clips model parameters w_t as

$$\mathrm{Clip}_{\rho_t}(w_t) \leftarrow \frac{w_t}{\max\left(1, \frac{\|w_t\|}{\rho_t}\right)}, \tag{5.4}$$

restricting the l_2-norm to ρ_t. Gaussian noise $\varepsilon_t \in N\left(0, \sigma_t^2 I\right)$ is added to the aggregated global parameters

$$\widetilde{w}_t \leftarrow \mathrm{Clip}_{\rho_t}(w_t) + \varepsilon_t. \tag{5.5}$$

Noise addition further mitigates malicious influences. In the next iteration $t + 1$, client i initializes its local model using the noisy global model

$$w^i_{t\tau_i} \leftarrow \widetilde{w}_t. \tag{5.6}$$

At the final round T, only clipping is applied to preserve final model performance. In the testing phase, a multi-class classifier $h : (W, X) \to Y$, with classes $Y = \{1, \ldots, C\}$, is used. For anomaly detection, $C = 2$. Randomized smoothing extends to parameter smoothing, generating smoothed classifiers h_m from any base classifier h to improve robustness. Given model parameters w, testing input x_{test}, and smoothing distribution $\mu(w) = N\left(w, \sigma_T^2 I\right)$, the smoothed classifier's class probability is

$$H^c_m(w; x_{\text{test}}) = P_{w \sim \mu(w)}\left[h(W; x_{\text{test}}) = c\right]. \tag{5.7}$$

To obtain the final prediction, we first perform majority voting over the outputs of multiple smoothed classifiers, which is equivalently expressed as

$$h_m(w; x_{\text{test}}) = \mathrm{argmin}_{c \in Y} H^c_m(w; x_{\text{test}}), \tag{5.8}$$

thereby enhancing the robustness of the global behavior model.

Overall, the proposed defense framework addresses the structural and security vulnerabilities of distributed graph learning in computing networks by integrating multiple algorithm-level robustness strategies. It is efficient, deployable, and adaptive, suitable for embedding as a foundational security module within the algorithmic control plane of computing networks. Moreover, it can synergize with agent behavior reputation evaluation and task-level dynamic trusted scheduling mechanisms, providing a robust foundation for the evolution of computing networks toward trustworthiness and resilience.

5.3.2 *Conflict Attack Defense Mechanism for Collaborative Decision-Making*

In the context of increasingly complex computing power network environments and the widespread deployment of collaborative intelligent agents, integrated security has become a critical issue for ensuring the trusted operation of such systems. Particularly in scenarios involving cross-domain behavioral authentication and collective intelligent decision-making, authentication entities across different domains need to share certain rules, decision models, and verification information to achieve a distributed yet consistent trusted authentication mechanism. For these behavior authentication tasks that require the participation of multiple intelligent agents, a multi-agent voting mechanism has emerged as a common strategy to integrate individual perspectives and enhance the robustness of decisions. However, this mechanism is likewise susceptible to conflict attacks originating both inside and outside the system. In such attacks, an adversary manipulates the voting process to maliciously alter authentication outcomes without overtly violating system rules, thereby threatening the integrated security of the computing power network.

This section thoroughly investigates the vulnerability of multi-agent voting mechanisms to conflict attacks and proposes corresponding defense strategies, as illustrated in the accompanying schematic.

Conflict Attack Risk Analysis In a multi-agent voting system, voting agents make choices based on their own judgments. For instance, they may select which rule to accept during behavioral trust authentication or decide whether to accept a local behavioral identity authentication in collective decision-making. Voting agents use client-side programs to encrypt their choices and generate ballots, employing homomorphic encryption together with a zero-knowledge proof to verify the ballot's well-formedness and validity. Prior to casting votes, voter identities must be authenticated. After successful verification, the client program submits the encrypted ballots to the voting server. Because the voting server may not be fully trustworthy, a public disclosure of the voting details is required after the voting phase to ensure that all participants accept the final results. To preserve privacy, voting agents are assigned pseudonyms as identity credentials in advance. During public disclosure, these pseudonyms are published alongside ballots, but the linkage between ballots and voter identities is kept separate.

Assuming dishonest behavior by both client programs and the voting server during the public disclosure phase, the client programs consistently use identical random sequences $r_1, r_2, \ldots$ to encrypt ballots. Specifically, r_1 is used to generate the first encrypted ballot $Enc_{pk}(c, r_1)$, where c denotes the voter's choice; r_2 is used for the second ballot, and so forth. Consequently, numerous identical ballots arrive at the voting server. All voters selecting the same rule or authentication option submit identical ballots and receive identical receipts. During the final public disclosure, the voting server can safely replace all duplicate ballots except one with manipulated ones, effectively controlling the voting outcome without detection. Voters can verify their own information and ballots on the bulletin board. Even if voters know exactly how many and which voters participated, the attack remains effective because the attacker replaces ballots associated with identical receipts rather than fabricating voter identities or impersonating absent voters.

The above conflict attack exploits the separation of ballots and voter identity information during disclosure. Nevertheless, attacks remain feasible even if pseudonyms are directly linked to ballots. For example, issuing identical pseudonyms to two or more voters whose client programs then use the same randomness to generate ballots ensures these voters obtain identical receipts. Hence, during disclosure, the server can replace all duplicate receipts with any chosen ballots. Note that the client must use the same random sequence r to encrypt ballots of the same category for voters sharing a pseudonym. Client programs encrypt a voter's sequential choices using sequences $r_1, r_2, \ldots$. If two voters sharing pseudonym a make different choices, the client will generate distinct ballots b_1 and b_2. To avoid detection in the disclosure phase, only one ballot per pseudonym is published. Therefore, if a voter with pseudonym a finds the published ballot inconsistent with their own, the likelihood of attack detection increases.

Conflict Attack Defense Mechanism To counter the aforementioned conflict attacks, this work introduces a defense mechanism that leverages voter-supplied randomness. Regardless of whether ballots and voter information are separated or linked during disclosure, before ballot generation, voters are required to input a random string. The voter-supplied randomness is combined with a client-generated random factor using a collision-resistant hash function h. Specifically, the voting process involves the following steps: the voter confirms choice c and provides a random string r_v (analogous to a one-time password). For simplicity, assume these random strings share the same length. The client selects a random factor r_b and computes the final encryption randomness as $r = h(r_b \| r_v)$, where $\|$ denotes concatenation. The choice c is encrypted using r. If the voter opts for ballot auditing, the client provides r_b to enable the voter to verify ballot correctness by recalculating the encrypted choice using r_b and r_v. This process significantly mitigates conflict attacks. Given two distinct voters' random strings r_v and $r_{v'}$, and client-generated factors r_b and r_b', the collision resistance of h makes $h(r_b \| r_v) = h\left(r_b' \| r_v'\right)$ computationally infeasible. However, the security level depends on the quality of randomness supplied by the voters: the stronger the randomness, the better the defense effect. During conflict attacks on disclosure procedures that link pseudonyms and ballots, the voting program must consistently use the same random factor to cause identical ballots. Consequently, voters may inspect all ballots generated by the client (including those submitted) to detect duplicates, for example, by recording ballot digests (e.g., MD5 hashes) and collaboratively comparing these records.

In summary, this section presents a systematic analysis and mechanism design to counter conflict attacks in collaborative authentication voting processes. Combined with the practical requirements of multi-domain cooperation in computing networks, it provides crucial support for building a cross-domain, trusted, and collaboratively secure computing power network infrastructure.

5.3.3 *Privacy Probing Protection Mechanism for Negotiation-Shared Systems*

Privacy probing protection mechanism for negotiation-shared systems Within the integrated security architecture of computing networks, behavioral data generated during network computing services serves as a crucial basis for authentication and coordination processes. While this data helps ensure service trustworthiness, it simultaneously introduces increasingly significant risks of privacy leakage. Although current behavioral authentication frameworks have incorporated various privacy-preserving strategies, such as employing distributed collaborative training to prevent direct exposure of user data and sharing only behavior fragments decoupled from business logic. These approaches remain insufficient in completely mitigating the security risks posed by behavioral data heterogeneity and differing privacy perceptions. This is particularly problematic in cross-domain sharing scenarios, where stakeholders often diverge in their understanding of what constitutes "non-sensitive" behavioral information, leading to inconsistent assessments of data credibility and privacy.

To address these challenges, there is a pressing need to establish a generalizable mechanism for privacy detection and protection that can automatically identify and assess the privacy sensitivity of behavioral data. Such a mechanism would enhance system-wide security and controllability while preserving utility.

This section concentrates on identifying privacy-sensitive elements within behavioral data produced during the use of network computing services, with the goal of balancing privacy protection and utility. The proposed framework is depicted in the accompanying figure.

Privacy Detection Currently, mainstream sensitive information detection techniques can be categorized into three primary approaches. The first involves keyword matching for identifying sensitive information, which, while simple, is prone to subjective bias and limited accuracy, making it suitable only for coarse initial screening. The second approach employs traditional machine learning algorithms, which extract handcrafted features and use classifiers such as logistic regression or random forests to identify sensitive content. However, this method is labor-intensive and time-consuming, requiring significant manual effort to curate effective features.

This section adopts a Text-CNN-based method for sensitive data detection. After preprocessing the behavioral data, the model is trained to predict privacy scores. Behavioral data from the terminal or system level, including user registration and resource request information, is first preprocessed through segmentation and vectorization. Given the strong interdependence among grouped behavioral records (e.g., jointly invoking a predictive model), pattern recognition within the data becomes essential for effective sensitivity identification. To this end, Latent Dirichlet Allocation (LDA) is used to uncover latent patterns in unstructured behavioral data, which are then fed as input features to the privacy detection model.

The degree of perturbation of a behavioral pattern is defined as:

$$R(D) = \exp\left(\frac{\sum_{i=1}^{d} \log\left[p\left(w_i \mid \alpha, \beta\right)\right]}{\sum_{i=1}^{d} N_i}\right), \tag{5.9}$$

where D denotes the behavioral dataset, $\sum_{i=1}^{d} N_i$ is the total number of data points, and $p\left(w_i \mid \alpha, \beta\right)$ is the probability of a behavioral sequence belonging to a latent pattern. Lower perturbation values indicate higher model robustness.

A privacy dictionary is also employed to automatically identify sensitive content by matching behavioral data against a predefined list of privacy-related fields and contextual keywords. Additional signals such as URLs, user handles, and hash tags are also considered, as they may contribute to information disclosure and thus assist in privacy detection.

Because vectorization may lead to the loss of important textual features, extracted features from the preprocessing stage are integrated with the vectorized data before training. Given the increasing latency constraints in modern network computing applications, a Text-CNN model is selected for its efficiency and performance. The fusion of vector and extracted features enables the model to achieve high privacy detection accuracy.

Privacy-Utility Trade-off In network computing behavioral authentication frameworks, all parties share the common objective of achieving high authentication accuracy with minimal privacy loss. Thus, a key challenge lies in optimizing utility gains under constrained privacy budgets.

Consider a pair of random variables $(X, Y) \in \mathscr{X} \times \mathscr{Y}$ (with finite cardinalities), jointly distributed according to $p_{X,Y}$, where Y represents the shared behavioral data and X denotes potentially sensitive information. Let U be a privacy-protected version of Y, derived via a privacy-preserving transformation. Privacy and utility are fundamentally at odds: the more heavily Y is perturbed, the less can be inferred about X, and the lower the resulting utility. The total variation distance between two probability distributions p and q over $\mathscr{X}$ is defined as:

$$\delta\left(p_X(\cdot), q_X(\cdot)\right) \triangleq \frac{1}{2}\|P - Q\|_1, \tag{5.10}$$

where P and Q are the respective probability vectors. Privacy leakage is quantified by the expected total variation distance

$$T(X; U) \triangleq E_U\left[\delta\left(p_{X|U}(\cdot \mid U), p_X(\cdot)\right)\right] = \frac{1}{2}\sum_{U} p_U(u)\left\|P_{X|U} - P_X\right\|_1. \tag{5.11}$$

Let $R(Y; U)$ denote a utility function based on the joint distribution $p_{U,Y}$. In this section, mutual information is adopted as the utility metric, allowing for a formal privacy-utility trade-off framework

$$m_{\varepsilon}(X, Y) = \max_{T(X;U)\leq\varepsilon} R(Y; U), \tag{5.12}$$

where $R(Y; U) = I(Y; U)$. As the actual behavioral data distribution across distributed participants is often unknown, this project proposes the use of a distributed Generative Adversarial Network (GAN) framework to optimize the privacy-utility trade-off. Each participant trains a local autoencoder on its own behavioral data to learn latent representations, while introducing controlled perturbations constrained by a privacy budget. These autoencoders serve as generators within a GAN framework, and a discriminator distinguishes real from synthetic samples. Through iterative adversarial training, the system produces data that maintains high utility while ensuring strong privacy.

Given the cross-domain and heterogeneous nature of modern network computing services, local data distributions vary significantly. Therefore, a federated learning paradigm is adopted in which participants share model parameters instead of raw data to collaboratively update models. This approach ensures fairness in privacy protection levels across parties while maintaining data locality.

This section addresses the privacy risks associated with sharing behavioral data in multi-party collaboration within computing networks. It proposes a privacy detection and protection mechanism that integrates sensitive information identification with federated learning. By incorporating behavior pattern modeling, perturbation quantification, and mutual-information-driven optimization, the mechanism adaptively balances privacy strength and authentication utility in cross-domain heterogeneous settings, thereby improving the overall robustness and controllability of integrated security systems.

References

1. W. Fan, F. Xiao, M. Lv, L. Han, J. Wang, X. He, IEEE Trans. Parallel Distrib. Syst. **34**(4), 1265 (2023)
2. T. Yu, X. Wang, J. Hu, IEEE/ACM Trans. Networking **29**(5), 2254 (2021)
3. Z.Y. Gong, S.S. Gao, Y.Z. Liu, B. Wang, Q.K. Li, C. Peng, in *2021 40th Chinese Control Conference (CCC)* (IEEE, New York, 2021), pp. 6512–6517
4. J. Zhu, R. Yang, X. Sun, T. Wo, C. Hu, H. Peng, J. Xiao, A.Y. Zomaya, J. Xu, IEEE Trans. Parallel Distrib. Syst. **33**(12), 4818 (2022)
5. L. Huang, T. Zhu, in *Proceedings of the ACM Symposium on Cloud Computing* (2021), pp. 76–91
6. P. Krishnan, K. Jain, R. Buyya, P. Vijayakumar, A. Nayyar, M. Bilal, H. Song, IEEE Internet Things J. **9**(9), 6611 (2021)
7. H. Zhang, Z. Cui, S. Huang, D. Guo, X. Wang, W. Wang, in *IEEE INFOCOM 2024-IEEE Conference on Computer Communications* (IEEE, New York, 2024), pp. 191–200

8. Z. Li, C. Xu, Q. Chen, J. Zhao, C. Chen, M. Guo, in *Proceedings of the 28th ACM International Conference on Architectural Support for Programming Languages and Operating Systems*, vol. 4 (2023), pp. 57–72
9. C. Zhang, S. Dang, B. Shihada, M.S. Alouini, in *IEEE INFOCOM 2021-IEEE Conference on Computer Communications* (IEEE, New York, 2021), pp. 1–10
10. V. Perifanis, N. Pavlidis, R.A. Koutsiamanis, P.S. Efraimidis, Comput. Netw. **235**, 109950 (2023)
11. L. Cheng, Y. Wang, R.H. Jhaveri, Q. Wang, Y. Mao, IEEE Trans. Netw. Serv. Manag. **20**(4), 4494 (2023)
12. C. Mommessin, R. Yang, N.V. Shakhlevich, X. Sun, S. Kumar, J. Xiao, J. Xu, J. Parallel Distrib. Comput. **177**, 1 (2023)
13. L. Cheng, Y. Wang, Q. Liu, D.H. Epema, C. Liu, Y. Mao, J. Murphy, IEEE Trans. Parallel Distrib. Syst. **32**(6), 1494 (2021)
14. G. Katz, C. Barrett, D.L. Dill, K. Julian, M.J. Kochenderfer, in *Computer Aided Verification: 29th International Conference, CAV 2017, Heidelberg, Germany, July 24–28, 2017, Proceedings, Part I 30* (Springer, Berlin, 2017), pp. 97–117
15. S. Wang, K. Pei, J. Whitehouse, J. Yang, S. Jana, in *27th USENIX Security Symposium (USENIX Security 18)* (2018), pp. 1599–1614
16. M.N. Müller, G. Makarchuk, G. Singh, M. Püschel, M. Vechev, Proc. ACM Program. Lang. **6**(POPL), 1 (2022)
17. X. Ling, S. Ji, J. Zou, J. Wang, C. Wu, B. Li, T. Wang, in *2019 IEEE Symposium on Security and Privacy (SP)* (IEEE, New York, 2019), pp. 673–690
18. L. Li, T. Xie, B. Li, in *2023 IEEE Symposium on Security and Privacy (SP)* (IEEE, New York, 2023), pp. 1289–1310
19. T. Hu, Z. Zhang, P. Yi, D. Liang, Z. Li, Q. Ren, Y. Hu, J. Lan, J. Parallel Distrib. Comput. **147**, 108 (2021)
20. Z.T. Sworna, C. Islam, M.A. Babar, ACM Trans. Softw. Eng. Methodol. **32**(1), 1 (2023)
21. P. Ranjan, S. Dahiya, Int. J. Commun. Netw. Inf. Security **13**(1), 185–196 (2021)
22. G. Baye, F. Hussain, A. Oracevic, R. Hussain, S.A. Kazmi, in *2021 International Symposium on Networks, Computers and Communications (ISNCC)* (IEEE, New York, 2021), pp. 1–6
23. Y. Zhang, M.M.A. Kabir, Y. Xiao, D. Yao, N. Meng, IEEE Trans. Softw. Eng. **49**(1), 288 (2022)
24. N. Cheng, H. Zhang, Z. Li, Soft Comput. **25**(23), 14573 (2021)
25. J. Hayase, W. Kong, R. Somani, S. Oh, in *International Conference on Machine Learning* (PMLR, New York, 2021), pp. 4129–4139
26. S. Liu, Z. Zhu, Q. Qu, C. You, in *International Conference on Machine Learning* (PMLR, New York, 2022), pp. 14153–14172
27. Y. Roh, K. Lee, S. Whang, C. Suh, Adv. Neural Inf. Proces. Syst. **34**, 815 (2021)
28. S. Kolouri, A. Saha, H. Pirsiavash, H. Hoffmann, in *Proceedings of the IEEE/CVF Conference on Computer Vision and Pattern Recognition* (2020), pp. 301–310
29. S. Wei, M. Zhang, H. Zha, B. Wu, Adv. Neural Inf. Proces. Syst. **36**, 25876 (2023)
30. L. Zhu, R. Ning, C. Wang, C. Xin, H. Wu, in *Proceedings of the 28th ACM International Conference on Multimedia* (2020), pp. 3173–3181
31. K. Wei, J. Li, M. Ding, C. Ma, H.H. Yang, F. Farokhi, S. Jin, T.Q. Quek, H.V. Poor, IEEE Trans. Inf. Forensics Secur. **15**, 3454 (2020)
32. S. Truex, L. Liu, K.H. Chow, M.E. Gursoy, W. Wei, in *Proceedings of the Third ACM International Workshop on Edge Systems, Analytics and Networking* (2020), pp. 61–66
33. L. Chen, D. Xiao, Z. Yu, M. Zhang, Inf. Sci. **667**, 120481 (2024)
34. Y. Cai, W. Ding, Y. Xiao, Z. Yan, X. Liu, Z. Wan, IEEE Trans. Dependable Secure Comput. **21**(4), 3817 (2023)
35. W. Wei, K.H. Chow, Y. Wu, L. Liu, IEEE Trans. Serv. Comput. **17**(1), 237 (2023)
36. C. Chen, Y. Gao, S. Huang, X. Yan, in *IEEE INFOCOM 2023-IEEE Conference on Computer Communications Workshops (INFOCOM WKSHPS)* (IEEE, New York, 2023), pp. 1–6
37. P. Rieger, T.D. Nguyen, M. Miettinen, A.R. Sadeghi, arXiv preprint arXiv:2201.00763 (2022)

38. A.R. Short, H.C. Leligou, M. Papoutsidakis, E. Theocharis, in *2020 IEEE 44th Annual Computers, Software, and Applications Conference (COMPSAC)* (IEEE, New York, 2020), pp. 1183–1188
39. M. Kesarwani, B. Mukhoty, V. Arya, S. Mehta, in *Proceedings of the 34th Annual Computer Security Applications Conference* (2018), pp. 371–380
40. M. Juuti, S. Szyller, S. Marchal, N. Asokan, in *2019 IEEE European Symposium on Security and Privacy (EuroS&P)* (IEEE, New York, 2019), pp. 512–527
41. A. Rashid, J. Such, IEEE Trans. Inf. Forensics Secur. **18**, 4361 (2023)
42. S. Szyller, B.G. Atli, S. Marchal, N. Asokan, in *Proceedings of the 29th ACM International Conference on Multimedia* (2021), pp. 4417–4425
43. M. Botta, D. Cavagnino, R. Esposito, Inf. Sci. **576**, 228 (2021)
44. T. Lee, Z. Lin, S. Pushp, C. Li, Y. Liu, Y. Lee, F. Xu, C. Xu, L. Zhang, J. Song, in *The 25th Annual International Conference on Mobile Computing and Networking* (2019), pp. 1–17
45. T. Shen, J. Qi, J. Jiang, X. Wang, S. Wen, X. Chen, S. Zhao, S. Wang, L. Chen, X. Luo, et al., in *2022 USENIX Annual Technical Conference (USENIX ATC 22)* (2022), pp. 723–738
46. H. Xiao, Q. Zhang, Q. Pei, W. Shi, in *2021 IEEE 41st International Conference on Distributed Computing Systems (ICDCS)* (IEEE, New York, 2021), pp. 751–761
47. C. Song, R. Huang, S. Hu, Neurocomputing **592**, 127794 (2024)
48. D.J. Han, D.Y. Kim, M. Choi, D. Nickel, J. Moon, M. Chiang, C.G. Brinton, IEEE Trans. Mob. Comput. **23**(6), 7048 (2023)
49. T. Lebrun, A. Boutet, J. Aalmoes, A. Baud, in *Proceedings of the 23rd ACM/IFIP International Middleware Conference* (2022), pp. 135–147
50. J. Chen, W.H. Wang, X. Shi, in *BIOCOMPUTING 2021: Proceedings of the Pacific Symposium* (World Scientific, Singapore, 2020), pp. 26–37
51. M. Du, X. Yue, S.S. Chow, T. Wang, C. Huang, H. Sun, in *Proceedings of the 2023 ACM SIGSAC Conference on Computer and Communications Security* (2023), pp. 2665–2679
52. S. Hu, L. Ke, X. Wang, S. Lyu, in *Proceedings of the IEEE/CVF International Conference on Computer Vision* (2021), pp. 7649–7657
53. S. Zhou, T. Zhu, D. Ye, W. Zhou, W. Zhao, IEEE Trans. Inf. Forensics Secur. **19**, 4130–4145 (2024)
54. T.A. Alves, F.M. França, S. Kundu, in *Proceedings of the 2019 Great Lakes Symposium on VLSI* (2019), pp. 411–415

Chapter 6
The Platform of Integrated Security and Safety

Abstract With the rapid digital transformation across industries, organizations face increasingly sophisticated security threats that transcend traditional security boundaries. We introduce the platform of integrated security and safety, a sophisticated architectural framework designed to address complex security challenges in modern digital ecosystems. This comprehensive platform integrates four specialized modules that work in synergy to create a robust, multi-layered security infrastructure capable of detecting, analyzing, and responding to diverse threats while preserving privacy across domains. The platform's modular architecture supports future expansion and industry-specific customization, making it applicable across security-sensitive domains such as financial services, healthcare, and critical infrastructure.

6.1 System Architecture

The Conceptual Platform of Integrated Security and Safety consists of four interconnecting modules: User Behavior Analysis and Monitoring, Cross-Domain Privacy Preserving, Behavioral Situational Awareness and Incident Response, and Transaction Security and Anomaly Detection. As shown in Fig. 6.1, the four modules contribute specialized capabilities to tackle the complex security challenges of modern digital environments while striking a balance between operational efficiency and privacy requirements.

The User Behavior Analysis and Monitoring module underpins the platform by capturing and analyzing user interactions to establish behavioral baselines and detect deviations. It employs advanced pattern recognition techniques to construct detailed user profiles, enabling continuous real-time monitoring of activities against established normal behavior patterns.

Complementing this, the Cross-Domain Privacy Preserving module implements cutting-edge privacy protection mechanisms, including data anonymization, federated learning algorithms, and privacy-preserving computation techniques. This ensures sensitive information remains protected while still enabling effective cross-domain collaboration and data sharing among different security components.

C. Wang, H. Tang, *Integrated Security and Safety of Intelligent Computing Networks*, https://doi.org/10.1007/978-981-95-5025-8_6

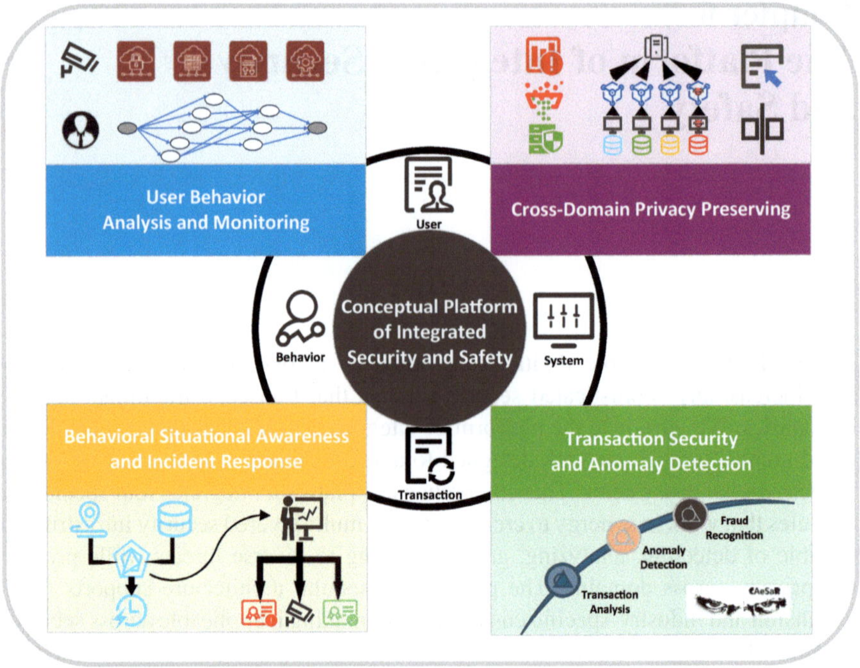

Fig. 6.1 Modules of conceptual platform

The Behavioral Situational Awareness and Incident Response module elevates the platform's capabilities by contextualizing detected anomalies within broader threat landscapes. It integrates threat intelligence feeds, performs comprehensive risk assessments, and orchestrates structured incident response protocols, allowing for rapid threat mitigation and coordinated security actions across organizational boundaries.

Finally, the Transaction Security and Anomaly Detection module specializes in identifying suspicious patterns within transaction flows, implementing sophisticated detection algorithms to recognize fraudulent activities, calculating risk scores for each transaction, and triggering real-time alerts when potential threats are identified.

The architecture facilitates a seamless workflow from data collection through processing and analysis to defensive response, establishing bidirectional information flows between modules through secure channels. This integrated approach enables more comprehensive threat detection capabilities than isolated security solutions, while the platform's modular design allows for scalability and adaptation to evolving security requirements. By balancing thorough security monitoring with strict privacy protections, the platform addresses both security effectiveness and compliance considerations in increasingly complex digital environments.

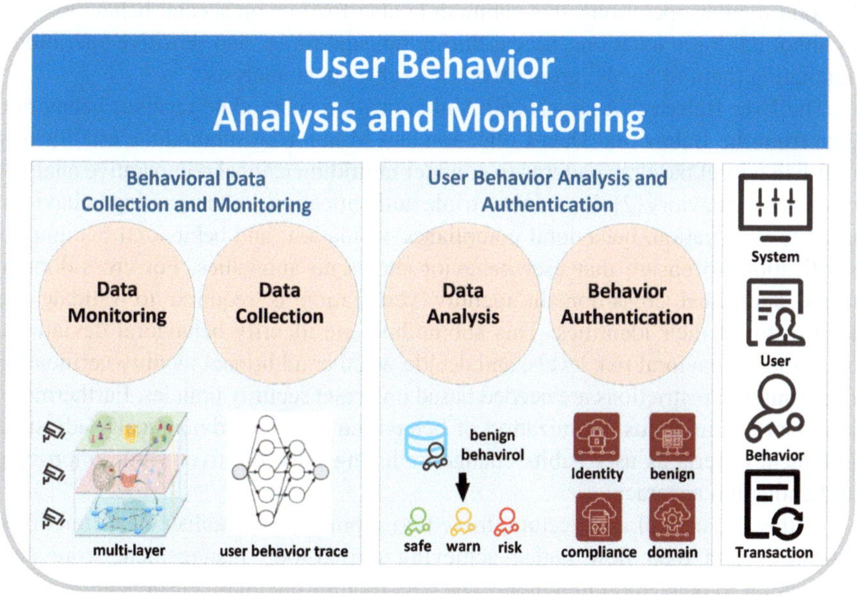

Fig. 6.2 Structure of user behavior analysis and monitoring

6.2 User Behavior Analysis and Monitoring

6.2.1 Module Structure

The User Behavior Analysis and Monitoring module, as a key component of the integrated security platform, aims to comprehensively capture, analyze, and evaluate user activities within the system, providing a decision-making foundation for user security, transaction security, behavioral security, and system security [1]. This module follows the complete business process of "data monitoring, data collection, data analysis, and behavior authentication". It achieves precise user profiling and risk assessment through the collaborative operation of two major functional sub-modules: Behavioral Data Collection and Monitoring, along with User Behavior Analysis and Authentication. Figure 6.2 demonstrates the overall structure of User Behavior Analysis and Monitoring.

The behavioral data collection and monitoring sub-module is responsible for the data collection process, designed to extensively monitor and collect multi-level behavioral data from users, including behavioral data from seven layers: transaction layer, application layer, scheduling layer, user layer, network layer, device layer, and operation layer. This sub-module conducts preliminary processing and complete lifecycle management of the collected multimodal data. Simultaneously, it possesses real-time monitoring capabilities, continuously tracking user activity trajectories and performing initial integration and classification of the raw behavioral data.

Beyond regular operations, this submodule also focuses on special behaviors such as abnormal login locations, access during unusual times, and sensitive operations, annotating them to lay the groundwork for subsequent analysis.

The User Behavior Analysis and Authentication submodule receives behavioral data from the Behavioral Data Collection and Monitoring submodule, establishing user behavioral baseline patterns to conduct multidimensional comparative analysis of current behaviors [2]. It performs triple authentication, encompassing behavioral identity verification, behavioral compliance validation, and behavioral benignness verification, to ensure that user behavior shows no anomalies. For cross-domain users, additional cross-domain identity verification is required to validate the legitimacy of their identities. This submodule can identify behavioral deviations, determine behavioral risk levels, and decide whether additional identity verification or permission restrictions are needed based on preset security policies. Furthermore, it supports continuous optimization of behavioral profiling, dynamically adjusting judgment criteria as user habits change, reducing false positives while improving authentication accuracy.

Within the overall architecture, these two submodules establish clear functional interfaces and data flow paths, achieving closed-loop management from data acquisition to behavioral judgment. The data monitoring phase ensures information timeliness and effectiveness; the data collection phase ensures behavioral information comprehensiveness and timeliness; the data analysis phase guarantees scientific and accurate judgment; while the behavioral authentication phase implements targeted and appropriate security measures. Additionally, this module maintains close business coordination with other security functional modules on the platform, jointly constructing a multi-level, multi-angle security protection system.

Through this modular functional design, the User Behavior Analysis and Monitoring module not only effectively identifies various potential security threats but also provides administrators with detailed behavioral audit reports, supporting root cause investigation and security reinforcement. Simultaneously, the module's design fully considers the special requirements of different business scenarios, allowing flexible configuration of monitoring scope and judgment rules based on the actual application environment, maximizing user experience fluidity while ensuring security.

6.2.2 Behavioral Data Collection and Monitoring

6.2.2.1 Multi-layer Data Stratification

The Behavioral Data Collection and Monitoring submodule employs a multi-layered data collection architecture, ensuring comprehensive capture of various user behavioral characteristics through systematic data layer classification [3]. This submodule is based on a seven-layer data model, covering the complete behavioral chain from underlying infrastructure to upper-level transaction behaviors, achieving comprehensive awareness and monitoring of user behavior. This layered design not only facilitates effective data organization and management but also provides structured data foundations for behavioral analysis, enabling the system to interpret the intrinsic meaning and external manifestations of user behaviors from different dimensions.

At the transaction layer, the system focuses on monitoring data directly related to user transaction behaviors, including abnormal transaction quantities, abnormal payment behaviors, abnormal order characteristics, account attack frequency statistics, transaction exception handling data, transaction anti-tampering data, and successful transaction counts. These data directly reflect users' financial activity patterns and can effectively identify high-risk behaviors such as account theft and abnormal fund movements. Transaction layer data demands the highest real-time requirements, with the system ensuring immediate capture of anomalous signals during transactions through deep integration of transaction engines and risk control systems. Additionally, transaction layer data includes derived indicators such as transaction frequency analysis, transaction amount distribution, and transaction entity correlation, which can precisely locate minor anomalies in transaction behaviors by comparing with users' historical transaction behaviors, providing early warnings for financial fraud prevention. Furthermore, transaction layer data collection also focuses on advanced features such as cross-account transaction pathways and transaction time characteristics, identifying potential money laundering behaviors and illegal fund flow chains through the construction of transaction network graphs.

Application layer data collection focuses on application program operational status and user interaction behaviors, primarily including process exception handling data, memory exception handling data, and port exception handling data. These data reflect abnormal user behaviors during application operations, such as unauthorized operations and abnormal API calls, serving as important bases for discovering application layer attacks. The system implements fine-grained tracking of user application operations through application behavior monitoring components, establishing baselines for normal application interaction patterns. In application layer data collection, the system particularly attends to software version compatibility issues, behavior sequences before application crashes, and abnormal permission requests, which often precede security vulnerability exploitation. Simultaneously, application layer data collection includes behavioral habit data such as user interface operation trajectories, function usage frequency distribution, and application switching patterns, which help establish operational fingerprints of users within applications, providing important references for behavioral identity authentication. Additionally, the application layer collects compliance-related data such as abnormal resource access records and sensitive data contact logs, ensuring user behaviors conform to application security policy requirements.

The scheduling layer focuses on behavioral data related to task execution and resource scheduling, with collection content encompassing scheduled task characteristics, scheduled task statuses, intercepted task information, and scheduling failure task analyses. Monitoring this category of data helps discover abnormal behavior patterns such as resource abuse and privilege escalation, while providing a basis for reasonable allocation of system resources. Scheduling layer data collection ensures comprehensive monitoring of critical task execution processes through seamless integration with task scheduling systems. Scheduling layer data analysis particularly focuses on signals that may indicate privilege abuse, such as task submission patterns, resource request characteristics, and task priority changes. Simultaneously, the scheduling layer collects performance-related indicators such as task execution duration distribution, resource consumption patterns, and task dependency relationships, which help identify abnormal task patterns that may lead to denial of service. Furthermore, scheduling layer data collection includes in-depth information such as task source analysis and component call chain tracking, through which a complete picture of user behavior and system resource interaction can be constructed, providing multidimensional references for abnormal behavior detection.

The user layer is the core level of behavioral data, where the system collects information such as user authentication anomalies, user behavior anomalies, overdraft consumption situations, and newly added risk users. These data directly reflect the authenticity of user identities and the compliance of behaviors, serving as fundamental materials for behavioral analysis and authentication. User layer data constructs user behavioral fingerprints through multi-dimensional feature extraction, providing data support for subsequent behavioral baseline modeling. In user layer data collection, the system particularly focuses on user login behavior characteristics, including login time distribution, geographical location changes, and device switching frequency. Simultaneously, the user layer collects authorization-related data such as permission usage patterns, sensitive operation trigger frequency, and data access scope changes, which help discover permission abuse and internal threat behaviors. Additionally, user layer data collection encompasses background information such as user social relationship networks, organizational structure positions, and historical security event correlations, through which a more complete user context can be established, improving the accuracy of behavioral determination. User layer data collection fully considers privacy protection requirements, adopting appropriate data desensitization and access control measures to ensure protection of user privacy while collecting sufficient behavioral data.

Network layer data collection focuses on users' network behavior characteristics, monitoring content including traffic data of various links in the network, throughput data of various nodes in the network, and packets related to abnormal access behaviors. Through analysis of network layer data, the system can identify network attacks, abnormal connections, data leakage, and other network security threats, while sensing changes in users' network usage patterns. Network layer data collection achieves non-intrusive monitoring of user network activities using distributed probe technology. In network layer data, the system particularly attends to communication behavior indicators such as connection establishment patterns, protocol usage characteristics, and data transmission frequency. Simultaneously, the network layer collects deep-level network fingerprints such as packet header characteristics, session duration, and communication encryption properties, which help identify abnormal patterns in network communications. Additionally, network layer data collection includes network activity characteristics such as traffic mutation analysis, periodic communication detection, and domain name resolution behaviors, through which advanced threats such as network tunnels and command and control channels can be discovered early. While ensuring comprehensiveness, network layer data collection controls the impact of data collection on network performance through intelligent sampling and traffic mirroring techniques, achieving efficient network behavior monitoring.

Device layer data focuses on the status and performance of devices used by users, with the system collecting and analyzing key indicators such as usage rates, failure rates, and runtime duration of various compute nodes in data centers and clusters. These data help identify device-level anomalies such as abnormal resource occupation and hardware failures, while also serving as important bases for determining changes in user device characteristics. Device layer data collection achieves real-time awareness of user device environments through collaborative monitoring between lightweight clients and servers. In device layer data, the system particularly focuses on device characteristic indicators such as hardware fingerprint changes, resource usage patterns, and device abnormal behaviors. Simultaneously, the device layer collects hardware environment data such as peripheral connection status, driver changes, and firmware version information, which help discover hardware-level security risks and device spoofing behaviors. Additionally, device layer data collection includes new computing environment indicators such as virtualization environment characteristics, container runtime status, and cloud resource scheduling situations, through which device behavior monitoring requirements in the cloud-native era can be adapted. Device layer data collection fully considers the differences between various types of devices, adopting an extensible data collection architecture to ensure effective behavioral data acquisition in heterogeneous device environments.

The operations layer, as the highest level of data collection, focuses on security risks in business operations, monitoring content including supplier violation data, load anomalies, malicious software attack characteristics, and network intrusion clues. Operations layer data reflects abnormal interaction patterns between systems and users from a business perspective, serving as an important means of identifying advanced persistent threats and internal risks. Operations layer data collection achieves precise capture of abnormal behaviors in business processes through deep integration with operations management systems. In operations layer data, the system particularly focuses on operational security data such as supply chain security indicators, third-party access risks, and service level anomalies. Simultaneously, the operations layer collects security operation indicators such as security incident response efficiency, risk disposal success rate, and security control coverage, which help evaluate the effectiveness of security control measures. Additionally, operations layer data collection includes governance-related information such as security policy implementation status, compliance requirement satisfaction level, and business continuity assurance level. This helps construct organization-level security situational awareness, providing macroscopic bases for security decisions.

Operations layer data collection fully considers the special requirements of different business scenarios, adopting flexible data collection strategies to ensure adaptation to changing business environments.

Through this seven-layer data architecture design, the Behavioral Data Collection and Monitoring submodule can construct complete user behavioral profiles. It perceives and records user behavioral characteristics from multiple angles, providing comprehensive and accurate data foundations for subsequent behavioral analysis and authentication. Data across various layers are interrelated and mutually verified, forming three-dimensional behavioral monitoring networks that significantly enhance the accuracy and comprehensiveness of abnormal behavior identification. The advantage of this multi-layered data collection framework lies in its focus not only on behavioral characteristics of a single layer but also on the consistency and coherence of behaviors across different layers, enabling the discovery of complex attack patterns and abnormal behavior chains across layers. Simultaneously, the seven-layer data model design also provides structured data views for security analysis, enabling security analysts to penetrate from different dimensions and gain insight into the essential characteristics of user behaviors. Furthermore, this layered design facilitates precise formulation and execution of security policies, allowing administrators to implement targeted security measures for specific layers of abnormal behaviors, improving the precision and efficiency of security protection. Ultimately, this complete data layer classification provides solid data support for the effective operation of the integrated security platform, ensuring that the platform can accurately perceive user behaviors and effectively prevent various security risks in complex and changing network environments.

6.2.2.2 Data Lifecycle Management

Data lifecycle management is an important function of the behavioral data collection and monitoring submodule, aimed at achieving systematic control and refined governance over the entire lifecycle of behavioral data. This function establishes a comprehensive data management framework, implementing all-around supervision and standardization over the entire process of behavioral data from generation to destruction, ensuring that data can maximize its value at different stages while meeting increasingly stringent data compliance requirements.

In the data collection phase, the system establishes diversified data acquisition mechanisms, formulating differentiated collection strategies based on different data sources and sensitivity levels. For high-value behavioral data, the system adopts an active collection approach to ensure data completeness and timeliness; for routine behavioral data, rule-triggered collection is employed to balance data acquisition and system performance. During the collection process, the system strictly implements data classification and grading standards, assigning corresponding sensitivity labels to different types of behavioral data. These labels accompany the entire lifecycle of the data, guiding subsequent processing flows. Meanwhile, all data collection activities must undergo compliance reviews to ensure collection behaviors comply with privacy protection regulations and internal policy requirements, preventing excessive collection and misuse.

The data storage phase adopts a multi-level storage architecture, allocating behavioral data to different storage areas based on data sensitivity, value, and access frequency. High-value, highly sensitive behavioral data is stored in the highest security level storage areas, equipped with enhanced measures such as encrypted storage and access control; medium and low sensitivity data is stored in storage areas of corresponding security levels, achieving reasonable resource allocation. The system implements dynamic timeliness management for all behavioral data in storage, setting clear retention periods for each piece of data and dynamically adjusting retention policies based on changes in data value. During storage, the system also automatically records data access history and processing logs, forming complete data lineage relationships to provide a basis for subsequent auditing and tracing.

In the data usage phase, the system implements strict authorization mechanisms and access control policies, ensuring only authorized personnel and groups can access corresponding behavioral data according to predefined permissions. For the use of highly sensitive data, the system requires additional identity verification and operation approval, while recording all data access activities in real-time. Simultaneously, the system enforces purpose limitation, ensuring that behavioral data are used solely for pre-declared legitimate purposes and preventing use beyond the intended scope. To enhance the security of the data usage process, the system also provides security audit and anomaly detection functions, capable of real-time discovery and blocking of suspicious data access behaviors, preventing risks of data misuse and leakage.

The data sharing phase adopts the minimum necessary principle, limiting the scope and granularity of shared data while ensuring business requirements. The system supports various sharing methods, including direct access, sharing after desensitization, and sharing of statistical results. All data sharing behaviors must undergo strict approval processes and establish data protection agreements with recipients, clearly specifying data usage scope, protection measures, and destruction requirements. At the technical level, the system uses measures such as encrypted transmission and digital watermarks to secure the sharing process and employs permission control mechanisms to ensure that the use of shared data strictly adheres to the authorized scope.

For archival management of behavioral data, the system establishes comprehensive archiving policies and processes. For behavioral data that has completed recent analytical value but needs to be retained, the system transfers it to archival storage areas, achieving a balance between data value and storage costs. During the archiving process, the system performs necessary compression and optimization of data to reduce storage overhead while maintaining data retrievability. Archived data is divided into multiple archive sets based on importance: behavioral data related to significant security events forms long-term preservation archives, supporting possible future retrospective investigations; general behavioral data forms short-term archives, entering the destruction process after a specified period. The management of archived data similarly follows strict access control principles, with only specially authorized personnel able to access archived data.

In the data destruction phase, the system implements differentiated destruction strategies. For behavioral data that has completed its entire value cycle and is permitted by regulations to be destroyed, the system employs secure destruction methods compliant with industry standards to ensure that data cannot be recovered or utilized. The destruction process executes strict approval and witness procedures, generating destruction certification documents as compliance evidence. For specific types of behavioral data that regulations require to be preserved long-term, the system transfers them to permanent archive areas and implements special protection measures. The system also supports condition-triggered destruction, automatically initiating the destruction process when certain data reaches preset retention periods or meets specific conditions, ensuring data is not retained beyond its period.

Throughout the entire lifecycle is a comprehensive data governance system. The system ensures appropriate control of behavioral data at various stages through means such as metadata management, data quality control, and data security assessment. For behavioral data of different levels, the system sets differentiated governance strategies, with high-value data receiving more governance resources and stricter control measures. Simultaneously, the system establishes a complete data lifecycle tracking mechanism capable of clearly displaying the complete journey of each piece of data, including collection sources, processing changes, usage records, archiving times, and destruction certifications. This fully traceable management approach not only meets compliance audit needs but also provides a basis for data value assessment and lifecycle optimization.

The data lifecycle management function also possesses high adaptability, capable of dynamically updating data processing flows based on external regulatory changes and internal policy adjustments. The system sets up compliance monitoring components to continuously track changes in data protection regulations across regions, automatically assessing impact scope and proposing adjustment recommendations when regulatory updates are discovered. At the same time, through data value assessment mechanisms, the system can identify the actual utilization value and retention necessity of data, providing a scientific basis for lifecycle policy optimization.

Through this comprehensive and refined data lifecycle management, the behavioral data collection and monitoring submodule maximizes the value of behavioral data while ensuring security and compliance. This capability satisfies stringent data protection regulations as well as the business needs of behavioral analytics, enabling the system to operate efficiently in complex and evolving regulatory environments and providing a reliable data foundation for user behavior analysis and security decision-making.

6.2.2.3 Data Storage and Desensitization

Data storage and desensitization is a critical component of the Behavioral Data Collection and Monitoring submodule, providing the platform with a secure and efficient data management foundation that ensures behavioral data meets analytical requirements while complying with privacy protection requirements. This functionality constructs a comprehensive data protection system by integrating advanced storage technologies, access control mechanisms, and data desensitization strategies, balancing data availability and security.

In terms of data storage architecture, the system employs a multi-level hybrid storage design, selecting the most appropriate storage medium based on data characteristics and access patterns. High-frequency, real-time behavioral data is stored in high-performance in-memory databases to ensure rapid response; recent historical behavioral data is stored in distributed file systems, balancing query efficiency and storage costs; long-term archived behavioral data utilizes object storage technology, optimizing storage efficiency for large-scale data. The storage system supports automatic data tiering and migration functions, dynamically adjusting data locations between different storage tiers based on data access frequency and importance, achieving optimal allocation of storage resources. Simultaneously, the system implements comprehensive data redundancy and backup strategies through mechanisms such as multi-copy storage, periodic snapshots, and off-site disaster recovery, ensuring the recoverability of behavioral data under extreme circumstances and preventing business impacts from data loss.

The platform provides standardized data access interfaces supporting various query modes to accommodate different business scenario requirements. For real-time monitoring applications, the system offers push-based data subscription interfaces, enabling clients to receive the latest behavioral data updates promptly; for statistical analysis applications, the system provides powerful aggregation query interfaces supporting complex data filtering, grouping, and calculation operations; for security audit applications, the system offers specialized time-series query interfaces, facilitating the tracking of historical changes and event chains in behavioral data. These interfaces adhere to unified API specifications, simplifying application integration complexity while supporting batch operations and asynchronous processing, improving the efficiency of large-scale data processing. Additionally, the system provides metadata query functionality, helping users understand the structural definitions, quality metrics, and processing history of behavioral data, offering guidance for correct data usage.

Role-Based Access Control (RBAC) serves as the primary security mechanism of the data storage system, ensuring that only authorized personnel and system modules can access behavioral data at the appropriate levels. The system defines multiple role templates, including security analysts, system administrators, and audit personnel, with each role assigned different data access permissions. Permission control granularity extends to the field level, allowing users of different roles to only view data content within their scope of responsibility. Permission allocation follows the principle of least privilege, with users by default only able to access the minimum dataset necessary to complete their work. The system supports dynamic permission adjustment functionality, temporarily elevating user permissions through strict approval processes to address emergency needs in special situations. All data access operations are recorded in detail in security logs, including accessor identity, access time, data scope accessed, and operation type, providing complete evidence for subsequent security audits.

To enhance data access efficiency, the system establishes dedicated indexes and data views for common query patterns. Through continuous analysis of user query behaviors, the system automatically identifies high-frequency query patterns and creates corresponding optimized indexes, significantly improving response speeds for these queries. For complex multi-dimensional analysis requirements, the system pre-constructs a series of data cubes and materialized views, transforming raw behavioral data into forms more suitable for analysis, reducing computational burden during queries. Concurrently, the system implements an intelligent query optimization engine that automatically selects the optimal query execution plan based on data distribution characteristics and system load conditions, avoiding the impact of resource-intensive operations on system performance. For behavioral data with obvious time-series characteristics, the system also employs specialized time-series database technology, optimizing the efficiency of time-range queries and trend analyses.

The system effectively reduces the pressure of frequent queries on the storage system through data caching mechanisms. The multi-level caching architecture includes application-level caches, service-level caches, and storage-level caches, capable of capturing and reusing hotspot data at different levels, reducing access frequency to underlying storage. Caching strategies employ intelligent adaptive algorithms, dynamically adjusting cache content and expiration policies based on data access patterns, update frequency, and business importance, maximizing cache hit rates. For distributed environments, the system implements cache consistency protocols, ensuring synchronized updates of cached data across nodes, avoiding analysis errors due to data inconsistencies. The caching system also features preloading functionality, predicting possible subsequent queries based on historical access patterns and preloading relevant data into the cache, further enhancing response speed.

Data desensitization processing is a key technical means of protecting user privacy, with the platform preventing improper disclosure of sensitive information while providing behavioral data necessary for analysis. The system implements various desensitization techniques, including data masking, data replacement, data transformation, and data aggregation, selecting the most appropriate desensitization strategy for different types of sensitive data. For example, irreversible hash processing is applied to user identification information (such as names and ID numbers); for location data, precision reduction is employed, preserving general area information while concealing exact locations; for behavioral sequence data, methods such as scrambling time orders or adding noise prevent the identification of specific users through behavioral patterns. The system supports multi-level de-identification strategies, dynamically adjusting desensitization levels based on data usage scenarios and user permissions to strike a balance between privacy protection and data utility. Furthermore, the platform implements differential privacy mechanisms, ensuring that sensitive information of individual users cannot be identified even under complex inference attacks by adding carefully designed random noise to query results.

To meet the data usage requirements of different business departments, the system provides flexible data export functionality, supporting various export formats and transmission methods. All export operations must undergo strict permission verification and security reviews, ensuring data flows only to authorized recipients. Exported data undergoes desensitization processing by default, with metadata marking data sensitivity levels and usage restrictions. The system also supports data watermarking technology, embedding invisible identification information in exported data to facilitate responsibility tracing in case of data leaks. For cross-system data sharing scenarios, the platform implements secure data exchange protocols, safeguarding data transmission security through encrypted channels and strong identity authentication.

The system's data storage and desensitization functionality also possesses high scalability and adaptability, capable of addressing continuously growing data volumes and changing privacy protection requirements. The storage architecture adopts a distributed design supporting horizontal scaling, allowing convenient addition of more storage nodes as data volumes grow. The desensitization engine is based on a plugin architecture, flexibly integrating new desensitization algorithms and privacy protection technologies to adapt to evolving privacy regulation requirements. Simultaneously, the system provides comprehensive monitoring and management tools, helping administrators understand data storage status, access patterns, and desensitization effects, providing a basis for optimizing storage strategies and protection measures.

Through this comprehensive and flexible data storage and desensitization mechanism, the Behavioral Data Collection and Monitoring submodule provides efficient data support for behavioral analysis and risk monitoring under secure and compliant premises. This functionality enables the platform to protect user privacy rights while fully extracting the value of behavioral data, providing reliable data foundations for security decisions. This design philosophy, balancing security and efficiency, allows the system to adapt to increasingly complex data protection environments and growing analytical requirements, becoming an important infrastructure for the entire platform.

6.2.3 User Behavior Analysis and Authentication

6.2.3.1 Behavior Analysis and Identification

Behavior analysis and identification is the core functionality of the User Behavior Analysis and Authentication submodule, providing scientific basis for security decisions by deeply mining patterns and correlations within user behavioral data. This functionality employs a multi-level analysis architecture, combining advanced machine learning algorithms with expert rules to achieve comprehensive perception and precise evaluation of user behaviors, effectively balancing security and user experience.

In terms of behavioral baseline modeling, the system first establishes multi-dimensional behavioral baseline patterns for each user. These baseline patterns cover multiple aspects including user operation habits, access patterns, transaction characteristics, and device preferences, forming a "digital fingerprint" of user behavior. The baseline establishment process adopts a progressive learning approach, building initial baselines through high-frequency sampling when users first use the system, then continuously absorbing new behavioral data to optimize and expand the baselines during continued use. The system supports multi-granularity baseline models, including both macroscopic behavioral trends and microscopic operational details, such as biobehavioral characteristics like keystroke rhythms, swipe trajectories, and visual attention areas. The baseline model employs a layered structure, distinguishing core invariant characteristics from peripheral variable characteristics, ensuring both model stability and sufficient flexibility to accommodate natural changes in user habits.

Behavioral comparison analysis is a key link in identifying abnormal behaviors, with the system conducting multi-dimensional real-time comparisons between currently captured user behaviors and established baseline patterns. The comparison process employs weighted similarity calculation methods, assigning different weights to behavioral features of different dimensions, highlighting the identification role of key behavioral features. The system implements various comparison algorithms, including Euclidean distance calculation, sequence pattern matching, and statistical distribution testing, selecting the most appropriate comparison method for different types of behavioral data. To improve comparison accuracy, the system also introduces context-awareness mechanisms, incorporating factors such as user historical behavior continuity, current business scenarios, and environmental factors, avoiding false positives caused by isolated judgments. Comparison analysis supports multi-level comparison strategies, from rapid coarse-grained screening to refined in-depth analysis, forming a progressive abnormality detection process that ensures both detection efficiency and judgment accuracy.

The deviation identification and risk assessment phase deeply interprets comparison analysis results, determining the nature and risk level of behavioral deviations. The system establishes a refined deviation classification system, capable of distinguishing between normal changes, environmental influences, accidental operations, and malicious behaviors. Risk assessment employs a multi-factor comprehensive judgment model, considering asset importance, operation sensitivity, and threat intelligence in addition to the degree of behavioral deviation, providing more comprehensive risk judgments. The system supports risk scoring mechanisms, expressing behavioral risk levels through quantifiable risk scores, facilitating subsequent decision processing. For different types of security risks, the system implements specialized detection models, such as account theft detection, internal threat identification, and automated attack identification, improving identification precision in specific risk scenarios. Simultaneously, the system possesses anomaly chain analysis capabilities, able to discover seemingly independent but actually related abnormal behavior sequences, identifying complex attack chains and threat scenarios.

Based on behavioral analysis and risk assessment results, the system executes corresponding security policies, achieving intelligent authentication and authorization control. Security policies adopt a risk-adaptive framework, dynamically adjusting security measure intensity according to behavioral risk levels, maintaining imperceptible verification in low-risk situations to enhance user experience, while triggering additional identity verification or imposing temporary permission restrictions in high-risk situations. The system supports various verification methods, including traditional password verification, biometric verification, knowledge question verification, and application push verification, flexibly selectable based on risk levels and scenario requirements. To enhance security policy precision, the system implements refined policy configuration functionality, allowing administrators to formulate differentiated security rules for different user groups, business scenarios, and asset types. Concurrently, the system possesses real-time response capabilities, able to immediately take measures when high-risk behaviors are detected, minimizing the impact scope of security threats.

Behavioral profile optimization is an important mechanism ensuring long-term effective system operation, enabling behavioral analysis to adapt to the natural evolution of user habits. The system adopts a continuous learning architecture, constantly absorbing new behavioral data to update user profiles, including newly added behavioral patterns, changing operation habits, and environmental factor changes. The profile optimization process implements decay memory mechanisms, gradually weakening the influence of historical data over time, ensuring profiles reflect users' latest behavioral characteristics. The system supports optimization strategies combining trigger-based updates with periodic updates, initiating profile reassessment when significant behavioral changes are detected or at fixed time intervals. To prevent malicious behaviors from being incorrectly incorporated into normal profiles, the system implements strict behavioral verification processes, with only confirmed trusted behaviors usable for profile optimization. Simultaneously, the system possesses behavioral trajectory analysis capabilities, able to identify gradual trends in user behaviors, anticipating changes in user habits, and reducing false positives during transition periods.

To improve behavioral analysis accuracy, the system integrates advanced machine learning technologies with expert knowledge systems. The machine learning module adopts a multi-model fusion strategy, combining supervised learning with unsupervised learning methods, both leveraging labeled historical data for pattern learning and discovering unknown abnormal patterns. The system implements automated feature engineering processes, able to extract and select the most distinctive feature combinations from raw behavioral data, enhancing model performance. To address data sparsity and cold start problems, the system employs transfer learning technologies, utilizing group behavioral models to provide foundation profiles for individual users, accelerating the personalized model building process. The expert knowledge system complements with rule-based analysis capabilities, incorporating security expert experience and industry best practices, remedying the shortcomings of purely data-driven methods. These two analysis methods complement and verify each other, forming a "human-machine collaborative" analysis framework, improving the accuracy and interpretability of behavioral identification.

The system also establishes comprehensive performance evaluation and optimization mechanisms, continuously monitoring and improving behavioral analysis effects. The evaluation metrics system covers security dimensions and experience dimensions, including false positive rates, false negative rates, identification delays, and user interference levels. The system implements automated model evaluation processes, periodically validating model performance using test datasets, identifying and correcting model defects. To balance security and user experience, the system supports sensitivity dynamic adjustment functionality, flexibly adjusting detection thresholds and risk tolerance based on security situations and business requirements. Simultaneously, the system possesses advanced anomaly explanation capabilities, transforming complex analysis results into understandable anomaly descriptions, helping security personnel quickly understand risk essences, improving response efficiency.

Through this comprehensive and refined behavioral analysis and identification mechanism, the User Behavior Analysis and Authentication submodule can effectively identify and prevent various security risks without affecting normal user experiences. This functionality enables the system to transcend traditional static authentication methods, establishing dynamic security protection based on the entire process of user behavior, laying the foundations for achieving "zero trust" security architecture. This intelligent behavioral analysis approach both enhances security protection effectiveness and improves user authentication experiences, providing solid security guarantees for organizational digital transformation.

6.2.3.2 Behavioral Multi-authentication

Behavioral multi-authentication is a key function of the User Behavior Analysis and Authentication submodule, building a multi-level, comprehensive behavioral verification system that ensures system security and compliance through integrated assessment of multiple dimensions of user behavior. This function breaks through the limitations of traditional single-dimension identity authentication [4], implementing a triple verification mechanism comprising behavioral identity verification, behavioral compliance verification, and behavioral benignness verification.

Behavioral identity authentication serves as the first line of defense in the multi-authentication system, verifying whether the current operator is the legitimate account holder through in-depth analysis of user behavioral characteristics. The system establishes rich behavioral identifiers across multiple behavioral dimensions, including user operation habits, interaction patterns, and cognitive preferences, constituting a unique "behavioral signature." The identity authentication process adopts a continuous evaluation model, not only verifying at initial login but also continuously monitoring behavioral consistency throughout the entire session, achieving end-to-end identity assurance. The system supports various behavioral identity feature extraction techniques, such as keystroke dynamics analysis, mouse operation trajectory, and touchscreen operation characteristics, covering different interaction scenarios and device types. To improve identity authentication accuracy, the system implements feature fusion mechanisms, integrating analyses of multiple behavioral characteristics to reduce the possibility of misjudgment from single features. Simultaneously, the system possesses environmental adaptability, dynamically adjusting identity feature matching standards according to changes in devices, networks, and physical environments used, avoiding misjudgments caused by environmental factors.

Behavioral compliance authentication constitutes the second layer of assurance in the multi-authentication system, ensuring user operations comply with organizational policies and regulatory requirements. The system incorporates a comprehensive compliance rule library covering multiple aspects including data access permissions, operation time restrictions, and function usage scopes, providing a foundation for behavioral compliance assessment. Compliance authentication employs real-time monitoring, conducting immediate compliance checks for each key user operation and intervening immediately upon discovering non-compliant behaviors. The system supports multi-level compliance policies, including both basic compliance requirements applicable to all users and specialized compliance rules for specific roles, departments, or business scenarios. To adapt to changing compliance environments, the system implements rule dynamic update mechanisms, promptly transforming new policy requirements into executable compliance check logic. Concurrently, the system possesses compliance risk early warning functionality, identifying behavioral trends that may lead to compliance issues, providing preemptive risk alerts and interventions to prevent problems before they occur. Additionally, the system establishes complete compliance authentication logs, recording all compliance check processes and results to provide detailed evidence for subsequent compliance audits.

Behavioral benign authentication forms the third layer of protection in the multi-authentication system, assessing whether user behaviors contain potential malicious or dangerous elements, preventing various attack and abuse behaviors. The system constructs a behavioral risk assessment framework, identifying potentially malicious intentions by analyzing user behavior characteristics such as purposiveness, consistency, and reasonableness. Benign authentication implements various abnormal behavior detection models, including abnormal access pattern detection, abnormal operation sequence identification, and sensitive behavior frequency monitoring, comprehensively covering various potential risk scenarios. The system supports context-aware risk assessment, incorporating users' historical behavior, current business scenarios, and overall system security status to provide more precise risk judgments. To address unknown threats, the system employs anomaly detection technology, capable of identifying behaviors deviating from normal patterns, even if these behaviors have not yet been explicitly defined as known threats. Simultaneously, the system implements behavioral chain analysis functionality, capable of correlatively analyzing seemingly independent multiple behaviors, identifying complex attack sequences and evasion strategies, enhancing protection capabilities against advanced threats.

For cross-domain users, the system implements additional cross-domain identity authentication mechanisms, resolving complex issues of user identity mutual trust between different security domains [5]. Cross-domain authentication adopts a federated identity framework, supporting various identity protocols and standards to achieve seamless integration between different identity systems [6]. The system establishes cross-domain trust evaluation models, dynamically adjusting initial trust levels for cross-domain users based on the source domain's security level, identity management maturity, and historical trust records. To enhance cross-domain authentication security, the system implements multi-factor verification mechanisms, requiring cross-domain users to provide additional identity credentials such as one-time passwords, digital certificates, or biometric features. Concurrently, the system supports progressive trust establishment, implementing strict permission controls for cross-domain users' initial access, gradually increasing trust levels and access permissions as usage records accumulate and behavioral characteristics are verified. To ensure cross-domain access traceability, the system implements complete identity mapping and behavioral audit mechanisms, recording cross-domain users' identity sources and all operational behaviors to facilitate accountability and evidence collection when security incidents occur.

The behavioral multi-authentication function employs risk-adaptive authorization strategies, dynamically adjusting user access permissions and operational restrictions based on triple authentication results and cross-domain authentication status. The system defines multi-level authorization results from full authorization to conditional authorization to denied authorization, corresponding to different risk levels and authentication result combinations. The authorization decision engine implements complex rule processing capabilities, comprehensively evaluating multiple authentication factors according to preset policy logic to generate final authorization decisions. The system supports progressive response mechanisms, adopting moderate measures such as increasing verification or restricting sensitive operations for medium-to-low risk situations, while executing mandatory measures such as session termination or account locking for high-risk situations. To enhance authorization decision flexibility, the system allows administrators to configure differentiated authorization policies for different business scenarios and user groups, balancing security requirements with business convenience. Simultaneously, the system possesses emergency authorization channels, allowing authorization administrators to temporarily override regular authorization rules in special circumstances to meet urgent business needs.

To support efficient behavioral multi-authentication operation, the system implements comprehensive performance optimization and reliability assurance mechanisms. Authorization processing adopts a distributed architecture, supporting horizontal scaling to address high-concurrency authentication requests, ensuring stable response times even during user surges [7]. The system implements authorization result caching mechanisms, reusing existing analysis results for repeated authentication requests within short timeframes, reducing computational resource consumption. To address potential component failures, the system designs degradation mechanisms, providing limited but secure authorization services based on available components and historical data when partial authentication services are unavailable, ensuring business continuity. Concurrently, the system establishes complete monitoring and alerting systems, real-time monitoring authorization service health status and performance metrics, promptly discovering and resolving potential issues.

Behavioral multi-authentication also provides comprehensive management interfaces and reporting tools, facilitating security administrators' understanding of authorization status and optimization of authorization policies. The management console displays detailed authorization statistics including key indicators such as pass rates for various authentications, risk distributions, and abnormal trends, helping administrators grasp overall security situations. The system supports in-depth authorization log analysis functionality, tracking authorization histories of individual users or user groups to identify potential problem patterns. To assist policy optimization, the system provides authorization simulation tools, allowing administrators to test new authorization policy effects without impacting actual users. Simultaneously, the system supports custom report generation functionality, generating authorization reports required for compliance audits by different dimensions and formats, meeting internal and external audit requirements.

Through this multi-level, comprehensive behavioral multi-authentication mechanism, the User Behavior Analysis and Authentication submodule can ensure system security while providing moderate user experiences, balancing contradictory requirements of security and convenience. This function breaks through the limitations of traditional authentication methods, establishing a dynamic authorization system based on comprehensive behavioral analysis, providing strong protection for secure access to organizational digital assets. This intelligent, risk-adaptive authorization approach not only strengthens the effectiveness of security protections but also improves the experience of legitimate users, thereby building a more secure and reliable information system environment for organizations.

6.3 Behavior Situational Awareness and Incident Response

6.3.1 Module Structure

The Behavior Situational Awareness and Incident Response module constructs a comprehensive closed-loop system for threat identification and handling, achieving full-process management of security events. Through a multi-layered architectural design, this module ensures seamless integration of every step from data collection

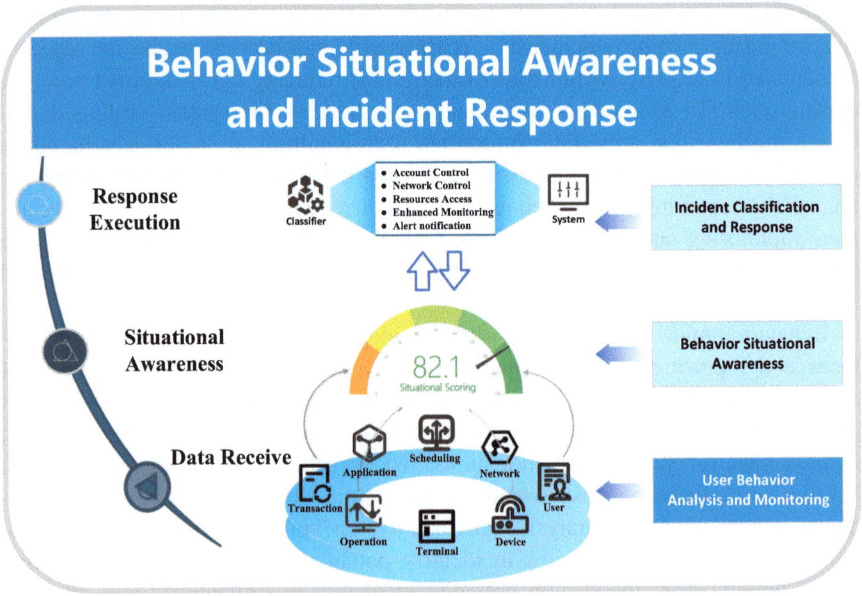

Fig. 6.3 Structure of behavior situational awareness and incident response

to incident handling, forming a "discovery-analysis-response-optimization" security operations loop. The module adheres to the design philosophy of "data-driven, situation-oriented, and response-focused", providing enterprises with real-time, precise security situational awareness and automated response capabilities. The structure is shown in Fig. 6.3.

The Data Reception Layer serves as the foundation of the entire module, responsible for acquiring pre-processed multi-layered behavioral data from the user behavior analysis and monitoring module, establishing a rich data source foundation. This layer implements seamless integration with the monitoring module through standardized interface protocols, ensuring real-time and complete data transmission. The Data Reception Layer also performs data cleansing and pre-standardization processing, conducting time synchronization, format conversion, and quality control on raw data to resolve heterogeneity issues from various data sources, providing consistent, high-quality data for upper-layer analysis. Additionally, this layer includes data buffering mechanisms to balance data collection and processing rates, preventing processing bottlenecks.

The Situational Analysis Layer is the core intelligence unit of the module, with its Behavior Situational Awareness sub-module undertaking the critical task of transforming discrete data into security situational cognition. This sub-module employs a situation graph-based analysis architecture, building comprehensive security awareness capabilities from low-level feature extraction to high-level situational understanding. During data correlation analysis, the system uses advanced correlation techniques to process multi-source heterogeneous data [8]. This includes entity correlation based on graph algorithms, constructing multi-dimensional relationship networks between users, devices, applications, resources, and other objects; temporal correlation analysis, capturing behavioral sequence patterns through sliding time windows and Markov chain models; and contextual correlation, integrating behaviors with business scenarios, historical baselines, and other background information. The system implements multi-granularity correlation analysis, comprehensively characterizing user activities from microscopic behavioral features to macroscopic behavior patterns. The system transforms correlation analysis results into structured user security situation graphs, providing intuitive visual representation for security analysis. The security situational scoring system is another core function of the analysis layer, quantitatively scoring the overall security status through real-time calculation of security metric matrices [9]. The scoring system designs a multi-level indicator framework, including basic indicators, composite indicators, and comprehensive scores. Basic indicators are directly extracted from raw data, such as abnormal login counts and sensitive operation frequencies; composite indicators are calculated by combining multiple basic indicators, such as user risk coefficients and asset threat indices; comprehensive scores integrate all dimensions, generating overall security situation scores through weighted algorithms.

The Response Execution Layer is responsible for transforming situational analysis into specific security measures, with its core component, the Incident Classification and Response sub-module, constructing a complete processing chain from event identification to response execution. This sub-module follows the principles of “rapid classification, graded response, automatic execution, and continuous optimization", ensuring efficient handling of security events.

The event classification system adopts a multi-level classification architecture, combining rule engines and machine learning models to achieve precise classification of behaviors. The rule engine handles clear threats with known patterns, quickly identifying common attacks through predefined expert rules; anomaly detection models concentrate on uncovering unknown threats by leveraging sequence anomaly detection to flag behaviors that deviate from normal patterns. The classification system also integrates contextual awareness, taking into account factors such as users, demands, resources, and historical behaviors to reduce false positives. Event classification results are risk-level categorized according to Common Vulnerability Scoring System (CVSS) scoring standards [10], from low to critical levels, providing priority references for subsequent responses. The automatic response strategy execution engine is the core execution unit of the response layer, responsible for transforming analysis results into actual security measures. This engine is designed based on a “response strategy library", containing preset response plans for different threat types and risk levels. Response measures cover multiple dimensions shown in Table 6.1.

Response execution adopts a progressive strategy, gradually escalating from low-impact to high-impact measures to avoid over-responses causing business interruptions. Meanwhile, the system supports manual intervention interfaces, allowing security teams to intervene or override automatic responses at critical decision points.

Table 6.1 Multiple measures in the incident response module

Type	Measures
Account control	Temporary account freezing, forced password reset, privilege reduction, etc.
Network control	IP blocking, traffic limitation, session termination, etc.
Resource access	Sensitive data access restrictions, operation approval escalation, etc.
Enhanced monitoring	Increasing monitoring granularity for specific users, initiating full session recording, etc.
Alert notification	Triggering security team alerts, generating event reports, etc.

The feedback optimization mechanism is a key component ensuring continuous system evolution through closed-loop design for self-improvement. This mechanism contains multiple levels of optimization loops: the event response effectiveness evaluation system records details and effects of each response operation, including whether threats were effectively controlled, false positive/negative situations, response times, and other indicators, through incremental learning methods, regularly updating model parameters using newly collected labeled data to adapt to constantly changing threat patterns. For complex scenarios, the system combines active learning strategies, intelligently selecting the most valuable samples for manual review and labeling to improve labeling efficiency. Through this series of feedback optimization designs, the system forms an adaptive, low-latency, high-precision security protection system that can continuously self-evolve with changing threat environments, effectively reducing manual intervention time for security events and improving overall security operation efficiency.

6.3.2 Behavior Situational Awareness

The Behavior Situational Awareness submodule serves as the core component of the situational analysis layer, fulfilling the critical responsibility of transforming the large volume of discrete data from the Behavioral Data Collection and Monitoring module into systematic security situational cognition. This submodule employs an advanced situational graph analysis architecture, achieving a comprehensive transformation process from raw data to high-level security awareness, providing a solid intelligent foundation for security decision-making.

In terms of fundamental architectural design, this submodule establishes a multi-dimensional and multi-granular analytical framework, beginning with low-level data correlation analysis, gradually progressing to mid-level situational graph construction, and ultimately achieving high-level situational understanding. This progressive processing method enables the system to gradually refine the security value embedded within the data, ultimately forming a global security situational awareness. The submodule integrates various advanced technologies, including graph computing, temporal analysis, machine learning, and knowledge representation, forming a complete security cognitive capability system.

6.3.2.1 Data Correlation Analysis Framework

In this submodule, the system implements a deeply integrated multi-dimensional correlation analysis framework, constructing a comprehensive security correlation network through collaborative analysis across three major dimensions: entity, temporal, and contextual. Entity correlation analysis employs graph representation methods to model the complex interaction relationships between various entity objects such as users, devices, applications, and resources as a dynamically evolving multi-dimensional relationship network. Simultaneously, the system utilizes Graph Convolutional Network (GCN) algorithms with message passing mechanisms that enable each node to aggregate information from its neighboring nodes, thereby learning node representations that simultaneously contain both intrinsic features and network structural information [11]. This approach facilitates learning association rules between entities from graph data, predicting potential entity interaction behaviors, and providing early awareness of potential risk behaviors. These graph neural network methods learn complex patterns directly from structured data, uncovering association rules that traditional methods often fail to capture.

Temporal correlation analysis revolves around the time series attributes of behavioral events, extracting valuable security insights from the temporal patterns of behavior occurrence. The system dynamically captures behavioral characteristics across different time spans through sliding time window techniques, enabling attention to both instantaneous anomalies and long-term evolutionary trends. In behavioral sequence modeling, Markov chain models are employed to describe the probability distribution of entity state transitions, characterizing the transition patterns of normal operation sequences and providing reference baselines for anomalous behavior identification. For deep-level behavior analysis, the system utilizes Long Short-Term Memory networks to process variable-length behavior sequences [12], with gating mechanisms that selectively retain or forget historical information, effectively capturing long-distance dependencies such as seasonal patterns in user operations or complex attack precursor sequences. This equips the system with deep understanding capabilities when mining behavioral sequence patterns, enabling it to identify various anomalous activity sequences in the temporal dimension, including operation sequence anomalies, time interval anomalies, periodicity disruptions, and gradual behavioral shifts. Through temporal analysis techniques, the system can precisely distinguish between legitimate but uncommon operation sequences and truly anomalous behaviors, significantly improving detection accuracy, reducing false positives, and providing security analysts with reliable temporal anomaly evidence.

The contextual correlation analysis framework achieves deep integration of behavioral data with multi-source contexts, enhancing the contextual understanding capabilities of anomaly detection from both static structural and dynamic environmental perspectives. Regarding static context, the system integrates domain knowledge such as organizational structure graphs, business process models, resource sensitivity classifications, and user permission matrices to establish a fundamental reference system for behavior judgment. Dynamic context includes real-time information such as current session states, environmental condition changes, and related event sequences, providing immediate background for behavior interpretation. The system employs a reinforcement learning-based context-sensitive anomaly scoring mechanism that assigns differentiated risk weights to identical behaviors under different contextual conditions, effectively reducing false positives. To handle uncertainties and incompleteness in contextual information, the model also possesses adaptive learning capabilities, continuously adjusting the influence weights of contextual factors based on feedback, achieving dynamic adaptation to organizational environmental changes.

These three correlation dimensions do not operate in isolation; the system has designed a multi-dimensional collaborative analysis mechanism that achieves cross-dimensional information complementarity and evidence aggregation, mutually verifying and enhancing the reliability of analytical conclusions. This multi-dimensional correlation analysis framework enables the system to comprehensively characterize all aspects of security events. It not only captures complex anomaly patterns that are difficult to discover based on a single dimension, but also provides richer evidence chains and explanatory paths, establishing a solid analytical foundation for security decision-making.

Concurrently, the submodule implements multi-granularity correlation analysis strategies, constructing comprehensive user behavior models through layered security perspectives. At the micro level, the system focuses on individual behavioral characteristics and short time sequence anomaly patterns. It precisely captures detailed features of each login attempt, resource access request, and system operation, such as operation speed, operation timing, and resource access sequence behavioral fingerprints. This enables rapid identification of burst anomalous operations and precisely targeted attack behaviors. At the meso level, the analysis engine associates discrete operation events into meaningful functional operation combinations. It understands users behavioral paths and operational habits for completing specific tasks, identifying abnormal changes in function usage such as business process bypassing, permission probing, and function abuse complex behavioral patterns. At the macro level, the system focuses on long-term behavioral trends, establishing stable long-term behavioral baselines by continuously monitoring seasonal changes in user activities, work responsibility evolution, and usage habit transformations. This approach helps discover slowly evolving anomalous behaviors such as advanced persistent threats and gradual privilege escalation by insiders. These three levels complement each other and work collaboratively, forming a complete behavioral analysis framework ensuring the system can comprehensively characterize user activity features. Through this multi-granularity analysis method, the system maintains high sensitivity while considering the global perspective. It ensures that subtle anomaly signals are not missed, while also capturing overall security situational changes. This provides security teams with a complete security cognition chain, from specific events to global trends, greatly enhancing the comprehensiveness and accuracy of threat discovery.

6.3.2.2 Security Situational Knowledge Graph and Scoring System

After conducting exhaustive analysis and processing of data correlations, the system transforms the complex results of correlation analysis into a structured security situational knowledge graph. This graph adopts a knowledge graph organizational form, clearly defining three core elements, including entities, relationships, and attributes, along with their interaction rules. At the entity level, the system defines multiple entity types including users, devices, applications, resources, behaviors, and events, with each type possessing specific attribute sets. At the relationship level, the system constructs rich relationship types, precisely describing interaction modes between entities. At the attribute level, each entity and relationship carries a series of descriptive attributes such as timestamps, risk scores, and confidence levels. This triplet structure (entity-relationship-entity) forms an expressive security semantic network, enabling precise expression and flexible querying of complex security scenarios. The system employs a multi-level ontology model to standardize the graph structure [13], forming a complete knowledge representation system from domain concepts to specific instances. The top-level ontology defines basic concepts and relationships in the security domain, the middle-level ontology provides refined extensions for specific business scenarios, while the bottom level consists of actual data instances. This layered design ensures the graph possesses good extensibility and adaptability, capable of continuously evolving with changing security requirements.

The security situational scoring system is another key function of the submodule, assessing and measuring the overall security status of the system through quantitative methods. The scoring system carefully designs a multi-level indicator framework, constructing a complete evaluation system from micro-events to macro situations, ensuring comprehensiveness and accuracy in security status assessment. At the fundamental level, the system directly extracts basic behavioral indicators from raw data, such as abnormal login counts, sensitive operation frequencies, and resource access patterns. These indicators directly reflect the most primitive security event characteristics in the system, establishing a data foundation for subsequent analysis. At the intermediate level, through fusion calculation and correlation analysis of multiple basic indicators, the system generates more insightful composite indicators such as user risk coefficients, asset threat indices, and behavioral anomaly degrees. These indicators can reflect concentrated manifestations of security threats from different dimensions, providing security analysts with more valuable threat awareness. At the highest level, the system integrates indicator data from all dimensions, applying hierarchical analysis methods to form a computational security indicator matrix [9], quantitatively scoring the system's overall security status through scientific calculation models. This scoring fully considers the mutual influence and comprehensive effects of various security factors. The system also employs dynamic weighting algorithms, automatically adjusting weight allocations for various indicators according to different environments and business scenarios, ultimately generating a comprehensive score that fully reflects the system's security situation. This quantitative scoring mechanism provides objective bases for security decisions, enabling security analysts to intuitively grasp trends in system security status and promptly discover security weaknesses. It transitions security management from traditional experience-driven approaches to more precise, data-driven modes, enhancing the scientific nature and effectiveness of security management. The scoring results not only support current security status assessment but also reflect evolutionary trends in security situations through historical data comparison, providing quantitative references for continuous security improvement, enabling organizations to systematically enhance their security protection capabilities.

The Behavior Situational Awareness submodule, through its situational knowledge graph, provides rich visualization expression and interactive analysis capabilities while preserving user behavioral information. It not only provides necessary information for security analysis algorithms but also enables security analysts to intuitively understand complex security situations. Analysts can flexibly explore graph contents through operations such as zooming, panning, and filtering, supporting multi-level analysis from global situations to individual behaviors. The system provides rich query functionalities, including keyword-based entity searches, path-based relationship queries, and pattern-based subgraph matching, enabling analysts to quickly locate security focal points of interest. Additionally, the system supports time retrospection functionality; through timeline controls, one can observe state changes in the graph at different time points, tracking the evolution processes of security events.

6.3.3 Incident Classification and Response

The Incident Identification and Classification Module functions as the analytical basis of the security system, converting raw behavioral data into security intelligence through advanced detection and classification capabilities. This module is architected to provide comprehensive threat visibility across the organization's digital environment, leveraging advanced analytical techniques to identify both known and emerging security threats with high precision.

The module consists of two primary functional components that work in tandem to deliver end-to-end incident management capabilities. The first component, the Incident Classification System and Risk Level Categorization, employs a multi-tiered classification architecture that progressively analyzes security events from basic behavioral patterns to sophisticated threat categories. This system utilizes a powerful rule engine for identifying known threats through expert-defined detection rules, while seamlessly integrating with anomaly detection capabilities to uncover novel attack patterns that evade traditional signature-based detection. A key strength of this component is its context-awareness framework, which enriches incident analysis with multidimensional contextual factors including user roles, resource sensitivity, temporal patterns, and historical behaviors. Once incidents are classified, the system applies the industry-standard CVSS methodology to assess risk levels, creating a graduated severity scale that considers both technical impact and business criticality, ensuring security teams can effectively prioritize their response efforts.

The second component, the Automated Response Strategy and Feedback Optimization Mechanism, extends the module's capabilities from detection to remediation through a sophisticated orchestration framework. This component enables the security system to automatically execute predefined response playbooks tailored to specific incident types and risk levels, significantly reducing time-to-response for critical security events. The response strategies range from non-disruptive monitoring actions for low-risk incidents to immediate containment measures for severe threats, with built-in safeguards to prevent disproportionate responses. What distinguishes this component is its closed-loop learning mechanism, which continuously evaluates response effectiveness by monitoring post-action security states and operational impacts. This feedback is systematically analyzed to refine future response strategies, optimizing both security efficacy and business continuity considerations over time. The system also maintains comprehensive incident documentation and metrics, providing valuable insights for security posture improvement and compliance reporting.

Together, these components create a robust, adaptive security framework that not only identifies and classifies security incidents with high precision but also ensures appropriate, measured responses that evolve through continuous learning. This holistic approach to incident management significantly enhances an organization's security resilience while minimizing operational disruption.

6.3.3.1 Incident Classification System and Risk Level Categorization

The incident classification system and risk level categorization are core functions of the incident identification and classification module, providing precise threat determination and priority guidance for security responses. The incident classification system employs a multi-level classification architecture, building a complete classification system from basic behavioral patterns to advanced threat categories, capable of adapting to continuously evolving security threat environments. This architecture includes three levels: behavior-level classification, incident-level classification, and threat-level classification, achieving precise classification of security incidents through a progressive approach. Behavior-level classification focuses on basic operation patterns, incident-level classification concentrates on specific types of security incidents, while threat-level classification categorizes incidents from the perspective of attack tactics and techniques, maintaining compatibility with threat frameworks such as MITRE ATT&CK [14]. The system achieves precise classification and comprehensive coverage of security incidents through a rule engine. The rule engine adopts a knowledge base-driven inference mechanism, supporting complex condition combinations and multi-level rule chains, capable of processing complex rule expressions containing logical relationships, temporal relationships, and dependency relationships. For known threat identification, the rule engine is responsible for handling security threats with clear characteristics, rapidly identifying common attack patterns such as identity theft, privilege abuse, data leakage, and unauthorized access through predefined expert rules, ensuring efficient processing of known threats. The expert rule library is continuously maintained and updated by security analysts, integrating industry threat intelligence and internal security experience to form a comprehensive and precise set of rules.

In the field of unknown threat discovery, the system relies on the anomaly detection module that will be introduced later. This module focuses on discovering potential unknown threats, employing sequence anomaly detection technology to identify abnormal patterns that deviate from normal behavioral baselines. It is capable of capturing complex behavioral anomalies such as account misuse, data access anomalies, and operation sequence anomalies, providing strong support for discovering advanced persistent threats. Sequence anomaly detection technology combines Markov models and sequence embedding methods, capable of capturing temporal dependencies and transition patterns in user operation sequences, precisely identifying operation sequences that violate normal behavioral patterns. This technology not only focuses on the anomaly of individual operations but also emphasizes overall pattern anomalies in operation sequences, capable of discovering complex attack behaviors that are compliant at individual steps but anomalous as a whole.

The classification system also integrates deep context-awareness capabilities, placing behavioral judgments within a complete environmental background. It comprehensively considers multi-dimensional contextual factors such as user roles, resource sensitivity, time factors, location information, device characteristics, and historical behavioral patterns to enhance classification accuracy, effectively reducing false positive rates and improving system practicality. The context-awareness mechanism establishes a multi-dimensional context model to build a complete background framework for each security incident. The system integrates static contextual elements including organizational structure information, role definitions, resource classification systems, and permission policies, while combining dynamic contextual elements such as current session states, environmental conditions, and related incident sequences, achieving a deep understanding of behavioral intent. The static context model precisely describes the organization's security knowledge system through concept hierarchies, relationship types, and attribute definitions, providing a reliable knowledge foundation for behavioral judgment. Dynamic context is captured through session tracking technology and real-time state monitoring, reflecting the instantaneous state of the current security environment. This context-awareness capability enables the system to distinguish the security significance of identical behaviors in different situations. For example, privileged operations performed by an administrator during working hours from an office network have completely different risk implications compared to the same operations performed by the same administrator during non-working hours from an unfamiliar location.

After incident classification is completed, the system categorizes security incidents into risk levels according to the Common Vulnerability Scoring System

(CVSS), establishing a grading system from low to critical levels, with each level corresponding to different risk characteristics and potential impact ranges. The CVSS scoring standard provides a systematic method for assessing the severity of security vulnerabilities and threats, including both base score vectors and environmental score vectors. The base score reflects the inherent harmfulness of the threat, considering factors such as attack complexity, required privileges, and scope of impact; the environmental score combines organization-specific security requirements and business importance to make environmental adjustments to the base score. This risk leveling not only considers the technical characteristics of threats but also integrates business impact assessments, providing security teams with clear response priority guidance, ensuring timely protection of critical resources, and effectively enhancing security operation efficiency. Business impact assessment automatically obtains the business value and criticality of affected assets through integration with core business systems, transforming technical risks into understandable business risks, aligning security response decisions with business priorities. The system's risk rating results are dynamically updated, adjusting with changes in threat contexts or the emergence of new evidence, ensuring that risk assessments always maintain timeliness and accuracy, providing reliable bases for security decisions. The dynamic update mechanism ensures security teams always have the latest risk status by continuously monitoring threat developments and environmental changes, promptly adjusting risk ratings.

6.3.3.2 Automated Response Strategy and Feedback Optimization Mechanism

The Automated Response Strategy and Feedback Optimization Mechanism is a sophisticated component of the security framework, designed to transform analytical insights into concrete security actions while continuously improving system performance. At its core, the Automated Response Strategy Execution Engine serves as the central operational unit, responsible for converting analysis results into actionable security measures. This engine operates based on a comprehensive Response Strategy Library, which contains meticulously crafted predefined response plans tailored to address various threat types and risk levels with appropriate countermeasures. These response plans are developed by security expert teams based on industry best practices and organization-specific requirements, ensuring that response measures comply with both technical security standards and business continuity requirements.

The system employs the Security Orchestration, Automation and Response (SOAR) technology framework, enabling the automation of complex response processes through visual workflow design and API integration capabilities, significantly reducing the time interval from threat detection to response execution. SOAR technology allows security teams to modularize complex multi-step response processes, creating reusable playbooks that can automatically execute complete workflows from initial investigation to threat mitigation. The system's response orchestration capability supports conditional branching and decision nodes, enabling dynamic adjustment of response paths based on real-time security contexts, ensuring that actions taken are most appropriate for the current threat situation. Additionally, the SOAR platform's integration interfaces enable the system to seamlessly collaborate with various security tools and enterprise systems, including firewalls, intrusion prevention systems, endpoint-protecting platforms, and identity management systems, achieving end-to-end response automation.

Response capabilities span multiple operational dimensions, including account control measures such as temporary account freezing, forced password resets, and privilege downgrading; network control operations including IP blocking, traffic limitation, and session termination; resource access restrictions that limit sensitive data access or escalate operation approval requirements; monitoring enhancement techniques that increase surveillance granularity for specific users or activate full session recording; and alert notification processes that trigger security team notifications and generate detailed incident reports. The execution framework employs a progressive response strategy, methodically escalating from low-impact to high-impact measures, carefully balancing security requirements with business continuity considerations to prevent unnecessary operational disruptions. The system first attempts to implement response measures with less impact on business operations, such as enhanced monitoring or sending warning notifications, and only gradually implements more restrictive measures when the threat level increases or initial response measures prove ineffective. This progressive approach effectively prevents the risk of business interruption that might result from overreaction, while ensuring that security protection matches the actual threat level.

Importantly, the system incorporates a manual intervention interface that enables security teams to intercede at critical decision points or override automated responses when human judgment is warranted, maintaining the optimal balance between automation efficiency and expert oversight. The manual intervention interface provides detailed event context information and system-recommended response options, while allowing security analysts to modify, pause, or replace automated response actions. This "human-in-the-loop" design ensures that critical security decisions remain guided by human professional judgment, especially in high-risk situations that may have significant impacts on core business systems.

Complementing the response capabilities is the Feedback Optimization Mechanism, a critical component that ensures the system's continuous evolution through a sophisticated closed-loop design. This mechanism encompasses multiple optimization cycles that systematically refine system performance. The incident response effectiveness evaluation component meticulously documents the details and outcomes of each response action, tracking key performance indicators such as threat containment effectiveness, false positive/negative occurrences, and response timing metrics. Response effectiveness evaluation focuses not only on security metrics but also covers business impact indicators, comprehensively assessing the overall effect of security responses and providing multi-dimensional reference for future strategy optimization.

The system uses learning methods based on Random Forest and Gradient Boosting Decision Trees, which automatically identify the most effective response strategy patterns through analysis of historical response data and recommend optimal response measures for similar scenarios, significantly improving the accuracy of automated decision-making. These machine learning models can extract key features and successful patterns from numerous historical response cases, establishing association mappings between threat types and optimal response strategies. The Random Forest model, with its excellent classification capabilities and robustness against noisy data, is particularly suitable for handling multi-feature judgments of security incidents, while Gradient Boosting Decision Trees provide more refined response effect predictions through iterative optimization. The integrated application of these models has achieved intelligent and precise response decisions, greatly reducing the workload of security analysts in handling routine threats.

Through incremental learning methods, the system regularly updates model parameters using newly collected and annotated data, enabling it to adapt to evolving threat patterns and emerging attack vectors. The incremental learning process automatically integrates new security event data and response result feedback, continuously optimizing decision models without requiring complete retraining, maintaining the system's timely adaptation capability to new threats. During model updates, the system pays special attention to misjudgment cases and edge cases, enhancing the model's judgment accuracy in complex scenarios through focused analysis of these cases.

For particularly complex security scenarios, the system employs active learning strategies to intelligently select the most valuable samples for human review and annotation, significantly enhancing the efficiency of human-machine collaboration while maximizing knowledge gain from expert input. The active learning mechanism can identify cases with high model uncertainty or rare threat patterns [15], prioritizing these cases for analysis and annotation by security experts, accelerating the model's learning process in new threat domains through targeted expert knowledge acquisition.

Comprehensive feedback channels extend beyond technical performance to include business impact assessments, tracking how security controls affect operational processes and adjusting response thresholds accordingly. The system records the degree of impact each security response has on business operations, including aspects such as user experience impact, service availability changes, and workflow interruptions. It incorporates these business impact data into response strategy optimization considerations to ensure that security measures minimize disruption to normal business while protecting assets. This business-sensitive optimization mechanism greatly enhances the organizational acceptance of security controls, making security protection an enabler rather than an obstacle to business development.

Through this sophisticated feedback optimization architecture, the system establishes an adaptive, low-latency, and high-precision security framework capable of continuous self-improvement in response to changing threat landscapes, effectively reducing manual intervention requirements while enhancing overall security operational efficiency. The system's adaptive capability makes it increasingly intelligent over time, with security response accuracy and efficiency continuously improving, forming a true security intelligence closed loop. This blend of automated response and continuous optimization not only strengthens the organization's defense against current threats but also lays a solid foundation for addressing potential new security challenges in the future.

6.4 Cross-domain Privacy Preserving

As network security threats become increasingly complex and global, the ability of a single organization to address security challenges in isolation has become increasingly limited. Current Advanced Persistent Threats (APTs), system vulnerabilities, and sophisticated cyber attacks often span multiple organizational boundaries, requiring collaborative defense to effectively counter them. Meanwhile, the introduction of data protection and privacy regulations such as GDPR (General Data Protection Regulation), CCPA (California Consumer Privacy Act), and PIPL (Personal Information Protection Law of China) has imposed strict compliance requirements on organizations handling sensitive data, with violations potentially leading to serious legal consequences and reputational damage. This dual challenge creates a seemingly contradictory need: organizations must both strengthen collaboration and share threat intelligence to enhance overall security posture, while strictly protecting sensitive data from exposure.

Traditional data sharing methods often face a dilemma between security and utility. On one hand, completely open data sharing may lead to sensitive information leakage, intellectual property risks, and violations of data protection regulations; on the other hand, excessive restrictions on data sharing hinder effective cross-organizational collaboration, weakening collective defense capabilities. Additionally, varying regulatory requirements across different industries and regions create complex compliance barriers for cross-border and cross-sector data collaboration. This challenge is particularly pronounced in highly regulated sectors such as finance, hospitals, and government, which both possess high-value security data and are subject to the strictest data protection constraints.

The Cross-Domain Privacy Protection Module is designed as a technical solution to address this core contradiction. Through advanced cryptographic technologies and access control mechanisms, it realizes the security paradigm of "data usable but not visible", enabling organizations to conduct meaningful collaborative analysis without exposing original sensitive data. This capability is critical for modern security operations, especially in scenarios such as threat intelligence sharing, cross-departmental security incident response, supply chain security management, and multi-party security analysis. For example, financial institutions can jointly analyze fraud patterns without disclosing their respective customer transaction data; healthcare organizations can collaborate on patient safety research without violating privacy regulations; government agencies can coordinate cyber defense without compromising national security information.

With the rise of the "zero trust" concept and the proliferation in distributed work environments, the need for cross-domain privacy protection has become more urgent. Organizational boundaries are increasingly blurred, and traditional perimeter-based security measures are no longer sufficient, requiring more granular and dynamic data protection approaches. Meanwhile, the application of intelligence methods in the security domain has amplified the demand for large volumes of multi-source data.

By implementing the Cross-Domain Privacy Protection Module, organizations can establish trusted collaborative networks to jointly address threats on a foundation of compliance and security. This capability not only enhances the security defense level of individual organizations but also brings positive impacts to the security ecosystem of entire industries and regions, promoting the formation of a more efficient and collaborative cybersecurity defense system.

6.4.1 Module Structure

The Cross-Domain Privacy Protection Module is a sophisticated security component designed to safeguard sensitive information while enabling collaborative computation and data sharing across multiple systems or organizations. This module implements advanced privacy-preserving technologies to ensure minimal data exposure and controlled usage while still enabling the extraction of valuable insights from multi-organizational datasets. The structure of Cross-domain Privacy Protection is shown in Fig. 6.4.

The Fine-grained Access Control sub-module is the most important sub-module, which employs multiple complementary control models including attribute-based access control, short for ABAC [16] and role-based access control, short for RBAC [17]. ABAC enables dynamic, context-aware authorization decisions based on user attributes, resource characteristics, and environmental conditions, allowing for highly precise and adaptable access policies. Meanwhile, RBAC simplifies administration by assigning permissions to roles rather than to individual users, streamlining permission management in large organizational structures. Together, these approaches enforce the principle of least privilege, ensuring that users access only the minimum data required for their legitimate duties and substantially shrinking the attack surface for potential data breaches.

The Secure Multi-Party Computation (SMPC) sub-module represents the technical core of cross-domain collaboration [18], enabling multiple organizations to compute functions over their combined data together without disclosing the underlying raw information to one another. Using cryptographic protocols such as garbled circuits, secret sharing, or homomorphic encryption, SMPC allows parties to contribute encrypted inputs to distributed computations while not leaking the information about their source data. This powerful capability enables cross-

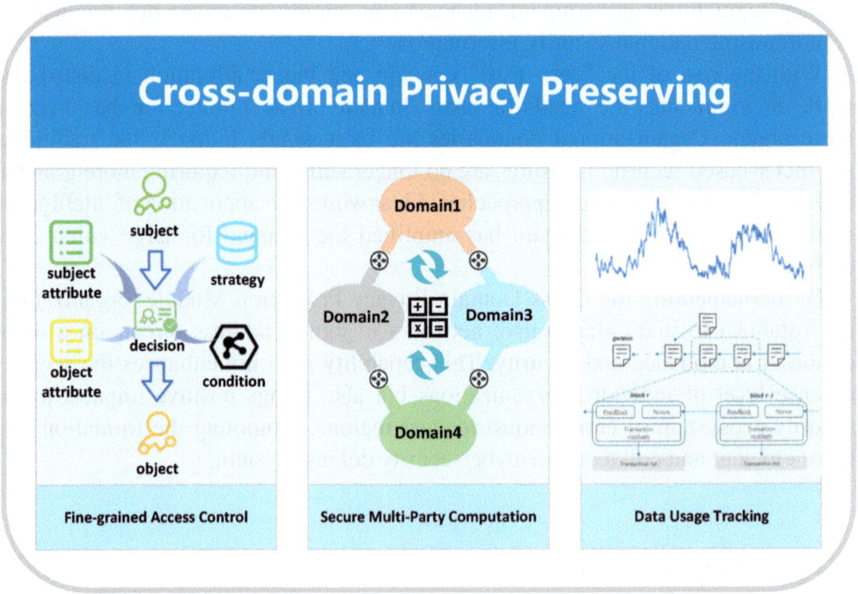

Fig. 6.4 Structure of cross-domain privacy preserving

organizational intelligence sharing, collaborative threat analysis, and joint security operations without compromising sensitive organizational data, which effectively makes data usable but not visible. For example, organizations can collectively compute statistical analyses across their combined datasets to identify common attack patterns while keeping their individual security incidents confidential.

Complementing these protection mechanisms, the Data Usage Tracking sub-module maintains comprehensive visibility over data utilization throughout its entire lifecycle. This component implements detailed logging and monitoring of all data access events, tracking who accessed what information, when, from where, and for what purpose. Advanced techniques such as watermarking and information flow tracking enable the system to trace data movement across boundaries and detect potential policy violations. The collected usage metrics not only support compliance verification with organizational policies and regulatory requirements but also enable forensic investigation in case of security incidents. Additionally, this tracking capability provides valuable inputs for continuous policy refinement, allowing security administrators to adapt access controls based on actual usage patterns and evolving security needs.

Together, these integrated sub-modules create a comprehensive privacy protection framework that enables secure cross-domain collaboration while maintaining strict data confidentiality and regulatory compliance. By balancing data utility with privacy protection, the cross-domain privacy protection module enables organizations to leverage the collective value of their data assets while controlling over sensitive information.

6.4.2 *Fine-grained Access Control*

The fine-grained access control sub-module emerged against the backdrop of increasingly complex cross-organizational data collaboration, where traditional single access control models have become inadequate for addressing challenges such as disparate identity authentication systems, inconsistent permission management approaches, and dynamically changing data sensitivity across multi-organizational heterogeneous environments. In response to these challenges, this submodule adopts an innovative multi-model fusion strategy that organically integrates the core advantages of multiple classical access control models to construct a comprehensive permission management system that maintains the unique strengths of each model while enabling their synergistic operation.

RBAC is a mature access control model whose core concept involves assigning permissions to roles rather than directly to users, with users indirectly obtaining permissions through assigned roles. The RBAC model comprises four fundamental elements: users, roles, permissions, and sessions. Users can be assigned multiple roles, roles can possess multiple permissions, and through the intermediate role layer, a decoupling between users and permissions is achieved. This design makes permission management more concise and maintainable, particularly suitable for large organizations with clear hierarchical structures and functional divisions. RBAC also supports role inheritance mechanisms, allowing child roles to inherit permissions from parent roles, further simplifying permission management in complex organizational structures.

ABAC is an access control model that makes access decisions using multidimensional information, including subject, object, environment, and action. Subject attributes encompass user identity information, departmental affiliation, security clearance levels, and other characteristics; object attributes describe resource classification, sensitivity levels, ownership, and other features; environmental attributes cover contextual information such as time, geographical location, and network security status; action attributes define specific types of access behaviors. ABAC combines and compares these attributes through policy rules, enabling the expression of complex access control requirements and supporting fine-grained permission control and dynamic authorization decisions. This attribute-based approach is particularly well-suited for handling complex access control scenarios across organizations and domains.

Context-Based Access Control, CBAC for short, focuses on leveraging environmental context information to enhance the accuracy and security of access control decisions [19]. Context information includes temporal context (access time, duration, and frequency), spatial context (geographical location, network location, and device location), technical context (device type, operating system, and network security status), and user behavioral context (historical access patterns, and current activity status). CBAC can change access policies by this contextual information dynamically, such as restricting sensitive data access during non-business hours, prohibiting access from insecure networks, or detecting anomalous access based on users' historical behavioral patterns. This context-awareness capability makes access control more intelligent and adaptive.

In the specific fusion implementation, the system skillfully leverages RBAC's advantages in simplicity and manageability for large-scale user permission management, handling hierarchical permission allocation within organizations through role abstraction mechanisms. When facing complex permission requirements across organizations, the system introduces ABAC's dynamic decision-making capabilities, performing precise permission judgments based on multi-dimensional information including user attributes, resource characteristics, and operation types. Meanwhile, CBAC's context-awareness features are integrated into the decision-making process, enabling the system to dynamically adjust permission policies based on environmental factors such as access time, geographical location, network environment, and device security status. This three-model fusion is not a simple overlay but rather a deep integration achieved through unified policy description languages and decision engines, ensuring that policies from different models can be executed in a coordinated and consistent manner.

The system's core innovation lies in establishing a layered decision architecture where RBAC provides the foundational permission framework and organizational structure mapping, utilizing its role inheritance and permission aggregation advantages to establish cross-organizational role mapping systems. ABAC performs fine-grained attribute matching and dynamic authorization on this foundation, leveraging its powerful attribute expression capabilities to handle complex cross-domain permission requirements and supporting precise access control based on multi-dimensional attributes such as data classification, user credentials, and project participation levels. CBAC provides environmental awareness and risk assessment capabilities by real-time monitoring and analyzing contextual information, offering important environmental evidence for the decision-making of the other two models. In actual permission decision processes, the system first determines users' basic role permission scope through RBAC, then employs ABAC's attribute matching mechanisms to verify whether users possess the necessary attribute conditions for accessing specific resources, and finally combines CBAC's contextual analysis to determine whether the current environment is suitable for executing the access operation.

Another important characteristic of the multi-model fusion is the achievement of flexible combination and dynamic adaptation of permission policies. The system supports selecting the most appropriate control model combinations for different types of data and access scenarios. For example, for structured internal organizational data, the system primarily relies on RBAC's role management for efficient permission allocation, while for sensitive data shared across organizations, it employs combination strategies that emphasize ABAC's attribute matching and CBAC's environmental monitoring. This model selection is not static configuration but rather intelligent dynamic selection based on factors such as data classification, user types, and access scenarios, ensuring optimal permission control strategies are employed in different situations.

Through this innovative multi-model fusion architecture, the Fine-grained Access Control submodule successfully addresses the limitations of single access control models in complex cross-domain environments. It forms a comprehensive permission management system that combines RBAC's simplicity and efficiency, ABAC's precision and flexibility, and CBAC's environmental awareness advantages. This system not only effectively addresses various permission control challenges in current cross-organizational data collaboration but also provides an extensible technical foundation for future more complex data sharing scenarios. The submodule collaborates with the Secure Multi-Party Computation submodule to ensure participant permission verification and result access control. It also integrates with the Data Usage Tracking module to form a complete data usage monitoring chain, collectively constituting the security control core of the cross-domain privacy protection framework and providing solid technical assurance for secure data collaboration among multiple organizations.

6.4.3 Secure Multi-party Computation

The Secure Multi-Party Computation submodule emerged from the need to resolve a fundamental contradiction in the modern digital economy: how to achieve cross-organizational data value mining and collaborative computation while protecting each party's data privacy. In traditional data collaboration models, participating parties often need to aggregate raw data to a centralized platform or mutually share plaintext data to conduct joint analysis, which poses serious privacy leakage risks and data sovereignty issues. As data becomes an important production factor, organizations both hope to gain greater value through data collaboration and are reluctant to expose their sensitive information. Particularly in highly sensitive domains such as finance, healthcare, and government, direct data sharing is often strictly restricted by laws and regulations. Meanwhile, different organizations lack sufficient trust foundations and worry about data being misused or leaked to competitors, which further impedes effective data circulation and value release.

The Secure Multi-Party Computation submodule applies cryptography-based secure multi-party computation to resolve this dilemma. Its core methodology is the design of sophisticated cryptographic protocols that allow multiple parties to jointly compute agreed-upon functions without revealing their private inputs. The implementation relies on advanced cryptographic primitives and protocols, with secret sharing serving as the foundational framework. Specifically, secret sharing uses polynomial interpolation or linear algebraic techniques to split each participant's private data into multiple shares with special mathematical properties. Any single share, or any subset below a threshold, reveals no information about the original data, and only when the preset threshold is met can the original data be reconstructed via Lagrange interpolation or matrix operations. During computation, participants perform the corresponding mathematical operations on their held shares; because addition and multiplication are homomorphic under secret sharing, computations on shares correspond directly to computations on the original data.

Garbled circuit technology provides another important implementation approach, particularly suitable for computational tasks involving complex logical judgments and conditional branches [20]. This technique first expresses the target function as a Boolean circuit composed of AND, OR, and NOT gates, then encrypts the circuit through Yao's garbled circuit protocol [21]. The specific process includes: the circuit constructor generates random key pairs for each wire in the circuit, representing the two possible values 0 and 1; for each logic gate in the circuit, the constructor creates an encrypted truth table where output wire keys are encrypted using input wire keys; the circuit evaluator obtains keys corresponding to their inputs through oblivious transfer protocols, then decrypts and computes layer by layer according to the circuit's topological order, ultimately obtaining the key corresponding to the output result. Throughout this process, the circuit evaluator can only see intermediate results related to the computation path and cannot obtain input information from other participants or information from unrelated computational branches.

Homomorphic encryption technology provides solutions for computational scenarios requiring high privacy protection, with its core advantage being the ability to directly perform mathematical operations on ciphertext [22]. Fully homomorphic encryption schemes such as BGV, BFV, and CKKS support arbitrary additions and multiplications on encrypted data, with the decrypted outputs matching exactly the results of performing the same operations on the plaintext. The CKKS scheme is particularly suitable for floating-point arithmetic and approximate computation, effectively handling continuous numerical computations in machine learning and statistical analysis through noise control and rescaling techniques. The implementation of homomorphic encryption involves complex lattice cryptography theory, building security guarantees by learning with errors assumptions [23] and ring learning with errors problems [24]. In practical applications, homomorphic encryption requires careful management of noise growth and ciphertext size expansion issues, achieving noise refresh through bootstrapping techniques and improving computational efficiency through batching techniques.

The sub-module's implementation also employs several key protocol optimizations and engineering techniques. Preprocessing optimization technology divides the computational process into offline and online phases: in the offline phase, participants can pre-generate large amounts of random numbers, correlated randomness, and cryptographic components such as multiplication triples and preprocessing results for comparison circuits; in the online phase, actual data input and computation execution time are greatly reduced because most cryptographic overhead has been completed in the offline phase. For communication optimization, the system implements vectorized batching techniques that package multiple scalar operations into vector operations, significantly reducing communication rounds and data transmission volume. The system also adopts a hybrid protocol framework that dynamically selects optimal cryptographic protocol combinations based on computational task characteristics: using secret sharing protocols for extensive numerical computations, garbled circuit protocols for conditional judgments and comparison operations, and homomorphic encryption protocols for scenarios requiring outsourced computation.

To support large-scale and complex real-world applications, the sub-module also implements distributed computing architectures and fault tolerance mechanisms. The distributed framework decomposes complex computational tasks into multiple parallel subtasks, executes them in parallel across multiple computing nodes through task scheduling algorithms, and processes large-scale datasets using MapReduce or similar programming models. Fault tolerance mechanisms include handling dynamic participant joining and leaving, network interruption recovery, computational checkpoints, and result verification functions. The system also implements privacy-preserving result verification protocols to ensure computational result correctness without revealing information about intermediate computational processes. For protection against malicious participants, the system employs zero-knowledge proof techniques to verify participants' honest behavior, uses commitment schemes to ensure input data consistency, and detects and excludes malicious behavior through majority verification mechanisms.

In actual deployment, the sub-module provides flexible API interfaces and programming frameworks supporting multiple programming languages and development environments. Developers can use high-level programming abstractions to describe computational logic, and the system automatically compiles these into corresponding cryptographic protocol executions. The system also provides rich predefined computational modules including statistical analysis functions, machine learning algorithms, and database query operations that users can directly invoke to build complex applications. Performance monitoring and tuning tools help users analyze computational performance bottlenecks and optimize protocol parameters and resource configurations. Through these comprehensive technical implementations, the Secure Multi-Party Computation sub-module successfully achieves the goal of making data usable but not visible, providing a solid technical foundation for secure cross-organizational data collaboration.

The sub-module collaborates with the Fine-grained Access Control module to ensure participant identity verification and permission management, and integrates with the Data Usage Tracking module to form complete computational process auditing. Together, these three components construct the core technical system of the cross-domain privacy protection framework.

6.4.4 Data Usage Tracking

The data usage tracking sub-module emerged from the increasingly stringent data protection regulatory requirements and complex cross-organizational data governance challenges. With the successive introduction of laws and regulations such as GDPR [25] and the Data Security Law, organizations need not only to protect data security but also to provide complete transparency and traceability for data usage processes. In cross-organizational data collaboration environments, data flow paths become extremely complex, involving multiple participants, various usage purposes, and multiple processing stages, making traditional logging and auditing mechanisms inadequate for such complexity. Meanwhile, data subjects are increasingly concerned about the use of their personal information, demanding to know who uses their data, for what purposes, and for how long. Regulatory authorities also require organizations to provide complete records of data processing activities to demonstrate compliance. Additionally, when data security incidents occur, organizations need to quickly determine the scope of impact, trace data flows, and analyze incident causes, all of which require comprehensive and precise data usage tracking capabilities.

The data usage tracking sub-module employs multi-layered, comprehensive tracking and monitoring methods to address these challenges. The core architecture of this sub-module is based on distributed data lineage tracking technology, achieving fine-grained tracking of data usage throughout its entire lifecycle by deploying monitoring agents at every critical node of data flow. The system employs Data Lineage technology to construct a complete data flow map, recording every stage from data creation, transmission, processing, storage to destruction. In specific implementation, the system assigns unique digital identifiers to each data object, similar to data identity cards, generated using hash function-based algorithms to ensure uniqueness and non-forgery. The identifier structure includes metadata such as timestamps, source organization identifiers, data type markers, and version information, forming a hierarchical namespace system. The system also implements fine-grained operational logging, using structured log formats to record complete contextual information for each data operation. This includes identity authentication details of operation subjects, attributes of operation objects, precise timestamps of operation times, standardized classifications of operation types, technical details of access methods, business classifications of usage purposes, and status codes of processing results.

At the technical implementation level, the sub-module employs advanced digital watermarking [26] and fingerprinting technologies to enhance data traceability. Digital watermarking leverages algorithms such as the Discrete Cosine Transform (DCT) and the Discrete Wavelet Transform (DWT) to embed watermarks and provenance history. For numerical data, the system employs Least Significant Bit (LSB) replacement methods to embed tracking information without affecting data precision; for textual data, the system uses semantic watermarking techniques to embed invisible identification information through synonym substitution and sentence structure adjustments. Data fingerprinting technology, based on perceptual hashing algorithms, generates compact fingerprint features for data content. Even when data undergoes minor modifications, fingerprints maintain similarity, enabling tracking of data changes. The system also implements a hierarchical fingerprinting mechanism, generating fingerprints for different granularity levels of data (such as document-level, paragraph-level, sentence-level), supporting fine-grained content change detection.

For structured data monitoring, the system employs a combination of database proxies and triggers. Database proxies are deployed as middleware between applications and databases, analyzing the semantics of each query statement through SQL parsing technology, extracting information about involved tables, fields, and conditions, and recording detailed access patterns. Database triggers automatically execute when data changes occur, recording data states before and after changes, types and parameters of change operations. The system also implements retrospective analysis functionality based on database log mining, reconstructing historical data change sequences by parsing database transaction logs. For unstructured data, the system uses file system hooks and content analysis technologies, monitoring file access, modification, copying, and deletion operations at the operating system level, while analyzing semantic changes in file content through natural language processing and machine learning technologies.

To address privacy protection requirements in cross-organizational environments, the sub-module innovatively employs various privacy-preserving auditing technologies. Zero-knowledge proof technology enables participating parties to prove that their data usage behaviors comply with established compliance policies without exposing specific usage details. The system implements compliance proof protocols based on Zero-Knowledge Succinct Non-Interactive Arguments of Knowledge (zk-SNARKs), allowing participants to generate compact proofs demonstrating that their data processing activities satisfy specific constraints, such as data usage frequency not exceeding limits, data access times within allowed ranges, and data processing purposes conforming to authorizations. These proofs possess zero-knowledge properties, enabling verifiers to confirm proof authenticity without obtaining any additional information. Differential privacy is applied to the generation and sharing of usage statistics: by adding carefully calibrated noise to true aggregates, it prevents the disclosure of individual records through statistical releases. The system adopts adaptive privacy budget allocation, dynamically tuning noise levels based on query sensitivity and importance to balance privacy protection and data utility.

The blockchain-based distributed audit log system provides tamper-proof guarantees for tracking records. The system adopts a consortium blockchain architecture where participating organizations serve as blockchain nodes jointly maintaining audit log integrity. Critical data usage events are encapsulated as transaction records on the blockchain, with each block containing the hash of its predecessor, forming an immutable chained structure. To protect sensitive information in audit logs, the system employs selective disclosure technology, recording only event hash digests and necessary metadata on the blockchain while storing detailed log content in encrypted off-chain databases. Smart contract technology is used to implement automated compliance checking, with contract code defining various compliance rules and violation response strategies. When data usage behaviors that do not conform to predetermined policies are detected, smart contracts automatically execute corresponding processing logic, such as recording violation events, notifying relevant personnel, and adjusting access permissions.

The system also implements efficient verification mechanisms based on Merkle trees, supporting rapid integrity verification of large-scale audit logs. Merkle tree leaf nodes contain hash values of individual log records, internal nodes contain combined hashes of child node hash values, and the root node provides an integrity digest of the entire log collection. This structure supports selective verification, allowing verifiers to verify only specific time periods or specific types of log records without downloading complete log data. To support privacy-preserving log queries, the system implements query processing protocols based on homomorphic encryption, enabling queriers to retrieve relevant log records without exposing query conditions, while log providers cannot understand specific query content.

The data usage tracking sub-module's significance lies in providing a foundation for transparency and accountability in cross-organizational data collaboration. Through comprehensive usage tracking and auditing, the sub-module not only helps organizations meet legal and regulatory compliance requirements but also establishes trust mechanisms for data usage, promoting data sharing cooperation between organizations. The detailed usage records furnished by the system provide a basis for fair allocation of data value, enabling data value accounting and revenue distribution according to actual usage conditions.

In collaborative relationships with other sub-modules, the data usage tracking sub-module plays an important supervisory and safeguarding role. Integration with the fine-grained access control sub-module forms a complete permission management closed loop: every permission decision and execution action of the access control module is detailed recorded by the tracking module, including authorization basis, decision processes, and execution results. The tracking module provides data support for optimizing access control policies by analyzing access patterns and permission usage, identifying overly strict or lenient permission settings and automatically generating policy adjustment recommendations. Collaboration with the secure multi-party computation sub-module ensures complete auditing of secure computation processes. The tracking module records detailed information for each secure multi-party computation process, including participant identity verification, data input confirmation, computation protocol selection, intermediate result generation, and final result output. The three sub-modules establish intelligent linkage mechanisms, forming an adaptive security governance system that provides comprehensive technical assurance for secure data collaboration between organizations.

6.5 Transaction Security and Anomaly Detection

With the rapid growth of digital financial services and the steady expansion of transaction volumes, financial systems are confronting increasingly complex and diverse security threats. Modern financial ecosystems have evolved from traditional single-channel service models to multi-channel, round-the-clock digital service systems, encompassing multiple business domains including mobile payments, online banking, digital currencies, cross-border remittances, and supply chain finance. This transformation has brought unprecedented challenges, with financial transaction frequencies surging from thousands of transactions per day to tens of thousands per second. Additionally, transaction amounts have evolved from traditional high-value, low-frequency patterns to a complex landscape where small-value, high-frequency and large-value, low-frequency transactions coexist. Meanwhile, the boundaries of financial services continue to expand, extending from closed internal banking systems to open internet environments, and from localized services to global operations. This openness and complexity pose significant challenges for security protection.

Traditional security protection measures have become inadequate for addressing the high-frequency, large-scale, real-time transaction demands of modern financial environments, as well as the continuously evolving fraud techniques and system attack methods. Traditional security systems primarily rely on static rules and manual review mechanisms, which prove insufficient when facing massive real-time transaction data, failing to meet millisecond-level response time requirements and unable to adapt to rapidly changing threat patterns. Modern cybercriminals employ increasingly sophisticated attack methods, including distributed denial-of-service attacks, advanced persistent threats, social engineering attacks, and intelligent fraud implemented using artificial intelligence technologies. These emerging threats are characterized by strong concealment, rapid changes, and large-scale attacks. Traditional signature-based detection methods and historical pattern-based protection mechanisms can no longer effectively identify and respond to these threats [27]. Furthermore, the increasingly stringent regulatory environment has placed higher demands on financial institutions' security protection capabilities, requiring the establishment of comprehensive security management systems covering entire business processes and complete data lifecycles.

The core significance of Transaction Security and Anomaly Detection lies in constructing a comprehensive, multi layered financial security protection system capable of simultaneously addressing fraud threats at the transaction level and technical risks at the system level. This comprehensive protection is manifested in the coverage of the entire financial business chain, incorporating every stage from user identity authentication, transaction authorization, and fund transfer to transaction confirmation within the security monitoring scope. Multi-layered protection is reflected in the three-dimensional security architecture spanning from network layer, system layer, application layer to business layer, ensuring that security threats at any level can be promptly detected and handled. The module establishes a trinity protection mechanism of transaction behavior analysis, system status monitoring, and anomaly event response, achieving dual protection against both internal threats and external attacks. At the transaction level, the module can identify various suspicious behaviors including account theft, transaction fraud, money laundering activities, and abnormal transfers. At the system level, the module can detect technical threats such as network intrusions, system vulnerability exploitation, malware infections, and data breaches.

This comprehensive security solution not only effectively reduces operational risks and compliance risks for financial institutions but also optimizes user experience while ensuring security, avoiding the impact of excessive security measures on normal business processes. The solution strikes a balance between security protection and operational efficiency through precise risk assessment and intelligent decision-making mechanisms. For low-risk transactions, the system can quickly approve them, ensuring users receive smooth service experiences. For high-risk transactions, the system initiates strict verification and review processes to ensure security. This dynamic risk control mechanism avoids “one-size-fits-all" security strategies, protecting both the asset security of financial institutions and maintaining customer convenience. Additionally, the security data and analysis reports generated by the module provide valuable business insights for financial institutions, helping them better understand customer behavior patterns, optimize product design and service processes, and enhance overall competitiveness.

6.5.1 Module Structure

The Transaction Security and Anomaly Detection module employs a layered and decoupled architectural design, constructing a comprehensive financial security protection system through three functionally specialized and collaboratively operating sub-modules. The entire module structure follows a data-driven design philosophy, establishing a complete pipeline from data collection, analytical processing to decision execution, ensuring that each processing stage has clearly defined responsibility boundaries and standardized interface specifications. Internally, the module adopts an event-driven architecture, where sub-modules achieve real-time data exchange and state synchronization via efficient message-passing mechanisms, forming a loosely coupled yet tightly integrated system design. The overall structure is shown in Fig. 6.5.

The fraud transaction monitoring sub-module sits at the front end of the module architecture, acting as the first line of defense for transaction data and specifically handling real-time transaction streams from various business systems. This sub-module employs a streaming computation architecture, utilizing distributed data processing engines to perform real-time ingestion, cleansing, and analysis of high-concurrency transaction data. The sub-module internally integrates multiple machine learning models and rule engines, including anomaly detection algorithms, behavioral analysis models, and risk scoring models, which work collaboratively to form a multi-dimensional transaction risk assessment system. The data processing workflow begins with raw transaction data, proceeds through feature extraction, model inference, and risk calculation steps, ultimately outputting structured risk assessment results and anomalous transaction identifications to provide foundational data support for subsequent decision-making.

The system anomaly detection and trace sub-module forms the monitoring layer of the architecture, tasked with comprehensive monitoring and analysis of the entire financial system's operational state. This sub-module adopts a multi-source data fusion architecture, simultaneously receiving monitoring data and log information from multiple layers including operating systems, applications, network devices, and databases. The sub-module internally establishes a layered anomaly

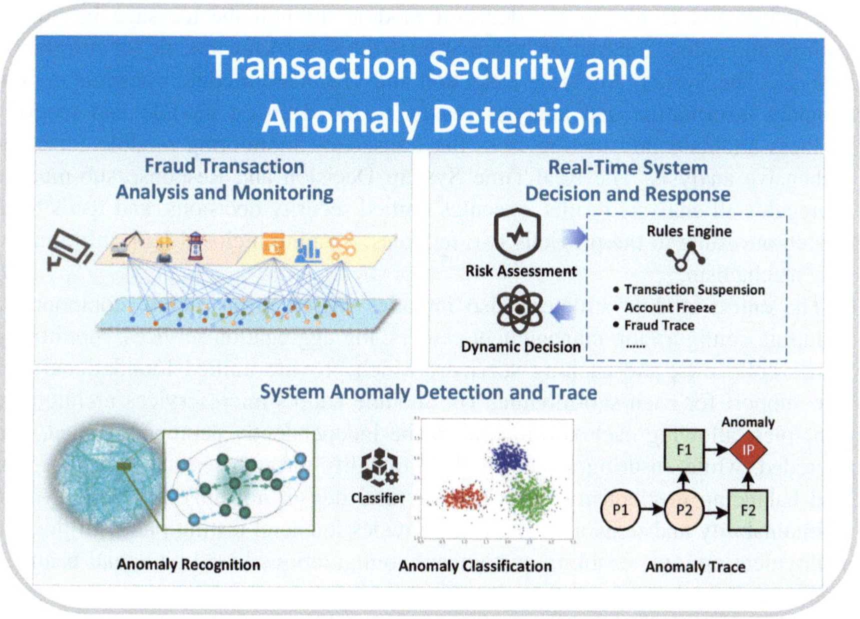

Fig. 6.5 Structure of transaction security and anomaly detection

detection system, encompassing different levels of detection mechanisms such as infrastructure monitoring, application performance monitoring, and business metric monitoring. By leveraging time-series analysis, statistical techniques, and machine learning algorithms, the system can detect diverse system anomalies, including performance degradation, resource exhaustion, and service failures. This sub-module also possesses powerful anomaly tracing capabilities, capable of quickly locating the root causes and propagation paths of anomalies through constructing system dependency graphs and call chain tracking mechanisms.

The real-time system decision and response sub-module serves as the decision center and execution engine of the entire architecture, receiving analytical results from the previous two sub-modules and making comprehensive judgments based on preset business rules and security policies. This sub-module employs an architecture combining rule engines and decision trees, supporting complex multi-condition judgments and hierarchical response mechanisms. The sub-module internally establishes a complete response action library, including various response measures such as transaction blocking, account freezing, security alerts, system isolation, and load adjustment. The decision-making process adopts priority queues and parallel processing mechanisms, ensuring that high-priority security events receive immediate response while maintaining overall system processing efficiency.

The three sub-modules achieve loosely coupled integration through standardized data interfaces and message queues, forming a complete data flow and control flow system. The Fraud Transaction Monitoring sub-module sends transaction risk assessment results to the decision module through the message bus while pushing anomalous transaction information to the monitoring module for correlation analysis. The System Anomaly Detection and Trace sub-module transmits system anomaly information and analysis results to the decision module and receives business anomaly information from the transaction monitoring module for comprehensive analysis. The Real-Time System Decision and Response sub-module aggregates all analysis results, executes unified security decisions, and feeds back execution results to the previous two modules, forming a closed-loop information flow mechanism.

The entire module structure also includes shared infrastructure components, including configuration management centers, log aggregation services, monitoring metric collectors, and caching services, which provide unified foundational service support for each sub-module. The module adopts microservices architecture principles, allowing each sub-module to be independently deployed, scaled, and upgraded, while ensuring system high availability through service discovery and load balancing mechanisms. This architectural design not only improves system maintainability and scalability but also provides financial institutions with flexible deployment options, enabling customized configurations based on actual business requirements and system resource conditions.

6.5.2 *Fraud Transaction Monitoring Module*

The Fraud Transaction Monitoring sub-module emerged from the background of increasingly severe fraud threats facing modern financial systems. With the proliferation of digital payments, mobile banking, online lending, and other financial services, traditional fraud methods are evolving toward more complex and covert directions. Modern financial fraud is no longer limited to simple identity theft or transaction forgery, but has developed into sophisticated attack patterns involving multiple accounts, spanning different time periods, and exploiting system vulnerabilities. These new fraud methods often exhibit characteristics of being distributed, collaborative, and progressive, making traditional protection mechanisms based on single transaction judgment unable to effectively identify and prevent such threats. Meanwhile, the real-time requirements of financial transactions necessitate that fraud detection be completed within extremely short timeframes, as any delay could result in financial losses and erosion of customer trust. Additionally, controlling false positive rates has become a critical challenge, as excessive security measures affect normal users' transaction experiences, while lenient controls may allow genuine fraudulent activities to slip through. Against this background, there is a need for an intelligent transaction monitoring system that can accurately identify complex fraud patterns, ensure real-time response, and maintain low false positive rates.

The Fraud Transaction Monitoring sub-module employs a multi-dimensional analysis method based on real-time stream processing, constructing a comprehensive transaction risk assessment system. The core methodology of this sub-module is built upon the deep integration of big data stream processing technology and machine learning algorithms. First, the sub-module ingests transaction data from various business systems in real-time through high-performance stream processing engines, including multi-dimensional information such as transaction amounts, timestamps, geographical locations, device information, and account history. Then, the system performs real-time feature engineering on this raw data, extracting hundreds of risk features including transaction frequency features, amount distribution features, temporal pattern features, geographical behavior features, and device fingerprint features. At the model analysis level, the sub-module integrates multiple machine learning algorithms, including unsupervised anomaly detection algorithms for discovering unknown abnormal patterns, supervised classification algorithms for identifying known fraud types, and reinforcement learning algorithms for dynamically optimizing detection strategies. The system also establishes association analysis mechanisms based on graph neural networks, identifying complex fraud networks involving multiple entities by constructing account relationship graphs and transaction network graphs. Furthermore, the sub-module employs ensemble learning methods [28], fusing prediction results from multiple models to improve detection accuracy and robustness. In terms of risk scoring, the system establishes dynamic scoring mechanisms that calculate comprehensive risk scores based on different feature dimensions of transactions and supports real-time model updates and parameter optimization.

The significance of this sub-module lies in constructing an intelligent transaction security defense line for financial institutions, achieving a transformation from reactive to proactive security protection modes. Through real-time transaction behavior analysis and risk assessment, this sub-module can identify and prevent fraudulent transactions before they cause actual losses, significantly reducing financial institutions' economic losses and reputational risks. The intelligent characteristics of the sub-module enable it to adapt to constantly changing fraud methods, with the system's detection capabilities continuously improving over time through continuous learning and model optimization. Additionally, the transaction risk data and analysis results generated by this sub-module provide valuable business insights for financial institutions, helping them better understand customer behavior patterns, identify high-risk customer groups, and optimize risk management strategies. From a compliance perspective, this sub-module helps financial institutions meet regulatory requirements for anti-money laundering and counter-terrorism financing through automated suspicious transaction identification and reporting mechanisms, significantly reducing compliance workload. Meanwhile, through precise risk assessment and personalized security strategies, this sub-module optimizes customer experience while ensuring security, avoiding customer attrition due to excessive security measures.

The fraud transaction monitoring sub-module forms close collaborative relationships with the other two sub-modules, constructing a multi-layered, comprehensive security protection network. Collaboration with the System Anomaly Detection and Trace sub-module manifests in multiple aspects: First, the Fraud Transaction Monitoring sub-module pushes detected anomalous transaction information to the system monitoring sub-module, which can perform correlation analysis combined with system operational status information to determine whether anomalous transactions are related to system failures or network attacks. Second, system anomalies detected by the system monitoring sub-module may affect the accuracy of transaction data and model judgment effectiveness, so it sends system status alerts to the transaction monitoring sub-module, helping it adjust detection strategies and confidence thresholds. Both parties also share timestamp and correlation information of anomalous events, identifying potential causal relationships through time series analysis. Collaboration with the Real-Time System Decision and Response sub-module is more direct and frequent: the transaction monitoring sub-module sends risk assessment results and anomalous transaction identifications to the decision response sub-module in real-time, which executes corresponding security response measures based on this information. Execution results from the decision response sub-module are fed back to the transaction monitoring sub-module for validating detection effectiveness and optimizing model parameters. Additionally, the decision response sub-module transmits processed case information back to the transaction monitoring sub-module as new sample data for model training, enabling continuous learning and improvement of the system. Through this collaborative mechanism, the three sub-modules form a self-evolving intelligent security system capable of continuously enhancing protection capabilities and response efficiency during actual operation.

6.5.3 System Anomaly Detection and Trace

The system anomaly detection and trace sub-module emerged from the background of increasingly complex IT infrastructure environments in modern financial systems and constantly evolving systemic threats. Today's financial institutions' IT architectures have evolved from traditional monolithic applications to complex distributed microservices architectures, involving hundreds of service components, multiple data centers, hybrid cloud environments, and numerous third-party integration systems. This architectural complexity makes system failures have broader impact, more complex propagation paths, and greater difficulty in localization. Meanwhile, modern cyberattack methods are continuously evolving, developing from simple DDoS attacks to composite, persistent advanced threats, including APT attacks, supply chain attacks, and zero-day exploit attacks. These attacks often exhibit characteristics of long-term stealth, multi-stage implementation, and difficulty in detection. Traditional threshold-based alert monitoring methods can no longer meet the security requirements of modern financial systems, unable to timely detect subtle abnormal behaviors or respond to unknown attack patterns. Furthermore, the 724 hour operational requirements and regulatory compliance demands of financial systems mean that any system anomaly could cause significant business impact and compliance risks. In this environment, financial institutions urgently need a comprehensive monitoring solution capable of intelligently identifying various system anomalies, quickly locating problem sources, and providing complete traceability capabilities.

The system anomaly detection and trace sub-module employs multi-layered, multi-dimensional intelligent monitoring methods, establishing a full-stack anomaly detection system covering from infrastructure to application layers. The methodology of this sub-module is based on the collaborative work of three core components: Anomaly Recognition, Anomaly Classification, and Anomaly Trace. In the Anomaly Recognition component, the system adopts unsupervised learning methods based on time series analysis, collecting multi-dimensional metric data including CPU utilization, memory usage, network traffic, disk I/O, database connections, and application response times to establish normal behavior baseline models. The system employs statistical methods, machine learning algorithms, and deep learning technologies, including LSTM neural networks, autoencoders, and isolation forest algorithms, to analyze real-time monitoring data and identify anomaly points that deviate from normal patterns. This module also integrates log analysis functionality, using natural language processing technology to intelligently parse system logs, application logs, and security logs to identify anomalous events and error patterns. Additionally, the system adopts graph analysis-based methods, constructing system component dependency graphs and detecting abnormal call patterns and propagation paths through graph algorithms.

In the anomaly classification component, the system establishes a sophisticated anomaly classification system that intelligently categorizes detected anomalies by severity level, impact scope, and anomaly type. Classification dimensions include anomaly severity levels (Critical, High, Medium, and Low), anomaly types (performance anomalies, security anomalies, functional anomalies, and resource anomalies), impact scope (single-machine anomalies, service anomalies, and system-level anomalies), and urgency levels (immediate response, priority handling, and routine processing). The system employs multi-label classification algorithms and decision tree models, combined with expert knowledge bases and historical case data, to automatically classify anomalous events. The classification process also considers business context information, such as transaction peak periods, system maintenance windows, and major event periods, ensuring the accuracy and business relevance of classification results. Furthermore, the system establishes dynamic priority adjustment mechanisms that real-time adjust anomaly priorities and classification labels based on anomaly development trends and business impact levels.

In the anomaly trace component, the system constructs comprehensive anomaly source tracing and tracking capabilities, quickly locating the root causes and propagation paths of anomalies through multiple technical means. The system establishes complete call chain tracking mechanisms, recording the complete execution paths of each request within the system, including service call relationships, database access records, and external interface calls. Through distributed tracing technology, the system can construct complete timelines of anomalous events, identifying anomaly origin points and propagation processes. The system also employs causal analysis algorithms, identifying possible causal chains by analyzing temporal relationships and dependencies between anomalous events. Additionally, the system integrates log correlation analysis functionality, constructing complete contexts of anomalous events by correlating log information from different components. Tracing results are presented in visualized formats, including anomaly propagation graphs, timeline views, and dependency relationship diagrams, helping operations personnel quickly understand the complete picture and impact scope of anomalies.

The significance of this sub-module lies in providing financial institutions with proactive system health management and security protection capabilities, achieving a transformation from reactive response to predictive prevention. Through real-time system monitoring and intelligent anomaly detection, this sub-module can discover and handle system problems before they evolve into business impacts, significantly improving system availability and stability. The intelligent classification and tracking capabilities of the sub-module significantly improve operational efficiency, reduce problem localization time, and minimize the impact of system failures on business operations. From a security perspective, this sub-module can detect sophisticated cyberattacks and insider threats, identifying potential security risks through abnormal behavior pattern recognition and providing early warnings for security teams. Additionally, the monitoring data and analysis reports generated by this sub-module provide valuable operational insights for financial institutions, helping optimize system architecture, improve operational processes, and develop capacity planning. From a compliance perspective, the complete traceability capabilities of this sub-module meet regulatory requirements for operational risk management, providing detailed evidence chains for audits and compliance inspections.

The system anomaly detection and trace sub-module forms synergistic collaborative relationships with the other two sub-modules, constructing a unified security situational awareness system. Collaboration with the Fraud Transaction Monitoring sub-module manifests in bidirectional information sharing and correlation analysis: when the transaction monitoring sub-module detects suspicious transactions, the system monitoring sub-module checks system status during corresponding time periods to determine whether anomalous transactions are related to system failures, network attacks, or malware infections. Conversely, when the system monitoring sub-module detects security-related system anomalies, it notifies the transaction monitoring sub-module to adjust detection strategies and increase monitoring intensity for transactions during related time periods. The two sub-modules also share characteristic information and pattern data of anomalous events, improving detection accuracy through cross-validation. Collaboration with the Real-Time System Decision and Response sub-module is more intimate and direct: the system monitoring sub-module sends anomaly detection results, classification information, and tracing analysis to the decision response sub-module in real-time, which executes corresponding response measures based on anomaly severity levels and business impact scope, such as system isolation, load adjustment, and service degradation. Execution results from the decision response sub-module are fed back to the system monitoring sub-module for validating response effectiveness and adjusting monitoring strategies. Additionally, the system monitoring sub-module provides system capacity and performance information to the decision response sub-module, helping it avoid causing additional load to the system when executing response measures. Through this collaborative mechanism, the three sub-modules form an intelligent, adaptive security protection ecosystem capable of comprehensively addressing various security threats and system risks.

6.5.4 Real-Time System Decision and Response

The Real-Time System Decision and Response sub-module emerged from the urgent need for immediate threat response and automated security management in modern financial systems. In the era of digital finance, the frequency and impact speed of security threats have grown exponentially, and traditional manual response modes can no longer meet the millisecond-level threat handling requirements. Modern financial fraud and cyber attacks often complete within extremely short timeframes, with the process from attack initiation to actual loss potentially taking only a few seconds, where any delay could result in irreversible damage. Meanwhile, the complexity of financial systems makes the impact of security incidents more widespread, as a seemingly localized anomaly could rapidly spread throughout the entire system, causing systemic risks. Furthermore, the globalization and 7×24 hour operational characteristics of modern financial business mean that security threats may occur at any time and location, with manual response modes showing obvious deficiencies in time coverage and response consistency. The increasingly stringent regulatory landscape also compels financial institutions to establish rapid, accurate, and traceable security response mechanisms, ensuring that appropriate protective measures are adopted promptly when threats arise. Against this background, financial institutions need an intelligent decision response system capable of real-time threat information analysis, automatic response strategy formulation, and rapid protective measure execution to achieve fully automated closed-loop protection from threat detection to response execution.

The real-time system decision and response sub-module employs a hybrid decision method based on rule engines and machine learning [29], constructing a comprehensive real-time threat response system. The core methodology of this sub-module is built upon a multi-layered decision architecture that integrates expert knowledge, historical experience, and intelligent algorithms. First, the system establishes a rule engine-based decision framework that transforms financial institutions' security policies, business rules, and compliance requirements into executable decision rules. These rules cover different types of threat scenarios, including transaction fraud, system attacks, and abnormal behaviors, while defining corresponding response measures and execution conditions. The rule engine supports complex conditional judgments and logical combinations, capable of processing multi-dimensional threat information and contextual data. Second, the system integrates machine learning decision models that learn optimal response strategy selection patterns by analyzing historical response cases and effectiveness data. Machine learning models can handle complex scenarios that are difficult for rule engines to cover, providing more flexible and adaptive decision-making capabilities. The system also establishes multi-level decision mechanisms that adopt different decision processes based on threat severity and urgency levels, ensuring high-priority threats receive immediate response. Additionally, the system employs dynamic response strategies based on risk assessment, adjusting response intensity according to potential threat impact and business importance to find the optimal balance between security assurance and business continuity maintenance.

In terms of response execution, this sub-module establishes a comprehensive automated response action library covering many response measures from lightweight alerts to heavy isolation. Response actions include transaction-level measures such as transaction blocking, delayed processing, enhanced verification, and risk marking; account-level measures such as account freezing, permission restrictions, enhanced monitoring, and user notifications; system-level measures such as service isolation, load adjustment, access control, and enhanced logging; and network-level measures such as IP blocking, traffic limitation, connection disconnection, and routing adjustment. Each response measure has clear trigger conditions, execution parameters, and rollback mechanisms, ensuring response precision and controllability. The system also supports combined response strategies, capable of simultaneously executing multiple response measures to form comprehensive protective effects. During execution, the system employs parallel processing mechanisms to ensure multiple response actions can proceed simultaneously, improving response efficiency. Furthermore, the system establishes response effectiveness monitoring mechanisms that real-time evaluate the execution effects of response measures and adjust subsequent response strategies based on feedback information.

The significance of this sub-module lies in constructing an intelligent, automated security protection execution engine for financial institutions, achieving seamless closed-loop from threat identification to protection implementation. Through real-time threat analysis and automated response execution, this sub-module significantly shortens threat response time from traditional minute-level to second-level or even millisecond-level, substantially improving the timeliness and effectiveness of security protection. The intelligent decision-making capabilities of the sub-module make response strategies more precise and adaptive, avoiding the impact of over-response on normal business operations while preventing security risks caused by insufficient response. From an operational perspective, this sub-module significantly reduces the workload of security operations teams by automating repetitive and procedural response tasks, allowing security experts to focus on higher-value threat analysis and strategy optimization work. The response data and effectiveness analysis generated by the sub-module provide valuable security operational insights for financial institutions, helping continuously optimize security strategies and response processes. From a compliance perspective, the automated response mechanisms of this sub-module ensure consistency and traceability of security measures, meeting regulatory requirements for operational risk management and providing complete evidence chains for compliance audits. Additionally, through rapid and effective threat response, this sub-module helps financial institutions maintain customer trust and brand reputation while reducing potential business impact from security incidents.

The Real-Time System Decision and Response sub-module forms highly integrated collaborative relationships with the other two sub-modules, constructing a complete security protection chain from detection to response. Collaboration with the Fraud Transaction Monitoring sub-module manifests in real-time threat information processing and response execution: the transaction monitoring sub-module sends risk assessment results, anomalous transaction identifications, and threat level information to the decision response sub-module in real-time, which immediately initiates corresponding response processes based on this information. For high-risk transactions, the decision response sub-module executes immediate blocking measures; for medium-risk transactions, it may initiate additional verification processes; for suspicious patterns, it may enhance subsequent monitoring. Response execution results are fed back to the transaction monitoring sub-module in real-time, including response measure execution status, effectiveness assessments, and related statistical information. This feedback information is used to optimize risk assessment models and adjust detection thresholds. Additionally, the decision response sub-module provides processed case information to the transaction monitoring sub-module as training samples, supporting continuous improvement of machine learning models. Collaboration with the System Anomaly Detection and Trace sub-module is equally intimate and frequent: the system monitoring sub-module sends anomaly detection results, classification information, severity assessments, and tracing analysis to the decision response sub-module, which executes corresponding system-level response measures based on anomaly types and impact scope. For critical system anomalies, it may trigger service isolation or system degradation; for performance anomalies, it may initiate load balancing adjustments; for security anomalies, it may strengthen access control and monitoring. Execution results from the decision response sub-module are similarly fed back to the system monitoring sub-module, helping validate response effectiveness and guide subsequent monitoring strategy adjustments. Through this real-time collaborative mechanism, the three sub-modules form a self-learning, self-adapting intelligent security ecosystem capable of continuously improving threat identification accuracy, response strategy rationality, and overall protection effectiveness during actual operation, providing financial institutions with truly intelligent security protection capabilities.

References

1. J.M. Stanton, K.R. Stam, P. Mastrangelo, J. Jolton, Comput. Secur. **24**(2), 124 (2005). https://doi.org/10.1016/j.cose.2004.07.001. https://www.sciencedirect.com/science/article/pii/S0167404804001841
2. Y. Chen, G. Liu, L. Yu, H. Kang, L. Meng, T. Wang, Expert Syst. Appl. **264**, 125811 (2025)
3. D. Haban, D. Wybranietz, IEEE Trans. Software Eng. **16**(2), 197 (1990). https://doi.org/10.1109/32.44382
4. P.K. Rayani, S. Changder, Multimedia Tools Appl. **82**(2), 1633 (2023)

5. J. Chen, Z. Zhan, K. He, R. Du, D. Wang, F. Liu, IEEE Trans. Dependable Secure Comput. **19**(5), 3301 (2021)
6. R. Miller, N.K. Banerjee, S. Banerjee, in *2021 IEEE Virtual Reality and 3D User Interfaces (VR)* (IEEE, 2021), pp. 140–149
7. Z. Shen, S. Li, X. Zhao, J. Zou, IEEE Trans. Inf. Foren. Secur. **17**, 1450 (2022)
8. Y. Zhang, S. Huang, S. Guo, J. Zhu, Procedia Environ. Sci. **10**, 1029 (2011)
9. A. Aigner, A. Khelil, in *2020 IEEE International Conference on Sensing, Communication and Networking (SECON Workshops)* (2020), pp. 1–6. https://doi.org/10.1109/SECONWorkshops50264.2020.9149779
10. K. Scarfone, P. Mell, in *2009 3rd International Symposium on Empirical Software Engineering and Measurement* (IEEE, 2009), pp. 516–525
11. X. Wang, M. Zhu, D. Bo, P. Cui, C. Shi, J. Pei, in *Proceedings of the 26th ACM SIGKDD International Conference on Knowledge Discovery & Data Mining* (2020), pp. 1243–1253
12. Y. Yu, X. Si, C. Hu, J. Zhang, Neural Comput. **31**(7), 1235 (2019)
13. B. Smith, *The Blackwell Guide to the Philosophy of Computing and Information* (Blackwell Publishing Ltd., Malden, MA, 2004), pp. 153–166
14. W. Xiong, E. Legrand, O. Åberg, R. Lagerström, Software Syst. Model. **21**(1), 157 (2022)
15. K. Konyushkova, R. Sznitman, P. Fua, Adv. Neural Inf. Process. Syst. **30** (2017)
16. E. Yuan, J. Tong, in *IEEE International Conference on Web Services (ICWS'05)* (IEEE, 2005)
17. E. Bertino, Comput. Secur. **22**(6), 511 (2003)
18. C. Zhao, S. Zhao, M. Zhao, Z. Chen, C.Z. Gao, H. Li, Y.a. Tan, Inf. Sci. **476**, 357 (2019)
19. B. Shebaro, O. Oluwatimi, E. Bertino, IEEE Trans. Depend. Secure Comput. **12**(2), 150 (2014)
20. M. Bellare, V.T. Hoang, P. Rogaway, in *Proceedings of the 2012 ACM Conference on Computer and Communications Security* (2012), pp. 784–796
21. Z. Jafargholi, D. Wichs, in *Theory of Cryptography Conference* (Springer, 2016), pp. 433–458
22. M. Naehrig, K. Lauter, V. Vaikuntanathan, in *Proceedings of the 3rd ACM Workshop on Cloud Computing Security Workshop* (2011), pp. 113–124
23. D. Micciancio, C. Peikert, in *Annual Cryptology Conference* (Springer, 2013), pp. 21–39
24. M. Rosca, D. Stehlé, A. Wallet, in *Annual International Conference on the Theory and Applications of Cryptographic Techniques* (Springer, 2018), pp. 146–173
25. S. Sirur, J.R. Nurse, H. Webb, in *Proceedings of the 2nd International Workshop on Multimedia Privacy and Security* (2018), pp. 88–95
26. S. Charles, V. Bindschaedler, P. Mishra, IEEE Trans. Very Large Scale Integr. Syst. **30**(7), 952 (2022)
27. M. Masdari, H. Khezri, Appl. Soft Comput. **92**, 106301 (2020)
28. H.V. Vo, H.P. Du, H.N. Nguyen, Comput. Secur. **136**, 103567 (2024)
29. T. Kliegr, Š. Bahník, J. Fürnkranz, Artif. Intell. **295**, 103458 (2021)

Glossary

Access Control Mechanism Techniques and policies that regulate which users, processes, or services can access specific resources, under what conditions, and what operations they may perform to minimize attack surfaces.

Access Control List A set of rules based on network attributes like IP addresses and ports used to permit or deny traffic at network devices.

Advanced Persistent Threat A long-term, targeted cyberattack in which an intruder gains ongoing access to a system to extract sensitive information.

AMD SEV AMD's solution for encrypting entire virtual machines, isolating them from hypervisors and other VMs.

Anomaly Detection Machine learning technique identifying patterns or behaviors that deviate significantly from established normal baselines, indicating potential security threats or system issues.

Audit-Evasion Attack A cyberattack in which the adversary manipulates audit trails to prevent detection of unauthorized behavior.

Behavioral Baseline Established patterns of normal user behavior used as reference points for detecting deviations and identifying potentially suspicious or anomalous activities.

Botnet A network of compromised devices controlled remotely to conduct coordinated attacks such as DDoS.

Chaos Engineering A practice of injecting faults or disturbances into systems to verify stability, fault tolerance, and identify hidden vulnerabilities.

Cloud-Edge-Terminal A hierarchical distribution model of computing resources from centralized clouds to edge nodes and end devices.

Container Engine A runtime platform that manages containerized applications, such as Docker or containerd.

Convolutional Neural Network A class of deep neural networks commonly used for processing grid-like data such as images, employing convolutional layers to extract features.

C. Wang, H. Tang, *Integrated Security and Safety of Intelligent Computing Networks*, https://doi.org/10.1007/978-981-95-5025-8

Coupling Instability A systemic phenomenon where optimization or degradation of one element (data, computing power, or algorithm) causes cascading performance issues in the others.

Data Lineage Complete tracking of data flow from creation through processing to destruction, recording transformations and usage throughout the entire data lifecycle.

Data Poisoning Attack A type of adversarial attack where malicious data is injected into the training process to degrade the performance or integrity of the resulting model.

DDoS Attack A cyberattack where multiple systems flood a target system's bandwidth or resources, rendering it unavailable to users.

Deep Neural Network An artificial neural network with multiple layers between input and output, capable of modeling complex patterns in data.

Differential Privacy A mathematical framework that ensures the privacy of individual records in a dataset by adding controlled random noise to query results.

Digital Watermarking Technology embedding invisible identification information into data using frequency domain algorithms to enable tracking and traceability of data usage.

Dynamic Defense Adaptive security strategies that evolve with ongoing threats rather than relying on static rules.

Edge Computing A distributed computing paradigm where computation and data storage occur closer to the data source to reduce latency and bandwidth usage.

Federated Learning A distributed machine learning paradigm where multiple decentralized devices collaboratively train a shared model while keeping raw data localized, thereby enhancing privacy and security during model training.

Generative Adversarial Network A machine learning framework where two neural networksthe generator and the discriminatorcompete against each other to improve data generation quality.

Graph Neural Network A neural network architecture designed to perform inference on data structured as graphs, aggregating node features and their relationships to learn representations capturing structural and attribute information.

Graph Structured Learning A machine learning approach that models data as graphs where nodes represent entities or events and edges represent relationships. It captures structural dependencies and interactions through graph neural networks (GNNs) for enhanced behavior analysis.

HIPAA/SOX/FISMA Regulatory frameworks: Health Insurance Portability and Accountability Act, Sarbanes-Oxley Act, Federal Information Security Management Act.

Homomorphic Encryption A form of encryption that allows computations to be performed directly on ciphertexts, producing encrypted results that can be decrypted to match the result of operations on the plaintexts.

Host Firewall A software firewall running on a device that monitors and controls incoming and outgoing network traffic based on security rules.

ICNs A unified architecture that integrates computing, networking, storage, and algorithmic resources across cloud-edge-terminal layers to support efficient execution of heterogeneous large-scale tasks.

Immutable Log Store A write-once, tamper-evident logging system that guarantees data integrity, often using WORM or blockchain.

Intel SGX A hardware-based TEE technology by Intel that creates isolated execution environments (enclaves).

Interface Layer Contamination A threat model focusing on how insecure or hijacked interfaces compromise the integrity of data pipelines.

Knowledge Distillation A model compression technique where a smaller student model learns to mimic the behavior of a larger, more complex teacher model, aiming to retain accuracy while reducing computational cost.

Label-Flipping Attack A data poisoning strategy in which the labels of certain training samples are intentionally misassigned to mislead the model.

Log Tampering The unauthorized alteration, deletion, or insertion of entries in system logs to conceal malicious activity.

Membership Inference Attack An attack method where the adversary attempts to determine whether a particular data sample was used in the training set of a model.

Metadata Poisoning Manipulation of metadata (e.g., timestamps, sensor IDs) to corrupt trust signals or inference results.

Mirai Botnet A type of malware first discovered in 2016 that infects IoT devices, turning them into remotely controlled bots to launch large-scale Distributed Denial of Service (DDoS) attacks.

Model Drift The gradual deviation of a model's behavior from its original logic due to poisoned or evolving data inputs.

Multi-tenant Isolation Security and resource partitioning techniques that ensure independent and secure operation of multiple tenants or users on shared computing infrastructure.

Oblivious RAM A method to hide access patterns to memory to ensure data privacy even when an attacker observes memory access.

Operating System Kernel The lowest layer of an operating system, responsible for managing hardware, processes, and system calls; a key target in system protection.

Pattern Poisoning A form of poisoning where adversaries manipulate data patterns to gradually bias model behavior.

Pervasive Sensing Technology A technology that enables continuous, automatic data collection through widely distributed and embedded sensors in everyday environments.

Phantom Data Stream Falsified or synthetic data streams generated by an attacker to deceive monitoring systems and upstream analytics.

Privilege Escalation A type of attack that allows a user or process to gain higher access rights than intended.

QoS A set of performance metricssuch as bandwidth, latency, jitter, and packet lossused to ensure service efficiency and responsiveness in networking or computational systems.

Red-Blue Team Exercise A security drill involving a Red Team simulating attacks and a Blue Team performing defense and response to test system security readiness.

Resource Scheduling The system's responsibility for allocating computing, memory, and I/O resources among competing tasks in real time.

Resource Silo A condition in which computing or network resources remain isolated and underutilized due to architectural fragmentation, physical separation, or lack of unified scheduling mechanisms.

Role-Based Access Control Access control model that assigns permissions to roles rather than directly to users, simplifying permission management through role inheritance mechanisms.

Searchable Encryption Encryption techniques that allow searches over encrypted data without revealing the plaintext.

Secure Multi-Party Computation A cryptographic technique that enables multiple parties to jointly compute a function over their inputs without revealing them to each other.

Security Feedback Loop A continuous monitoring and response mechanism that connects abnormal findings across layers to enable coordinated defense.

Semantic Trigger Injection A backdoor attack in which inputs containing specific features (triggers) cause the model to produce incorrect outputs.

SIEM A platform that provides real-time analysis of security alerts generated by applications and network hardware.

SLA A formal agreement between service providers and users that defines expected service performance, availability, and penalties for failure to meet agreed-upon levels.

Software Defined Network A network architecture that separates the control plane from the data plane to enable flexible, programmable network management.

TEE A secure area of a processor that ensures the code and data loaded inside are protected with respect to confidentiality and integrity.

Triadic Coupling The structural interdependence among data, computing power, and algorithms that jointly shape system behavior and performance in intelligent computing networks.

Unsupervised Learning A type of machine learning that identifies patterns or anomalies in data without relying on labeled training samples, often used for anomaly detection in complex environments.

Vehicle Networks A networked system where vehicles communicate with each other and with infrastructure to support autonomous driving, traffic optimization, and safety.

VPN A secure communication channel over public networks that encrypts data between endpoints.

WireGuard A modern, high-performance VPN protocol known for simplicity and cryptographic strength.

Zero-Trust Architecture A security model that assumes no implicit trust for any entity inside or outside the network and enforces strict identity verification and access controls at every stage.

MIX
Papier aus verantwortungsvollen Quellen
Paper from responsible sources
FSC® C105338

If you have any concerns about our products,
you can contact us on
ProductSafety@springernature.com

In case Publisher is established outside the EU,
the EU authorized representative is:
Springer Nature Customer Service Center GmbH
Europaplatz 3, 69115 Heidelberg, Germany

Printed by Libri Plureos GmbH
in Hamburg, Germany